The Commonwealth and
Restoration Stage

LONDON : HUMPHREY MILFORD

OXFORD UNIVERSITY PRESS

THOMAS KILLIGREW (AGED 26)

(From the original, an old copy from a painting by Sir Anthony Van Dyck,
in the National Portrait Gallery.   41¼ in. by 38⅜ in.)

THE COMMONWEALTH AND RESTORATION STAGE

By LESLIE HOTSON

CAMBRIDGE

HARVARD UNIVERSITY PRESS

1928

PRINTED AT THE HARVARD UNIVERSITY PRESS
CAMBRIDGE, MASS., U. S. A.

TO

M. M. P. H.

Prefatory Note

OF THE two periods of London stage history with which this book deals, the first, 1642–1660, has been generally regarded as a homogeneous blank. We have been taught to think that at the outbreak of the Civil Wars "long locks were converted to large ears; Masques and Playes to Conventicles and Psalm-singing." It is true that Malone and Collier, two great pioneers, uncovered certain lively and disturbing facts which tended to show that the theatrical life of London was not extinct throughout these eighteen years. Yet little was written since their time, aside from the paragraphs of C. H. Firth in *Notes and Queries* and those of J. Q. Adams in his *Shakespearean Playhouses*, until the important contributions made by Hyder E. Rollins in *Studies in Philology* (1921 and 1923). Mr. Rollins has performed a notable service in re-awakening interest in the period, and in bringing to light more of the rich material to be found in the Thomason Collection of Tracts in the British Museum. The present study combines his discoveries with a quantity of additional and corrective data obtained from a minute examination of all the newsbooks and many of the pamphlets included in Thomason's Collection. For clearness of reference in the notes, I have distinguished each document discovered and printed by Rollins with an *R*, placed after the document's press mark (*e.g.*, B.M., E412.27. *R*.).

With the purpose of securing new material bearing on the history of the theatres and actors of the Commonwealth and Restoration, I undertook an extensive and careful search through the Chancery Proceedings, Bills and Answers, Six Clerks' Divisions, 1649–1714, preserved in the Public Record Office. The fruits of this search far exceeded my expectations. Of new Chancery suits alone concerned with theatrical matters, I found some one hundred and twenty of the greatest importance for stage history. A numbered list of these records will be found in the Appendix. So voluminous were the documents discovered that the mere reading of them was a serious task, and their reproduction *in extenso* quite out of the question. In order, therefore, to bring this book within a reasonable compass, I have been obliged not only to forego some of the amenities of Restoration stage gossip, and to limit my chapters for the most part to a presentation of new material, but also to defer publication of some of the facts discovered. I have made no consistent attempt to distinguish every piece of fresh information. The discriminating reader will note them for himself, as he will the many passages in which I have profited by the valuable work of R. W. Lowe, W. J. Lawrence, and Allardyce Nicoll, to mention only three recent laborers in the field. In the matter of presentation I have uniformly retained the oddities of spelling in the selections from the Thomason newsbooks. On coming to the quotations from Chancery documents, however, I concluded that legal phraseology was difficult enough, and have modernized the spelling at my peril. Material contained in two parts of the book has been already published: "Bear Gardens and Bear-baiting During the Commonwealth" appeared in the *Publications of the Modern Language Association of America*, 1925, vol. xl, no. 2, and "George Jolly, Actor-Manager" in the North Carolina *Studies in Philology*, 1923, vol. xx, no. 4. For courteous permission to use these papers, I have to thank the editors of the two journals.

This study was begun in 1922 as a doctoral dissertation. Since that time I have been enabled to carry on the work through the generosity of the authorities of Harvard University, who appointed me Charles Dexter Scholar for the summers of 1922 and 1925, and Sheldon Travelling Fellow for the year 1923–1924. Finally, the officers of Yale University, by nominating me Sterling Senior Research Fellow for 1926–1927, provided the means of bringing the book to completion.

There remains the pleasure of acknowledging the expert assistance of Mr. Hilary Jenkinson and Mr. J. J. O'Reilly, Assistant Keepers of the Public Records; and the helpful suggestions of Miss Lucy Drucker and of Dr. Arthur Sprague. My colleague, Dr. A. S. Borgman, has very kindly read and criticized the proof sheets. Without the cordial encouragement of Professor H. E. Rollins I should hardly have undertaken this work, to which his labors have so largely contributed. Especially am I indebted to Professor G. L. Kittredge, whose alert and friendly interest from the beginning has furthered my researches in every way; and above all, to my wife, who has not only made the labor a pleasure, but assumed no small part of it herself.

L. H.

New York University

Contents

Illustrations

The Commonwealth and Restoration Stage

CHAPTER I

PLAYERS AND PARLIAMENT

Surreptitious Drama, 1642–1655

Ald. Players! thou foolish profane Boy, Players!
Sq. If you be not read in the History of Players, both men and women,
   't will call your Breeding in question.
—John Lacy, *Sir Hercules Buffoon*, I, 1.

WE ARE not to think of Parliament's first ordinance against stage plays, in 1642, as a blight which suddenly struck a flower in full bloom. The London theatres had been going through hard times; plagues had closed their doors in 1635, and again, for eighteen months, in 1636–1637. This latter period, in spite of occasional relief (such as acting before the King at Hampton Court), had drained the players' pockets and helped to disorganize their forces. When they were again permitted to "exercise their quality," the actors showed characteristically poor judgment in offending the powers of the state.

The Fortune company outraged the bishops in May, 1639, by acting a play in contempt of the ceremonies of the Church. I find an amusing account of the incident and its sequel, by a Puritan scribbler, in *A Second Discovery by the Northern Scout.*[1] *

> In the meane time let me tell ye a lamentable Tragedie, acted by the Prelacie, against the poore Players of the Fortune Play-house, which made them sing
>
> *Fortune my foe why dust thou frowne on me?* &c.
>
> for having gotten a new old Play, called *The Cardinalls Conspiracie,* whom they brought upon the Stage in as great state as they could, with *Altars, Images, Crosses, Crucifixes,* and the like, to set forth his pomp and pride.

---

* The notes will be found at the end of each chapter, with an indication in parentheses of the number of the page to which each note refers.

But wofull was the sight to see, how in the middest of all their mirth, the Puesevants came and seazed upon the poore Cardinall, and all his Consorts, and carried them away. And when they were questioned for it, in the high Commission Court, the[y] pleaded Ignorance, and told the Archbishop, *that they tooke those examples of their Altars, Images,* and the like, *from Heathen Authors.* This did somewhat asswage his anger, that they did not bring him on the Stage: but yet they were fined [2] for it, and after a little imprisonment got their liberty. And having nothing left them but a few old Swords and Bucklers, they fell to act the valiant *Scot,* which they played five days with great applause, which vext the Bishops worse than the other, insomuch that they were forbidden playing it any more, and some of them prohibited ever Playing againe.

Thus the unfortunate Fortune lost money, dresses, and liberty by ridiculing the Church.

The Red Bull players under Andrew Cane (of whom we shall hear more later) got into trouble with the Privy Council on 29 September, 1639. On this day a complaint was brought that they had acted "for many days together" *The Whore New Vamped,* "a scandalous and libellous" play, in which they had "audaciously reproached . . . and personated not only some . . . aldermen . . . but also scandalized . . . the whole profession of proctors belonging to the Court of Probate, and reflected upon the present Government." [3] The Attorney-General was ordered to proceed roundly to bring those who were guilty to sentence; thus the Red Bull had the worse in its attack upon aldermen, monopolies, and government.

The Phoenix, or Cockpit in Drury Lane, sheltering the King's and Queen's Boys under William Beeston, offended the King in the spring of 1640 by acting an unauthorized play referring to his journey into Scotland. Sir Henry Herbert, Master of the Revels, at the King's complaint shut the theatre for several days. Beeston was not only imprisoned but for a time removed from his position as governor of the company, Davenant being installed in his place, 27 June, 1640. The Phoenix learned that it could not beard the King with impunity.

In themselves these mishaps were not desperate. Troubles of a like nature had afflicted the theatres often enough before.

But now there was something ominous of civil war in the air; and in September, 1641, when the players were hindered from acting by the pestilence,[4] they issued the well-known *Stage-Players Complaint. In A pleasant Dialogue betweene Cane of the Fortune, and Reed of the Friers.*[5]

Cane takes a gloomy view, reflecting on the fate of many of the institutions of royal prerogative under the smashing attack of the Puritan Parliament: "For Monopolers are downe, Projectors are downe, the High Commission Court is downe, the Starre-chamber is downe, & (some think) Bishops will downe; and why should we then that are farre inferior to any of those not justly feare least we should be downe too?" But Reed rejoins: "Pish! . . . we are very necessary and commodious to all people: First for strangers, who can desire no better recreation, then to come and see a Play: then for Citizens, to feast their wits: then for Gallants, who . . . doe find a great delight and delectation to see a Play." It is well to keep these "infallible reasons" of Reed's in mind during the stormy period that follows.

After the pestilence, by February, 1642, the playhouses were again performing, and at such a rate as to call forth a protest from some of the increasingly powerful Puritans in Parliament. On Friday, February 4, "there was a great complaint made against the Play-houses, and a motion made for the suppressing of them."[6] Nothing was done, however, at this time. June came, and Sir Henry Herbert, after licensing *The Irish Rebellion,* closed his books, for the season; but he never reopened them until the Restoration.

On September 2, when the long-gathering war cloud had broken, a resolution originating in the House of Commons and agreed to by the Lords solemnly put down all stage plays, "to appease and avert the Wrath of God":

Fasting and Prayer having bin often tryed to be very effectuall . . . are still enjoyned; and whereas publike Sports doe not well agree with publike Calamities, nor publike Stage-playes with the Seasons of Humiliation, this being an Exercise of sad and pious solemnity, and the other being Spectacles of pleasure, too commonly expressing laciuious Mirth and Levitie: It is therefore thought fit, and Ordeined by the Lords and Commons in this Parliament Assembled, that while these sad Causes and set times of Humiliation doe continue, publike Stage-playes shall cease, and bee forborne.[7]

The alarm of battle, as well as this grave prohibition, shifted the actors' scene to the stage of war. Many of them, notably the King's Company of the Blackfriars and Globe, enlisted at once with the King. On the other side, some soldiers of fortune anxious to serve the Parliament preferred an amusing petition, which shows the part played by some of the actors' costumes in this warlike time. These "poore Gentlemen Souldiers" humbly beseech the House "that they may be intrusted in some office of credit in this present Expedition"; because

for want of habit, money, and friends [they] cannot get preferment so soone as many rawe giddy youth handicrafts-men, as Taylors, Barbers, players, nay Butchers now are imployed through the meanes of their money, or the loane of players garments, before such as have served an apprentiship in forraigne Nations.[8]

We shall see later that the King's Company, on the closing of the theatres, sold off their stock of "Apparell, hangings, books, & other goods." [9]

The government's act in closing the playhouses was looked upon, I find, with hearty approval by those who agreed with John Vicars, the author of *God in the Mount*. In praising the ordinance, this semi-official spokesman of Parliament calls playhouses "those most dirty and stinking sinks or lestalls of all kinds of abominations, those odious Hell-houses of the land." [10] A less solemn view of the behavior of the authorities is displayed in *A Discourse Between a Citizen and a Country-Gentleman*, published 12 October, 1642:

Count. Why, I thought that playes & play-houses had beene put downe:
Cit.   Yes so they were in the Suburbes, but they were set up in the City, and Guild-hall is made a Play-house.
Count. But I pray, what Play was it that was Acted?
Cit.   In troth, I cannot well tell, I saw it not I thank God; there were none but great ones there: the Marshall that kept the door would let no honest men come in.
Count. But could you by no meanes here the name of it?
Cit.   Some say it was called *a King or no King*, or *King Careo*.[11]

New powers were given to the city officials by Parliament, which, on being exercised, stirred revolt in the breasts of some of the townspeople. While the Lord Mayor and the Court of Common Council were sitting at Guildhall on 12 December, 1642, the populace, intent on obtaining a hearing for their petitions, surged in and made a riot: "some Proctors, some Tapsters, some Players, witnesse Cain the Clown at the Bull, and others came in great multitude, and filled the Hall and Yard." [12]

This "Cain the Clown at the Bull" is, of course, the famous actor, Andrew Cane. *Mercurius Britanicus*, the Parliament newsbook, gives us a further trace of him two years after this riot, in a curious reference to him as engraver, at Oxford, of the dies for the debased coinage of the Royalist Army:

I could wish that the Coine for his Majesties souldiers might not come too fast that way to this City, which is graved in the West, by the *quondam* foole of the Red Bull, now stampt for a knave in brasse, I mean farthing tokens, made now in the West. . . . The losse the Subject sustaines by Farthings is so great that it deserves a redresse. [13]

That Cane is here meant is clear from the fact that he was a goldsmith by trade. After the wars, we find him, under the name of "Andrew Decayne," signing a goldsmiths' petition to Parliament. [14] And that the goldsmith Decayne was identical with the actor Cane is again shown by the Chancery suit, *De Caine* v. *Wintershall*, 1654. [15]

But to return to the Guildhall riot of 1642. Many of the ringleaders were imprisoned, among them Tom Godfrey, the Master of the Bear Garden. He was convicted by the Commons of getting subscribers to his petition by threatening that "he would cut the Throats of those that refused" to sign. [16] They committed him to Newgate, and also ordered

that the Masters of the *Beare Garden*, and all other Persons who have Interest there, be injoined and required by this House, That for the future they do not permit to be used the Game of Bear-baiting in these Times of great Distractions, till this House do give further Order herein. [17]

It has been supposed that this order constituted a real prohibition; but *The Actors Remonstrance or Complaint* for "the filching of their profession, and banishment from their several Playhouses" (24 January, 1643),[18] charges that "Stage-playes, only of all publike recreations are prohibited; the exercise at the Beares Colledge, and the motions of Puppets being still in force and vigour." [19]

It is worth noting that this *Complaint* is written by the actors of the "private" houses, — the Blackfriars, the Cockpit, and Salisbury Court, — where, as they boast, "none use to come but the best of the Nobility and Gentry." They are inclined to look down on the Red Bull and the Fortune as being large, cheap, and rowdy places. But we shall find that, in spite of these ostensible disadvantages, the Red Bull was more successful than any of the other theatres in keeping open during the Commonwealth. The private houses, however, says the *Complaint*, are badly off. The sharers and housekeepers are living on their rapidly diminishing savings; the "Hired-men are disperst, some turned Souldiers and Trumpetters, others destin'd to meaner courses, or depending upon us, whom in courtesie wee cannot see want for old acquaintance sakes." The tire-men are out of service; "our stock of cloaths, such as are not in tribulation for the generall use, being a sacrifice to moths." And "some of our ablest ordinarie Poets [are] compelled to get a living by writing contemptible penny-pamphlets."

We have seen that the Blackfriars (King's) Men joined the Royalist forces. I now discover that at the Oxford headquarters these soldiers were occasionally called upon to act plays, and that in 1642 a Parliament newsbook knew of it: "Friday, the *16 of December* [1642]. The Cavaliers intend to be merry this *Christmas* at *Oxford*, for they have sent for Musick, Players, and Ladies to entertain the time with."[20] Whereas in London "the delicious buxsome young widowes of fifteen and twenty . . . have no . . . man to carry them to . . . Play-houses, which are now as solitary as they are." [21]

The Cavaliers at Oxford knew how to enjoy themselves in a way that horrified the Puritans. I find a report that on a Sunday evening in October, 1643,

Prince *Rupert* accompanied with some Lords and other Cavaliers, danced
through the streetes openly with musick before them, to one of the Col-
ledges, where after they had stayed about halfe a houre ["hearing of a
Play," admits a Royalist newsbook [22]], they returned back againe dancing
with the same musick before them, and immediately there followed them a
pack of women, or Curtizans it may be supposed, for they were hooded
and could not be knowne.[23]

Puritan George Wither, in his *Mercurius Rusticus* [24] (October, 1643), gives us some further light on the doings of the
Cavaliers:

It is, there, thought also by some of his Majesties servants . . . that
the Queen will not have so many Masks at Christmas and Shrovetide this
yeare as she was wont to have other yeeres heretofore; because *Inigo Jones*
cannot conveniently make such Heavens and Paradises at *Oxford* as he did
at White-hall; & because the Poets are dead, beggered, or run away, who
were wont in their Masks to make Gods and Goddesses of them.

The Parliament newsbooks could never have enough of bitter references to the masques which had been such a costly
amusement at the court of Charles:

. . . in time they [the Cavaliers] will go neere to put downe all *preaching*
and *praying*, and have some *religious Masque* or play instead of Morning
and Evening Prayer; it has been an old fashion at Court, amongst the
Protestants there, to shut up the *Sabbath* with some wholesome Piece of
Ben Johnson or *Davenant*, a kinde of *Comicall Divinity*.[25]

She [the Queen] cared for nothing but playing with little Dogges . . .
and Masquing, Dancing, revelling . . . it was but a Scene of Volup-
tuousnesse, a Stage of Luxurie and Pride.[26]

The Royalist Junto at Oxford, according to the satirical *Mercurius Britanicus*, is "a three daies wonder, a kind of an *Anti-
masque*, one of her *Majesties mock-showes*, which hath cost the
Kingdome as much as all those at *White-hall*, that were maintained with *Ship-money*." [27] *Britanicus* is not without a certain pungent wit, too, in his scarification of the Royalists. We
come upon him quoting the Court newsbook:

This day sayes he, the *Queen* began her journey; . . . I could tell ye
the *Stages* she hath made in this *journey*, from *France* to *White-Hall*,
from *White-Hall* to dancings, Masquings, and little dogs, from thence to
Friers, and Jesuits, from Jesuits to Jermins, and Gorings, and Digbies, from

thence to *Holland*, and from *Holland* to Gunpowder, Ordnance, and Ammunition, and from thence to *England*, and so on to fighting, *Plotting, killing, murdering* the *Protestants* of *England*, and Ireland.[28]

Yet, despite the legion of accusers of royalty, there were those in London who were sorry to see the palace of the King deserted. One such loyal soul put forth *A Deep Sigh Breathed Through the Lodgings at White Hall Deploring the absence of the Court, and the Miseries of the Pallace.*[29] After taking us to "the Lodgings of the severall Lords and Gentlemen," where, he assures us, "the smell and odour of the perfumes and tinctures of a mornings curling, and dressing, made your attendance not to seem tedious but gave a delight to your frequent and long solicitation," he regrets that "now there's nothing but the raw sent of moist walls, and all as silent as midnight." He continues in a kind of ecstasy:

In the Cockpit and Revelling Roomes, where at a Play or Masque the darkest night was converted to the brightest Day that ever shin'd, by the luster of Torches, the sparkling of rich Jewells, and the variety of those incomparable and excellent Faces, from which the other derived their brightnesse, where beauty sat inthron'd in so full glory, that had not *Phaeton* fir'd the world, there had wanted a Comparative whereunto to paralell the refulgencie of their bright-shining splendor, Now you may goe in without a Ticket or the danger of a broken-pate, you may enter at the Kings side, walke round about the Theaters, view the Pullies, the Engines, conveyances, or contrivances of every several Scaene And not an Usher o' th Revells, or Engineere to envy or find fault with your discovery, although they receive no gratuitie for the sight of them.

It is only fair to the Londoners, after this outburst of enthusiasm, to hear a denunciation, couched in the sizzling Puritan phrase, of

many of our late wanton Courtiers, men and women of debaucht consciences and conversations, impudent, impenitent, jearing, mocking and scoffing at all means of recovery, wasting their precious times in Plays, Pastimes, Masks, and such fooleries, spending their wits and parts in Complements and Courtships, rising up in the morning wreaking from their beds of lusts, no sooner up but their lustful drinks are tempered for them, then to their powdering, trimming and tiring, then to their devotion to their bellies, I mean their gluttonous dinners; then to Black-fryers, or other places, to see Plays, to offer up their evening sacrifices to the Devil.[30]

THE SUCKLINGTON FACTION; OR, SUCKLINGS
ROARING BOYES

A Puritan attack on the typical young Cavalier — "a painted Puppet on
the stage of vanity" who "hath the Devill to his conducter. . . . Now he
acts his ryots, anon his revels, and forthwith ferries to a Play-house. . . ."

(From a single sheet, 1641, in the Thomason Collection.)

Glapthorne, in his elegiac poem of *White-Hall*,[31] written in 1642, before the storm of bitterness broke, took a pleasanter view, seeing in the delights of the personified palace the art of Ben Jonson and of Inigo Jones:

The Muses then did florish, and upon
My pleasant mounts planted their Helicon.
Then that great wonder of the knowing age,
Whose very name merits the amplest page
In Fames faire book, admired *Iohnson* stood
Up to the chin in the Pierian flood,
Quaffing crownd bowles of Nectar, with his bayes
Growing about his temples; chanting layes,
Such as were fit for such a sacred Eare
As his majestick Masters was; to heare,
Whom he so oft pleasd with (those mighty tasks
Of wit and judgement) his well laboured Masks.
Then those two thunderbolts of lively wit,
Beamont and *Fletcher* gloriously did sit
Ruling the Theatre, and with their cleane
Conceptions beautifying the Comick Scene.
And noble *Donne* (borne to more sacred use)
Exprest his heavenly raptures; As the juice
Of the Hyblean roses did distill
Through the Alembeck of his nectard quill.
Chapman like *Homer* in me often reads
His Odisses, and lofty Iliads.
That I did rather then appeare to be
The worlds best furnishd learnedst Academy,
Then the Kings pallace: who when fatall fire
In its malicious fury did conspire
To ruine part of my faire buildings; He
Great *Iames* renewed with State and Majesty,
Like to himselfe, that goodly Fabrick, which
Is for materialls, as invention rich;
On polishd marble pillars, which shall stand
To speak his fame, while this renowned Land,
Free from the invasion of all forraigne harmes,
Is walld about with Oceans watry armes.
For which faire ornament I must bestow
My gratitude on worthy *Inigo*,
Whose skill in Fabrick did direct each part
Of that excelling frame with powerfull art.

> Yet should I silent be, the very stones,'
> So quaintly laid, will speak the praise of Jones.

Mention of the masques and of the "powerful art" of Inigo
brings us to a consideration of the fate, hitherto unknown,
under the Commonwealth, of the huge masque house built
by King Charles. The purpose of this structure was to provide a place for masques other than the Banqueting House,
where the smoke of the stage lights threatened damage to
the elaborate ceiling paintings. These had been designed by
Rubens, and cost £3000. The Reverend Mr. G. Gerrard describes its erection in a letter to the Lord Deputy dated
9 November, 1637:

> A great Room is now in building only for this Use betwixt the Guard-
> Chamber and the Banqueting-house, of Fir, only weather-boarded and
> slightly covered . . . which will cost too much Money to be pulled down,
> and yet down it must when the Masks are over.[32]

In a later letter he tells us that "it cost the King 2500 *l.*" [33]
The edifice was really huge, measuring 120 feet in length, 57 in
width, and 59 in height.[34] Instead of coming down, however,
after the last masque, it stood as a remembrancer for several
years. *Mercurius Aulicus*, the Royalist newsbook written by
John Berkenhead, in rehearsing the vaunts of the London
scribblers, gives under date of July, 1643:

> Lastly . . . they say, if *they want wood this Winter in* London, *neither
> the Masquing-house at* White-Hall, *nor the timber of any Malignants house
> shall stand;* But [he retorts] *Tyburne* shall stand, where I leave ye all six
> together.[35]

In spite of the London newsbooks, the masque house stood
two years longer; and a Parliament man, in a categorical
counter-blast to Cleveland's *Character of a London Diurnall*,[36]
— a satirical attack on the Parliament scribblers, — writes:

> *The onely Play-house is at Westminster.* You say very true, it is the great
> Barne in Whitehall, since the State hath pulled downe [37] the Globe, Black-
> fryers, the Fortune, and I make no question that wooden Babell shall be
> no eye-sore to you; there shall be no more playing or dancing there beleeve
> it.[38]

He was right. On 16 July, 1645, the Commons ordered that

the Boarded Masque House at *Whitehall*, the Masque House at *St. James'*, and the Courts of Guard, be forthwith pulled down,[39] and sold away; and that the Proceed thereof shall be employed towards the Payment of the King's poor Servants Wages.[40]

Apparently the timber was not disposed of at once but lay for at least two years piled in Scotland Yard. In *A Dialogue . . . Concerning our present* [Church] *Government by Elders* (14 May, 1647) one of the disputants says that his party intends

to dig and root out all shrubbed Elders . . . and so convey them by Cart to *Scotland* yard, there to remaine with the superstitious timber of the late erected Play house in White Hall, but this wood must lye in the posture of a very large Bonfire ready to welcome the King and his Nobles.[41]

We shall leave it there and return to the players and their part in the war. The *locus classicus* for details about them is the often-quoted *Historia Histrionica*, by James Wright (1699).[42] The actors, as he remembers,

most of 'em, except *Lowin*, *Taylor*, and *Pollard*, (who were superannuated) went into the King's Army. . . . *Robinson* was Kill'd at the Taking of a Place (I think *Basing House*) by *Harrison* [43] . . . who refused him Quarter, and shot him in the Head when he had laid down his Arms . . . *Mohun* was a Captain, (and after the Wars were ended here, served in *Flanders*, where he received Pay as a Major) *Hart* was a Lieutenant of Horse under Sir *Thomas Dallison*, in Prince Rupert's, Regiment, *Burt* was Cornet in the same Troop, and *Shatterel* Quartermaster. *Allen* of the *Cockpit*, was a Major, and Quarter Master General at *Oxford*.

According to *A Perfect Diurnall* (24 October, 1642), a player named Shanks deserted from the Parliament forces rather than fight the King.[44]

A satirical pamphlet addressed to Parliament in December, 1642, advocated religious stage plays with psalm-singing between the acts, and assured the august body that, if plays could be made to edify, "Captaine *Trig*, and the rest of the Players which are now in service, would doubtlessely returne to their callings, and much lessen the King's Army." [45]

In 1643 one of the players who remained in London addressed an ironical "Players' Petition" to the "Hoghen Moghens" of Parliament. Professor Rollins has discovered two manuscript copies [46] of this (earlier than that printed by Hazlitt [47]), one of which — the Ashmolean — runs in part as follows:

> O wise, misterious Synod, what shall we
> Doe for such men as you, ere forty-three
> Be halfe expir'd, & an vnlucky Season
> Shall set a *p*eriod to Trienniall treason?
>
> .   .   .   .
>
> But whilst you liue, our lowe peticon craues
> That the King's true Subjec*tes* & your Slaues
> May, in our Comick Mirth & tragick rage,
> Set vp the Theater & shew the Stage,
> The shop of truth & Fancy, where we vow
> Not to act any thing you disallow.
> We will not dare at your strange votes to ieere,
> Or *p*ersonate K[ing] P[ym] *w*hich your State Steeres.
> Aspiring Cataline shalbe forgott,
> Bloody Sejanus, or who ere would plot
> Confusion to a State; the warrs betwixt
> The Parliament & iust Henry the sixt
> Shall haue no thought or mencan, cause *thei*r power
> Not only plact, but lost, him in *th*e Tower;
> Nor like the graue advice of learned Pim
> Make a Malignant & then plunder him.
>
> .   .   .   .
>
> We make the people laugh at some vaine show,
> And as they laugh at vs, they doe at you.
> But then, in the Contrary, we disagree,
> For you can make them cry faster than we:
> Your Trajedies are more really exprest,
> You murder men in earnest, we in iest.
> .   .   .   . give vs leaue to play
> Quietly before the King comes, for we wood
> Be glad to say w'aue done a litle good.
> Since you haue satt, yo*u*r play is almost done
> As well as ours — wood it had nere begun;
> For we shall see ere the last act be spent,
> Enter the King, exunt the Parliament.

Records of players who took the side of the Parliament are scanty. James Wright says, "I have not heard of one of these Players of any Note that sided with the other Party, but only

Swanston, and he profest himself a Presbyterian, took up the Trade of a Jeweller, and liv'd in *Aldermanbury*. . . . The rest either Lost, or exposed their Lives for the King." From *A Key To the Cabinet of the Parliament, By Their Remembrancer* (1648), Professor Rollins has extracted a corroborative passage which shows that Swanston was a Parliament's man: "What need is there of any Playes? will not these serve well enough, especially when they have gotten *Hillyar Swansted* the Player to be one?"

As an additional point of interest, I have found Swanston's will,[48] which was dated 24 June, 1651. He died before 3 July of that year, and is described as "Eylaeardt Swanston, of St. Mary Aldermanbury, London, gent." Another actor who took the Parliament side seems to be John Harris, variously described as "sometimes a Players Boy", [49] "once a Strowlers boy, or a Players boy of the Company of the Revells", [50] or "a Players Boy, knowne by the name of *Jack of Oxford*." [51] He became a printer in Oxford after the rigorous ordinance against playhouses in London was issued; then, turning his coat, he came back to London and wrote an anti-Cavalier newsbook called *Mercurius Militaris*. As might be expected, the Cavalier papers vie with each other in execrating him, and his later career seems to justify their contempt. For we find that in 1654, by forging Oliver Cromwell's signature, he swindled three merchants out of £900.[52] He was committed to prison, and in 1660 (for other crimes) hanged.[53]

Some of the Royalist pamphleteers are fantastic in the accusations they hurl at prominent members of the Puritan government. For example, *Mercurius Pragmaticus* in 1647 said of Hugh Peters, the famous Independent divine: "he has a fine wit I can tell you, *Sam Rowley* and he were a *Pylades*, and *Orestes*, when he played a womans part at the Curtaine Play-house, which is the reason his garbe is so emphaticall in the Pulpit." [54] And in 1649 John Crouch, in his erratic and extravagant anti-Parliament *Man in the Moon*, referred to Peters as a "*Book-holder* at the Bull-play-house"; [55] but as there is nothing of which he was not accused,[56] it is impossible to take these references seriously. Their interest for us is in the mention of these playhouses.

Apropos of play-acting in war-time, I discovered the following incident, much too good to omit here. We are told that, "to prevent sin," two whole regiments of Roundheads were turned into actors for one day. It seems that in Kent the country folk were much attached to their custom of celebrating May Day with "pastimes, and drinking matches, and May-poles, and dancing and idle wayes"; and, it is added, "sin hath been acted on former May dayes." Colonel Blunt, a Roundhead officer who was sharper than his name, thought of a holy stratagem to prevent the good people of Kent from again falling into such sin. Accordingly, without taking any repressive measures which might give "the Malignants occasion to mutinie," he summoned in

two Regiments of his foot Souldiers to appear the last May-day . . . at Black-heath, to be trained, and exercised . . . and places provided to pitch in, for the Souldiers to meet in two bodies, which promised the Countrey much content. . . .

For on May day when they met, Colonell *Blunt* divided them into two parts, and the one was as Rounheeds, and the other as Cavaliers, who did both of them act their parts exceeding well, and many people . . . were present to see the same.

The Roundheads they carried it on with care and love, temperance and order, and as much gravity as might be, every one party carefull in his action, which was so well performed, that it was much commended.

But the Cavaliers they minded drinking and roaring, and disorder, and would bee still playing with the women, and compasse them in, and quarrell, and were exceedingly disorderly.

And these had severall skirmishes one with another, and took divers prisoners one from another, and gave content to the Countrey people, and satisfied them as well as if they had gone a maying in an other way which might have occasioned much evill.[57]

This exploit may be said to be the only godly play on record staged by two regiments of infantry.

Surprising as it may appear, even during the height of the war, plays were given with remarkable frequency at the regular playhouses in London. Relying on the cockney's ineradicable love of the theatre, the actors went on performing in defiance of the ordinance against them. To begin with, Sir Henry Mildmay notes in his *Account-book* and *Diary,*

20 Aug. 1643.   To a playe and other foleyes, 2*s*. 1*d*.
16 Nov. 1643.   To a playe of warre, 9*d*.

At the latter play, he adds laconically, "there was a disaster." [58]

"Disasters" at these illegal performances were not uncommon. They took the shape of a sudden irruption of Parliament soldiers into theatre, stage, and tiring house, and a serious plunder of the actors' costumes. For example, on 2 October, 1643,

The Players at the Fortune in Golding Lane, who had oftentimes been complained of, and prohibited the acting of wanton and licentious Playes, yet persevering in their forbidden Art, this day there was set a strong guard of Pikes and muskets on both gates of the Play-house, and in the middle of their play they unexpectedly did presse into the Stage upon them, who (amazed at these new Actors) it turned their Comedy into a Tragedy, and being plundered of all the richest of their cloathes, they left them nothing but their necessities now to act, and to learne a better life.[59]

This raid, or another like it, was the occasion for a letter from Thomas Forde to his friend "Mr. E. B.," in which he writes:

The Souldiers have routed the Players. They have *beaten* them out of their *Cock-pit*, *baited* them at the *Bull*, and *overthrown their Fortune*. For these exploits, the Alderman (the Anagram of whose name makes *A Stink*) moved in the House, that the Souldiers might have the Players cloaths given them. *H.M.* stood up, and told the Speaker, that he liked the Gentlemans motion very well, but that he feared they would fall out for the *Fools Coat*.[60]

The Fortune, I find, was used for fencing-matches at this time as well as for plays, and the raids by the soldiers were by the state made a means of drafting [61] men into the Parliament army. *Mercurius Veridicus* for 19–26 April, 1645, tells of one such encounter:

The same day a Waterman and a Shoomaker met at the Fortune Play-house to play at severall Weapons, at which (though they had but private summons) many were present, and in the middest of their pastime, divers of the Trained Bands beset the house and some Constables being present, had choise of fit men to serve the King and Parliament.[62]

With this ignominious affair should be compared the Parliament's rather contemptible trick at the Bear Garden in the same year.[63]

Even while continuing to break the law against stageplaying, the players probably still plied the Parliament with requests for permission to act. For unless we make some such assumption, it is difficult to feel the force of a phrase in the following pseudo-Welsh prophecy:

> There shall also crete inflammations of Lightning happen tis yeare about the fortune in Colding Lane, if the players can get leave to act the tragedies of Doctour *Faustus*, in which Tempest shall be seen shaghaired Tivills runne roaring with squibs in teir mouthes, while drummes make thunder in the tiring house, and the twelve pennie hireling make artificiall lights in her heavens.[64]

This extract, which is nothing but a piece of John Melton's *Astrologaster* (1620) brought up to date and turned into "Welsh," was printed in February, 1643, and reprinted with the reference to the players unchanged in 1647.[65]

It is obvious, however, that this surreptitious acting could not support all the pre-war theatres. One of the most celebrated of these was the first to be sacrificed to the hard times: the Globe Playhouse, which in 1644 was "pulled downe to the ground, to make tenements in the roome of it." [66] The loss of this stage further narrowed the attention of London on the houses which were still putting on plays.

England in the winter of 1645–1646 had grown war-weary. There had been bloody battles, and the end was not yet in sight. On 12 February, 1646, a Parliament newsbook [67] spoke in a sober key:

> The stage of War is like a maske at Court full of the croud, and of noyse, and gallantry at the first, but on the next morning (the rich intention and the furniture that brought Heaven and earth together to a conference being taken downe) it appeares a very spectacle of confusion, and all about it are silent as sleepe or midnight, so hath the War declared it selfe to be; the Musick and the glory of it hath delighted and deluded many, but the conclusion hath bin fatall, and left many great and gallant personages low as the grave, to enjoy a long rest in the silence and sloth of death.
> This hath bin the motive that hath caused so many Trumpets to come

from Oxford unto London, the last came in mourning and was clad in black. It seemes that the adverse party repent of their colours, and now do mourne in earnest that so much bloud is shed.

To cheer the King, the Royalists at Oxford not infrequently acted plays before him. We find a report in *The Moderate Intelligencer* for 16 January, 1646: "There came with this News a Play-book, made by some of Sir *Thomas Overburies* men in Black: we conceive its acted before His Majesty, to keep up his spirit in stead of good successes from his Souldiery." [68] We have record too of an old play — "*Exchange Ware at the Second Hand:* viz. Band, Ruffe, and Cuffe, lately out, and now newly dearned up" — which was acted at Oxford, 24 February, 1646. [69]

But neither of these plays was acted by the King's Men, for they had been heartily tired of the war by August, 1645, when the Cavalier *Mercurius Anti-Britannicus* [70] spoke for them:

For when the Stage at *Westminster*, where the two Houses now Act, is once more restored back againe to *Black-Fryers*, they have hope they shall returne to their old harmlesse profession of killing Men in Tragedies without Man-slaughter. Till then, they complaine very much that their profession is taken from them: and say 'twas never a good World, since the Lord *Viscount Say and Seale* succeeded *Joseph Taylor*.

(Here the anti-Parliament scribblers are at their old trick of likening the new state rulers to the old stage players.) For the actors in the King's army the discouragement of the defeat at Naseby was too great. In September they threw down their arms and came to London to give themselves up:

Nay the Kings very players are come in, having left Oxford, and throwne themselves upon the mercy of the Parliament, they offer to take the Covenant, & (if they may be accepted) are willing to put themselves into their service. [71]

Evidently the King's Men were in hard straits and ready to go to any length to maintain themselves.

Of the two Houses of Parliament, the Lords were less hostile to plays and players than were the Commons. The latter on 3 December, 1645, proposed to the Lords, as one of the conditions of future peace with the King, that, to continue and confirm their suppression of the theatres, he sign an act "for the putting downe of stage-playes." [72] It was to the Lords therefore that the Blackfriars (King's) Players presented their humble petition in March, 1646. They desired Parliament to pay them the arrears of salary which had been owing to them, before the wars, from King Charles. It speaks highly for the justice and generosity of the Roundhead Lords that we find the following entry in their Journal:

> March 24, 1646. Upon reading the Petition of the King's Players: it is *Ordered*, To be specially recommended to the House of Commons, that they may have their Monies paid them, expressed in their Petition.[73]

The Commons received,[74] and in all probability granted, the petition.

In spite of the defection of the Blackfriars players, however, there were still plenty of actors, and dramatists as well, in the Royalist ranks. The Roundhead scribblers loved especially to gird at William Cavendish, Marquess of Newcastle, who, besides having had command of the northern army, was a well-known playwright. In February, 1645, *Mercurius Britanicus* announced:

> First, Enter *Newcastle;* one that in time of peace tired the stage in *Black-Fryers* with his *Comedies*; and afterwards, one that trode the stage in the *North* with the first *Tragedies*, travers'd his ground between *York* and *Hull* . . . help't *Rupert* to a sound beating, and Exit.[75]

Another writer developed the theme:

> But the Earle of *Newcastle*, the brave Marquesse of *Newcastle*, which made the fine playes, he danced so quaintly, played his part a while in the North, was soundly beaten, shew'd a paire of heels, and *exit* Newcastle.[76]

The King's journalist retorted sharply, for Newcastle was a brave man, and all the world knew that the Cavalier disaster of Marston Moor was attributable least of all to him:

> Only to that passage concerning the Marquesse of *Newcastle*, whom this wretched creature . . . prayses for an eminent deserving Person in one place, and dispraises, as a writer of *Dramaticke* Poems in another; all I shall say, is this, I would have him remember (if he be so good a Scholar) that the *Roman* Empire, never atchieved greater victories by any Generall,

then by him who writ foure of the sixe Comedies in *Terence*. Nor do I despaire to see the day, when this Noble Lord, shall prove as fatall to this punicke Parliament, as that noble *Roman* was to *Carthage;* A City where the Publique Faith, grew to be a proverbe for perfidiousnesse.[77]

But Newcastle, disgusted with the lack of judgment on the part of the Royalist high command, had withdrawn to the Continent. This is the "exit" spoken of above.

Prince Charles, who was now with the Queen Mother at Paris, had maintained up to this time, as we now learn, a company of English comedians in Paris for the amusement of the exiled English. What actors these were is unknown. It is possible that some of them had been members of the English company which resided at the Hague at least from November, 1644, to about February, 1645, whose names, "recorded in an act passed by notary, were: Jeremiah Kite, William Coock, Thomas Loffday, Edward Schottnel, Nathan Peet and his son."[78] Of these, Thomas Loveday had been a member of the King's Revels company in 1635, and at the Restoration in 1660 he was to join Mohun and Hart's company at the Red Bull. Edward Shatterell ("Schottnel") also later made one at the Red Bull, where he acted as early as 12 May, 1654. But whoever the actors in the Paris company may have been, they had little luck. *Mercurius Candidus*[79] for 11–20 November, 1646, gives us interesting news of them, with his own caustic comment:

From France thus: The company of English Actors that the Prince of Wales had, are for want of pay dissolved —: That's newes not strange . . . It is probable, that the Prince thinkes it may concern his present condition to mind something else. . . .

The English audience being there so poor and few, that they were not able to maintaine the charges of the Stage —: It is wonder sufficient to me, how they can maintain themselves.

Newcastle, I find, was intimately connected with this company before its dissolution, and wrote for it. *The Kingdomes Weekly Intelligencer,*[80] speaking of Newcastle, says:

He has writ severall things for the English Company that did lately act in *Parris* which sheweth in him either an admirable temper and settlednes of mind . . . or else an infinite and vaine affection unto Poetry, that in the ruines of his Country and himselfe to can be at the leisure to make Prologues and Epilogues for players.

Besides regular companies such as this of Prince Charles, the Royalists at their headquarters at home as well as abroad habitually got together players for the major festivals — Christmas, New Year's Day, and Shrove Tuesday. Sometimes, as in the following case at Oxford, the plays given were satires directed against the Roundheads. We have the story from a Puritan pamphleteer:

December 8, 1646. Malignants have stollen as much Holland of late from the Presbyterians, and the Independants, as hath made a thousand sheetes for the *Oxford* old Juglers to wrap their evill spirits in at *Aulicus* his Maske (who it is said hath contracted a Company for *Newcastle*, to shew Gamballs at Court this Christmasse). The Mummers parts were drawne from a publike Conference, betwixt six Presbyterian Ministers, and some Independants, held at *Oxford* on Thursday, *Novem*. 12. 1646 (as one of his Disciples saith).[81]

In Paris, too, on New Year's eve, the defeated Royalists regaled themselves with a masque. *Mercurius Candidus* for 28 January, 1647,[82] is found to contain a very detailed account of it:

There must needs have been store of mirth (this Christmas) in France; or else some of her Majesties Poets have a great deale of wit. . . . From private intelligence thus; On New-Years day eve last, a conceited Masque (or shew) in this manner.

A Banquet prepared.

Enter 3 grand old Seigniours, *Janus* and *Christmas* ushered in by *Time*. Janus attended by the 4 seasons. Two conceited dances: The first by three, *Shuffle, Cut* and *Trumpe:* Shuffle represented in the habit of an old sage Pettiffogger, run mad with eating of *Alopodridas*, and studieng to invent new arguments for Anarchy and the Philosophers Stone. *Cut* a factious Lady, and Widdow of an an [*sic*] old Souldier of the Queens. *Trumpe*, a young wag-taile, and Madam Cuts own Chambermaid.

The other dance was by eight, and alike madly conceited, in which the 4 *Aces* rob the 4 *Knaves*. The 4 *Knaves* expressed in their severall conditions. *Spades*, the country knave, an Ingrosser, *Clubs* the Camp-knave, a Sutler. *Diamonds*, the Citie-knave, a Promooter: *Hearts*, the Court-knave, an Informer.

4 Conceited dances presented by each knave. The *Spade-knave*, Coun-

try sports in a Wassaile bowle. The *Campe-knave* a *Matachine* or sword dance. The *Diamond-knave* a Mumming. The *Heart-knave* a *Cornucopia*. The 4 *Aces* were Elder Brothers to the 4 *Knaves*.

However witty this masque appeared to its makers, its description falls rather flat on our ears. But no doubt we are ignorant, or spoiled for "conceited" diversions.

The Puritans in their thoroughgoing fashion tried to abolish Christmas and its celebration, as a Popish festival. But it was hard, even for their own newsbooks, to get on without the name. *Perfect Occurrences* for 17–24 December, 1647,[83] announces, "From *France* little of newes; but that the Queen of Great *Brittaine* hath provided for two Playes this *Christmasse* (as they call it)."

Before we return to London in 1647 to witness the new skirmishes between Parliament and the poor players, we are arrested by a small but highly significant notice, which I came across in a Roundhead newsbook of 7 May, 1647: "Stage-Playes are still acted at *Knightsbridge:* Whither go we!"[84] This last exclamation must mean something like "What are we coming to!" And the reader's impression from the passage is that players had gone to Knightsbridge, then a hamlet outside of London, to be freer from the danger of raids, and had there given plays more or less frequently. Where did they set their stage in Knightsbridge? If they played publicly, they may have used the Rose and Crown, the largest inn of the village,[85] later known as the Oliver Cromwell, from the tradition that the Protector's body-guard was once quartered there; or perhaps they made use of the Swan,[86] the ancient and disreputable hostelry to which Otway refers in *The Soldier's Fortune* (1681), III, 1:

Sir *Davy Dunce:*— . . . she may be . . . taking the Air as far as *Knights-bridge*, with some smooth-fac'd Rogue or another: 'T is a damn'd House, that *Swan*, that *Swan* at *Knights-bridge* is a confounded House.

I think it much more probable, though, that we should here follow Wright, who in his *Historia Histrionica* (1699) tells us that "in *Oliver's* time they used to Act privately, three or four

Miles, or more, out of Town, now here, now there, sometimes in Noblemens Houses, in particular *Holland-house* at *Kensington*."

Now although 1647 is in no strict sense of the word "Oliver's time," yet in this year the Parliament army was encamped about Knightsbridge, and Fairfax had headquarters near by at Holland House. It is not impossible that the gentlemen of the neighborhood and the less fanatical of the officers were not averse to seeing a play. Such an explanation would account for the discreetly shocked tone of the Parliament newsbook's ejaculation, "Whither go we!" and the use of the first person plural.

The periodicals of 1646 are meagre in news of the doings of players in London. It is probable that many of the actors had not yet returned to the city, and that therefore Thomas May, a former playwright turned Parliament's historian, in this year could pen the smug remark that the playhouses were "fitly silenc'd by the Lawes." [87] There is a record, too, which seems to indicate that the Cockpit in Drury Lane was used as a school.[88]

Sixteen hundred and forty-seven, however, is an exciting year in the history of the English stage. The actors began their trade at the Salisbury Court, the Cockpit, and the Fortune, in quite an open and public manner — treating the ordinance of 1642 as a thoroughly dead letter. In the pamphlet entitled *The Parliament of Ladies* (18 May, 1647) we find a ribald and satirical picture of Parliament framing a new law against plays:

A motion was then made for putting down of playes, whereupon the Lady *Munmouth* desired it might be explained what playes were meant . . . answer being made, Stage-playes were only understood, shee declared shee would concurre with the House in that.[89]

More details are given in a highly scurrilous continuation, dated 2 August, 1647. Here *The Ladies, A Second Time, Assembled in Parliament* [90] consider

a Complaint that was made against Players, who contrary to an Ordinance, had set up shop againe, and acted divers Playes, at the two houses, the Fortune, and Salisbury Court. Whereupon it was demanded what Plaies they were, and answer being given, that one of them was the scornefull Lady, the house tooke it in high disdaine, and as an absolute contempt of their power; and therefore ordered that Alderman *Atkins* should make a journey on purpose to suppresse them.

Before the date of these squibs, however, on 16 July, the House of Commons had drawn up an order to the Lord Mayor and the justices of the peace "to take effectual Care speedily to suppress all publick Plays and Playhouses, and all Dancings on the Ropes." [91] The House of Lords, against the protest of six of its members — Manchester, Kent, Warwick, Pembroke, Mulgrave, and Howard — who regarded stage plays as ever-lastingly unlawful, amended the order to run only until 1 January, 1648, and added the words "and Bear-baitings" to it.[92] The Commons passed the ordinance as amended,[93] but the players evidently took no notice of it. Their contempt of the law, in acting plays publicly at the Fortune and at Salis-bury Court, when complained of to Parliament on 11 August, caused the House to wonder at the "neglect of the justices of the peace."[94] It was moved on that day that the Commander-in-Chief of the Guard of Parliament take care to suppress all plays; but the House, deciding to give the justices an-other chance, ordered them and the sheriffs "to be very diligent and strict in improving their Authority, for the suppressing and preventing any Stage Plays, Dancings of the Ropes, Bear-baitings, or Bullbaitings." [95]

The players held these ordinances in slight esteem. They agreed with *Mercurius Melancholicus*, who remarked,

Ordinances are dayly discharg'd by whole volleyes, but they give no great report, onely a flash and away; they are like a man of clouts, more to terrifie then endanger.[96]

One stray shot, however, hit the Fortune; and *Mercurius Mel-ancholicus* reminds the Parliament scribbler, "Luke Har-runey" (alias *Carrot-beard*), of

somethings he forgot . . . of the unfortunate accident which happened at the Fortune Play-house, the Actors instead of *Actus primus, Scaena prima*, being taken away by some industrious Officers, to prevent such dangerous Assemblies, and so the Play was spoyled.[97]

There was evidently strong feeling in favor of the players. Nothing less can explain the extraordinary vitality of the stage under the fusillade of repressive ordinances. One gentleman gave voice to his sentiment in *A true account and character of the times*, suggesting [98] "That it were a good way to mollifie peoples minds to suffer Play-houses againe, and that it would be a considerable addition to the education of the Gentry."

The authorities nevertheless again attempted to enforce the ordinance when the players had grown so bold as to set up bills announcing a performance by a company (probably made up largely of the King's Men) at Salisbury Court. The choice of the play *A King and No King* was in itself an affront to the Parliament. *Perfect Occurrences* [99] (Henry Walker) gives a triumphant account of the raid on the playhouse:

A Stage-Play was to have been acted in Salisbury Court this day [100] (and bills stuck up about it) called *A King and no King*, formerly acted at the Black-Fryers, by his Majesties servants, about 8. yeares since, written by *Francis Beaumont*, and *Iohn Fletcher*.

The Sheriffes of the City of *London* with their Officers went thither, and found a great number of people; some young Lords, and other eminent persons; and the men and women with the Boxes, (that took monies) fled. The Sheriffes brought away *Tim Reade* the Foole, and the people cryed out for their monies, but slunke away like a company of drowned Mice without it.

But the Royalist newsbook *Mercurius Pragmaticus* [101] assures the Parliament that its follies will receive their due reward:

Though the House hindred the Players this weeke from playing the old Play, *King*, and no *King*, at *Salisbury* Court, yet believe me,

> *He that does live, shall see another Age,*
> *Their Follies* stript *and* whipt *upon the* Stage.

The ordinance against unlicensed newsbooks had routed for a time some of the Royalist pamphlets, and among them our friend *Mercurius Melancholicus*.[102] In his place appeared a counterfeit *Melancholicus*, really favorable to Parliament. The true nature of this bogus sheet comes out in its comment on the raid which we have witnessed at Salisbury Court and in its complaint against the restrictions on uncontrolled printing:

The Common Inns of sin, and Blasphemy the *Playhouses* began to be custom'd again, and to act filthinesse and villanny to the life; but on Tuesday last there appear'd more Actors then should be, (yet no Devills) at *Salisbury-Court*, the Lord Mayjor and Sheriffe was there, who put the puppy-Players so out of countenance, that they had not one word to say; why should *Play houses* be cry'd up, and *Pamphlets* be cry'd down; are they bawdy-houses too? [103]

But in spite of such occasional disasters the actors made definite plans to maintain three theatres, and also (an important fact which has never been noticed) the King's Men had begun to put their old Blackfriars playhouse into condition for reopening. The Parliament newsbook called *The Perfect Weekly Account* confesses that

Plays begin to be set up apace neverthelesse not without disturbance yet they give out that it shall go forward at three houses, and blacke Fryars is repairing to the end that may be one. [104]

In view of this impudent activity, more complaints were made to the Commons; and that body, with the assent of the Lords, passed a severe measure on 22 October, 1647, which provided that all actors caught *flagrante* should be imprisoned and proceeded against at the General Sessions as rogues. [105] The text of this order, which is referred to in Wright's *Historia Histrionica* (1699), runs as follows:

[16 October, 1647.] For the better Supression of Stage-plays, Interludes, and Common Players: It is this Day *Ordered*, by the [blank] and Commons, in Parliament assembled, That the Lord Mayor, Justices of the Peace, and Sheriffs of the Cities of *London* and *Westminster*, the Counties of *Middlesex* and *Surrey*, or any Two or more of them, shall and may, and are hereby authorized and required to enter into all Houses, and other Places, within the City of *London*, and Liberties thereof, and other Places within their respective Jurisdictions, where Stage-plays, Interludes, or other common Plays, are or shall be acted or played; and all such common Players, or Actors, as they, upon View of them, or any one of them, or upon Oath by two credible Witnesses (which they are hereby authorized to minister) shall be proved before them, or any Two of them, to have acted or played in such Playhouses or Places abovesaid; and all Person and Persons so offending, to commit to any common Gaol or Prison; there to remain until the next General Sessions of the Peace, holden within the said City of *London*, or Liberties thereof, and Places aforesaid, or sufficient Security entered for his or their Appearance at the said Sessions; there to be punished as Rogues, according to Law.

The Lords Concurrence to be desired herein. [106]

[21 October, 1647.] Sir John Hippisley brings Answer, That the Lords do agree . . . to the Order for Supressing of Stage Plays.[107]

One cannot deny that here are provided harsher penalties than any which had gone before. Yet even this latest measure was not thoroughly effectual, as we shall see.

But the Roundhead papers hailed its appearance with joy:

There's an end of those Gamesters, there's Tragedies (though not Comedies) enough besides in *England* and *Ireland*.[108]

I would counsell them [the actors] to imitate the heroick acts of those they have personated, and each help destroy his fellow, since they are not onely silenced, but branded with a name of infamie, ROGUES; but this word perhaps doth the lesse distaste them, on consideration that a famous Queen bestowed upon them the same Epithete.[109]

The Cavaliers responded sharply with their inexhaustible gibe at the Parliament:

Unlesse the *houses* take some speciall Order, *Stage-playes* will never downe while the heavenly *Buffones* of the Presbyterie are in Action, all whose *Sermons* want nothing but *Sence* and *Wit*, to passe for perfect *Comedies*. And therefore seeing the *houses* condemne all Stage-players in an Ordinance, to be prosecuted as *common-Rogues* at the *Sessions*, I see no reason why *Rogues* should be parted.[110]

Mercurius Elencticus, in the same jeering vein, lets us know incidentally that the Cockpit was one of the houses that had been playing. He says that the Commons

... have thundred out an Ordinance, for the Lord Mayor, and the Justices of the Peace, to suppresse Stage Playes, Interludes, and Common-Players: Wherein wee may observe how malicious men are one to another, that be of the same Profession. They of Westminster have Acted their parts now seaven yeares upon the stage of this Kingdome; insomuch that they have even tyred and wearyed out the Spectators, and are themselves ready to be hissed off the Stage, and yet they cannot endure that their Elder brethren of the *Cock-pit* should live by them; because their Actions consist of Harmelesse mirth and Loyalty, whilst themselves Act nothing but tragicall and treasonable Scenes of mischiefe and ruin to the whole Kingdome.[111]

Here I find a reference in a satire on the disagreement between Parliament and the army agitators, which makes it seem that the King's Men, after this last severe order, had petitioned for leave to act:

The Comedy of Errors, had been so often presented in publicke to the rabble that it grew common and out of fashion, whereupon the Houses commings in, began to impaire, and was not so full as it had wont to bee; which perceived by his Majesties servants of the Blacke fryers, they petitioned for leave to set up their old trade againe; no sooner was this motion of theirs whispered to the Army those men of Action, but they conceived that it came to their turne by succession to enter, and to play their parts now or never. . . . May it please yee, this selected fraternity had been often at rehearsall, and intended their first show should be a King and no King, personated to the life, but wholy Tragicall, altered into a new forme by their Poet, H. Peters.[112]

Once more we are presented with the familiar equation between stage players and "state mountebanks." The proceedings of the Commons are a series of amusing mistakes; the army men, on the other hand, are grimly determined to bring the King to trial.

When—on 1 January, 1648—the ordinance of 17 July, 1647 expired, the players presumed that they were free to open shop again on a large scale. Their bad judgment in beginning again so openly was later shown by the harshness of the next repressive order. But for a time they played unhindered. To make matters worse, however, they acted so well that they drew many more prominent persons to hear them than went to listen to the preachers. *The Kingdome's Weekly Intelligencer* says:

. . . it is very observable, that on Sunday *January* 23, there were ten Coaches to heare Doctor *Ushur* at *Lincolns* Inne, but there were above sixscore Coaches on the last Thursday in Golden lane to heare the Players at the Fortune.[113]

The Royalist *Elencticus* remarks with satisfaction that

the *Members* are *perplexed* with the *Play-houses:* for since *Orthodox* Preaching was laid aside, the *People* find that they can *edifie* much more in hearing one *play*, then twenty of their best *Sermons*. . . . So that where a dozen Coaches *Tumble* after *Obadiah Sedgewick;* Threescore are observed to *wheele* to the *Cockpit*, which is very offensive to the Brethren.[114]

It is amusing to see how frequently the pulpit and the stage were bracketed in the writings of the time. Here are a few passages in point:

Snarl. There was an age . . . before . . .
  So many plays, and Puritan preachings,
  That women might be chaste; now 't is impossible.[115]

As for Clergie men . . . some of them have, as it is generally knowne, preacht in the Pulpit like Players on the Stage, only to get themselves rich wives. . . .[116]

. . . Parson *Fowler* standing up above the people, in the Maiors presence, vaunting as in a stage-play. . . .[117]

  From a precise Player and a Club-Divine . . .
    Libera nos [Domine].[118]

On 22 January, on complaint that "many Stage Playes were acted in the severall parts of the City, [and] County of Middlesex, notwithstanding the Ordinance of Parliament to the contrary," [119] the House told off Mr. John Stephens to prepare and bring in with all speed an ordinance "for the effectual Suppressing of Stage Plays, with a severe Penalty upon such as shall offend against it; and for the Pulling down of the Stages, Galleries, and Seats; and making all those Houses unfit for Stage Plays." [120] At the same time they renewed their exhortations to the justices, and authorized the committees of the militia to "take effectual Course."

Anti-Pragmaticus applauds the Parliament's new measure, and girds at the actors:

. . . if those proud parroting Players cannot live, let them put their hands to worke, they are most of them a sort of Superbious Ruffians given to all manner of wickednesse, and because sometimes the Asses are cloathed in Lions skins, the Dolts imagine themselves some body, walke in as great State, as *Caesar*, and demeane themselves as loftily as any of the twelve noble spirited Beasts of the wildernesse; away with them and their actions on the publike Stage.[121]

Pragmaticus, on the other hand, jeers at the Parliament and prophesies a bad end to the high and mighty Players of State who

have new vamp't an *old Ordinance* for abolishing *Stage-Playes*; and to prevent the acting of any hereafter, the *Boxes* and *Scaffolds* in each *Playhouse*, must be pull'd downe, except it be in their owne; because they have not plaid out all their parts yet, nor I neither, nor will I till they give over:

  For, though in *Tragick* Plots they all combine,
  Yet know the *Comick* part shall still be mine.[122]

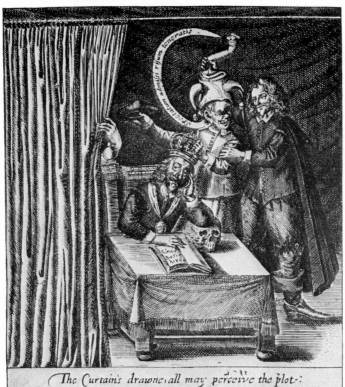

The Curtain's drawne, all may perceive the plot:

A CAVALIER CARTOON

The drawn curtain discovers a significant group on the stage of England. On
the head of the Puritan, who is in the act of taking the crown from the royal
martyr, the Cavalier places a fool's cap surmounted by a cockscomb from
which proceeds an appropriate but misquoted line from Horace.

(From Εἰκών ἡ πιστή, 1649.)

In bitterer vein, *Melancholicus* [123] pretends that Parliament puts down the players because they reveal on their stages the iniquity of the law-givers:

On *saturday* last the house acted their parts against all stage-players, commanding the boxes stages, and seates, (except their own) to be made unserviceable for further acting; for to say the truth, Play-houses are worse then whipping-schooles, or the houses of correction; for there they lay open truth and falshood, in their naked colours, and scourge Iniquity untill he bleeds againe; there you may read the Parliament in print, there you may see Treason courting *Tyranny*, and Faction prostituted to *Rebellion*, There you may see (as in a Myrrour) all State-juglings, cleanly conveyances, and underhand dealings pourtray'd to the life; therefore Players and Pamphleteers, they must, they shall come down, the Parliament playhouse is sufficient to lead the Kingdom a daunce without these, and to lick up all the profitable Customers into their own Brothell, and let 'em out again unto the publick at eight *per centum.*

While the Commons were awaiting the report of Mr. John Stephens on the new ordinance, the Lords prepared an ordinance of their own [124] for suppressing plays for twelve months, and passed it down, on 31 January, to the Commons for approval. After some debate, however, the Commons ordered it laid aside, and called for a report from their committee of one; whereupon Stephens's ordinance was read for the first time and ordered to be read again the following day.[125] But some delay occurred and the ordinance was not reread until 9 February, on which day it was passed by the Commons, and agreed to by the Lords.

We must pause here for a moment to consider some new and important disclosures of the doings of the King's Men which come from a Chancery suit brought by the actor Theophilus Bird in 1655.[126] Bird begins by showing that about 1635 he was admitted to the King's Company at Blackfriars. At that time the company had "a stock consisting of apparel, books, hangings, and other goods of the value of £3000 and upwards." On his admission, Bird says, he deposited £200 "towards the said apparel, books, goods, and other things, being £150 at least more than others of the said company had done, and was more than his proportion of the said clothes and stock did amount unto." But since Michael Bowyer [127] (one of the chief actors) had advanced £200 for the company's use, Bird was persuaded to join with eleven other members in a bond of £400 to Richard Perkins, in trust for Bowyer, for the payment of the £200. Bird insists that in his lifetime Bowyer never demanded payment of him on this bond.

Continuing, he alleges that, when the company was dissolved on the suppression of playhouses in 1642, Bowyer, Pollard, and others of the company being in London, in Bird's absence "seized upon all the said apparel, hangings, books, and other goods . . . and sold and converted the same to their own uses." Bowyer, he says, got most of the profits of the sale. Later Bowyer died, and his widow Elizabeth married one Thomas Morrison. When Bird came back to London in 1647, he went to Morrison and "Pollard and others who survived of the said company," and demanded his share in the money raised by sale of the stock. Instead of giving it to him, Morrison and his wife threatened to sue him on the old bond.

From this point on it is clearer to follow the answer of Morrison and his wife to Bird's complaint. Elizabeth Morrison mentions the £400 bond which she says was never discharged. Bowyer (her late husband), she says, made her his executrix by his will in September, 1645, and died shortly after. She proved his will, and later married Thomas Morrison, 1 April, 1646.

Morrison confesses that before January, 1647/8, he had received £50 from Bird and the others as a part payment of the £200 and interest, and in January they paid an additional £48. At this time they admitted that there was still £180 due, and asked for an abatement. Morrison reduced the debt some £30 or £40, and on 28 January, 1647/8, John Lowen, Richard Robinson, Robert Benfield, Thomas Pollard, Hugh Clarke, Stephen Hamerton, and Theophilus Bird entered on a new bond of £300 conditioned on the payment to Morrison of £147 12s. on or before 30 July, 1648. This sum never being paid, Morrison brought suit for recovery against Bird at common law in Easter term, 1655.

Morrison and his wife deny that the Blackfriars stock was worth anything like £3000 and insist that Bird deposited only £50. Further they deny that Bowyer had any of the profits of the sale of the stock.

They do not know whether it is true (as Bird alleges) that Pollard died worth £500 and that "one Richard Perryn of the town of Buckingham, saddler" is administrator to his estate. They deny that Benfield also died worth more than £1500 and that a London apothecary named Warburton and his wife Ann (Benfield's only daughter) are his heirs. Bird, they insist, was a principal obligor, not a mere surety, and ought by right to discharge the bond.

This suit dragged on through 1656 and 1657. Elizabeth Morrison died 28 August, 1656, and by the number of court orders it is clear that Morrison delayed his appearance in Chancery to end the suit. What the upshot was, I cannot discover.

Nevertheless there is much new information in these parchments. Besides the testimony concerning Bowyer's and Pollard's deaths (which should furnish a clue to their wills), we have an interesting light on the money value of a share in the Blackfriars company, which seems to have been £50. Further, in the presence of Richard Robinson as an obligor with the others in 1648 we have another proof to add to Cunningham's, that General Harrison did not kill "Dick Robinson" the player,[128] and a correction to Lowe's statement [129] that Robinson died in 1647. All these seven actors had taken part in publishing a folio of Beaumont and Fletcher's plays in 1647.

More important is the light this document throws on the clouded question of the membership of the Queen's and King's companies in and after the closing of the theatres, because of the plague, in 1636 and 1637. That the Queen's Men united with the Revels Company at Salisbury Court when the theatres reopened in 1637 seemed probable from Sir Henry Herbert's undated entry, which runs: "I disposed of Perkins, Sumner, Sherlock, and Turner, to Salisbury Court, and joyned them with the best of that company." [130] Our Bird–Morrison suit illuminates this entry by showing that three other leading members of the Queen's Company at this period went over to the King's Men — Michael Bowyer, Theophilus Bird, and Hugh Clark.[131]

In January, 1648, then, while Parliament was preparing an ordinance which should crush stage players, Lowen, Robinson, Benfield, Pollard, Clark, Hamerton, and Bird, calmly looking forward to an era of prosperity, were promising to pay off an old Blackfriars debt to Michael Bowyer's heirs. And as if careless of the imminent blow, the actors proceeded to play with vigor unabated. On 5 February, John Evelyn was one of the spectators of a tragi-comedy at the Cockpit.[132] And on 3 February, the Red Bull put on Beaumont and Fletcher's *Wit Without Money*.

Here we have the earliest record, so far as I know, of the method of advertising plays by scattering bills in the coaches of the quality:

Tickets were thrown into Gentlemens Coaches, thus. At the Bull this day you may have Wit without Money, meaning a Play.[133]

It is interesting to compare this bill with the facsimile, published by Mr. W. J. Lawrence,[134] of the earliest known English playbill (1692). Both notices are brief and to the point, and the order of announcement in each is the same:

At the Bull this day you may have Wit without Money.

At the Theatre Royall, in Drury Lane, this present Wensday being the nineth day of November, will be presented, a new play called, Henry the Second of England.

These bills, or "tickets," are evidently of exactly the same type. As Mr. Lawrence remarks, the presence of four such bills dated in 1692, 1693, and 1694, in the Verney family archives shows that they must have been delivered at the houses of the noble patrons of the theatre. The custom of throwing the bills into coaches, which we here see practised a half-century earlier, is even more picturesque. One wonders whether the customary *Vivat Rex!* appeared on the Red Bull's ticket when Parliament was gathering its strength to execute Charles I.

The ordinance passed on 9 February, 1648,[135] affected the actors, the playhouses, the money taken for seats, and lastly the pockets of the auditors. The "Players shall be taken as Rogues" and punished [136] according to the statutes of Elizabeth and James. The lord mayor and sheriffs are authorized to "pull down and demolish all Stage-Galleries,[137] Seats and Boxes." Money gathered of persons coming to see stage plays shall be forfeited to the churchwardens for the poor of the parish in which it was collected. Every spectator at any play (if caught!) "shall for every time he shall be so present, Forfeit and Pay *Five Shillings* to the Use of the Poor" of his parish.

While there is no record that the authorities set about demolishing the stages of the actors at once, there is no doubt that the penalties to be imposed on the spectators had an instant effect upon the flourishing profession. *Mercurius Elencticus* [138] (Sir George Wharton), who was in a position to know, thought that this order would prove the death of the actors and their families. He says that the Commons

have pronounced the *Players* to be *Rogues*, thinking by this Meanes to make them *Theeves*, and then theile find out an easier way to be rid of them. These poore Men were most of them initiated, and bred up in this *quality* from their *Childhood* for the service of *King* and *Quen*, and very few of them have any other meanes of subsistence; so that they and their Families (being about 100. Persons) must inevitably starve: But this is all the *Charity* I ever heard of, that yet they afforded to the *Kings* servants, *plunder* them of what they had, and then turne them a *grazing*.

Another Royalist paper, *Pragmaticus*, also recognized the harshness of the ordinance:

And to witnesse unto the world how perfectly they hate a *King*, they are resolved for the time to come, after the *Tragedy* of this, never to admit of one, so much as in *Comedy* again. And therefore on *wednesday* last the grand *Ordinance* against *Stage-playes* was hastened into the *House*; which ordains, that all *Players* shall, for the first offence, be *committed* & *and Fined*, and for the second, be *whipped*. And though this course seem too harsh against such harmlesse *recreations*; yet, as some thinke,

> *The reason why* Playes *must be lash't downe,*
> *For feare themselves be* whipt *about the* Towne.[139]

Mercurius Bellicus,[140] while admitting that the heavy artillery-men among the law-givers have "mounted their roaring *Meg*," encourages the players to laugh at them:

> But now farewell Playes for ever, for the Rebels are resolved to bee the onely Tragedians, none shall act *Cataline* but themselves; and therefore (they being angry) that their former Ordinance did no execution, have now mounted their roaring *Meg*, with which they intend to beat downe all the Stages, Galleries, and Boxes, in the severall Theatres; the Players for the first Contempt, are to bee Imprisoned and fined for Malignants; for the second, to bee whipt about the Towne as Rogues, but the Actors may well laugh at them, and despise this their Edict as themselves, since they have the faith to believe that the time is comming when *Barkstead*, cannot protect them for [*sic*] tasting the lash themselves.

Better enforced than those that had gone before, this enactment no doubt caused the actors much hardship. At the end of the first month of its operation they were driven to the pass of begging the House of Lords for relief and for permission to leave England:

> A Petition was presented to their Lordships by the Players lately put downe by an Ordinance of Parliament, desiring something to be bestowed upon them from the State, and to have passes to goe beyond the Seas, but this Petition was utterly rejected.[141]

Meanwhile — a fact which we now learn for the first time — the exiled English colony at The Hague wrote to announce that a company of actors had come to divert its members:

> Wednesday, March 8. By Letters . . . from the Hague March 6. new stile [that is, 24 February, 1648] is thus certified:
> Hither are come a pack of Players from France, who are to help away the time spent formerly in Martiall actions, so that what you pull down in England, we are setting up.[142]

It seems likely that this was George Jolly's company of English actors, and perhaps identical with the company formerly supported by Prince Charles in Paris.[143]

The harshness of the English House of Lords in granting the unfortunate actors neither relief nor passports doubtless enlisted more sympathy from those who patronized the players, and nerved the latter to play at all costs. The Parliament had made plenty of enemies by its acts. *Mercurius Insanus In-*

sanissimus [144] gives an exhilarating list of its high crimes and misdemeanors:

> . . . besides all this they have put downe Bishops, Players, Saints, spirituall Courts, & in their roomes they have erected and set up the Excise, Courts of Sequestrations, Confiscations, Compositions, Examinations, Abhominations, &c.

Some of the opponents of Parliament professed not to feel the lack of comedies while they could watch the antics of the Parliament farce:

> Indeed we need not any more *Stage-playes*, we thanke them for suppressing them, they save us money; for Ile undertake we can laugh as heartily at *Foxley*, *Peters*, and others of their godly Ministers as ever we did at *Cane* at the *Red Bull*, *Tom: Pollard* in the humorous Lieutenant, *Robins* the Changeling, or any humorist of them all. [145]

But that stage plays were not properly put down as yet even by this ordinance is shown by the renewed activities of Parliament. On 23 June, 1648, the Commons instructed the Committee of Complaints to take into consideration the breaches of "the Ordinances concerning Playhouses," and ordered that the Committee should have power to put the said ordinances "in speedy Execution." [146] That this order had little effect appears from the sequel which was passed on 26 July:

> That it be referred to the Committee of the Militia of *Westminster*, with such Forces as they shall think fit, to take Care, that the Stages, Boxes, Scaffolds, Seats, and Forms, in the several Playhouses within the County of *Middlesex*, be forthwith taken down; and the Materials thereof made unuseful for that Service for the Future: And that Major General *Skippon* be desired to advise with the said Committee about the same; and to assist them with Horse, if Need be. [147]

At the same time, a committee under a certain Mr. Scott, sitting *de die in diem*, was to put into execution the laws "for suppressing of Stage Plays and Interludes."

Nothing drastic was done, however, on these orders; but Parliament, in a letter to the General Assembly of the Church of Scotland, complacently numbered among its proceedings "in the Work of Reformation," an ordinance "for suppressing all Stage-Plays and Interludes (the Nurseries of Vice and Prophaness)." [148]

Complaints were preferred on 1 September that these "nurseries" were still functioning. The House thereupon again jogged the elbow of Mr. Scott's committee.[149] But it was only after another two weeks, when information was brought that "Stage-plays were daily acted either at the *Bull* or *Fortune*, or the private House at *Salisbury-Court*," [150] that the Commons resolved to do something effective. The only hopeful course was to *pay* someone for doing that specific job. Adding thereto the duty of suppressing newsbooks, on 13 September, 1648, they commissioned Francis Bethan as Provost Marshal for three months within a radius of twenty miles of London. Bethan's duties were "to apprehend and surprise all . . . Persons as sell, sing, or publish, Ballads or Books, scandalous to the Parliament . . . and to suppress Playhouses, and apprehend the Players." [151] He was allowed

for himselfe five shillings a day, and for his Deputy three shillings and foure pence a day, and twenty men whom he is to make choice of for this particular service, to be alwayes ready at his command are to have eighteen pence a day.[152]

As may be imagined, the putting on of a paid sleuth-hound fluttered the fugitive writers. *Mercurius Elencticus* [153] speaks straight to Bethan, appealing to his better nature:

Come Master *Bethen*: thy worth (if such as they report it to be from *Derby-House*) assures me thou wilt not be so injurious to *Truth*, as to stop, or abuse her *Messengers*. Surely we that in these Dayes of *Mis-rule* and *Danger*, dare yet execute her Commands, deserve rather thy Assistance and Encouragement, then thy Threats, and Indeavours for Suppression. Our *Truth* is naked & open *Day-light*, that does present the *Masques* and *Mummeries* of thy great Masters, and shew their severall *Triumphs* over the Kingdome.

A touching appeal, but hardly strong enough to outweigh duty and five shillings a day. Another Royalist paper, *The Parliament Porter*,[154] boldly condemned Bethan's work while making a stout defence of good plays:

[My language will] perhaps hasten Capt. *Bethen* . . . to the performance of his odious task, *viz.* the seizing upon all honest books and ballads which speak plain English to the people . . . the suppressing of Stage-playes, honest and harmlesse recreations, as that renowned *Q. Elizabeth* stiled them, (I speak not in the justification of that prophane vile Commedy, called the *Puritans of Amsterdam*, or any of that kind) knowing that the people of themselves are too apt to scoffe at the profession of godlinesse, but I say that it is the lustre and glory of our Nation to have vertue extolled and vice deprodated even upon the publike Theater, for to no other end an illaborate Comedy or Tragedy ought to be written or presented to the view of the vulgar, and I wish it may be the care of both present & future Actors to condemn to silence all obscaene or irreligious plays, so shall the Commick Sock and Tragick Buskin be an adornment, & not a badge of contempt, as their ignorant enemies maliciously divulge.

But if *Bethen* go on his imployment, what a wretch will he remain upon record?

Melancholicus,[155] setting up for a "gentleman playwright" rather than a fugitive scribbler, bears away the bell for rhetoric and self-assurance:

But what becomes of the mighty Captaine over twenty the mighty Mahound, called the provost Marshall, whom the Machivillians voted five shillings a day to suppresse me and Stageplaies, hold up my Roscians of the Red Bull; for you and I must fall together, there is some of you whom I love, and a party of proud Princoxes amongst you whom I scorne, more then a tinkers t . . . d, or a Committee mans taunt; I would have each Actor to know that he is at most but the Poets ape, and speakes like a Parrot, those words he puts in his mouth; 'tis we Gentlemen that are you creators, 'tis we that advance you to the Dignity of Kings, Dukes, Earles, and Knights; and sometimes least you should (inspired with ignorance) imagine your selves to be those whom you personate, we abate your overweening thoughts, putting on you the habit, and prescribing unto you the language of Beggars, sometimes of Thieves, conspirators of Rebells, and miscreants.

> What is it lies not in Poetick art?
> Verses have magick in them and impart
> Celestiall Rhapsodies and charm men more
> Then those wise Jigs the Sybills sung of yore.

But it seemes our deformers will have no Tragedie presented but that of their own; I confesse they are exquesite Tragedians, and play their parts to the amazement of all mankind; they have worn the Buskins so long, that they have changed the face of beauteous Britain into a charnell or Golgotha, yet were there any love of learning in them they would not be so eager for the suppressing of plaies, the lustre and glory of our Nation, is by all consequence benificiall even to the vulgarre, to see vice lasht till she bleed, with her own whip that she bears at her girdle, and vertue enthronized and deified, even on the publike theater, but they shew by this what sordid soules they harbour; I say no more.

The Red Bull players will agree with us that he has said quite enough for once.

Whatever the activities of Bethan and his crew, they were not sufficient to satisfy the House of Commons. On 4 November the Commons, going over Bethan's head, ordered the sheriffs of London and Middlesex to work more execution on the offending players and playgoers and "to give this House an Account of their effectual Proceedings herein." [156]

It was in this winter of 1648, as James Wright tell us, [157] that a company which numbered among its members the great actors Lowen, Taylor, Pollard, Burt, and Hart, was acting with as much caution and privacy as possible at the Cockpit. But after several undisturbed performances, while they were doing *Rollo, or the Bloody Brother,*

a Party of Foot Souldiers beset the House, surprized 'em about the middle of the Play, and carried 'em away in their habits, not admitting them to Shift, to *Hatton-House* then a Prison, where having detain'd them sometime, they Plunder'd them of their Cloths, and let 'em loose againe.

Mercurius Elencticus (December 19–26) admits that "the *Red Bull* and *Cock-pit* are silenc'd." [158] But these houses must have reopened at once, for I find a most circumstantial account of a grand raid carried out by the soldiers on 1 January, which shows all four theatres in full career:

The Souldiers seized on the Players on their Stages at Drury-lane, and at Salisbury Court. They went also to the Fortune in Golden-lane, but they found none there, but John Pudding dancing on the Ropes, whom they took along with them. In the meane time the Players at the Red Bull, who had notice of it, made haste away, and were all gone before they came, and tooke away all their acting cloathes with them. But at Salisbury Court they were taken on the Stage the Play being almost ended, and with many Linkes and lighted Torches they were carried to White-Hall with their Players cloathes upon their backs. In the way they oftentimes tooke the Crown from his head who acted the King, and in sport would oftentimes put it on again. Abraham had a black Satten gown on, and before he came into the durt, he was very neat in his white laced pumps. The people not expecting such a pageant looked and laughed at all the rest, and not knowing who he was, they asked, what had that Lady done? They made some resistance at the Cockpit in Drury Lane, which was the occasion that they were bereaved of their apperell, and were not so well used as those in Salisbury Court, who were more patient, and therefore at their Releasement they had their cloaths returned to them without the least diminution: After two days confinement, They were Ordered to put in Bayle, and to appear before the Lord Mayor to answer for what they have done according unto Law.[159]

This is the best description yet found of one of these raids on the actors; and we see by the tone of the report that the law was not harshly enforced. The players were not robbed of their costumes except when they resisted arrest. Mr. W. J. Lawrence makes the attractive suggestion that the player Abraham appearing here as the "Lady" is probably identical with the Abraham Ivory, mentioned in Buckingham's *The Rehearsal*, who, according to Briscoe "had formerly been a considerable actor of women's parts."[159a] *Perfect Occurrences* [160] adds to the picture of the raid: the "Ladies were in a great fear, but had no hurt: Some of the exempted Members of Parliament were there."

A writer who was in sympathy with the players seized upon this opportunity to rush into print with an attack on the army and all those opposed to plays, under the guise of William Prynne, cleverly naming his squib *Mr. William Prynn His Defence of* STAGE-PLAYS, *or A Retractation of a former Book of his called Histrio-Mastix*.[161] Here, in Prynne's well-known conscientious and energetic style, his facetious mimic takes back his wrong-headed arguments against plays, and attacks

this Tyrannicall, abominable, lewd, schismaticall, haeretical Army, [which] did lately in a most inhumane, cruell, rough, and barbarous manner take away the poor Players from their Houses, being met there to discharge the duty of their callings; as if this Army were fully bent, and most traytterously and maliciously set to put downe and depresse all the Kings Friends, not onely in Parliament but in the very Theaters.

George Thomason's copy of this exhilarating tract is dated 10 January; and on that same day the outraged Prynne hurried out a broad-sheet [162] to disabuse the public mind. He declares to all the world that the scandalous paper has been "newly printed and published in my name by some of the imprisoned Stage-Players, or agents of the army." Some simple-minded

persons may have been deceived by the hoax. As late as
2 October, 1649, a writer pretended to think that the *Retractation* was genuine. In *A Serious Epistle to Mr. William
Prynne* [163] he holds that it is an easy matter to confute the
Histrio-Mastix,

. . . when by so many *Presidents Records Journalls, Historyes, Diarys,
Ledgeer Books, Annalls Poems, Orations,* &c. it can be prov'd that plays
have been in former times acted and entertained into the delights of
Princes, as your self write, confesse, declare, acknowledge, manifest, and
prove by Authors in your *Retractation* to that purpose.

On 1 January, 1649, Parliament resolved that for Charles I
to levy war against the Parliament and kingdom was treason.
The same day, marching to Whitehall with the captured players, the soldiers "oftentimes tooke the Crown from his head
who acted the King, and in sport would oftentimes put it on
again." In less than a month Charles was sentenced to the
block at Whitehall. *Pragmaticus,* [164] likening the event to a
monstrous tragedy, vainly hopes that some power will inter-
vene (as the soldiers did at Drury Lane) before the catastrophe:

Yes, the feat is now done, and Law and Equity must both give way: the
Trayterous Tragedie[n]s are upon their *Exit,* and poor King CHARLES at
the Brinke of the *Pitt;* [165] The *Prologue* is past, the *Proclamation made,*
His Sentence is given, and we daily expect the sad *Catastrophie;* and then
behold! The Sceane is *chang'd:*

England but now [a] glorious *Monarchy*
Degraded to a base *Democracy.*

The *Play* thus done, or rather the WORKE *Finish'd;* the Epilogue remains, to wit the Epitaph of a slaughter'd King; which I reserve to another
Opportunity; hoping Heaven may prevent you, ere your Sceane be finish'd;
(as you did those poor Players lately in the middle of their's; not onely de-
priving them of their present subsistance, but of the meanes of the future)
but what doe we talke of such slight Injuries to them that are now undoing
Kingdomes . . .?

After the King's execution a Puritan writer [166] found it "re-
markable, that he should end his dayes in a Tragedie at the
Banqueting-house, where he had seene, and caused many a
Comedy to be acted upon the Lord's Day." One can almost

see the sagacious readers wag their heads over the miraculous fitness of things.

It was not until March, 1649, that the earlier Draconian ordinances against the playhouses were revived and actually put into effect, and the interiors of the Fortune, Cockpit, and Salisbury Court — stages, boxes, seats, and galleries — dismantled.

The play house in Salsbury Court, in fleetstreete, was pulled downe by a company of Souldiers, set on by the Sectaries of these sad times, On Saturday the 24 day . . . of March. 1649. The Phenix in Druery Lane, was pulled downe also this day . . . by the same Souldiers. . . . The Fortune . . . now pulled downe on the in-side by the Souldiers this 1649.[167]

Although the Salisbury Court and Cockpit, with their interiors made over, were to take part again in dramatic history, the Fortune never survived the wrecking in 1649. Tobias Lisle, who leased it from its owner, Dulwich College, being in arrears of the yearly rent of 120 pounds, in 1649 wished to put the house to some other use in order to make it pay; but the college refused any rent except "in the nature of a Playhouse" and entered into costly suits at law.[168] The playhouse returned into the hands of the college, which in 1650 refused to let the poor of the parish of St. Giles without Cripplegate use it as a place of worship. In 1656 it was reported to be in a ruinous condition, and by March, 1662, it was totally demolished.[169]

This wrecking of the interiors of the playhouses, the most serious blow sustained by the players, doubtless drove some of them to seek other employment. While the Red Bull, which had somehow escaped the military wrecking parties, continued to play,[170] the Cockpit and Blackfriars players, and probably those of Salisbury Court, were in want. Their pitiful condition is set forth in an appeal of 1650 or thereabouts to Parliament.[171] Asking a term of probation in acting, they offer to submit to a Parliament censor and to contribute a portion of their takings to the state:

To the Supream Authoritie the Parliament of the Commonwealthe of England The humble Petition of diverse poor and distressed men, heretofore the Actors of Black-Friers and the Cock-Pit. Sheweth,

That your most poor Petitioners, having long suffered in extream want, by being prohibited the use of their qualitie of Acting, in which they were trained up from their childhood, whereby they are uncapable of any other way to get a subsistance, and are now fallen into such lamentable povertie, that they know not how to provide food for themselves, their wives and children: great debts being withall demanded of them, and they not in a condition to satisfie the creditours; and without your mercifull and present permission, they must all inevitably perish.

May it therefore please this Honourable House to commiserate their sad and distressed condition, and to vouchsafe them a Libertie to Act but some small time (for their triall of inoffensiveness) onely such morall and harmless representations, as shall no way be distastfull to the Commonwealth or good manners. They humbly submitting themselves to any one of knowing judgement and fidelitie to the State, appointed to oversee them and their actions, and willing to contribute out of their poor endeavours, what shall be thought fit and allotted them to pay weekly or otherwise, for the service of Ireland, or as the State shall think fitting.

And as in dutie they are ever bound, shall pray, &c.

But despite this humble appeal, nothing was done for their relief. We must look for them after this time acting privately in houses and tennis courts in London, and at the mansions of the gentry in the suburbs. James Wright [172] tells us that

in *Oliver's* time they used to Act privately, three or four Miles, or more, out of Town, now here, now there, sometimes in Noblemens Houses, in particular *Holland-house* at *Kensington*, where the Nobility and Gentry who met (but in no great Numbers) used to make a Sum for them, each giving a broad Peice, or the like. And *Alexander Goffe*, the Woman Actor at *Blackfriers* (who had made himself known to Persons of Quality) used to be the Jackal and give notice of Time and Place.

Such are the performances at Knightsbridge already referred to. Abraham Cowley tells us in a preface that his *Guardian* (afterward *Cutter of Coleman Street*) was acted several times "privately during the troubles." We shall hear later of the use of Gibbons's Tennis Court (which after the Restoration became the first Theatre Royal) for private performances during the Interregnum. Some of the dispossessed actors from the other playhouses also occasionally used the Red Bull.

At *Christmass* and Bartlemew fair, they used to Bribe the Officer who Commanded the Guard at *Whitehall*, and were thereupon connived at to Act for a few Days, at the Red *Bull*; but they were sometimes notwithstanding Disturb'd by Soldiers.[173]

As a rule, however, the "Roscians of the Red Bull" used their playhouse themselves. It argues well for the strong love of the drama in the English people that (after the dismantling of the other playhouses) we find lords, ladies, and gentlewomen frequenting the Red Bull, which had had the reputation of being a turbulent, rowdy place, patronized chiefly by "citizens and the meaner sort of people." The elocution at the large open-air theatres, as may be imagined, was not of the finest. Edmund Gayton says, in 1654,

I have heard, that the Poets of the Fortune and red Bull, had alwayes a mouth-measure for their Actors (who were terrible teare-throats) and made their lines proportionable to their compasse, which were *sesquipedales*, a foot and a halfe.[174]

Further, he gives us a lively picture of the boisterous character of the audiences before the war (especially on holidays), the plays they clamored for, and their behavior when displeased:

. . . men come not to study at a Play-house, but love such expressions and passages, which with ease insinuate themselves into their capacities. . . . To them bring *Jack Drumm's* entertainment, *Greens tu quoque*, the *Devill of Edmunton*, and the like; or if it be on Holy dayes, when Saylers, Watermen, Shoomakers, Butchers and Apprentices are at leisure, then it is good policy to amaze those violent spirits with some tearing Tragoedy full of fights and skirmishes: as the *Guelphs* and *Guiblins*, *Greeks* and *Trojans*, or the three [sic] *London Apprentises*, which commonly ends in six acts, the spectators frequently mounting the stage, and making a more bloody Catastrophe amongst themselves, then the Players did. I have known upon one of these *Festivals*, but especially at *Shrove-tide*, where the Players have been appointed, notwithstanding their bils to the contrary, to act what the major part of the company had a mind to; sometimes *Tamerlane*, sometimes *Jugurth*, sometimes the Jew of *Malta*, and sometimes parts of all these, and at last, none of the three taking, they were forc'd to undresse and put off their Tragick habits, and conclude the day with the merry milk-maides. And unlesse this were done, and the popular humour satisfied, as sometimes it so fortun'd, that the Players were refractory; the Benches, the tiles, the laths, the stones, Oranges, Apples, Nuts, flew about most liberally, and as there were Mechanicks of all professions, who fell every one to his owne trade, and dissolved a house in an instant, and made a ruine of a stately Fabrick. It was not then the most mimicall nor fighting man, *Fowler*, nor *Andrew Cane* could pacifie; Prologues nor Epilogues would prevaile; the Devill and the fool were quite out of favour.[175]

We may believe, however, that this description fits better the period before the strict laws against plays, and that in the time we are studying the audience was more grateful for what it could get. Besides, the private announcements must have helped to keep away the most disorderly element. On the other hand, "the most fighting man," Cane, and his fellows had now as much or more to fear from the soldiers as formerly from the mob. On Tuesday, 22 January, 1650, they were surprised at a performance at the Red Bull. The soldiers took down the names of the lords, ladies, and gentlewomen, for the purpose of imposing fines or other penalties, and after a bloody encounter marched off seven or eight of the principal actors. *Mercurius Pragmaticus (for King Charls II)* [176] recounts this latest infringement of the Parliament "crack," as he calls it:

> If you [Parliament] be destitute of something to do, you may go hang your selves for a pastime to the people; I believe you would have more spectators then the *Players* in *St. John's street;* yes and Lords and Ladies too would laugh more to see the *Juncto* and State hang, then any Play in the world Acted.
>
> But your own Play-houses at *Westminster, Whitehall, Darby-house, Somerset-house, &c.* are the only Stages where Players must come, and who those players must be, I'le tell you; all in Parliament Robes K——s F——s and Rebels; those are the men now in request: *Andr. Cane* is out of date & all other his complices: alas poor players they are acting their parts in prison, for their presumptions to break a Parliament Crack. On Tuesday *Janu.* 21 [177] 1649. bee it known unto all men, the State *Janizaries* rob'd the Play-house in *St Johns streete,* imprisoned the Players, and listed all the Lords, Ladies and Gentlewomen, who are either to serve the States or pay money, if their mightynesse please to command it for so great a contempt as breaking an Act made upon the Stage at *Westminster.*
>
> Me thinks the Supreme Poppet-players of State should have somthing else in their minds then suppressing Playes.

The Man in the Moon's account [178] is still more amusing and circumstantial:

> Sure the *Play* at *Westminster* is almost at an end, for the *Foole* hath done his *part,* and is fetch'd off the *Stage* with a *vengeance;* Exit *Philip* the *Foole,*[179] but a knavish one Ile promise you; which made the *Tragedians* at *Westminster*-Hall presently so mad for him; that they thought, the hideous *Storm* that fetch'd him away, had carried him to those other *Comedians* in Saint *Johns* street: which drove them presently thither, with two or three

Companies of the *Rebells;* seized on the poore *Players,* uncased them of their Cloaths, disarmed the Lords and Gentlemen of their Swords and Cloakes; but finding him not to be there, they hung the poore *Players* Cloathes upon their Pikes, and very manfully marched away with them as *Trophies* of so wonderfull a *victory:* there was taken at this Fight about seven or eight of the chiefe Actors, some wounded, all their Cloaths and Properties, without the losse of one man on our side; onely at their returne with their *spoiles* and *prisoners,* one of our Souldiers being left behind by reason of some plunder, was taken up with the sight of a *Riding* at *Smithfield-Barres;* where, one that acted Sir *Thomas* a horse-back, with a *Ladle* in his hand, two Baskets of *Prides* Graines before him, and his *Doxie* riding with her face to the horse tayle behind; one of them flung a Ladle of Graines in our Commanders face: which he took to be a great affront to a Souldier that had so lately routed the *Players,* that he furiously drew his Sword (he had stole from the Play-house) and began to sweare and vapour: which a Butchers Boy perceiving, presently disarm'd him, made him swallow his Graines and be thankfull, and after some certain *Kicks* of *Indignation,* broke his sword over his Coxcombe, and sent him to *Pauls* to complaine to his Fellowes: and if this Souldier scape (as the Surgeon is something doubt-full) there will questionlesse come forth an *Act* for a *Thanksgiving* for this wonderfull Victory over the poore *Players,* and the Souldiers deliverance.

He goes on to tell how the soldiers "brought their *Spoiles* (and the poore Carrion *Players,* that look'd like *Pharoahs* leane Kine on one another) to their *Slaughter-house* at White-hall."

These raids, so costly for the actors in fines, imprisonment, and occasional loss of costumes and properties, were un-doubtedly the cause of the development of the shortened form of entertainment known as the "Droll." The name is evidently an abbreviation of "Droll Humours" (which, with "Humours," "Drolleries," and the like, was also used). When full-length plays with complete paraphernalia had become too difficult and expensive to give regularly, some of the best actors pitched upon a method of selecting short, racy, comic scenes from the plays most in favor, and treating them as little farci-cal pieces rounded off with dancing, in the manner of the well-known jigs at the end of comedies, which "shut up the scene with mirth." And for lack of better, these little dramatic pieces were eagerly attended by the hungry public. The familiar preface by Francis Kirkman to his edition of a collec-tions of drolls is worth quoting here:[180]

When the publique Theatres were shut up . . . then all that we could divert ourselves with were these humours and pieces of Plays, which passing under the Name of a merry conceited Fellow, called *Bottom the Weaver*, *Simpleton the Smith*, *John Swabber*, or some such title, were only allowed us, and that but by stealth too, and under pretence of Rope-dancing, or the like; and these being all that was permitted us, great was the confluence of the Auditors; and these small things were as profitable, and as great getpennies to the Actors as any of our late famed Plays. I have seen the Red Bull Play-House, which was a large one, so full, that as many went back for want of room as had entred; and as meanly as you may think of these Drols, they were then Acted by the best Comedians then and now in being; and I may say, by some that then exceeded all now living, by Name, the incomparable *Robert Cox*, who was not only the principal Actor, but also the Contriver and Author of most of these Farces.

Cox was rather contriver than author of most of these twenty-seven drolls (printed in *The Wits*), which are largely from Beaumont and Fletcher, with some borrowings also from Shakspere, Jonson, and Shirley. His "contriving" had begun as early as 1646, with a Shaksperian droll, *The Merry Conceits of Bottom the Weaver*.[181]

Professor Rollins has performed an important service in discovering new facts concerning Cox — notably records of his acting and of the date of his death — which cast light on an obscure and interesting figure. One of the documents is a bold advertisement published by *Mercurius Democritus* in June, 1653, inviting one and all to the Red Bull to see rope-dancing, a sword trick, a new country dance, and a droll: [182]

At the *Red-Bull* in *St. Johns street* on Thursday next, being the Ninth of *June*, 1633 [1653]. There is a Prettie Conceited fellow that hath challenged the *Dromedary* lately come out of *Barbary*, to dance with him *Cap a Pee*, on the Low Rope. . . . As also running up a board with *Rapiers*, and a new countrey Dance called the *Horn-Dance*, never before presented; performed by the ablest Persons of that *Civill quality* in *England*. There will also appear a merry conceited Fellow which hath formerly given content. *And you may come and return with safety.*

But in spite of this confident assurance, the auditors and the "merry conceited fellow" (who was Robert Cox acting in the ancient jig or droll of *John Swabber*) were betrayed by some actors jealous of Cox, to the military, with disastrous consequence. *Mercurius Democritus* was obliged to print the sad news: [183]

The Rope dancers having implyed one Mr. *Cox* an *Actor*, (a very honest though impoverished man, who is not only as well as others, put by the practice of his Calling, but charged with a poor Wife, and 5 helplesse Infants) to present a modest and ha[r]mless jigge, calle[d] *Swobber*, yet two of his own quallity, envying their poor brother should get a little bread for his Children, basely and unworthily betrayed him to the Souldie[r]s, and so abused many of the Gentry that formerly had been their Benefactors, who were forced to pay to the Souldiers 5s. a piece for their comming out, as well as for their going in,

> An Action, so superlatively base,
> Would bush [184] the Devil in an Anticks face.

The next record we have of this "incomparable" actor is of his death in Clerkenwell: [185]

1655, Dec. 12. Robert Coxe, a Player.

Before his death Cox had written his *Actaeon and Diana*, to be published with four of the old popular jigs which he had contrived into drolls. Presumably this book came out before he died: *Printed at London by T. Newcomb, for the use of the Author, Robert Cox.*[186] We may hope that the proceeds of its sale (if any there were) went to the widow and five orphans.

Leaving Cox's "implyers," the rope-dancers, let us return to the vicissitudes of the companies which still tried to act complete plays. That the latter were still in existence as such is shown by a nonsensical announcement in *The Laughing Mercury* for 22 September, 1652: [187]

When they return back the *Players* are to meet them as they come from *Sturbridge-Faire* in a *Galley-Foyst*, and to sayle back with them to the *Red-Bull*, where they are to Act a *bloody-Sea-fight* before them in a Land *Water-worke*, written by the Ghost of Fryar *Bacon*.

A most interesting record which I found is the account of a performance of Killigrew's tragi-comedy *Claracilla* at Gibbons's Tennis Court, near Lincoln's Inn Fields: [188]

The poor *Comoedians*, (whose sad condition ought to be look'd upon with a pittying *Eye*, as being debarr'd of that livelyhood, to which they were bred up) adventuring not long since to Act a Play called *Claracilla* at one Mr. *Gibbions* his *Tennis Court*; an ill *Beest*, or rather Bird (because the rest denyed him a share of their profits) be——t his *own nest*, causing the poor *Actors* to be routed by the *Souldiery*, though he himself hath since the prohibition of *Playes*, had divers *Tragedies* and *Comedies* acted in his own house; a deed so base, that it were pitty but all Persons of Honor would take Notice of him.

> How powrfull's *Lucre*, that can make one brother,
> Basely betray, and ruine one another? [189]

Who was this "ill *Beest*" who so basely betrayed the rest of the company? In the first place, what company of actors was this? We have a clue to their identity in the name of the play which they acted. *Claracilla* was the property of the Cockpit company, and was first produced by them before 1641.[190] Assuming, then, that it was the Cockpit players who acted at Gibbons's Court, which one of their number is an "ill *Beest*" who has a "house" or theatre of his own? I cannot escape the conclusion that it is [W]ill Beest[on], formerly governor of the King's and Queen's Servants at the Cockpit in Drury Lane, and now lessee of the playhouse in Salisbury Court.[191] "His own house," where plays were acted since the prohibition of acting, probably refers to the Cockpit,[192] of which Beeston's mother, Dame Elizabeth Beeston Kirk, held a lease. In the winter of 1650–1651 Beeston had repaired the Drury Lane house for plays and had begun to train a company of boys. Failing, however, to obtain the expected reversion of the lease from the landlord Rolleston, he transferred his attention to the Salisbury Court playhouse, the lease of which he found means to purchase on 25 March, 1652. But by the date of this raid on Gibbons's Tennis Court — eleven months or so after his purchase — it is doubtful that the dismantled building had yet been suitably fitted up for playing.

Democritus felt so strongly the baseness of Beeston's treachery that he printed his *exposé* two weeks in succession, to make sure that "all Persons of Honor would take Notice of him." A month later (27 April, 1653) *Democritus* made a further and more direct appeal for the players: [193]

It were much to be desired (since some harmlesse, moderate recreation takes off mens minds from hatching Treason, fellonies, whordoms, murders and the like) . . . that the poor Comedians, whose sufferings have been very great, were permitted to represent some modest and harmless *Pastoralls*, so that no offence might be in them either against the present Government, Religion or Modesty.

Edmund Gayton, in his *Pleasant Notes upon Don Quixot*, 1654 (page 270), argues in a similar vein:

Where the minds of the vulgar are not busied in some such pleasant arguments, they fall upon matters which lesse concerne them, and become troublesome Judges of the State and Church wherein they live; wherefore it hath been accounted great policy to divert these mens fancies, by licensing Plaies, sports, and divers recreations from businesses above their capacity, and not of common ventilation. For want of these *chimeras*, (which had no more harm in them, then their impossibility) reall phantasmes, and strong delusions have succeeded and possessed not a few, who transported with their owne imaginations, doe not write Romances, but act them, and fill the world with substantiall Tragœdies.

Just how far the government winked at the surreptitious performances is hard to say. But to judge by the large number of raids which occurred only because the actors were betrayed (often by jealous members of their own profession), one would say that the actors were safer from the soldiers than they were from themselves; and that the routs happened only often enough to appease the Puritan die-hards. The other main difficulty of the players besides these raids was lack of patronage among the upper classes to support so many companies with private performances alone (for a part of the play-going wealthy was in exile). On the other hand, public performances at the Red Bull, with their increased danger, were left more and more to Andrew Cane and his fighting band of Roscians. As we have seen, this company, if warned of the approach of the soldiers, ran away to save their costumes; but if caught, made a tough fight for it, and brought the theatrical swords and staffs into play in hard earnest. In the midst of these alarms and excursions, how much time could old Cane, "the most fighting man," devote, under the name of "Andrew de Caine, Goldsmith," to his more peaceful profession? One might suppose, too, that he had borne the brunt of enough attacks *vi et armis* without being obliged to defend himself at law.

But in 1654 William and Margaret Wintershall brought an action of debt against the veteran actor on an old bond. Cane retaliated by complaining in Chancery.[193a] His story runs that about 1624 he and several others entered into a bond of £80 to "Richard Gunnell, late while he lived of . . . St. Giles Cripplegate." The bond was conditioned "for doing of some collateral thing." Cane asserts that this was done; for Gunnell, knowing that the bond was equitably discharged, never asked for any money on it although he often conversed with Cane. Gunnell died in 1634, and only of late have his executors "unconscionably commenced an action of debt" on this 31-year-old bond, pretending that it was absolute for the payment of £40. This Cane denies, maintaining that

no money was ever lent or paid, or ever intended to be secured thereon; but the said bond was only entered into by your orator and the said other obligors, being then the then Prince of Wales his Servants that played and acted at the Fortune Playhouse in Golding Lane . . . unto the said Richard Gunnell (another of the said Prince's then Servants and Players in the same house) only to oblige themselves to the said Mr. Gunnell to stay and play there: it being usual for them to become mutually bound to each other in like manner, for that they were advised a covenant to play there would not bind them. And it was agreed betwixt your orator, the said other obligors, and the said Mr. Gunnell that no money (notwithstanding the said bond was absolute) should be paid thereon unless your orator and the said other obligors by discontinuance or departure should break the Company (which neither of them did), it being also customary for the said Mr. Gunnell and the rest of the said late Prince's Servants to do and agree to the like terms.

For answer Wintershall and his wife Margaret say that Gunnell died intestate in 1633 or 1634, leaving his widow Elizabeth with two daughters, Margaret and Anne. The widow administered to the estate and afterwards married a certain John Robinson (who may be identical with the prominent actor of that name in the King's Revels Company at Salisbury Court and the Fortune [194] — with both of which houses, of course, Gunnell was closely associated). However that may be, Elizabeth (Gunnell) Robinson made her will about 1641, leaving the estate to her daughters. Margaret had married William Wintershall; Anne, William Clarke. Anne is recently deceased, and the Wintershalls say they are therefore entitled to this "unadministered principal debt" of £40, secured by an obligation dated 30 April, 1624, "wherein the said complainant by the name of Andrew Caine of London, gentleman, (by which name the said complainant was then commonly called and known) together with Charles Massey, William Cortwright, William Stratford, Richard Price, and Richard Fowler, of London, gentlemen, became jointly and severally bound unto the said Richard Gunnell" in the penal sum of £80 conditioned for the payment of £40 before 1 October, 1624. The Wintershalls allege that the money was "often demanded" by Gunnell's widow and by themselves, but in vain, "by reason of the death and insolvency of the said obligors and the absence of the said complainant, who being at Oxford in the late king's army could not be proceeded against." (How cleverly they bring Cane's being a Royalist to the notice of Cromwell's Chancery commissioners!) Finishing with some aspersions on the truth of Cane's allegations, they hope they shall not be enjoined from recovering the debt at law.

Though it would be satisfying to learn that this dispute ended in Cane's favor, I can trace no further proceedings. Wintershall's marriage to Margaret Gunnell makes an interesting link between the Restoration and the Jacobean stage. Richard Gunnell was long and well known as actor and manager, and as one of the two builders of the Salisbury Court Theatre. His son-in-law Wintershall, having begun in the Queen's Company at the Salisbury Court before the wars, lived to be a versatile and valuable player in Killigrew's company at the Theatre Royal until 1679. He shone as Cokes in *Bartholomew Fair*, and is mentioned in Buckingham's *Rehearsal*. Gunnell's players at the Fortune, styled by Cane "the Prince's Servants," were in fact not so called until 1631. In 1624, the date of the bond, they were known as "the Palsgrave's Men"; but that is no great slip for Cane to make after so many years. Also of importance is this additional evidence of the method then in use to secure the cohesion of a company, that is, by mutual bond and an agreement not to sue unless the company were broken. The penal sum in this case, £80, may be compared with the £100 bond given by each member of Pembroke's company in 1597 to Francis Langley,[195] and the enormous joint and several obligation of £5000 of the Duke of York's sharers, who received a patent in 1610.[196]

Returning to our story of the stage in Cromwell's London, we find in Daniel Fleming's notes of expenses in London and Oxford from January to September, 1653,[197] an entry which seems to refer to a public performance, perhaps at Andrew Cane's Red Bull: ". . . for the seeing of a play, 2d." Private performances were much more expensive.

In 1654, plays were of such frequent occurrence as to call forth new repressive measures from the government. In February, "instructions were given for suppressing of a wicked sort of people called Hectors,[198] and Playes, and other wicked disorders; and larger power will bee given if need require." [199]

This order, added to their other distresses, made life so hard for those players who had no regular theatre that, when certain persons asked that the actors be suppressed more rigorously, *Mercurius Fumigosus* [200] was moved to write in pity and indignation:

> The Bawdes in the Suburbs are Petitioning to put down the poor *Actors*, who have a long time lingered under the heavy yoke of Poverty, and fed themselves and families with hunger, sighs, and tears; yet not one of these poor men during this long Winter of many years debarment from the exercise of that Quallity wherein they were bred, but have continued alwayes Civill and honest in life and conversation, not one of them branded with any foul *Crime* (which such exigences as *Poverty* commonly produces) and truly Playes have better recreated the mindes of ingenious men, then any other exercise; and with modest Presumption, may doubtless gain the affection of the Noblest Spirits in any City or Country.

Indeed, compared to the gay ante-bellum days some of the playhouses presented a sad picture. Flecknoe said in 1653: [201]

> Passing on to Black-fryers, and seeing never a *Play-bil* on the Gate, no *Coaches* on the place, nor *Doorkeeper* at the *Play-house* door, with his *Boxe* like a *Church-warden*, desiring you to remember the poor *Players*, I cannot but say for *Epilogue* to all the *Playes* were ever Acted there (that the Puritans)
>
> Have made with their Raylings the *Players* as poore
> As were the *Fryers* and *Poets* before.

Two years after this epilogue of Flecknoe's, Blackfriars playhouse "was pulled down to the ground on Monday the 6 day of August, 1655, and tenements built in the room."[202]

But to return to the irrepressible Red Bull, which seemed able to survive anything, we find *Fumigosus* reporting that the players, to turn an extra penny, had been giving lessons in elocution to a couple of tailors!

Two *cross-legg'd Creatures* called *Sutorians*, having a great minde to learn the right Art of Preaching, would the other day needs go the *Red-Bull* to learn *speech* and *Action* of the *Players* before they came to Exercise or hold *forth*.[203]

The Roscians of the Red Bull were playing so regularly and with such supreme disregard for the ordinances of Parliament that a raid on 30 December, 1654, when they were acting *Wit without Money*, came as a surprise.

The players at the *Red-bull* were on the last Saturday despoiled of their acting cl[o]aths by some of the soldiery, they having not so ful a liberty as they pretended.[204]

A Perfect Account says:[205]

This day the Players at the Red-Bull (being gotten into all their borrowed gallantry, and ready to act) were by some of the Souldiery dispoyled of all their bravery; but the Souldiery carryed themselves very civilly towards the Audience.

Mercurius Fumigosus caps the story with a couplet:[206]

The next day the *Players* presuming to Act *Witt without money*, were rowted by the Souldiers,

> *Who Acting better then the Players, yet,*
> *Left them* sans *money, Cloaths or Witt.*

Daniel Fleming's accounts for expenses in February and March, 1655,[207] include heavier items for plays than two years earlier; which may indicate private performances of a more sumptuous nature:

Spent with Sir W.D. and Sir G[eorge] F[letcher] at the Playhouse, 15 s.
Spent in going into a play, 1s. 4d.

This "Sir W.D." is in all probability Sir William Davenant, whose work in establishing the production of plays under a new guise demands a chapter by itself.

The Red Bull players in these latter years were involved in internal difficulties which sometimes prevented them from acting, or resulted in their betrayal to the soldiers. I am fortunate to find *Mercurius Fumigosus* for 9–16 May, 1655, reflecting in verse on the sad consequences of their quarrels: [208]

A Dumb *Comedy* is next Week to be Acted at the Red-*Bull*, if the *Players* can but agree and be honest amongst themselves; which will be the best, though hardest Sceane they can Act.

> *Pitty that those that Act in various shapes,*
> *Should 'mongst themselves prove worse then Mymick Apes.*
> *True* Roscians *learn by Action, and Civill be*
> *To all; but those Act ill, 'can't with themselves agree.*
> *For whilst they quarrell which the most should share,*
> *They are tane napping, as* Moss *did take his Mare.*

Another great raid, and the last we shall notice here, was carried out at the Red Bull on 14 September, 1655. As was to be expected, the actors fought for their possessions, and it looks as if some of the spectators joined in the fray. Says J. Bankes to Joseph Williamson in a letter: [209]

There were many put to the rout this weeke by the souldiers at the play house; and could not come off without a hole or broken-crowne. Had not the Corporall bin somewhat uigelent he had bin entrapt alsoe.

Bankes's pun makes the sense obscure. What he meant was "could not come off except by fighting, and getting a broken crown, or peaceably, with the loss of a whole crown [that is, five shillings fine]." And in those days a crown was worth from eight to ten times as much as it is to-day. *The Weekly Intelligencer* gives a lively story of the rout: [210]

This Day proved Tragical to the *Players* at the *Red Bull*, their Acting being against an Act of Parlament, the Soldiers secured the persons of some of them who were upon the Stage, and in the Tyrin-house, they seized also upon their cloaths in which they acted, a great part whereof was very rich, it never fared worse with the spectators then at this present, for those who had monies payed their five shillings apeece, those who had none to satisfie their forfeits, did leave their Cloaks behind them, the Tragedy of the Actors, and the Spectators, was the Comedy of the soldiers. There was abundance of the Female Sex, who not able to pay 5*s*. did leave some gage or other behind them, insomuch that although the next day after the

Fair, was expected to be a new *Faire* of Hoods, of Aprons, and of Scarfs, all which their poverty being made known, and after some check for their Trespasse, were civilly restored to the Owners.

Mercurius Fumigosus adds that the Jack-Puddings of Southwark Fair were also raided: [211]

The *Players* at the *Red-bull*, and all the *Jack-Puddings* of *Southwark Faire*, last Friday listed themselves for Souldiers, a little after, a great *Rowt* was given, some Prisoners taken, which presently paying their *Ransoms*, were released.

> So were the Puddings, and the Fiddlers,
> The Actors and the hy-down Diddlers,
> Put by their Action, and their Parts,
> And led away with heavy hearts.
> The reason was, as some do say,
> 'Cause they can't work, but live by Play.

This raid inspired a ballad which was later included in the collection *Sportive Wit* (1656): [212]

A SONG

1

The fourteenth of September
I very well remember,
   When people had eaten and fed full,
Many men, they say,
Would needs go see a Play,
   But they saw a great rout at the red Bull.

2

The Soldiers they came,
(The blinde and the lame)
   To visit and undo the Players;
And [from] women without Gowns,
They said they would have Crowns;
   But they were no good Sooth-sayers.

3

Then *Jo: Wright* they met,
Yet nothing could get,
   And *Tom Jay* i' th' same condition:
The fire [213] men they
Wou'd ha' made 'em a prey,
   But they scorn'd to make a petition.

4

The Minstrills they
Had the hap that day,
    (Well fare a very good token)
To keep (from the chase)
The fiddle and the case,
    For the instruments scap'd unbroken.

5

The poor and the rich,
The whore and the bitch,
    Were every one at a losse,
But the Players were all
Turn'd (as weakest) to the wall,
    And 't is thought had the greatest losse.

Here we shall leave the Red Bull, which continued its stormy existence until after the Restoration, acting "unreformed" plays. Some writers indeed thought of creating a purified drama which would be acceptable to the Parliamentary Babes of Grace. In 1654, the immortal Richard Flecknoe wrote *Love's Dominion*, which he describes as "full of Excellent Morality, written as a Pattern for the *Reformed Stage*." In his dedication to the Lady Elizabeth Claypole, the author "insinuates the use of Plays, and begs her Mediation to gain License to act them." [214] Edmund Gayton, in the same year, hits off "good" plays: [215]

The Canon and the Curate find out waies,
To make Romances good, and write good plaies.
Such as may edifie; such I have seen
Of holy subjects, and with Psalmes between
The Acts of *Dives* and of *Lazarus;*
Of *Hester* good, and great *Ahasheverus:*
Which now, through Poets vanity and sloth,
Are seen in Puppet plaies, or painted cloth;
The stage reform'd (as they say 'tis thought on)
Time may be spent there well, as reading *Broughton.*
No fooles with *Harry Codpieces* appeare,
Nor Souldiers suffered in their parts to sweare:
No Lady vitiated o' th' stage before us,
But let *Susannah's* bathing be by *chorus.*

With the rise of the opera and elaborate scenery in 1656, under Davenant, the stage *was* reformed, but not in Gayton's sense.

BEAR GARDENS AND BEAR-BAITING

I

The attack of the Puritans and of the city authorities upon the amusements of London under Charles I and the Interregnum was directed primarily against plays and playhouses. The sport of bear-baiting — one of the favorite entertainments of the Londoners — was allowed to continue almost without interruption throughout the Commonwealth.[216]

Just before the Civil War, the attitude of the English toward the sport was much the same as that of the Spanish to-day toward the *corrida*. Nobility and mob were its chief supporters. Citizens of the better class frowned upon it. Two opinions of the Bear Garden, written in the decade 1630–1640, illustrate the divergent points of view.

The first is a digest of a letter in Latin from "Honest William" (a name given to the writer by Francis Lord Cottington) to the same lord, in 1639:

Was much delighted to hear that his lordship had recently visited the bear garden, commonly called Paris Garden, which last was certainly a misnomer, for notwithstanding all that Frenchmen might say, there was not such a charming place in all Paris. Our ancestors called it the Garden of Paradise, so great is the variety of its charms, as witnessed by the learned (Sir) Robert Cotton in his *Antiquities*, and before him by John Stow in his *Survey of London*. Enumerates amongst its attractions the scent of the shrubs and flowers, the music, and the bear-baiting. There you may hear the shouting of men, the barking of dogs, the growling of the bears, and the bellowing of the bulls, mixed in a wild but natural harmony. This appears to the writer a picture of the world, for "All the world is but a bear-baiting." There are some men who do not endure to see the bears, but they are generally rustics, and of little judgment, who do not know how to regard this business, nor do they approve of recreation.[217]

Against this enthusiastic impression we have D. Lupton's account in 1632 under the heading "Paris-Garden":

This may better bee termed a foule Denne then a faire Garden. It's pitty so good a piece of ground is no better imploied: Heere are cruell

Beasts in it, and as badly vs'd; heere are foule beasts come to it, and as bad or worse keepe it, they are fitter for a Wildernesse then a City: idle base persons (most commonly) that want imployment, or else will not be otherwise imploy'd, frequeut [*sic*] this place; and that money which was got basely here, to maintaine as bad as themselues, or spent lewdly; here come few that either regard their credit, or losse of time: the swaggering Roarer, the cunning Cheater, the rotten Bawd, the swearing Drunkard, and the bloudy Butcher haue their Rendeuouz here, and are of chiefe place and respect. There are as many ciuil religious men here, as thei're Saints in Hell.²¹⁸

Before coming, however, to a consideration of the fortunes of the "royal sport" from 1642 to 1660, we may profitably cast a hasty glance over the history of the Hope or Second Bear Garden on the Bankside.

It was built in 1613 as a playhouse with a double purpose: "for players to play in, and for the game of bears and bulls to be baited in." ²¹⁹ But the combination was not happy. On the one hand, the noses of even hardy Jacobean playgoers were outraged by the proximity of the beasts; and on the other hand, some of the devotees of the royal sport resented the intrusion of the play actors:

> When Ize came there, Ize was in a Rage,
> Ize rail'd on him that kept the Bears,
> Instead of a Stake, was suffer'd a Stage,
> And in *Hunks* his House a Crew of Players.²²⁰

The players sought other quarters; and the house was used after 1617 almost entirely for animal-baitings, challenge matches between champion beasts, prize bouts of fencing, and the like. The name "Hope" was gradually replaced by the older and handier "Bear Garden," or the looser "Paris Garden."

In the year 1638, according to John Taylor the Water Poet, the Bear Garden was flourishing. In his *Bull, Beare, and Horse*,²²¹ dedicated to "Mr. *Thomas Godfrey*, Keeper of the Game for Beares, Bulls, and Dogges," he says:

> There's three couragious *Bulls*, as ever plaid
> Twenty good Beares, as er'e to stake was taid.
> And seventy Mastives. . . .

And that we have obtain'd againe the Game,
Our *Paris-Garden* Flag proclaimes the same.
Our *Beares*, and *Bulls*, and *Dogs* in former state,
The streets of *London* do perambulate,
And honest sport, and lawfull merriment,
Shall thrice a weeke be shew'd, to give content.

On 12 December, 1642, for making a riot and threatening to cut the throats of those who refused to sign a petition of his, Tom Godfrey was sent for an indefinite term to Newgate. At the same time the House of Commons enjoined and required "the Masters of the *Beare Garden* and all other Persons who have Interest there" to forbid "the Game of Bear-baiting in these Times of great Distractions."

This order, while not couched in the solemn language of the ordinance against stage plays, was of a like nature and, if possible, was less well enforced. Bear-baitings continued as usual, and the players who were hindered from acting complained bitterly that the Bear Garden was permitted to stand "in statu quo prius," referring to it as "that Nurse of barbarisme and beastlinesse . . . where upon their usuall dayes those Demy-Monsters are baited by bandogs." [222]

The complaint had no effect in diminishing the sport. But the large and often dangerous crowds which assembled on the Bankside caused the authorities much uneasiness. In November, 1643, Parliament ordered the Southwark sub-committee to put down the game of bear-baiting; directing further "that they do permit there, hereafter, no Concourse of People to the Bear Garden; and that they apprehend such loose and suspicious Persons as come thither." [223]

Some attention was paid perhaps to this order. At any rate, whether because of the closing of the Garden or because of his confinement in Newgate, Godfrey was evidently in straits by 17 April, 1644. On that date the Commons referred a petition of his to the sub-committee in Southwark "for his Relief." [224]

Southwark's Bear Garden, however, was not long closed. In 1645 it must have been open, for in July of that year the Royalist, John Berkenhead, accuses the Parliament of even stooping to lure young men to the Bear Garden under guise of showing a new kind of bear-baiting, and then impressing them into the army:

Such a decoy as this they lately made the *Beare Garden*, for on divers Posts in *London* and *Westminster* they set up bills, for such a day there should be a Bull and Beares bayted a new better way then any had beene formerly; The common Youths and inferior 'Prentices went thither very plentifully, but came not so fast home; for the Constables and Officers (according to the Designe) stood ready at the doore to wait their comming forth, and in an instant pressed as many for Souldiers as filled 4 or 5 Barges. Now if people refuse to be often cosened the same way, and the *Beare-Garden* faile, you'l see Constables come to Lectures, and presse a man in his very *Thanksgiving* clothes.[225]

Of course the Parliament newsbook countered with the quip modest: "Now Sirrah, *Mall Cut-purse* her selfe sayes thou art a *Liar*."[226] But this denial by Mall Cut-purse (one of the bears), and the blustering tone of the writer, carry little conviction. It is more than likely that the Parliament was guilty of using this low expedient for recruiting its forces.

In 1645, too, we find an interesting passage on the Bear Garden which informs us that one of the officers of the place was a "clerk of the challenges." It is contained in the satirical *Last Will and Testament of P. Rupert*.[227]

Item. My last Legasie is, my admonition to *Aulicus* my Secretary, which is, with speede to repaire to *Britanicus*, and desire his assistance in drawing a Petition for him to the Baregarden, for the man is very ingeneous, and in time may come to be Clerke of the Challenges.

When (on 16 July, 1647) the House of Commons forwarded to the Lords an ordinance requiring the lord mayor and justices of the peace "speedily to suppress all publick Plays and Playhouses, and all Dancings on the Ropes,"[228] the Lords sent it back with an amendment: "after the Word 'Ropes' to add the Words 'and Bear-baitings.'"[229] The amendment being accepted, the order was passed to continue in force until 1 January, 1648.

How little effect it had can be judged by the complaints that came to Parliament's ears, and the necessity for another order in less than a month's time. The House was surprised at the neglect on the part of the justices, especially during "the dangerous season of the plague." The House hoped that the justices would observe its orders, and again enjoined them to suppress all plays, rope-dancings, "Bear-baitings, and Bull-baitings." [230]

The tone of this order shows the weakness of Parliament in London matters. If the city had obeyed the first order, there would have been no need for a second. *Mercurius Pragmaticus* in a satirical passage allows us to see that despite this second order the Bear Garden was open in October, 1647: "Neverthelesse, it's my desire in the mean time, that *Tuesday* should be the constant day of *Beare bayting*." [231] And on 30 November he prophesies that "*Paris-garden* shall bee translated from the *Banke-side* into the *City*, and the *Colonels* of the Army shall . . . *whip* the *blinde-Beares* of the *Common Councell* into better manners." [232]

Melancholicus, on 28 July, 1648, mixes just enough sense with his nonsense to make a meaning possible:

Shall we never be delivered of this Monstrous burden called plotts? no, for I tell you, there was a plot conceiv'd . . . in the *Beare-Garden*, but that it prov'd abortive, for the *Bears*, the honest *Bears* had conspired to a Gaol-delivery. [233]

And James Taswell, in his *Ten necessary Quæries*, 7 August, 1648, relates that "to continue this sport and pastime the Gentlemen [*sic*] hath fetched two or three brace of Beares, roaring meg and her Squadron from *Paris* garden." [234] In the same month *The Parliament Kite* has some ironical praise for the law-givers: "You have suppressed . . . Bear bayting, and . . . that Babylonish sport of the Jack-an-apes, and the whiping of the blind Bear." [235] But that this is mere irony is proved by a passage from *A Bartholomew Fairing*, which appeared a year later:

> Deer was the *Tyrant's* game; but Buls is ours,
> *Bishops* and *Plays* were in a day put down,
> I well remember; and *Bull baytings* allow'd. [236]

There seems to be no lack of new evidence to show that the Bear Garden was one of the most uninterrupted and satisfactory amusements of London during the Interregnum. We find continual reference to it in the newsbooks. *Mercurius Britanicus*, for instance, threatens to have Hercules lead a certain adversary whom he likens to a dog "Captive to the Beare-Garden, and there shall learn to baite bulls and beares, and shall be cheyned up from baiting Christians any more." [237] In *A Hue and Crie after Cromwell* Oliver is an unruly bull; his pursuers are resolved ". . . in case they can tame him, to convey his loathed Carkasse in a Wheel-barrow to the *Bear-garden* in *London*, that all the Butchers in *Middle-Sex*, and *Surrey*, may play a match at *the Town-bull of Ely*." [238]

The ancient custom of printing bills for the performances at the Bear Garden, it appears, was still in use. *The Man in the Moon* (13–20 February, 1650) publishes a typical bill with amusing alterations:

A Match, a match; Gentlemen, pray stand off: *Be it known unto all men by this presents, that I the* Man in the Moon, *in behalfe of my Dog* Towzer, *doe challenge all the Dogs, Bitches, Puppies, and all in the Citie of* Westminster; *to play with them all one after another, severally three Courses at the* Winsor-Bull, *at the* Hope *on the Bank-side, on* Thursday Feb. 28. *for three* Crownes *a Dog; and that* Dog *that hits, or fetches* Blood *first, to winne the* Wager, *and be rewarded with a* Parliament Collar: *hee desireth* Godfrey *to see that his* Bull *be ready, and his* Seats *and* Galleries *strong, for I intend to bring many* Friends, *and there all my* Enemies, Pusivants, Dogs, Setters, Bitches, &c. *if they have any* Warrants, *or any other matter else against me, shall be sure to find me; else hereafter let them not presume to come in my presence under the penalty of a stab at least. There shall also be seen the most excellent sport of an old* Munkey *dancing on a* Rope, *and riding on a* Tukesbury Hobby-horse *for a* wager *of three pounds of the* States-money, *to please the Sisters of the* Separation, *and some other rare* Tricks *shall make you merry.* VIVAT REX. [239]

Other extracts from the Royalist newsbooks add more evidence on this head. *Mercurius Democritus* announces that a certain she-bear

. . . will now beat all the doggs that come to the *Bare-Garden* . . . Mr. *Faithfool Scout,* hath sent his *Jenny* to her [that is, the bear] with a Present of a brace of *Wood-cocks* and a *Petition,* to see if she can procure him the favour to print her Ladyships Bills for the *Bare-garden.* [240]

DANCING BEARS

(From *Recreation For Ingenious Head-peeces*, London, 1650.)

And on 16 June, 1652, *Democritus* tells a very circumstantial story:

I hoopt and hollowed half a year for a Water-man to set me over the water, at last came a woman Waterman, who set me clean over the water up to the knees in durt, so I went up the bank, and looking over the Park-pales into the *Bear-Garden*, I spy'd a fellow in a long fools coat a hors-back upon a Bull . . . I heard a great noise of stop Thief, stop, where at last I perceived it to be *Pragmaticus*, which was apprehended by the Bear-wards for creeping in at the windows, and robbing the blind Bear of her dinner . . . he was . . . committed a close prisoner . . . where he is to write weekly Bills for the *Bear-garden*.[241]

From all this it is manifest that the Bear Garden was still open. But, although the Butchers' Company still contributed the offal and waste meat for the bears' food,[242] and although Thursday was still bear-baiting day on the Bankside, there is no denying that the sport did not flourish as it had in the days before the war. According to John Taylor, there were in 1638 about twenty bears and four bulls. In the pinching times following the war, however, it was found impossible to maintain so many; some were killed and were not replaced. *Democritus*, in his Baron Munchausen manner, tells an extravagant tale with perhaps a grain of truth:

The *Blind-Bear* being at the *stake* last Thursday-night, gaped so wide, that no lesse then six *Mastiffs* ran all down her throat one after another . . . the *Bearwards* deny to tye up the *Blinde Beare*, or keep her fasting, in hopes (now many of the Bears be kill'd) before Easter Term next she will bring forth a new *litter* of *Bear-Whelps*.[243]

Some of the most famous bears, however, were still alive: among them this Blind Bess and the great Ned of Canterbury. *Mercurius Fumigosus* prints a bit of satire on Sir Balthazar Gerbier's Academy, in which he mentions Ned:

An *Italian High German-Portuguize* . . . reads *Anatomie Lectures* . . . to *Tom Godfrey's* Beares; the Beares are so Docible (especially *Ned* of Canterbury) that 't is thought . . . they will sing Ballads by *Bartholomew-tyde*.[244]

In the spring of 1653, the animal-baitings had grown to such proportions that the Council of State ordered "The bear baiting, bull baiting, and playing for prizes by fencers hitherto practised in Southwark and other places, which have caused great evils and abominations, to be suppressed from this time. Cols. Cooper and Pride, Mr. Hyland, and Major Allen to carry out this order." [245]

II

We must pause before witnessing the downfall of the Bear Garden (for the Hope, as well as the House of Commons, had its Pride's Purge) to consider a phenomenon which has not, I think, ever been noticed: namely, "private" bear-baiting in London. It has always been supposed that at this period there was but one bear garden — the Hope on the Bankside. In the course of my research, however, I have brought to light facts which show that there was another, a private bear-baiting, in St. John's Street, Clerkenwell.

Its beginning is to be found in a grant to Sir Sanders Duncombe. This gentleman, reputed to be a great traveller and curio-hunter, is the man who popularized the sedan-chair in England.[246] Charles I in 1634 granted him a monopoly for fourteen years of manufacturing and "putting forth to hire" these chairs "for carrying . . . our loving Subjects . . . in and about . . . *London* and *Westminster.*" [247] In 1635, John Evelyn's mother died after the doctors had given her up, although "Sir Sanders Duncombe tried his celebrated and famous powder" on her.[248]

On 11 October, 1639, Sir Sanders Duncombe received a patent for "the sole practisinge and makinge profitt of the combatinge and fightinge of wild and domestick beasts within the Realm of England for fowertene yeres." [249] It is doubtful whether this patent gave Duncombe any rights in the Bank-side Bear Garden. The game there was supposed to be a royal monopoly, and, as we know, had been maintained as such by former sovereigns. Indeed in 1638 John Taylor says:

> The Game hath been maintain'd, and will, we hope,
> Be so againe (now favour gives it scope)
> For Kings, for Princes, for Ambassadors. [250]

Furthermore, I have found nothing which connects Sir Sanders with the Hope. On the other hand, I have found direct evidence of a bear garden of his, built almost immediately after his patent was issued in 1639. The evidence is contained in a sensational account of how one of his bears slew his gardener:

Strange and horrible NEWES *Which happened betwixt St.* Iohns *street, and* Islington *on Thursday morning, being the eight and twentieth day of this instant moneth of October. Being a terrible murther committed by one of Sir* Sander Duncomes *Beares on the body of his Gardner, that usually came to feed them, where thousands of people were eye-witnesses. Printed at London for T. Smith 1642.*

. . . This worthy Knight delighting in the sport, had built an house some 2. yeares since betwixt the Red Bull and *Islington*, but not quite finished in the full manner of a beare-garden, had purchased beares to have them bayted for his recreation, but the building, beeing but weak, and the winde being rough and high, blew it downe flat and layd it with the earth, which he never built again, nor never will, but his two beares he hath kept there two yeares since these combustious times, thinking when they were over to make some further use, and there caused this man daily to feed and look unto these beares, which he has done these 2 years till this day, without least touch of danger, but fatall day be ordained to be his last! Comming to the place where the beares were kept, which is a great spacious yard payled round betwixt *Islington* and the *Red Bull*, to feede them in the morning, betwixt 9 and ten of the clocke, the great bear had broken out of his den. [251]

The story goes on to tell how the bear killed the man, and then how the populace, for revenge, killed the bear.

Such a terrible mishap as this may well have dampened Duncombe's zeal for bear-baiting and animal shows, although it must have done much to advertise his place. At any rate, we have no record of his activities until after the "combustious times." When conditions were better after the war, he built a bear garden of some kind and gave performances.

The Faithful Scout, 9–16 April, 1652, prints a satirical announcement of "a Duel on *Wednesday* next in Sr *Alexander Duncams* Bear-Garden near *Islington*." [252] About this time, too, the knight began to fit his place up as a zoölogical garden with strange and remarkable beasts; but before he had been collecting very long he died. *Mercurius Democritus* affords us some curious details:

At the *Half-moon* neer the *halfway-House* going to *Islington*, is to be seen the rarest Creature ever eye beheld; It is bodied, horned and hoofed like a *Bull,* with a large pair of *wings* growing out at each *shoulder.* . . . He is newly sent over out of *Arabia* by a Merchant that hath been a long Travel-ler, and Directed to Sir *Sander Duncom,* who at the Merchants *going over,* was *storing* that ground with *raryties* of all *living Creatures;* and he being dead, it was sent to be kept at the place before mentioned, where for the satisfaction of those that desire they may see it every day in the week, my self and many others having already been spectators of the same.[253]

Strictly speaking, Sir Sanders's patent expired shortly after its owner, in 1653; but the privilege once obtained was un-doubtedly handed on to his heirs and assigns. We find that this private bear garden of his near the Red Bull Playhouse was used at certain times as the headquarters of bear-baiting in London when for any reason the Hope was closed. For in-stance, a Parliament newsbook (29 December, 1654 to 5 Janu-ary, 1655) contains the notice: "Yesterday a man was killed by a Bull at the Bear Garden." [254] This revolting accident, or a later one, moved the authorities to close the Hope for a time; and the devotees of the sport went over to Duncombe's private bear garden in Clerkenwell. *Mercurius Fumigosus* recounts that,

a great Bull-bayting being lately in *St. Johns street,* there hapned a strange but true Accident, for the Bull breaking from the stake, bitt a Souldier quite thorow the legg, which putts the *Butchers* in great fear, that their Doggs will this Summer all die of the *Scurvy* for want of Exercise, if *Private Bull-bayting* should be put down as the *publick Bear-garden* was, because *Ned* of *Canterbury* had flung a Man quite from the stake into the *upper Gallery,* and broake the shoulder of the huckle-bone of his left Buttock;

> *A sad Prediction, and enough to make*
> *Us leave both* Bull *and* Beare, *and bayt the stake.*[255]

In spite of this doleful foreboding, however, the Hope soon got leave to open again, as appears by a note in *Fumigosus* (29 August to 5 September, 1655) concerning tallow, "which they doe want at the *Beare-Garden,* to annoint the *Bulls Nose,* that *was pinched last Play day.*" [256]

The most shocking accident of all was the killing of a child by a bear at the Hope in September, 1655. The child had come with others to see the bears, as nowadays at the zoo; and after the others had come out, it was discovered that the child had been locked in with the beasts. On returning, the bearward found that a bear had caught the child and killed it. Let the state newsbook tell the rest of the story:

The Bear for killing the Child fell to the Lord of the Soil, and was by the Bearward redeemed for fifty shillings; and the Bearwards told the Mother of the Child that they could not help it, (though some think it to bee a design of that wicked house to get money) and they told the Mother that the Bear should bee bated to death, and she should have half the money, & accordingly there were bills stuck up and down about the City of it, and a considerable summe of mony gathered to see the Bear bated to death; some say above 60 pound, and now all is done, they offer the woman three pound not to prosecute them; some other have been lately hurt at the Bear-garden, which is a sinfull deboyst profane meeting.[257]

The baitings at the Hope came to a temporary and inglorious end on 9 February, 1656:

Seuen of Mr. Godfries Beares, by the command of Thomas Pride, then hie Sheriefe of Surry, were then shot to death, On Saterday the 9 day of February 1655 [that is, 1656], by a Company of Souldiers.[258]

The Diary of Henry Townshend gives a slightly different account of the massacre:

Feb. (1656). Col. Pride, now Sir Thomas Pride, by reason of some difference between him and the Keeper Godfrey of the Bears in the Bear Garden in Southwark, as a justice of the peace there caused all the bears to be fast tied up by the noses and then valiantly brought some files of musketeers, drew up and gave fire and killed six or more bears in the place (only leaving one white innocent cub), and also all courts [that is, cocks] of the game. It is said all the mastifs are for to be shipt for Jamaica.[259]

In a little more than a month after this fatal event, the Hope was converted into tenements "by Thomas Walker, a Peticoate Maker in Cannon Streete." [260]

As may be supposed, after the closing of the Hope, bear-baiting in London was continued at the private bear garden in St. John's Street. This fact is shown beyond a doubt in a most touching and hitherto unnoticed epitaph, by the *Man in the Moon*, on Blind Bess. The date is 26 November, 1660.[261]

Here lyes old Bess *the ransome of* Prides *fury,*
Who was condnmn'd [sic] *without a Judg or Jury.*
A valiant Champion was she, many prize
'Gainst Butchers Dogs she won, till that her eyes
She lost in service, Godfrey *then lament,*

'Twas she that got thy food, and paid thy Rent.
And Butchers *all keep you that fatal day*
When Pride *and* Hewson *took her life away;*
Your very Dogs shall not forget her name
That many years together kept the Game.
You that the sport now keep in St. Johns-street,
Will never such a Bear or Garden meet
As Godfreys *was, for such as did resort*
To see her, will extol the place and sport.
Then Butchers *mourn, for you have lost a prize*
Of her that here entomb'd in Hony lyes.

Immediately upon the Restoration of Charles II, the game reverted to its old status as a royal sport; but it remained for some time in its new quarters in St. John's Street. An interesting petition preferred on 28 November, 1662, illustrates the standing of the Bear Garden by royal grant:

Petition of George Murray, His Majesty's coachman, to the King, for the keeping of such outlandish beasts as shall be presented to His Majesty by the Russian Ambassador. With reference thereon to Thos. Killegrew, as to whether the request may be granted without prejudice to the apes and bears of the bear garden and their masters.[262]

Manifestly there was some doubt whether the royal sport had always been granted as a monopoly and whether the Duncombe grant, which gave a monopoly for fourteen years from 1639, was still valid.

It may be that Tom Godfrey went to practise his old profession at the Clerkenwell bear garden, for in 1662 his burial is entered in the register of St. James's: "Oct. 19, 1662. Thomas Godfrey, who formerly kept the Beare garden ouer the bankside, buried in the Church." [263]

In the third year of the Restoration, however, Charles II decided to reopen the venerable Hope Playhouse; and accordingly the establishment in Sir Sanders Duncombe's bear garden in St. John's Street was ordered to be moved to its old home. On 27 July, 1663, Thomas Davies petitioned

. . . for repayment of part of the expense incurred in removal of the game of bears, bulls, &c., to the ancient place on the backside [that is, bankside], as ordered in Council, and in erecting a theatre at his own expense for better seeing the diversion.[264]

NOTES FOR CHAPTER I

1 (3). 1642. British Museum, E239.2.

2 (4). Edmund Rossingham gives the amount of their fine as 1000 pounds — a sum incredibly large. *Calendar of State Papers, Domestic, 1639*, p. 140. Cf. Adams, *Shakespearean Playhouses*, p. 288. I can find no other mention of *The Cardinalls Conspiracie*. Greg, in his *List of English Plays* (1900), p. 137, mentions *The Valiant Scot*, by "J. W. Gent.", printed 1637.

3 (4). *Cal. State Papers, Dom., 1639*, p. 529. Cf. Malone Society, *Collections*, v, 394.

4 (5). "In June," says Professor Rollins, "had appeared satirical broadsides called *The Late* [and *The last*] *Will and Testament of the Doctors Commons*, which contain these provisions:
  'Item I will and bequeath all my large Bookes of Acts, to them of the Fortune Play-House . . . in regard they want good action.
  'All my great Books of Acts to be divided between the Fortune and the Bull; for they spoyle many a good Play for want of Action.'"
  B. M., 669.f4.(18, 20). *R. Studies in Philology*, 1921, p. 270.

5 (5). B. M., E172.23. Reprinted by W. C. Hazlitt, *English Drama and Stage, 1543–1664* (1869), p. 253.

6 (5). *The True Diurnal Occurrances*, B. M., E201.15.

7 (6). B. M., E115.15. Knight, in his edition of Downes's *Roscius Anglicanus*, prints a facsimile.

8 (6). *A Perfect Diurnall*, 5–12 Sept., 1642. B. M., E239.20.

9 (6). See below, p. 32.

10 (6). B. M., E73.4.

11 (6). B. M., E124.11. *King Careo* means "I lack a king."

12 (7). *An Exact and True Relation*. B. M., E130.15.

13 (7). 17–24 June, 1644. B. M., E52.8.

14 (7). 9 Dec., 1652. W. S. Prideaux, *Memorials of the Goldsmith's Company*, ii, 23. For this reference I am indebted to Professor Rollins.

15 (7). No. 6. See below, pp. 52–54.

16 (7). *Journals, House of Commons*, ii, 885a. Collier (*History of English Dramatic Poetry*, iii, 102) has a rather inaccurate account of this affair, in which he is followed by Ordish, *Early London Theatres*, p. 237.

17 (7). *Journals, House of Commons, loc. cit.*

18 (8). Not 1644, as Professor Thaler says, *Shakspere to Sheridan*, p. 218.

19 (8). B. M., E86.8. Facsimile in Hazlitt, *op. cit.*, pp. 259 ff.

20 (8). *England's Memorable Accidents*. B. M., E244.26.

21 (8). *The Widowes Lamentation*, 8 Feb., 1643. B. M., E88.26.

22 (9). *Mercurius Urbanus*, 9 Nov., 1643. B. M., E75.16.

23 (9). *Certaine Informations*, 30 Oct.–6 Nov., 1643. B. M., E75.3.

24 (9). B. M., E73.2.

25 (9). *Mercurius Britanicus*, 9–16 Nov., 1643. B. M., E75.38.

26 (9). *The Second Part of the Spectacles*, 5 June, 1644. B. M., E53.21.

27 (9).   28 April–5 May, 1645.   B. M., E281.14.

28 (10).   29 April–6 May, 1644.   B. M., E45.11.

29 (10).   4 Oct., 1642.   B. M., E119.30.

30 (10).   *Tyrants and Protectors Set forth In their Colours*, by J. P., London, 1654.   B. M., E738.18.

31 (11).   White-Hall. / *A Poem*. / Written 1642. / *with* / *Elegies* / *on* / The Right Honourable *Francis* Earl / of *Bedford*. / And *Henry* Earle of *Manchester*, Lord Privy / Seale: both deceased during this present / Session of Parliament. / . . . The Authour *Hen. Glapthorne*. / London, printed for *Francis Constable*, 1643. [MS. "March 4. 1642." B. M., E91.33.]

32 (12).   *Strafford Papers*, ed. Knowler (1739), ii, 130.

33 (12).   *Ibid.*, p. 140.

34 (12).   Reyher, *Les Masques anglais*, p. 345.   Reyher gives "yards" for all these dimensions, which is certainly a mistake for "feet." The Banqueting Hall itself measures 115 feet in length, 60 in width, and 55 in height.

35 (12).   23–29 July, 1643.   B. M., E64.11.

36 (12).   Feb., 1645.   B. M., E268.6.

37 (12).   A figurative use, equivalent to "put down." Compare "it is a great measure to *pull downe* sinne . . . and to *pull downe* sin is alwaies a seasonable worke." *Mercurius Civicus*, 22–29 May, 1645. B. M., E286.8.

38 (12).   *The Oxford Character of the London Diurnall Examined and answered*, 31 March, 1645.   B. M., E274.32.

39 (13).   Literal enough here.

40 (13).   *Journals, House of Commons*, iv, 210a.

41 (13).   B. M., E387.3.

42 (13).   Reprinted in Hazlitt's Dodsley, xv, 399 ff.

43 (13).   Cf. Cunningham, "Did General Harrison kill 'Dick Robinson' the Player?" *Shakespeare Society's Papers*, ii, 11–13, and Collier, *Hist. Eng. Dram. Poetry* (1879), iii, 478.   Collier's argument, in which he demonstrates that this Robinson must be William Robinson, a Queen's man (cf. Murray, *English Dramatic Companies*, i, 266) is borne out by a reference in *A Diary or an Exact Journall*, 9–16 Oct., 1645; "Robinson the Player . . . he was in Drury Lane a Comodian, but now hee acted his own Tragedy." Other notices are: "Robinson the Fool slain, as he was turning and acting like a Player" (*Perfect Occurrences*, 10–17 Oct.); "*Slaine*. Major *Robinson*" (*Perf. Diurn.*, 13–20 Oct.); and another, which may link William Robinson with Richard, or (less probably) John Robinson: "Slain . . . *Robinson* the Players son" (*The Kingdomes Weekly Intelligencer*, 14–21 Oct.).

44 (13).   Collier, iii, 486.

45 (13).   B. M., E179.28.   Reprinted, *Antiquarian Repertory* (1808), iii.

46 (14).   MS. Ashmole 47, f. 132; MS. Rawlinson poet. 71, pp. 164–168.   R.

47 (14).   *Eng. Drama and Stage*, 272.

48 (15). Prerogative Court of Canterbury, Grey, No. 151.

[Abstract.] Nuncupative will. He left all he possessed to be divided among his children, and he desired his daughter Sarah, wife of Joseph Wilson, to see the same carried out. Witnesses: Joseph Wilson, Elizabeth Vasely, Elizabeth Swanston, Sarah Wilson (*her mark*), Joseph Wilson Junior.

3 July, 1651, commission to Sarah Wilson *alias* Swanston, to administer the goods, &c.

18 April, 1666, the like to Joseph Wilson husband of Sarah Wilson *alias* Swanston, to administer the goods left unadministered by her, now deceased.

49 (15). *Mercurius Impartialis*, 12 Dec., 1648. B. M., E476.3.

50 (15). *Royall Diurnall*, 25 Feb., 1650. B. M., E594.6.

51 (15). *Man in the Moon*, 13–20 March, 1650. B. M., E596.3.

52 (15). *Mercurius Fumigosus*, 28 Feb.–7 March, 1655. B. M., E829.13.

53 (15). "J. B. Williams" (pseudonym of J. G. Muddiman), *History of English Journalism*, pp. 106 ff.

54 (15). 21–28 Sept., 1647. *R.*

55 (15). 24–31 Oct., 1649.

56 (15). Peters in early life "came to be the jester (or rather a fool) in Shakespeare's company of players," according to the scurrilous biography by Dr. William Yonge, called *England's Shame* (1663).

57 (16). *Perf. Occurr.*, 9–16 May, 1645. B. M., E260.37.

58 (17). Collier, ii, 38.

59 (17). *The Weekly Account*, 4 Oct., 1643. B.M., Burney 17. *R.* Cf. *Cal. State Papers, Dom., 1641–43*, p. 564.

60 (17). *Fœnestra in Pectore, or Familiar Letters* (1660), p. 56. *R.* Rollins, who discovered this letter (*Stud. in Philol.*, 1923, p. 53), dated it as being before 1644, on the ground that Atkins was alderman up to 1644 (A. B. Beavens, *The Aldermen of London*, p. 64). This delimitation is too exact. Atkins was called "alderman" at least down to 1656. For example, in May, 1649, "Alderman Atkins," in a speech in Parliament, boasted that he personally had "smelt out many plots" (*Cal. State Papers, Dom., 1649–50*, p. 167.) In June of the same year "Thomas Atkins, Alderman, and former Lord Mayor" was to be knighted by the Speaker (*ibid., 1649–50*, p. 175). On 5 Aug., 1656, "Dr. Savery, carried before Alderman Atkins; the Alderman liberated him" (*ibid., 1656–57*, p. 58). So that, while 1643 is as good as any date for this letter of Forde's, it is far from being the only possible one.

"H. M.," for whom Rollins suggests Henry Mildmay, is much more probably Harry Marten, whose numerous jests in the House are notorious.

61 (17). *An Ordinance of the Lords and Commons Assembled in Parliament, For the speedy Raising and Impresting of Men for the Defence of the Kingdom. 10 August, 1643.* (Harvard College Library, Gay, 643. 587.) The men were to be "not under the age of eighteen, nor over the Age of fifty."

62 (17). B. M., E279.1.

63 (18). See below, pp. 61–62.

64 (18). *Wonders Foretold*, etc., 1643. B. M., E245.34.

65 (18). The 1647 edition is included in Ashbee's *Occasional Facsimile Reprints*. Cf. Rollins, *Studies in Philol.*, 1923, p. 56.

The *Astrologaster* (1620), which is not primarily humorous, but against charlatanry in figure-casting, says: "Another will fore-tell of Lightning and Thunder that shall happen such a day, when there are no such Inflamations to be seene, except men goe to the *Fortune* in Golding Lane, to see the Tragedie of Doctor *Faustus*. There indeede a man may beholde shagge-hayr'd Deuills," etc. (p. 31).

66 (18). F. J. Furnivall (*Academy*, xxii, 315) printed this MS. note from the Phillipps copy of Stow's *Annales*, 1631.

67 (18). *Mercurius Civicus*. B. M., E322.20.

68 (19). B. M., E317.10.

69 (19). *Harleian Miscellany*, x, 204. Cf. *Hist. MSS Comm., Rep. III*, App., p. 295*b*.

70 (19). B. M., E296.9. *R*.

71 (19). *Perf. Occurr.*, 19–26 Sept., 1645. Quoted by Collier, ii, 40.

72 (20). *Merc. Civicus*, 27 Nov.–4 Dec., 1645. B. M., E311.6. *The Kingdomes Weekly Post* (B. M., E311.15) refers to it as "an Act against Enterluds."

73 (20). *Journals, House of Lords*, viii, 234*a*.

74 (20). "Also a Petition of the *Black Friars* Players: Which they refer to your consideration." *Journals, House of Commons*, iv, 496*a*.

75 (20). 10–17 Feb., 1645. B. M., E269.25.

76 (20). *The Oxford Character of the London Diurnall Examined and Answered*, 31 March, 1645. B. M., E274.32.

77 (21). *Mercurius Anti-Britannicus*, 11 Aug., 1645. B. M., E296.9. *R*.

78 (21). L. P. C. van den Bergh, *Gravenhaagsche Bijzonderheden* (1857), p. 22; translated by J. H. van Lennep, *Notes and Queries*, Second Ser., ix, 48.

79 (21). B. M., E362.21.

80 (21). 23 Feb.–2 March, 1647. B. M., E378.18.

81 (22). *Diutinus Britanicus*. B. M., E365.11.

82 (22). B. M., E372.18.

83 (23). B. M., E520.18.

84 (23). *Perf. Occurr.*, 30 April–7 May, 1647. B. M., E386.8.

85 (23). E. B. Chancellor, *Knightsbridge and Belgravia*, p. 265. H. G. Davis, *Memorials of the Hamlet of Knightsbridge*, 1859, pp. 104, 105.

86 (23). Davis, *op. cit.*, p. 176.

87 (24). In commendatory verses prefixed to James Shirley's *Poems*.

88 (24). "1646. Pd. and given to the teacher at the Cockpitt of the children, 6*d*." John Parton, *Some Account of the Hospital and Parish of St. Giles in the Fields*, p. 235.

89 (24). Bodleian, Wood 654 A, pp. 12, 13. *R*. (Another copy, B. M., E388.4.)

90 (24). B. M., E406.23. *R*.

91 (25). *Journals, House of Commons*, v, 246*a*.

92 (25). *Journals, House of Lords,* ix, 334*b*.

93 (25). *Journals, House of Commons,* v, 248*a*. (17 July, 1647.)

94 (25). *Perf. Occurr.*, quoted in *Cal. State Papers, Dom., 1645–1647*, p. 599.

95 (25). *Journals, House of Commons,* v, 272*a*.

96 (25). 11–18 Sept., 1647. B. M., E407.25.

97 (25). 4 Sept., 1647. B. M., E405.24. Cf. J. G. Muddiman in *Nineteenth Century and After*, March, 1908. "Luke Harruney" was the anagrammatized pseudonym of Henry Walker.

98 (26). 9 Aug., 1647. B. M., E401.13.

99 (26). B. M., E518.42. *R.*

100 (26). 6 Oct., 1647. (The false *Melancholicus* gives Tuesday, 5 Oct., as the date.)

101 (26). 5–12 Oct., 1647. B. M., E410.19. *R.*

102 (26). *Mercurius Anti-Pragmaticus* exults over their fall: "That new broome (the late Ordinance against Printing) which in all probability was likely to sweep so cleane, which purged the Exchange of those dusty cobwebs, *Melancholicus, Clericus,* and *Diabolicus,* left *Pragmaticus* in some odd corner, as a trap for flies." 12–19 Oct., 1647. B. M., E411.10.

But *Medicus* was not dead yet; he roused himself sufficiently to denounce the impostor: "I see the Fates will not suffer me to dig my owne grave, I had thought to have laine still, and intombed my selfe with deceased *Melancholicus:* but as I was administering a draught of Mandragora into my owne bodie, *Mercury* touched me with his wand, and presented to my view an Asse cloathed in a Lions skin, whom but for his braying, I should have taken for the beast hee resembled, who baul'd out naming himselfe *Melancholicus.*" 15–22 Oct., 1647. B. M., E411.17.

The real *Melancholicus,* Parson John Hacklet, or Hackluyt, after breaking prison twice in the spring of 1648, reappeared in May, 1649, with "Gentlemen, I was a long time abused with variety of Counterfeits, which brought such an *odium* on the true *Melancholicus,* that I chose rather to leave off writing, then longer to hazard my reputation with such beetle-heads as weekely tooke upon them to personate me." B. M., E557.8.

This explanation removes the difficulty experienced by Professor Rollins, *Studies in Philol.*, 1921, p. 283.

103 (27). 2–9 Oct., 1647. B. M., E410.12. *R.*

104 (27). 6–13 Oct., 1647. B. M., E410.22.

105 (27). *Perf. Occurr.*, 22–29 Oct., 1647. B. M., E518.48.

106 (27). *Journals, House of Commons,* v, 335*a*.

107 (28). *Ibid.*, 339*b*.

108 (28). *The Moderate Intelligencer,* 21–28 Oct. B. M., E412.2. *R.*

109 (28). This is a reference to Queen Elizabeth's statute which made strolling, unprotected players rogues and vagabonds. *Merc. Anti-Pragmaticus,* 28 Oct.–4 Nov. B. M., E412.27. *R.*

110 (28). *Merc. Pragmaticus,* 26 Oct.–2 Nov. B. M., E412.16. *R.*

111 (28). 29 Oct.–5 Nov., 1647. B. M., E412.30. *R.*

112 (29). *Mercurius Vapulans*, 27 Nov., 1647. B. M., E417.6.

113 (29). 18–25 Jan., 1648. B. M., E423.23. *R.* Cf. Gardiner, *History of the Great Civil War*, iii, 308.

114 (29). 19–26 Jan., 1648. B. M., E423.25. *R.*

115 (30). Marmion, *Holland's Leaguer* (1632), i, 1.

116 (30). *A Remonstrance of Londons Occurrences*, 1642 (14 Dec.). B. M., E130.21.

117 (30). *An Admirable Speech Made by the Maior of Reading*, 1654. B. M., E745.17.

118 (30). *Universall Madnesse: or, A new merry Letany*, etc., 1647. B. M., E412.14.

119 (30). *A Perfect Diurnall*, 17–24 Jan., 1648. B. M., E520.28. *R.*

120 (30). *Journals, House of Commons*, v, 439*b*. Cf. *Mod. Intell.*, 20–27 Jan. (B. M., E423.28), which says that "many eminent persons" resorted to stage plays.

121 (30). 20–27 Jan., 1648. B. M., E423.29. *R.*

122 (30). 18–25 Jan., 1648. B. M., E423.21. *R.*

123 (31). 22–29 Jan., 1648. Bodleian, Hope 634, p. 130. This reference was recently discovered and kindly communicated to me by Professor Rollins.

124 (31). "for putting downe of Stage-Players, to punish them as *Rogues.*" *Perf. Occurr.*, 28 Jan.–4 Feb., 1648. B. M., E520.32. Cf. *Journals, House of Lords*, x, 3.

125 (31). *Journals, House of Commons*, v, 450*b*. Cf. *The Kingdome's Weekly Account*, 25 Jan.–2 Feb., 1648. B. M., E425.4.

126 (31). No. 5. See Appendix.

127 (32). For notes on Bowyer's earlier history, see Miss E. M. Denkinger's article in the *Publications of the Modern Language Association*, xli (March, 1926), 98, 99.

128 (33). See above, p. 13, and Note 43.

129 (33). *Thomas Betterton*, p. 2.

130 (33). Malone, *Variorum*, iii, 240.

131 (34). Fleay surmised that Clark had gone over at some time between 1635 and 1642. *A Biographical Chronicle of the English Drama*, ii, 210. Cf. Murray, i, 266–269.

132 (34). John Evelyn's *Diary*, ed. Bray, i, 246.

133 (34). *Perf. Occurr.*, 28 Jan.–4 Feb., 1648. B. M., E520.32.

134 (34). *The Elizabethan Playhouse* (Second Ser.), pp. 72, 240.

135 (35). But was not printed until 11 Feb. Cf. Firth and Rait, *Acts and Ordinances of the Interregnum*, i, 1070. Hazlitt, *Eng. Drama and Stage*, p. 65. An incomplete copy is preserved in Rushworth's *Historical Collections*, vol. iv, pt. 2, p. 991. The contemporary newsbooks printed the law in full: *Kingd. Weekly Intell.*, 8–15 Feb.; *Perf. Diurn.*, 7–14 Feb.

136 (35). *Perf. Occurr.*, 11–18 Feb., says, "The Actors to be whipt (in the Market) as Rogues."

137 (35). So printed officially; but see the better reading, "Stages, Galleries," above, p. 30. See below, pp. 36, 37, 101.

138 (35). 9–16 Feb., 1648. *R.*

139 (35). *Merc. Pragmaticus*, 8–15 Feb., 1648. B. M., E427.7. *R.*

140 (36). 14–20 Feb., 1648. B. M., E428.4.

141 (36). *Kingd. Weekly Intell.* (B. M., E432.6) gives the date as Wednesday, 8 March, while *Perf. Occurr.* (B. M., E522.3) gives 6 March.

142 (36). *Perf. Diurn.*, 6–13 March, 1648. B. M., E522.4.

143 (36). See below, pp. 167–168.

144 (37). 28 March, 1648. B. M., E433.29.

145 (37). *A Key to the Cabinet of the Parliament*, 1648 (MS. June 20). Cf. Collier, ii, 38.

146 (37). *Journals, House of Commons*, v, 612a.

147 (37). *Ibid.*, 648a.

148 (37). London, 3 Aug., 1648. B. M., E457.13.

149 (38). *Perf. Occurr.*, 1–8 Sept., 1648. B. M., E526.3.

150 (38). *Kingd. Weekly Intell.*, 12–19 Sept., 1648. B. M., E464.18. Cf. Rollins, *Studies in Philol.*, 1921, p. 291, who, however, gives a mistaken reference.

151 (38). *Journals, House of Commons*, vi, 20b.

152 (38). *Kingd. Weekly Intell.*, 12–19 Sept., 1648.

153 (38). 13–20 Sept. B. M., E464.22.

154 (38). 18–25 Sept., 1648. B. M., E464.36. *R.*

155 (39). 25 Sept.–2 Oct. B. M., E465.14.

156 (40). *Journals, House of Commons*, vi, 69b.

157 (40). *Historia Histrionica*, Hazlitt's Dodsley, xv, 410.

158 (40). B. M., E477.31.

159 (41). *Kingd. Weekly Intell.*, 2–9 Jan., 1649. B. M., E537.22. The date is here given as 2 Jan.; but this is probably a mistake for 1 Jan., the date given by *Perf. Occurr.*

159a (41). *Times Literary Supplement*, April 26, 1928.

160 (41). 29 Dec.–5 Jan., 1648–1649. B. M., E527.3. *R.* Another short account of the raid is to be found in *Perf. Diurn.*, 1–8 Jan., 1649, B. M., E527.4, and is quoted in Rushworth's *Historical Collections*, iv, 1381. Cf. Whitelocke's *Memorials*, 1732, p. 366a.

161 (41). B. M., E537.31. Cf. Hazlitt, *Eng. Drama and Stage*, pp. 266 ff.

162 (41). *Ibid.*, p. 271.

163 (42). B. M., E575.4.

164 (42). 16–30 Jan., 1649. B. M., E540.15.

165 (42). One of the two senses of "pit" here is the theatrical one. While this is not the earliest recorded use of the term—Chambers (*Elizabethan Stage*, ii, 555 n.) cites the use of the word "cock-pit" in 1640 for the parterre of a theatre — yet it is worth noticing.

166 (42). *Gleanings, or, A Collection of Memorable Passages*, London, 1651.

167 (43). *The Academy*, xxii, 315. See above, p. 12. "Pulled down" here certainly means "dismantled on the interior" and not "levelled with the ground," for the Cockpit and Salisbury Court were subsequently fitted up and used for plays. See below, pp. 96, 108 ff.

168 (43). *Notes and Queries*, Tenth Ser., i, 85.

169 (43). Adams, *Shakespearean Playhouses*, pp. 290 ff.

170 (43). Witness the raid on 20 Dec., 1649, when one of the actors betrayed the rest who were "privately playing neer St. *Iohns* street," to some soldiers, who "seized upon the Players, and took away their Sword and Cloths." *Perf. Diurn.*, 17–24 Dec., 1649. *R.* Mentioned also in Whitelocke's *Memorials*, 1732, p. 435*a*.

171 (43). Discovered by Professor Firth, who describes it as "from a broadside bound up in a volume of pamphlets belonging to that year [1650] collected by William Clarke, Monk's secretary." *Notes and Queries*, Eighth Ser., v, 464.

172 (44). See above, pp. 23–24.

173 (44). *Historia Histrionica, loc. cit.*

174 (45). *Pleasant Notes upon Don Quixot*, p. 24.

175 (45). *Ibid.*

176 (46). 22–29 Jan., 1650. B. M., E590.6. *R.* A short account is printed also in *Severall Proceedings in Parliament*, 18–25 Jan. B. M., E534.2.

177 (46). An error for "22."

178 (46). 23–31 Jan., 1650. B. M., E590.12. *R.*

179 (46). Evidently Philip, Earl of Pembroke, recently deceased. He was one of the six Lords who on 17 July, 1647, had objected to limiting the ordinance against plays, preferring to suppress them forever. See above, p. 25.

180 (47). *The Wits, or Sport upon Sport*, 1672.

181 (48). Reprinted by Halliwell-Phillipps, 1860. Cf. his *Shakespearean Drolls*, 1859.

182 (48). 1–8 June, 1653. *R.*

183 (49). 22–29 June, 1653. *R.*

184 (49). That is, "bash."

185 (49). *A True Register of all the . . . Burialles in the Parishe of St. James, Clerkenwell*, ed. Robert Hovenden, iv, 336 (Harleian Society, 1891). *R.*

186 (49). But Thomason's copy is dated 1 Sept., 1656 — eight months after Cox's death. He may, of course, have acquired it after the book had been on the market for some time. A second edition, with one additional droll (*Simpleton the Smith*), also appeared in 1656. Rollins (*Studies in Philol.*, 1923, p. 59) erroneously describes Thomason's copy as "the second edition."

187 (49). B. M., E675.17.

188 (49). See above, p. 44.

189 (50). *Mercurius Democritus*, 2–9 March, 1653. B. M., E689.15. *Democritus* reprinted this account, without the verses, in the following week: B. M., E689.25.

190 (50). Greg, *A List of English Plays*, p. 59.

191 (50). Adams, *Shakespearean Playhouses*, pp. 358–362.

192 (50). See above, pp. 24, 28, 29, 40. And compare below, p. 95.

193 (50). B. M., E693.8.

193*a*. (52). No. 6. See Appendix.

194 (52). Murray, i, 279–281.

195 (54). Wallace, *Englische Studien*, xliii, 340 ff. Cf. Chambers, ii, 131.

196 (54). Wallace, *Globe Theatre Apparel*, p. 2. Cf. Thaler, "Elizabethan Dramatic Companies," *P. M. L. A.*, xxxv (March, 1920), 123 ff.

197 (54). *Hist. MSS Comm.*, *Rep. XII*, App., part 7, p. 21.

198 (54). *The Faithful Scout* tells us what "Hectors" are: "The first thing that presents it self to publike view, is, a bloody Tragedy from sundry parts of the Nation; the Scene is Murder; but the Actors are called by the name of Hectors, *alias* Highway men; who have committed several notorious Robberies." 24 Feb.–3 March, 1654. B. M., E225.18.

199 (54). *Severall Proceedings*, 23 Feb.–2 March, 1654. B. M., E225.16.

200 (54). 1–8 Nov., 1654. B. M., E816.8. *R.*

201 (54). *Miscellania*, 1653.

202 (55). *The Academy*, xxii, 314.

203 (55). *Merc. Fumigosus*, 15–22 Nov., 1654. B. M., E817.14. *R.*

204 (55). *Kingd. Weekly Intell.*, 26 Dec.–2 Jan. B. M., E821.13. *R.* The Saturday mentioned is 30 Dec.; not, as Rollins says, 1 Jan.

205 (55). 27 Dec.–3 Jan. B. M., E821.16. Copied in *Certain Passages of Every Dayes Intelligence*, 29 Dec.–5 Jan., (B. M., E237.17). Noted by C. H. Firth in *Notes and Queries*, Seventh Ser., vi, 122.

206 (55). *Merc. Fumigosus*, 27 Dec.–3 Jan. B. M., E821.15. *R.*

207 (55). *Hist. MSS Comm.*, *Rep. XII*, App., part 7, p. 22.

208 (56). B. M., E838.18.

209 (56). State Papers, Domestic, Interregnum, vol. c, p. 124.

210 (56). 11–18 Sept., 1655. B. M., E853.16. *R.* Firth called attention to this account in *Notes and Queries*, Seventh Ser., vi, 122.

211 (57). 12–19 Sept., 1655. B. M., E853.19. *R.*

212 (57). Bodleian, Malone 391. *R.* Cf. a reprint by J. W. Ebsworth, *Choyce Drollery*, 1876, p. 285.

213 (57). Read "tire."

214 (58). Langbaine, *English Dramatic Poets*, 1691, p. 201.

215 (58). *Pleasant Notes*, p. 270.

216 (59). J. Q. Adams (*Shakespearean Playhouses*, pp. 336, 337) erroneously assumes that the sport was put down from 1642 until the Restoration.

217 (59). *Cal. State Papers, Dom.*, *1639*, p. 420.

218 (60). *London and the Countrey Carbonadoed*, p. 66.

219 (60). Greg, *Henslowe Papers*, p. 19.

220 (60). *Pills to Purge Melancholy* (1714), ii, 96. Harry Hunks was a famous bear in Shakspere's time.

221 (60). Spenser Society, 1876.

222 (61). *The Actors Remonstrance, or Complaint*, 24 Jan., 1643. B. M., E86.8.

223 (61). *Journals, House of Commons*, iii, 325*b*.

224 (61). *Ibid.*, p. 463*b*.

225 (62). *Mercurius Aulicus*, 13–20 July, 1645. B. M., E296.33.

226 (62). *Merc. Britanicus*, 11–18 Aug., 1645. B. M., E296.34.

227 (62). 7 Oct., 1645. B. M., E304.4.

228 (62). *Journals, House of Commons*, v, 246*a*.

229 (62). *Ibid.*, 248*a*. Cf. *Perf. Occurr.*, 16–23 July, 1647.
230 (63). *Cal. State Papers, Dom., 1645–1647*, p. 599. *Journals, House of Commons*, v, 272*a*. *Perf. Diurn.*, 9–16 Aug., 1647. B. M., E518.8.
231 (63). 19–26 Oct., 1647. B. M., E411.23.
232 (63). B. M., E417.20.
233 (63). B. M., E455.1.
234 (63). B. M., E457.8.
235 (63). 24–31 Aug., 1648. B. M., E461.30.
236 (63). 30 Aug., 1649. B. M., E572.7.
237 (64). 15–22 May, 1649. B. M., E556.8.
238 (64). 24 July, 1649. B. M., E565.24.
239 (64). B. M., E593.17. For a real Thursday performance, compare the Bear Garden bill, preserved among the Alleyn papers, which is reprinted by Adams, *Shakespearean Playhouses*, p. 133.
240 (64). 13–21 April, 1652. B. M., E660.3.
241 (65). 8–16 June, 1652. B. M., E667.17.
242 (65). *Merc. Democritus*, 7–14 April, 1652. B. M., E659.25. Cf. Ordish, *Early London Theatres*, p. 241.
243 (65). 3–10 Nov., 1652. B. M., E681.3.
244 (65). 8–15 Nov., 1654. B. M., E817.4. Ned of Canterbury is at the top of the list of bears in Taylor's *Bull, Beare, and Horse*, 1638.
245 (66). 5 May, 1653. *Cal. State Papers, Dom., 1652–1653*, p. 307.
246 (66). Evelyn says that Duncombe got the chairs from Naples. *Diary of John Evelyn*, ed. Wheatley, i, 192.
247 (66). Rymer, *Foedera* (1732), xix, 572.
248 (66). Evelyn's *Diary*, i, 7.
249 (66). *Notes and Queries*, Eleventh Ser., ii, 152.
250 (66). *Bull, Beare, and Horse*, p. 59.
251 (67). B. M., E124.24.
252 (67). B. M., E794.23.
253 (68). 2–9 Nov., 1653. B. M., E718.3.
254 (68). *Certain Passages of Every Dayes Intelligence.* B. M., E237.17.
255 (68). 9–16 May, 1655. B. M., E838.18.
256 (68). B. M., E852.29.
257 (69). *Perfect Proceedings of State Affairs*, 20–27 Sept., 1655. B. M., E854.2.
258 (69). *The Academy*, xxii, 315. Cf. Adams, *Shakespearean Playhouses*, p. 337.
259 (69). Edited by J. W. W. Bund, i (1920), 31. Cf. *The last Speech and dying Words of Thomas (Lord, alias Colonel) Pride; being touched in Conscience for his inhuman Murder of the Bears in the Bear-garden, when he was High-Sheriff of Surrey. Taken in Short-hand, by T. S. late Clerk to his Lordship's Brew-house*, 1680 (*Harleian Miscellany* [1809], iii, 136). Both mentioned by Rollins, *Studies in Philol.*, 1923, pp. 60, 61.
260 (69). *The Academy*, xxii, 315.
261 (69). Printed for John Johnson, 1660. B. M., E1050.4.
262 (70). *Cal. State Papers, Dom., 1661–1662*, p. 574.

263 (70). *A True Register* . . . *of St. James, Clerkenwell*, ed. Robert Hovenden, iv, 347 (Harleian Society, 1891). Discovered by Rollins. Cf. *Studies in Philol.*, 1923, p. 61.

264 (70). *Cal. State Papers, Dom., 1663–1664*, p. 217. For the later history of the Hope, see J. Q. Adams's *Shakespearean Playhouses*, pp. 337–341. The first document he quotes after the Restoration is a letter from the Earl of Manchester, 29 Sept., 1664. This letter says that the game is "now removed to the usual place on the Bankside"; but, until now, no one has discovered *from where* it was removed.

CHAPTER II

THE PLAYHOUSES

I. The Red Bull

IN this short section I shall deal with two matters bearing on the history and structure of the Red Bull Playhouse. Although the first of these falls outside the limits of our period, the fresh material I have to offer is of sufficient importance to be included here. The second point needs no explanation; it affects our understanding of the physical form of the theatre throughout our study.

I

Until now, for knowledge of the beginnings of the Red Bull, we have had to rely on the documents in the case of Woodford v. Holland, 1613 and 1619, in the Court of Requests, published by J. Greenstreet and Professor C. W. Wallace.[1] I have found, however, later documents in the same dispute, which not only provide new information but also correct our notions of the meaning of these earlier records.

No one has known the result of Woodford's suit against Holland, over a share in the profits of the Red Bull, in the Court of Requests in 1619. From the new data it is now clear that Woodford carried his claim into the higher court of equity, the Chancery, where his bill was filed 25 October, 1623. Aaron Holland put in his answer on 6 November following. The text of the bill and answer, with the decree of the court, will be found in the Appendix. I shall content myself here with the gist.

From Woodford's bill of 1619 it was known that Holland had leased a house and land called the Red Bull, in the parish of St. James at Clerkenwell, from Anne, relict and administratrix of Christopher Beddingfield, and had built a playhouse in and upon some part of the property. In the present Chancery bill of 1623, to the description of the property as "known by the name or sign of the Red Bull at the upper end of St. John Street," is added "with the Gardens Courts Cellars Ways & liberties thereunto belonging . . . sometimes in the tenure of one John Waintworth or his assigns." This description of the building suggests an inn. It would be interesting if we could learn Waintworth's occupation.

The history of the Woodford–Holland affair is briefly as follows. To Thomas Swynnerton, an actor in the Queen Anne's Company, Aaron Holland had leased a certain owner's or proprietary share of the profits in the Red Bull. Swynnerton later sold this lease for £50 to one Philip Stone, whereupon Holland granted the latter a new lease of the share, to run for $25\frac{3}{4}$ years from Christmas, 1608, at an annual rent of 50 shillings. On 17 June, 1612, Stone made over his lease to Woodford. The latter complained in the Court of Requests that Holland refused to pay him the profits of his share, and also a certain sum of threepence a day which he said accrued to him by reason of a "gatherer's place which belonged to" his share. Holland replied that Woodford had forfeited the share by failing to pay his rent, and that the "gatherer's place" did not belong to the share. A "gatherer's place," it should be said, means the office and pay of one of the receivers of admission charges at the playhouse.

We come now to the confusion which has arisen in the minds of scholars concerning the size of the said share in the Red Bull profits, and the question of the "gatherer's place," which were the matters in dispute between Woodford and Holland from the beginning. Professor Wallace's reading of the 1619 bill gave them as "a seventh part of the said playhouse and galleries with a gatherers place there[to] belonging or appertaining." [2] This reading obliged him to regard as an error the following statement of the arbitrator, Clement Goldsmith (to whom the case was referred): "the cause . . . touching an interest claimed by the plaintiffs bill in the 18th part of the profits of the playhouse." [3] To reconcile these two conflicting statements, one giving the share as one-seventh, and the other as one-eighteenth, of the profits of the house, Sir Edmund Chambers is led to think that "the gallery profits were divided in the proportion of seven-eighteenths to the house-keepers and eleven-eighteenths to the players." [4]

The Chancery suit of 1623 clears up the matter by revealing the fact that the share in question was not a seventh but an eighteenth share. The reading "seventh" is an error. Naturally this revelation alters our conception of the total value of the owners' or "housekeepers'" shares. Since the profit on one share was reckoned at £30 a year (or, as Woodford put it in his bill of 1623, "amounting sometimes to Twenty shillings a week sometimes more & sometimes less"), the total annual profit on 18 shares would come to £540, which is a good deal more than seven shares at £30, or £210 a year.

The description given in our new documents of the basis and method of payment of profits is interesting. By the terms of the lease, Holland promises

. . . well & truly [to] pay & deliver or cause to be delivered unto the said Phillip Stone his executors or assigns at the said Play house the Eighteenth penny & just Eighteenth part of all such sum & sums of money and other commodities profits & benefits whatsoever that at [all times within] the said Term of Twenty & five years & three quarters of a year should be collected had made gotten or received of all & every or any person or persons whatsoever that should or did come into and sit stand or be placed or take place in any the Gallery or Galleries or [rooms belonging] to the said Play house or upon the Stage of the said Play house or in or upon any part or parcel of the said Play house weekly or at the end of every week The said Phillip Stone or his assigns demanding the same of the said Aaron Holland his executors [& assigns at the] Great Gate leading into the said Play house called the Red bull the Actors & Players parts & duties and all other ordinary charges & duties arising to be paid out of the same And the whole profit of the selling of bread beer ale & fruit being first deducted.

As to the gatherer's place, which was said to "belong to" the share, Woodford's bill has a clear statement:

To which Eighteenth part there was then & still is incident & belonging by the usual Custom a Gatherers place whereby in respect of certain orders made by & between the said Company [of Players and Partners and] Sharers or owners of the said house for the avoiding of all differences & controversies concerning their daily charge of Gatherers there did arise & grow due unto the said Eighteenth part Three pence profit a day amounting to Eighteen pence a week to be paid daily or at the end of every week [to the said] Swynnerton or to such Gatherer as he should nominate or appoint during . . . the time of their playing.

Obviously the threepence-a-day gatherer's fee was payable to the owner of the share, in addition to his share of the gallery profits. It was a perquisite, in return for which he had to provide an employee to "gather." [5]

Holland, in his answer to Woodford, denies that the latter had any right to the gatherer's place, insisting that there is no mention made of it in the deed, and that it belonged by right to him (Holland); and as an excuse for his having taken the forfeiture of the eighteenth share, he asserts that the three-pence-a-day profit to the gatherer's place "was far more worth than the said eighteenth part." If this assertion be true, then the income of the share could not have been anything like £30 a year. But the answer in another respect appears untrustworthy and inclined to exaggeration: Holland asserts that the arbitrators awarded twenty marks (£13 6s. 8d.) to be paid him by Woodford, whereas the award as printed by Professor Wallace [6] gives the sum as £6 13s. 4d., which is only half as much.

I shall not attempt to determine the relative truthfulness of the litigants. Their allegations will be found at large in the Appendix, including Holland's assertion that Woodford, moved by "a desire and delight to variety of suits and controversies," exhibited his second bill in the Court of Requests, "thinking himself . . . to be an excellent Tragedian and purposing to vex and undo this defendant (being an aged man)"; and his complaint that he (Holland) had been forced, for lack of money

. . . not only to sell his whole benefit and profit in the said Playhouse, but also all his interest and term of years in the said Messuage called the Red Bull and in divers tenements thereunto near adjoining for the sum of one hundred Pounds reserving a small Annuity for the maintenance of him and his wife for the term of their several lives.

An end was put to the suit on 3 May, 1624, by the court's adjudging Woodford to pay to Holland 46s. 8d. costs "for want of a Replication," and dismissing Woodford's bill.

As a result, then, of the discovery of this suit we are enabled to solve a puzzle of long standing as to the value of the owners' or housekeepers' shares in the Red Bull, and further to shed light on the institution of the "gatherer's place."

II

Perhaps by the time of this suit we have just studied (1624), the Red Bull Playhouse had been rebuilt and enlarged.[7] Certainly Prynne tells us in 1633 that the remodeling had been carried out.[8] But I cannot follow Mr. Lawrence[9] in thinking that the rebuilt edifice was provided with a roof which turned the open-air yard into a protected pit. Wright's clear statement, in the *Historia Histrionica*, that it "lay partly open to the weather," can now find confirmation in some unnoticed passages which I have gleaned from the Thomason newsbooks. John Crouch, as usual writing nonsensical sense in his weekly *Mercurius Fumigosus*, in 1654 and 1655 scribbled some paragraphs on the famous ropedancer called "the Turk," which throw light on the physical disposition of the Red Bull:

> *News from St* Johns *Street is,*
> That the *Turk* the other day, dancing so high, in capering on the upper Rope, discovered a *Myne of Gold* in the Ayre. [23–30 August, 1654.][10]

> The *Turk* . . . hath imployed the Company of *Scive-makers* to *make a great Scive* . . . to draw up with *Pulleys* over the Ropes, to *keep off the Raine;* that he may Dance dry-shod all the *Winter*, So that the gaining of the *Gold Myne* in the Aire, is now laid aside, and by the *wisest*, thought but a meer fable, his meaning being, *by shewing his tricks in the Aire, he would quickly gather much gold to himself.* [30 August–6 September, 1654.][11]

> The climbing *Turk*, finding the *Red-bull* Play-house is not for his turn, is now about to take one of the Twelve Houses of the Heavens to dance in. [20–27 September, 1654.][12]

> The *Rope-dancing Turk*, finding much inconvenience in the high Winde and the *raine*, is about drawing up a Petition to *Jupiter*, to bannish the *Winde* and the *Raine* into another Country for a year. [25 April–2 May, 1655.][13]

Since the acrobatic equilibrist was hindered by wind and rain from performing on the high rope in the Red Bull, it is pretty clear that the house lay "open to the weather" as late as 1655.

As for the state of the house under the Restoration, Mr. Lawrence argues persuasively for a roof. He points out that Thomas Jordan's *Nursery of Novelties* contains "A Speech . . . to those who would rise out of the Pit at the Red Bull . . . and disturb the Conclusion by going on the stage, June 23, 1660," in which the turbulent are exhorted to "keep their seats." The term "pit" (except in the case of the unroofed Hope Theatre on the Bankside, which was used for bear-baiting) [14] referred ordinarily to the *parterre* of the private or roofed theatres; and we have no other evidence of seats being set up in the yard of a public or unroofed theatre. Moreover, Mr. Lawrence notes that Pepys, on his visit to the Red Bull, 23 March, 1661, saw Rowley's *All 's Lost by Lust* from "the pitt."

Yet, in spite of these references to pit and seats, I doubt very much that the Red Bull was ever roofed. Considerations of strength of materials alone argue emphatically against it. The Red Bull and the Fortune were considerably larger than any of the roofed private houses. Taking the interior dimensions of the first Fortune for an example, the mere weight of a roof to cover an opening 55 by 55 feet, would be enormous, and the additional burden would necessitate a rebuilding of the walls. That the owners of the enlarged Red Bull undertook any such great expense in the lean years between 1655 and 1660 is more than doubtful; and since we have no mention or evidence of a roof at any time, the presumption is that there was none. It is not impossible to conclude that benches were set in the yard in good weather, and that the "seated yard," in the last of the un-roofed houses, under the influence of private theatres, or per-haps in emulation of them, came to be called the "pit."

Under the persuasion of his belief that the Red Bull in Com-monwealth times was a roofed theatre, Mr. Lawrence has reaccepted the picture in Kirkman's *The Wits* (1672) as actu-ally representing "the Interior of the Red Bull." [15] But if I have demonstrated that this theatre lay open to the weather, the Kirkman picture, which shows a stage lighted by a chan-delier and footlights, cannot have anything to do with the Red Bull.

II. The Phoenix, or Cockpit in Drury Lane

Excellent as it is, Professor J. Q. Adams's chapter on the private playhouse in Drury Lane [16] affords no clear account of the origin of the building. For lack of definite evidence, the author was led to suppose that the playhouse was built on the site of an old cockpit. Thanks to new material from the Chancery records, I can supply some cardinal facts as to its origin. These will be found to corroborate Howes's remark that one of London's theatres was a "cockpit," [17] and to provide a basis in fact for Randolph's turgid figure: [18]

> When thy intelligence on the Cockpit stage
> Gives it a soul from her immortal rage,
> I hear the Muse's birds with full delight
> Sing where the birds of Mars were wont to fight.

The fresh information presented in the following pages is extracted from a number of suits in Chancery hitherto unknown to the stage historian.

I

On 28 April, 1607, one Henry Holdford, Esq., and Jane his wife granted to Walter Burton (a gardener) a lease of a large plot of ground in the parish of St.-Giles-in-the-Fields, to run for fifty-one years from the preceding Christmas. The holding is described as "a plot newly enclosed from the west side of Aldwich Close adjoining Drury Lane." [19] We find that Burton, by two indentures, — 30 April, 1607, and October, 1609, — made over all but two months of his fifty-one years' term in this plot to John Best, a member of the Grocers' Company, at a total rental of £4 9s. a year. Shortly after October, 1609, the enterprising Best built seven or eight houses on the plot, among which was "one messuage house or tenement called a Cockpit and afterwards used for a play house & now called the Phenix with divers buildings thereto belonging, And one other messuage house or tenement with the appurtenances adjoining to the said Messuage." [20] This second house, next to the Cockpit, provided a lodging for the keeper of the gamecocks.

For six years the building housed the devotees of cockfighting, and the audiences in the amphitheatre followed the bloody encounters of the spurred and winged gladiators.

The Drury Lane Cockpit must have been a well-constructed amphitheatre of a respectable size to have then attracted the attention of a theatrical manager. In 1616 Christopher Beeston,[21] *alias* Hutchinson, was at the head of the Queen Anne's Men at the Red Bull. Unroofed theatres, such as the Red Bull, in spite of their greater capacity, were subject to serious disadvantages. Exposed to rain and wind, they could not draw audiences in bad weather. Plays had to be acted almost exclusively by daylight; and because of the theatre's size and bad acoustic properties — not to mention the turbulence of the penny groundlings or "understanders" in the yard — the actors were fain to shout their lines, a deplorable practice which drove away auditors of discretion and refinement. Beeston, in the summer of 1616, in order to secure better acting conditions and to attract a more elegant and manageable clientele, hired the Cockpit from Best, with a view to turning it into a "private" playhouse. We learn therefore that, on 9 August, John Best and six trustees let to Christopher Beeston, under his alternative name of Hutchinson,

. . . All that edifices or building called the Cockpits, and the Cockhouses and sheds thereunto adjoining, late . . . in the tenure or occupation of John Atkins gentleman or his assigns; Together also with one tenement or house and a little Garden thereunto belonging next adjoining to the Cockpits then in the occupation of Jonas Westwood or his assigns, and one part or parcel of ground behind the said Cockpits, Cockhouses, sheds, Tenement, and garden.[22]

Beeston's annual rent was fixed at £45, and his lease was to run for thirty-one years, from 29 September, 1616. He entered on the premises and began alterations without delay, for I discover that by the middle of October the Council of the Society of Lincoln's Inn was disturbed by his activities. The Cockpit was not far from Lincoln's Inn Fields; and the prospect of a theatre drawing crowds so near the sanctuary of the law alarmed the Solons. A committee of the society was formed on 15 October to attend "the Queene's Councell, with others of the Innes of Courts, touching the convertinge of the Cocke Pytte in the Feilds into a playe house." [23]

Objection even by such an august body proved fruitless. By the end of the winter Beeston had finished fitting up the Cockpit as a playhouse. On 4 March, however, just after he had opened in Drury Lane with his company brought from the Red Bull, the London mob entered a more violent protest, in the form of a Shrove Tuesday assault, which left the interior of his theatre a wreck. Ordinarily, the mob attacked only the brothels; and the one reason I can think of for their extending their attentions to the playhouse is that the latter was an innovation in the neighborhood. Whatever the cause of destruction, it was three months before repairs were complete and the persevering Beeston could once more bring his company from the Red Bull to begin afresh at the Cockpit. [24]

To rehearse the story of the successive companies of players at the Cockpit, so well told by Professor Adams, [25] would be superfluous; but there is much new material to be included here touching the theatre itself, and the family of Beestons who controlled its destiny.

The small house already mentioned close adjoining the Cockpit now furnished a lodging for the keeper of the theatre. We find that this officer at the Cockpit was not Beeston the manager, but a leading member of his company. William Sherlock, spoken of as a chief actor at the Phoenix in 1622, [26] occupied this house first, followed at some time before 1644 by John Rhodes. Thus the dwelling of the manager or his deputy on the premises — the prime distinguishing feature of the earliest "private" playhouses — [27] is shown to be a characteristic of the "private house in Drury Lane," as we shall find it was later to be of Salisbury Court, Rutland House, the first Lincoln's Inn Fields, the Theatre Royal in Drury Lane, and the Duke's Theatre in Dorset Garden.

As to the position of the buildings in the Cockpit group, while we have no documented details, it is possible to place them fairly accurately within the quadrilateral formed by

Drury Lane, Great Queen Street, Great Wild Street, and Prince's (now Kemble) Street. The playhouse itself, whose site is now said to be marked by Pit (formerly Cockpit) Court, was set back some distance from Drury Lane, and had a yard which extended (as late as 1623) to Great Wild Street.[28]

I find that a house in Drury Lane abutted "on the Cockpit on the East" and on the south adjoined another house in Drury Lane, known as the "George." This "George" was also let by Best to Christopher Beeston. After Beeston's death it was apparently occupied in 1639 by a certain George Lillgrave, whose attempts to convert it into a tavern aroused the better class of inhabitants of Drury Lane to secure his arrest, and to desire the government

. . . that power may be given to the next justices of the peace to commit any person who shall be found drawing and selling wine there, or attempting to hang up a sign or a bush, or doing any work there towards making that house a tavern, the disorder being likely to be such in the tavern joined to the playhouse as will not be possible to be suppressed.[29]

Nevertheless, within a short time after this protest we discover that Elizabeth Beeston sublet the house to Knightley Lucas, who in spite of opposition converted it into the "George" Tavern. Very likely this same house is identical with "the Cockpit ordinary in Drury Lane," where Captain Godolphin, "a very wild young gentleman," was killed in 1682.[30]

Unfortunately we have no graphic information as to the shape and appearance of the Cockpit Theatre. I fully expected to find a clear representation of it in Hollar's Bird's-eye View of West Central London, drawn in 1657, but I was disappointed; unless indeed we are to take a three-gabled structure, which stands where the Cockpit should be, for the theatre.

II

By 1633 John Best had died; and on 4 May of that year Beeston obtained from Best's widow Katherine an additional term of nine years, making his holding in the Cockpit, the small dwelling-house, and the George forty years in all — to expire 28 September, 1656. Only five years after the signing of this lease, Christopher Beeston "of St. Giles-in-the-Fields, gentleman" died — in 1638, between 7 October and 3 December. On 4 October, when making his testament,[31] he was "sick and weak in body." By his will, proved on 3 December, he bequeathed to his son William some freehold land and houses in St. Leonard's, Shoreditch, and a plot of ground in Lincoln's Inn Fields (parish of St.-Giles-in-the-Fields), enclosed with a brick wall. From a later suit in Chancery[32] I have extracted some new information concerning Christopher Beeston's holdings in Shoreditch. Besides some property in Hog Lane, Shoreditch, he owned several houses in King's Head Yard, between Hog Lane and a ten-acre plot known as "the Curtain." Katherine Crosse, who owned this large property, let a piece of it to Christopher Beeston. The Curtain estate included the site of the Curtain Playhouse, one of the first two public theatres erected in London.[33] Beeston, as we know, acted with Queen Anne's Company at this theatre in and after 1604. The last mention of the Curtain hitherto discovered is from the year 1627: "the common shoare near the Curtain playhouse."[34] I have uncovered another record which testifies that the building was still standing in 1660, some thirty-three years later. In the unsavory list of "Common Whores, Wanderers, Pick-pockets and Night-walkers" compiled by John Garfield,[35] I find the following item: "Mrs Mails by the Curtain Playhouse."

But to return to the matter of Christopher Beeston's will. To his eldest daughter Anne, wife of Theophilus Bird the actor, and to her son Christopher Bird, he left £300, in case his (Beeston's) "two houses lately erected and built in Covent garden . . . shall be assured to amount" to £600.

Elizabeth his wife he made sole executrix, and named as overseers his "Noble friend Captain Lewis Kirk" and his "Worthy respected friend Thomas Sheppard esquire," entreating them "in the love of a true and dying friend" to help her carry out his will.

The passages relating to the Cockpit Theatre and to his company of young actors there, known as "Beeston's Boys," run as follows:

And whereas I stand possessed of four of the six shares in the Company for the King and Queen's service at the Cockpit in Drury lane, I declare that two of my said four shares shall be delivered up for the advancement of the said Company, and the other two to Remain unto my said executrix as fully and amply as if I lived amongst them. And I will that my said executrix shall for the said two shares provide and find for the said Company a sufficient and good stock of apparel fitting for their use, she allowing and paying to my said son William Hutchinson for his care and industry in the said Company twenty pounds of lawful money of England per annum. And I do hereby charge him by the love of a Child to his Father that he for my sake do all good concerning this or any other business to my said wife and her two daughters.

On 7 October Beeston added the following codicil:

Memorandum that whereas the within named Christopher Hutchinson have willed ordered and devised by my last will and testament within written that my executrix within named should pay unto my within named son William Hutchinson the yearly sum of Twenty pounds of lawful money of England for his Care and industry to be taken in and about the Company within mentioned, Now my will and mind is and I do hereby order and devise that my said Executrix in lieu of the said twenty pounds per annum shall allow unto him my said son William Hutchinson one half share of the two shares in the said Company within mentioned for his care in the business, she finding and providing a stock of apparel for the said company as is within declared. Witness my hand the day and year above-said CHRISTOPHER HUTCHINSON.

Christopher Beeston, then, as manager held a two-thirds interest (four shares out of six) in the profits of the company. But being sole lessee of the building, he carried the entire responsibility of the rent, and had furthermore to provide the players with dresses.[36] To encourage the boy actors, he gave up to them by his will half of his two-thirds interest, or two of his four shares. The codicil is interesting; as we have seen, it alters his son William's remuneration as governor of the company from £20 a year to a half-share out of the two remaining shares: an arrangement which would better engage William's diligence, and one which incidentally gives an approximate notion of the value of a share. If a half-share were roughly equivalent to £20 a year, the annual income of the two shares to be divided among the King's and Queen's Boys at this period (1638) would be about £80.

Elizabeth Beeston had some difficulty in meeting her late husband's obligations. On 7 July, 1640, she was obliged to borrow £150 of the actor William Wilbraham, and for security make over to him the Cockpit property by way of mortgage. Subsequently she married her husband's "noble friend," Captain Lewis Kirk, a gentleman pensioner and Royalist officer in the Civil War. Charles I knighted Kirk at Oxford on 23 April, 1643, and in 1645 he was colonel and governor of the castle at Bridgnorth, Salop.[37]

Here we must pause a moment in order to introduce two men, Hussey and Rolleston, who were destined to contend with each other for possession of the Cockpit. In 1633 Katherine Best, landlord of the Cockpit, having borrowed a large sum of money from Thomas Hussey, a prothonotary of Chancery, made over the rents of several houses to him, including that of the Cockpit, for a term of years ending Christmas, 1653.[38] And further, a year before she died in 1645, she assigned, among other property, to her son-in-law Robert Rolleston the remaining four years of her lease, which expired 25 December, 1657.

Elizabeth Beeston, before and after her marriage to Kirk, paid the £45 rent of the Cockpit to Katherine Best up to 29 September, 1643 — that is, for more than a year after the suppressing of stage plays. At Mrs. Best's death in May, 1645, the Kirks owed her eighteen months' rent. Hussey, Mrs. Best's creditor, came up to London at the close of the first Civil War and took the administration of her estate in June, 1647. He arrived at an agreement with the Kirks, who alleged "that they were disabled to pay their said arrears of rent by reason they were not suffered to use the premises as a play house." Hussey remitted the arrears in consideration of £22 10s. cash, on the Kirks' verbal promise to pay him the growing rent to the end of his term. Actually they paid one year's rent, to Michaelmas, 1648. On 25 March, 1650, Hussey asked them in vain to settle their eighteen months' arrears. In his complaint in Chancery, Hussey says that they refuse to pay him,

. . . although they . . . do make a very great constant yearly profit of the said messuages, Tenements, & premises, & sometimes a very extraordinary profit, for in several nights since the said feast of Saint Michael 1647, they have gained by acting of plays there about xxx or xl^l a night.

These statements are no doubt exaggerated, after the manner of bills in Chancery; but it is interesting to get confirmation of surreptitious acting at the Cockpit from this quarter. As a result of his suit it appears that Hussey obliged the Kirks to pay the Cockpit rent to him.

Meanwhile, Robert Rolleston, an upholsterer and a man of substance, decided that the Cockpit was a good piece of property. Accordingly he went to the ground landlord, now Richard Holdford, Esq., and purchased among other things the reversion of the playhouse, which was to come 25 December, 1657.

Upon this, William Beeston, with a view to getting the playhouse for himself, free from the hold of his mother and his stepfather, opened negotiations with Rolleston. As he says in a complaint [39] which he later made against Rolleston to the Chancellor,

. . . your said Orator, having taken much pains for advancement of the said Playhouse and the said Messuage or tenement, and being desirous also, in regard the same was formerly his said late father's, to contract for and purchase the same, and one small messuage or tenement thereunto adjoining. . .

Beeston alleges that he agreed in October, 1650, with Rolleston for the purchase at a price of £351; that he paid 20s. earnest money, and provided 40s. for a sealing dinner "at a tavern in Catteaton Street London, near the said Rolleston's house." After paying another £10 and sealing the articles without reading them, Beeston found they were not according to agreement; whereupon he tried to get Rolleston to correct them. Rolleston refused, and Beeston says he was obliged to sign harder conditions on 2 January, 1650/1, by which, if he paid £141 more in hand and the remainder, £201, by 24 March following, Rolleston assigned all his interest in the "Cockpit Playhouse & a tenement or house thereunto adjoining . . .

late in the occupation of John Rhodes," to give possession 28
December, 1653; if he did not give possession on that date, he
would pay Beeston £45 a year rent for four years.[40] On the
sealing of this agreement, Beeston says that he

. . . entered upon the premises & laid out near Two hundred pounds about
the repairing & fitting the same for [his] occasions. And after that [he] took
Prentices, & Covenant Servants to instruct them in the quality of acting,
& fitting them for the Stage, for which the said premises were so repaired
& amended, to his great charge & damage.

In the face of Beeston's admitted difficulty in finding enough
cash to fulfill his agreement, this estimate of his expenses for
repair work sounds exaggerated. But let him proceed with his
tale.

About two weeks before 24 March, 1651, when the remaining £201 was to be paid, Beeston found himself a prisoner in
the Fleet for debt, and unable to raise the sum. He offered to
pay £100 on 24 March, and the rest in six months, with eight
per cent interest. Rolleston promised to accept this proffer,
but on the day of payment put Beeston off with an excuse. In
hope of finding Rolleston, Beeston danced attendance daily at
his creditor's place of business, until he annoyed the upholsterer's partner into a threat that if he "did not forbear coming to the shop they would set a Sergeant upon [his] back to
arrest him." Beeston closed his complaint in Chancery by
charging that Rolleston intended to defraud him of the £150
already paid, and to sell the reversion of the playhouse to the
Kirks.

For answer, Rolleston quickly stopped Beeston's suit by
pleading an outlawry. Dame Elizabeth Kirk, who was also a
defendant, disclaimed all knowledge of any agreement between
her son and Rolleston, and denied that she had made a bargain
with the latter for the Cockpit.

As we have seen, Hussey's right to the rent of the Cockpit
was to expire at Christmas, 1653. It appears, however, that he
continued to receive the Kirks' rent beyond that date, and
Rolleston brought suit against them all in May, 1655.[41] By his
complaint he seeks to force Hussey to relinquish the premises,

and to oblige the Kirks to attorn to him. Replying, Hussey alleges that he came to an agreement with the Kirks for the rent of the Cockpit, by which they agreed to pay the £45 a year, provided that he should make allowance "for taxes and other extraordinary payments and some further abatement in respect the same house was not used for a play house." Hussey claims £250 still due him on Katherine Best's debt, and insists that he should be paid somehow. For their part, the Kirks say that they are ignorant of any title that Rolleston has in the Cockpit, and in a further answer[42] in February, 1656, they aver that they have paid Hussey rent until Christmas, 1655.

The depositions in this case throw an amusing light on the attempts of Rolleston to be recognized by the Kirks as the landlord of the Cockpit. One of Rolleston's witnesses, Thomas Benson, an "oil man" of Catteaton Street, on 23 April, 1656, deposed as follows: [43]

That about a year ago as he remembereth the time, he . . . was present with the Complainant when as he the Complainant did require the now defendants Kirk and his wife to Attorn Tenants to him and to pay to him the rents by them payable for the houses in their possession, and did acquaint them with his title to the same and did offer to secure the said defendants for so doing against the defendant Hussey; Whereupon the defendant Kirks wife made the Complainant this or the like answer in effect: that she was confident that he the Complainant had the just right and title to the said houses and that Mr. Hussey had nothing to do therewith; and if in case the Complainant would abate one half year's rent of a whole . . . year's rent that was then in arrear, she would solely become tenant unto him and utterly deny to have any thing to do with Mr. Hussey; the which the Complainant thought unreasonable and took time to Consider thereof and made no more words at that time of the business.

A certain Martin Higgins, who had been Rolleston's agent, gave on 19 May a lively report of a further encounter between Dame Elizabeth Kirk and himself:

. . . this deponent did by the plaintiff's direction wait on the said Lady Kirk again for her & her husband's resolution, whereupon the Lady Kirk demanded what abatement the plaintiff would make her for the time past; to which this deponent replied that the plaintiff would abate her 5ˡ (or some such sum) of the arrears of rent that were behind & unpaid & would not grant any further term in the said premises until she had paid the rent arrear; to which she replied, "If that is all you will do, I thank you for nothing," & so kissed her hand, & made a leg like a man & went her way, & utterly refused to pay any part of the said arrears of rent or to attorn Tenant to the Complainant, although the plaintiff & this deponent on his behalf did offer to secure the said defendants from the defendant Mr. Hussey for their so doing; & this deponent did on his behalf offer the said Lady Kirk that if she thought the rent of her house were too dear, that she should deliver up her house to the plaintiff & he would take the same into his hands.

The case came up for hearing on Friday, 24 April, 1657, and was referred to "the final end and determination of Edmond Prideaux Esq. attorney general," and the parties were ordered to attend him the following morning.[44] While I have not learned the details of his decision, it is clear that Rolleston was later in possession of the Cockpit.[45]

We have come to the end of the story of the Cockpit as I found it in the records of the Chancery. After such a flood of detail, however, it may be useful to give in brief summary the leading points now established for the first time.

The Phoenix, then, was originally a cockpit, built in 1609 by John Best, who in 1616 leased it at £45 a year to Christopher Beeston. The latter converted it — over the protest of the Society of Lincoln's Inn — into a "private" playhouse, utilizing the house adjoining the cockpit as a lodging for the keeper of the theatre. At his death in October or November, 1638, Beeston owned house property in Hog Lane and King's Head Yard, Shoreditch, near the Curtain Theatre (which, by the way, was standing as late as 1660). He owned also two thirds of the profits of his Cockpit company, — "Beeston's Boys," — or, as he said, four shares out of six. Two of these he made over by will to the company for their encouragement. Another half-share went as salary to his son William, who was to succeed him for a short time as their manager. His widow Elizabeth got the Cockpit lease and the remaining share and a half of the profits, out of which she was to provide costumes for the company.

During the hard times of the Interregnum and suppression of acting, Elizabeth (who had now married Sir Lewis Kirk, Beeston's "noble friend") found it difficult to pay the rent as before, although they made some money from plays in the autumn of 1647. In 1650 William Beeston tried to wrest control of the playhouse from his mother and stepfather by a bargain with the landlord, Rolleston, whose right, it should be said, the Kirks refused to recognize. Beeston went so far as to pay money down, to repair the theatre, whose interior had been dismantled by the government's orders in 1649, and to begin to train a company; but the agreement with Rolleston fell through, partly, no doubt, because Rolleston's title had not been yet established in the courts. This is the last we hear of William Beeston in connection with the Cockpit. Thereafter the theatre was apparently let to John Rhodes, who, as we now know, was living at the Cockpit for several years after 1644.

I may round off this account of the Phoenix with some new facts about Rhodes, who managed the theatre at the Restoration. We find him, then, as another witness for Rolleston in the latter's suit against Hussey and the Kirks. On being sworn, 23 April, 1656, he is described as "of St. Martin's-in-the-Fields, Citizen and Draper of London, aged 50 years and upwards." This is the first clue we have had as to his age. His address shows that in 1656 he was no longer occupying the dwelling-house at the Cockpit. To hear him described as a "Draper" is somewhat disconcerting when one recalls the often-quoted passage of Downes, "Mr. Rhodes, a bookseller, being wardrobe-keeper formerly (as I am informed) to King Charles the First's company of commedians in the Blackfriars." But the difficulty is easily removed. In a further document in Chancery,[46] dated 1668, John Rhodes is described as "of St. Martin-in-the-Fields, Bookseller." And when one turns to the records of the Drapers' Company,[47] one finds in the list of members assessed for the poll tax in 1641, under the heading "Those of the generality or Yeomanry of the said Company wch allege they are not able to pay three pounds,"

	Trade or Profession	Number of Apprentices held
		During lifetime
RHODES JOHN		
in little brittaine	Bookeseller	7.

Rhodes, then, born about 1606, was a bookseller, who had joined the Drapers' Company probably for special privileges to be gained from membership. He had long been associated with the Cockpit before he set up his young company of actors there on the eve of the Restoration — a company which, under the leadership of Davenant and Betterton, was to play to the admiration of Pepys and his fellow playgoers.

III. Salisbury Court

To the researches of Peter Cunningham we owe the greatest part of what has been known of the Salisbury Court Theatre. By following the clues afforded by his documents published in 1849,[48] I have collected a good deal of new and rather lively material, presented in the following pages.

I

First there is the complaint[49] of William Beeston, after he had given up hope of securing the Cockpit for himself. We find him here complaining in Chancery, 25 June, 1658, against Richard Sackville, Earl of Dorset. Giving his abode as the parish of St. Bridget's, or Bride's, London, Beeston recites the lease of 6 July, 1629. (This lease corroborates the details given in Cunningham's document.) By its terms Sir Henry Compton, Sir John Sackville, and others, in trust for Edward, Earl of Dorset, let to Richard Gunnell and William Blagrove a plot of ground in Salisbury Court [50] for a term of forty-one and one-half years from 24 June, 1629. Rent for the first half-year was to be £25; thereafter, £100 annually.[51] Under this lease,

> Gunnell and Blagrove by the consent of the said Edward Earl of Dorset did erect and build upon the said premises one dwelling house and playhouse wherein plays and interludes were usually acted: the building whereof cost the said Gunnell and Blagrove the sum of one thousand pounds.

This is the first estimate that we have had of the initial cost of the Salisbury Court Theatre. Continuing his recital, Beeston rehearses Dorset's sale of the rent and reversion of this property to John Herne of Lincoln's Inn. The price, as we already knew from Cunningham's document, was £950; and the lease was to run for sixty-one years from 8 July, 1629. We now learn that Gunnell and Blagrove paid to Herne their yearly rent of £100 until stage plays were forbidden by Parliament, in 1642; and that afterwards, being by this prohibition

. . . disabled to pay the said rent . . . [they] did intend and was [*sic*] resolved to make the same into a brewhouse: which the said Earl perceiving and withal considering the same would be a great annoyance to him being so near his dwelling . . . did earnestly importune him your said orator [Beeston] to agree with the said Mr. Herne about the premises and buy the said latter lease of the said Mr. Herne, promising your orator that for so doing your orator should have a new lease of the said playhouse and premises for eighty years at the rent of a peppercorn. Whereupon [your orator, not] doubting of the performance, agreed with . . . Mr. Herne [52] for the same for seven hundred pounds and paid him . . . one hundred pounds in part of payment of the said 700*li*.[53] And your orator was to pay the remainder of the said sum about six months after; but before the remainder was paid . . . divers soldiers by force and arms entered the said playhouse, cut down the seats, broke down the stage, and utterly defaced the whole buildings: in regard whereof your orator did not pay the residue of the said money to the said Mr. Herne.

This circumstantial passage not only confirms but also elucidates the well-known note, already quoted,[54] written by Howes into the Phillipps copy of Stow's *Annales* (1631): "The playhouse in Salisbury Court, in Fleet Street, was pulled down by a company of soldiers set on by the sectaries of these sad times, on Saturday, the 24 day of March, 1649." In the presence of Beeston's detailed report, it is no longer necessary to point out that "pulled down" means merely "wrecked on the interior" and not "razed." But let Beeston continue his complaint:

. . . within a short time after, he the said John Herne died and left the premises to his son John Herne, who sealed a lease of ejectment upon the premises; whereupon the assigns of the said Gunnell and Blagrove finding plays [still forbidden, gave up the premises] unto the said John Herne . . . who . . . shortly after contracted with one Lightmaker, a brewer, for the converting of the said playhouse into a brewhouse.[55] And thereupon the said John Herne designed to return your orator his 100*li* disbursed as aforesaid. . . . Whereupon the said Earl of Dorset, knowing what an annoyance a brewhouse would be so near his own house, tried many ways to prevent it; and, finding he could not prevail therein, sent for your orator and told him . . . that if [he] would go on with [his] former bargain, [and would assure] him the said Earl the said house should not be made a brewhouse, your orator should find him the said Earl his great friend. But your orator excusing himself did allege to the said Earl (as the truth was) that the aforesaid bargain was worse by two hundred pound than at the time your orator did give the [100*li* to Mr. Herne]. Whereupon the said Earl promised . . . that in case your orator would conclude his said bargain with ·. . . Herne . . . your orator should have the said John Herne's time, which was then unexpired forty years or thereabouts, made up [that is, extended to] eighty years . . . and . . . have a passage to the water stairs through Dorset Garden (then the said late Earl's), and also have the place where the dunghill now is in Salisbury Court with a coach house adjoining to [it. And the said Earl] also promised that, so soon as he could receive the money which was due to him from the Earl of Middlesex, he would pay your orator seven hundred pounds which he . . . did owe to Thomas [?]Bowen, Mercer, of London, for wares — whose relict and executrix your orator married.

Beeston crowds a quantity of information into one breath. To me most of it seems credible enough, if I discount some of the numerous "promises" which he puts into Dorset's mouth. He further represents himself to be the earl's creditor for £700, as the husband of Bowen's widow. Let that pass for the moment. We have not done with the brewhouse project.

Armed with all the promises Dorset had made him, Beeston says he waited on the earl's heir (Richard, Lord Buckhurst) with an eye to extracting a promise from him to join with his father in the lease which he, the theatrical manager, sought. We have Beeston's word for it that Buckhurst promised to comply; considering that if "the making the said playhouse a brewhouse would be offensive to his father whom he did believe would very seldom stir out of his chamber,[56] it would be much more inconvenient to him the said Lord Buckhurst and to his posterity." Buckhurst went to Herne, we are told, in Beeston's behalf, and persuaded him to treat with the manager. After much negotiation Herne consented to let Beeston have the buildings for the sum (not specified) which was agreed upon by his late father, John Herne, Senior. Relying on the nobleman's word, Beeston accepted the bargain, "and two months after, in the presence of the . . . Earl of Dorset, your orator, having sold and pawned his most necessary goods and having took up money upon ill conditions, he paid Mr. Herne for the premises all the money agreed upon except eighty pounds." Another two months after, in June, 1651, when the Earl of Dorset was dangerously ill, Beeston avers that Buckhurst reiterated his promise to make good the lease, with the additions mentioned above. But a month after the old earl's death,[57] when Beeston called on Richard, the new Earl of Dorset, to keep his word, the latter replied that what he had "promised or said was to please his father."

At this critical moment, Lightmaker, the annoying and inconvenient brewer, hearing of Dorset's reply to Beeston, took prompt advantage of it and of the fact that the final £80 had not been paid by Beeston to Herne. Once more treating with Herne, Lightmaker closed the bargain, "entered upon the said house and premises, and took down the roof of the said house and was disposing of it to a brewhouse." For choice of neighbors, Dorset really preferred a playhouse to a brewery; and according to Beeston, he had a letter sent to the prison where the unfortunate manager was temporarily confined, — probably again for debt, — offering to let Beeston supplant Lightmaker as lessee if he "would be tied by covenant in the . . . lease not to make the same a brewhouse." Borrowing from his friends, and "selling or pawning all that he could," Beeston prevailed on the brewer to resign the premises to him, and "also paid the present John Herne his eighty pounds; whereupon the said John Herne, by the direction of your orator, did the five and twentieth day of March [written over the word *May*] One Thousand Six Hundred Fifty Two,[58] assign the said playhouse and premises to Theophilus Bird." Bird was Beeston's brother-in-law, and here acted as his agent. [59]

So far, good; but Beeston had still to obtain the eighty-year lease promised by Dorset; and the next six years witnessed a lamentable series of efforts and disappointments. To begin with, the earl, using the hoped-for lease as a lure, persuaded Beeston

. . . to repair the ruined buildings of the playhouse and to make a convenient house to entertain persons of honor in . . . and . . . promised if your orator would build the house as aforesaid, the said Earl would make it worth all of three hundred pounds a year to your orator; upon which encouragement your orator upon several engagements procured three hundred pounds and laid it out [in reparations upon the said house].

In view of later facts this seems an exaggeration. Repairs to the Salisbury Court at this time could not have cost him £300.

But he goes on to complain that the earl referred the matter of the lease and his promises to his counsel. Counsel informed Beeston that he might have the lease and the earl's encouragement if he would agree to pay 40 shillings a year for the eighty years. Being "in miserable want and not . . . willing to contest with the said Earl," Beeston agreed; yet even then Dorset failed to grant the lease. Petitioning, beseeching letters followed, which brought a suggestion from the earl that Beeston might make a garden about the theatre (for the sake of appearances, no doubt). "Whereupon your orator did take the said house according to the said Earl's desire and made a garden of the ground belonging to the playhouse." But having no money to finish refitting the theatre, and no means of raising it except by a mortgage, he again applied for the lease, that he might engage it for money. Many months passed. In 1654, Beeston's wife Alice, the former widow Bowen, bore him a son. The manager seized on this as a further possible means of placating the earl, and christened the infant "Sackville," after the family name of the Earls of Dorset. But even this delicate attention bore no fruit.[60] Finally Beeston in 1655 applied to Lightmaker, the brewer, for a loan of £300 to carry out his repairs, and Lightmaker promised to advance him the money. Beeston represents Dorset as "much displeased" at this development, and accuses him or his agents of introducing a crew of plumbers into the house "who digged up the ground [and broke the conduit] which conveyed water to your orator."

Here the document is rotted away. One can, however, make out that Beeston represents Frances, Countess of Dorset, as wishing him well and abhorring the thought of a brewery:

"[she would rather] have the house and ground made into a fishpond than that a brewhouse should be so near her dwelling; and did engage herself that whatsoever your . . . [blank] . . . should be forthwith made good."

As a further diversion we have Sir Kenelm Digby, who, according to Beeston, was entrusted with the earl's business during Dorset's absence from London. To Sir Kenelm, then, Beeston repeated Earl Richard's promises. Their reception was so encouraging that the manager "did lay out a hundred pounds more on the said building." Digby caused a letter to be written to Dorset, urging the lease; but nothing came of that. Beeston now says he petitioned to have the case go to referees, "whereupon his highness [Cromwell?] forthwith referred the same to Colonel Daniel Pudsey and others."

Dorset returned to England in 1657. In the following spring he decided to test his title to the Salisbury Court premises, which Beeston claimed, and brought suit in the Common Pleas to eject Beeston in favor of a certain Wheeler. The manager's complaint ends by asking an injunction to stay the proceedings at law, and challenging Dorset to show Wheeler's lease.

In his answer of 19 August, 1658, Dorset insists that his father's demesne in Salisbury Court was of freehold for life only; and that the leases to Gunnell and Blagrove, and to Herne, should terminate on Earl Edward's death. He maintains further that Beeston would not agree to be tied by covenant in the lease not to convert the theatre into a brewery; and that consequently the oral agreement, if any were made, is not valid. Denying any promises made to Beeston, and knowing of none made by his father, he admits that upon Earl Edward's death he requested Beeston

. . . to put the said playhouse and other the demised premises into reparations, . . . as he was bound to do by his lease, or to deliver the possession thereof up unto this defendant; and thereupon the complainant did bestow some reparations upon the . . . premises, but not near to the value (as this defendant believes) set forth in the bill of complaint, nor so much as the complainant by his lease ought to do.

Therefore, since Beeston refused to resign the premises, Dorset has begun an action at law to recover possession. As to Beeston's charges

touching the words or discourse used by the defendant's wife or Sir Kenelm Digby . . . and the reference gained by the plaintiff to Colonel Pudsey . . . this defendant is advised they nothing at all concern him or his title, and are nothing at all conducing to the matters in question; and in case they were, yet doth this defendant know nothing thereof other than by hearsay. But whereas 't is by the bill surmised that this defendant should say that he would give the complainant seven hundred pounds to release his interest in the demised premises, this defendant saith that the said suggestion is false, feigned, and untrue.

Note that Dorset denies none of Beeston's charges except the numerous promises including the engagement to pay the manager the £700 alleged to be owing to him in his wife's right. There is, we may presume, considerable truth at least in the undenied portions of the complaint. According to his own account, Beeston was treated very shabbily; and although no doubt he exaggerated his sufferings, his complaint is quite circumstantial.

The court [61] granted Beeston one injunction to stay Dorset's proceedings at law, and another injunction to secure him in possession of the property, as he had "for above 5 years last past quietly enjoyed the premises without any molestation." For more than a year the suit dragged on. Yet, though I can find no record of the final hearing of the case, it is certain that Beeston kept his hold on the building.

II

Heretofore students of the theatre have had practically no information concerning the structure of the Salisbury Court Theatre. Through Cunningham we have known only that the plot on which the theatre was built measured 140 by 42 feet, and Wright told us in his *Historia Histrionica* that for "form and bigness" it was almost exactly like the Blackfriars and the Cockpit. Again it is from the Chancery that we have a most interesting body of new material bearing, in this case, on the structure of the Salisbury Court playhouse. The clue to the existence of this new light is found in the document of 1667 printed by Cunningham,[62] which records a dispute in the Court of Judicature over the right to build on the site of the Salisbury Court playhouse, destroyed in the Fire of London. Edward Fisher and Thomas Silver, William Beeston, and Richard, Earl of Dorset, were the contending parties. By their petition Fisher and Silver alleged that Beeston had mortgaged his lease to them as security for payment for repair work carried out on the playhouse, and added "that there was a suit depending in the High Court of Chancery concerning the equity of redemption." This guided me in my search to the suit in question: Beeston *v.* Fisher and Silver, 1666.[63] Our unlucky William Beeston was again in prison for debt, and had to sue *in forma pauperis.* His bill of complaint, filed 8 May, 1666, begins by showing that, after Herne had taken a lease of

. . . all that great messuage or tenement and certain yards, stables, sheds, and outhouses thereto belonging, situate and being in the lower end of Salisbury Court near the River of Thames . . . then used for a Common Theatre or playhouse . . . your orator — being bred up in the art of stage playing, and being skilled in that science — did . . . purchase the premises of and from the said John Herne.

We have already seen that the date of this purchase was 25 March, 1652, at which time not only had the interior of the playhouse been unfitted for theatrical use, but Lightmaker had "lowered the roof." Yet Beeston seems to say next that plays were acted here at some period between 1652 and 1659:

. . . your orator entered thereinto and held and enjoyed the same, and there was used in the said house for some time the said Art of Stage playing, until Stage playing was forbidden by the powers that then were: so that and by the means thereof the said house lay neglected and unused and became ruinous, and wanted repair.

If such acting did occur between 1652 and 1659 we have no other record of it. No other, I should say, aside from the possibility that the "ill *Beest's*" own house where, after the prohibition of plays and before March, 1653, he had had "divers *Tragedies* and *Comedies* acted," [64] was not the Cockpit, but

Will Beeston's Salisbury Court, newly hired and hastily repaired for performances.

On that rather dim possibility we shall leave the matter, and return to Beeston's complaint. He now shows that

. . . on or about the latter end of the year 1659, — when it was known that his Majesty was like to return and the times for such ingenuous exercises began to be open, — your orator was minded to repair and amend the said house, and make it fit for the use aforesaid. Whereof one Thomas Silver and Edward Fisher, carpenters, having notice and being desirous to do the said work (or rather, indeed, to defeat your orator of his interest in the premises, as by the sequel it will appear), they or one of them repaired to your said orator and desired to be employed in the said work, and proffered to take a view thereof, and that they would do the same upon very reasonable terms, and would stay for their money till such time as your orator could with conveniency pay the same, or to that effect.

The carpenters thereupon went over the building, and came to an agreement with the manager which gives us unique information about the structure. Fisher and Silver were bound by articles within six months or so to

build and erect over the said theater or stage a large Room or Chamber for a dancing school, forty foot square, which was to be done with good, sufficient, and substantial timber; and . . . firmly repair and amend the said Theater and all the seats and boxes and viewing rooms thereto belonging, and . . . also raise the roof of the said house thirty foot higher than it was; and some other things agreed upon.

For this work, Beeston alleges, he was to pay Silver £120, and goes on to say that for security the carpenters persuaded him to make over to them the original lease granted by the Earl of Dorset to Herne, and by Herne assigned to him. On the understanding that they "would only make use thereof for the recovery of their just debt . . . they did shortly after enter upon the said work, and they pretended that they had honestly and perfectly finished the same, and according to the said Agreement." But

. . . when your orator and some friends and workmen of his came to view and consider of the said building and new alteration, your orator and his friends and workmen found that they had done the said work contrary to the said Agreement . . . for whereas they were . . . to raise the said roof, and to make such great large room for a dancing school as aforesaid, the said workmen had not only not raised the said roof, but had also instead of the said large room made eight little rooms with partitions and posts thereto that went up to the roof, to help support the roof because the scantlings that they had put in were so weak that they would not support the roof. And the upper room [*sic*] in the said theater were framed and fixed so low that the spectators on the second seats could not discern the actors on the [st]age; and in many other particulars the said Theater was made so inconvenient and incommodious and unfit for the use intended, that a Company of good able players who had fixed themselves therein, after a short time for that very reason deserted the said place and went and acted at another house; whereby your orator was able to make no rent or benefit at all of the said house, nor hath been since able to make any benefit thereof; by means whereof your orator was damnified near one thousand pounds which he might have made even in the very Rent of the said house. And your orator was forced at his own costs and charges to make the said room three foot higher, which cost your orator near fifty pounds or thereabouts. And your orator was also forced at his own costs and charges to alter all or most of the boxes and seats in the said house, and the galleries there, and the stage, and most of the said house, which cost your orator near one hundred pounds. And all or most of the joists in the pit, and the chiefest pieces of strength that supported the fabric, and all the timber belonging to the Cellars and private rooms, and the timber belonging to the dwelling house and over the stage, and many other pieces of timber in other places of the said house were his (your said orator's) own materials; and yet the said Silver and Fisher do reckon for the same to your said orator as if they had been brought and provided by them.

Altogether, by the carpenters' "falseness and unworthy actions," Beeston alleges that he has been damaged at least £2000. Moreover, while they were doing "this their unhappy work, and before it was quite finished, the said Silver and Fisher would be every foot calling to your orator for money." By several payments, for which he says he took no receipt, he believes he paid nearly £200. He therefore maintains that "very little reason the said workmen have . . . to have any more money from your said orator, but rather your orator hath good cause to sue them for the great wrongs and injuries they have done him."

Beeston claims his lease back again, on the ground that he has paid and suffered enough; he is quite "undone, and . . . a poor prisoner in Ludgate for debt." But the carpenters "being enraged against your orator, have of late sealed lease of

ejectment upon the said premises." Beeston therefore prays
that the suit at law upon the said ejectment may be stopped.

Fisher and Silver in their answer say they neither know nor
believe that Beeston "was bred up in the art of stage playing,
or that he was skilled in the said science." They agree, however, that he bought Herne's interest about 1652, and that the
Salisbury Court house "was used for Acting of stage plays
therein until forbidden by the powers that then were."

As for their alleged eagerness to do the repair work, they
deny it, and say that on the contrary they came in at Beeston's
request. Having viewed the premises, they arrived at the
written agreement of 5 April, 1660, to which Beeston referred
above. By its terms they agreed to carry out the following
work on the playhouse,

. . . the walls thereof, whereof were then already built or almost built
with brick, that is to say:

(a) the two upper floors and the roof thereof the full extent of the same
building, and

(b) a stair case without the walls;

[These] were to be of such height and bigness as the said complainant
should appoint; and [they] should ashlar the same roof and make

(c) seats or degrees and

(d) doors, and hang the same with iron hinges in the same playhouse as
the said complainant should likewise direct and appoint, and make

(e) windows therein, both transom and clear story lights as occasion
should require. . . .

That the scantlings of the timber thereof should contain upon the square
as followeth, *viz.:*

(a) the beams or girders, and posts supporting those girders, 10″ x 10″ [65]
(only the girder which should support the dwelling house of the
complainant should contain 12″ x 10″);

(b) and the joists of the same floor, 6″ x 3″ and the joists to lie not above
14″ asunder;

(c) and that the railing plates, principal rafters, and purlin of the roof
should contain 8″ x 6″;

(d) and the single rafters 4″ x 3″, and should not stand above 13″
asunder;

(e) and the collar beams of the roof to contain 8″ x 4″;

(f) the upright posts of the ashlaring, 6″ x 4″;

(g) the quarters, 4″ x 2″;

(*h*) the principal posts of the staircase should be 6″ x 6″;

(*i*) the interlices [tie-beams ?] and braces thereof, 6″ x 4″;

(*j*) the quarters, 4″ x 2″;

(*k*) the rafters, 4″ x 3″;

(*l*) and that the stairs should be made of inch thick elm boards;

and that all the rest of the said work should be done with fir or deal timber;

and that these defendants should cover and lay all the floors and seats or degrees with whole deal boards;

and find and provide the nails wherewith the same work should be nailed;

and should finish the same by or before the four and twentieth day of June the next following [that is, 24 June, 1660].

Further, the carpenters insist "that they did finish the same according to the agreement above mentioned; and that the said complainant did order them instead of the dancing school to make it into several little rooms with partitions therein." They deny that they ever agreed to do the work for £120 or any such sum; and declare that by the articles Beeston was to pay according to the rates which follow:

(*a*) for flooring the seats or degrees, ...   40*s*. a square

(*b*) "   the roof, ...   30"   "   "

(*c*) "   the ashlaring and doors, ...   18"   "   "

(*d*) "   the ceiling joists, ...   12"   "   "

(*e*) "   the staircase, ...   30"   "   "

and so proportionally for less than 1 square.

(*f*) for every window light, ...   2*s*. 6*d*.

[and] for the stairs, door cases, and all other works, such rates as should be thought fit by two indifferent men who should view the same.

Payment was to be made without interest, within six months after the work was finished, or at the end of twelve months with interest at 6 per cent for the last six months.

They took the mortgage as security only because Beeston had nothing else to offer; and, insisting that their work was carried through in workmanlike fashion, they refuse to believe that Beeston could possibly be damaged to the extent of anything like £1000.

Moreover, they deny "that all or any of the joists in the pit, or the chiefest pieces of strength that supported the fabric, or that all or any of the timber belonging to the cellars and private rooms, or that the timber belonging to the private house and over the stage, or any other pieces of timber in other places of the said house were the complainant's," maintaining that they "did provide and buy the same at their own costs and charges."

Beeston, they say, was never damnified by their negligence to the amount of £2000, or any sum whatsoever. They have received not over £100 or so, and they gave receipts for all payments. They think they ought not to redeliver Beeston's lease to him until they receive the balance due them, which is £229 2s. 6d. It is true that they delivered a declaration in ejectment to Beeston, but only to get their money; and they are ready to forego the interest which he agreed to pay. So ends the carpenters' reply.

On 20 June, 1666, some unspecified exceptions that Beeston took to the answer were accepted for consideration.[66] The suit was still depending when the Salisbury Court property was "totally burned down and consumed" by the Fire of London.

Cunningham's documents show the dispute which followed the fire, over the right to build on the site. The court decided against Beeston, and, with Dorset's consent, awarded the right to Fisher and Silver. It is evident from the wording of the carpenters' petition that they intended to build a new theatre on the site of the old, at an estimated cost of £1000. (This sum, it will be recalled, is precisely the same as Beeston's figure for the original cost of Gunnell and Blagrove's playhouse.) But the plan was never carried out. If they did build anything, it was not a theatre.[67]

Several facts which the above documents disclose are of prime importance. In the first place, we now know that the walls of the building were of brick.[68] Secondly, we find the basis for calling the Salisbury Court a "private theatre" in its description as "one dwelling house and playhouse." This lodging of the owner probably extended over the stage, and lay behind the upper stage. My ground for this conclusion is the reference to the great girder, 12 by 10 inches, "which should support the dwelling house," and the fact that certain timbers are described as "belonging to the dwelling house and over the stage." Constructions of this kind at the back of the theatre, in the long dimension of the plot, 42 by 140 feet, would bear out Mr. Lawrence's theory of the doors and windows at the back of the stage which did not open on the outer air.[69]

Lightmaker must have lowered the roof to the first story, for Beeston's plan included raising the roof "thirty foot higher than it was." Thirty feet is a serious alteration in the height of a building about forty feet in width. We must remember, however, that this height included a proposed dancing school forty feet square, to be built over the theatre, taking up all the width and a good part of the length of the edifice. But with the means at hand, the roof could not be supported over so large an open space, and the plan of the great dancing hall had to be abandoned in favor of eight little rooms. To these the staircase outside the walls no doubt gave access.

If we may trust Beeston, the "upper room[s] in the said theatre were framed and fixed so low that the spectators on the second seats could not discern the actors on the [st]age." Because of this and other inconveniences "a Company of good able players who had fixed themselves therein, after a short time for that very reason deserted the said place and went and acted at another house."

What company of players was this? The two troupes that we know acted at Salisbury Court were (1) Davenant's company, from 5 November, 1660, until the following June; and (2) George Jolly's company, in the autumn of 1661. Davenant's company used the Salisbury Court merely for a stopgap until their new theatre with scenes — Lisle's Tennis Court — should be ready. Their departure can hardly be laid to the inconvenience of the Salisbury Court. With Jolly's company the case is different. Professor Nicoll has shown [70] that Beeston preferred a petition to the Lord Chamberlain against Jolly, and that on 13 November an order was issued to "George Jolly and his company, actors or comedians at the Cockpit."

Jolly was hereby bidden to cease playing until the differences between his company and Beeston should be settled. After hearing the dispute, the Lord Chamberlain issued an order on 26 November which begins with the words:

> Whereas his Majesty ordered George Jolly's company of players should act at Wm. Beeston's theater in Salisbury Court, and for that the said George Jolly and Wm. Beeston have referred themselves to me [to decide] what he the said George Jolly shall give for his said company of players to act stage plays in the theater belonging to Wm. Beeston in Salisbury Court and not elsewhere . . .

On the evidence, I should say that Jolly's was the "company of good able players" which had deserted the Salisbury Court, because of its inconvenience and the high rent charged by Beeston, and "acted at another house," that is, the Cockpit, where, on Beeston's complaint, they were ordered to cease playing[71] and later commanded by the King to go back to Salisbury Court. Beeston's statement that he made no profit out of the theatre after that time is probably not far from the truth. We have no record of long-continued acting at the Salisbury Court after Jolly left it, although Beeston was ordered to be apprehended for playing there without a license in both August, 1663, and September, 1664.[72] Two years later, in the great Fire of London, the theatre was reduced to ashes.

IV. GIBBONS'S TENNIS COURT

PRIG. Engag'd! no, Faith, let's make a Match at Tennis to Day. . . . How will that Gentleman and you play with *Stanmore*, and I keep his back Hand, at *Gibbons's!*   —Shadwell, *A True Widow*, Act I.

"The finest playhouse, I believe, that ever was in England." Such was Samuel Pepys's enthusiastic verdict upon his first visit to Killigrew's new Theatre Royal, formerly Gibbons's Tennis Court.[73] And yet the origin and early history of this famous theatre, the last of the Elizabethan order, have been wrapped in an unpenetrated obscurity. Some light, nevertheless, can now be thrown on them by the aid of records from Chancery Lane.

Tennis courts have had a long and intimate association with the drama. A tennis-court building, as the accompanying pic-

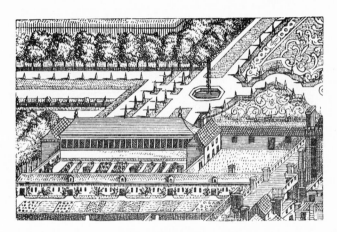

HENRY VIII'S TENNIS COURT AT HAMPTON COURT

(From Julian Marshall's *Annals of Tennis*)

ture of Henry VIII's "court tennis" at Hampton Court will show, might without much pains be converted into a theatre. The large, unencumbered oblong hall, well lighted by a row of windows in the upper part of the side walls, made good raw material. By the middle of the seventeenth century it had become a common practice for players to hire tennis courts in which to set up their stages. George Jolly, the last great English stroller on the Continent, performed, as we shall see, "with all propriety and decency" in a tennis court in Cologne; and, at the Frankfort Fair, he put on his plays in the *Ballhaus* adjoining the *Gasthof zum Krachbein*. In France as well, during the classical period, most of the theatres were fitted up in converted *jeux de paume*.[74]

Gibbons's Tennis Court had its beginning in the spring of 1633, thanks to the enterprise of a certain Charles Gibbons, who saw his opportunity to make money. The Earl of Clare owned a large piece of open ground in Clement's Inn Fields, which adjoined Lincoln's Inn Fields on the southwest. To borrow the words that Ned Ward makes use of in his *London Spy*, we may picture Gibbons as resolved to build on this spot a "Conveniency for the Noble Game of *Tennis*, a very Delightful Exercise, much used by Persons of Quality and . . . attended with these extraordinary good Properties; it is very *Healthful* to him that plays at it, and is very *Profitable* to him that keeps it." [75] Opening negotiations with the earl for a lease, he applied at the same time to Charles I for a license to build. In both of these designs he was successful. On 10 May, 1633, Clare leased [76] to Charles Gibbons, "of St Clement Danes, gentleman," an irregular piece of land in Clement's Inn Fields, the description of which may be summarized thus: "adjoining to a ditch there between Louch his houses and certain other houses built in or near the place where the gunpowder house stood in Clement's Inn Fields," containing north and south on the northeast, 216 feet, and on the southwest, 240 feet; and in breadth east and west, on the north (next the new buildings where the gunpowder house stood) 190 feet, and south (toward Louch's buildings) 120 feet. This plot is included in the small block subsequently bounded (see Strype) on the north by Duke (later Sardinia) Street, west by Vere Street, south by Sheffield Street, which separated it from Louch's buildings, and east by the St. Clement's parish line behind Arch Row in Lincoln's Inn Fields.

Gibbons was to have "free ingress from Clement's Inn Fields, both on horseback and on foot, with Carts and Carriages," and his lease was to run for thirty-one years, beginning 25 March, 1633. Rent was fixed at £10 a year, and Gibbons paid £140 fine on receiving the lease.[77] Royal license under the Privy Seal was granted to him and his assigns on 11 May, 1633, to

make, frame, erect, build, and set up . . . in and upon the field called Clement's Inn Field, in and upon his and their own lands . . . two Tennis Courts, the one covered, the other uncovered, with a house at each end for his and their private habitation to attend that service; and the same to increase [read enclose] with such walls and other fences as he or they should think best.[78]

As a further encouragement to his undertaking, Gibbons obtained from Lord Haughton (the earl's heir) a written promise that, on coming into the property, he would extent the 31-year lease by ten years.[79] But since he had far from enough capital to carry the project through, Gibbons borrowed £800 of his wife's stepfather, John Poole, and as security set over the lease to him 21 July, 1634. On the strength of this loan he built "one fair capital messuage and a tennis court, and other buildings" — among which was a bowling alley — at a cost of more than £1200. His license, it will be recalled, allowed him to build two courts; but for the moment his funds were sufficient only for one.

Tennis and bowls were not the sole attractions of the establishment. Gibbons was clever enough to provide a sumptuous table and French *cuisine*, thus winning for his house the most elegant patronage. We hear of the French cook of "Mr. Gibbons, who keepeth the Tennis Court in the fields, unto whose house many noblemen resort, and there eat."[80] To one Christopher Sorrell, a butcher, Gibbons let one of the houses he had built; and "bought Cates of him: as Beef, mutton, Lamb, and Veal." [81]

Clients flocked to him so plentifully that by the summer of 1636 Gibbons felt the need of adding a second tennis court. No doubt London's unsatisfactory weather led him to abandon the project of an uncovered court and to petition the King to be allowed to erect, instead, another roofed building for the pastime. His special license,[82] procured from the King by Henry Rich, Earl of Holland, on 4 August, 1636, quotes the petition showing "that he hath built the said covered Court with a house at the end thereof; but, for the open Court, he finding that it will be of little use and not worth his charge, therefore he hath forborne to build the same." The new patent authorized him to set up (instead of the open court) "upon his own ground near adjoining to his house aforesaid between the said East end of Princes [that is, Duke] street and Louch's buildings aforesaid, in and upon the said field of Clement's Inn, one other covered Tennis Court, with rooms at each end thereof fit for the nobility's and gentry's accommodation."

Some years elapsed, it will be seen, before Gibbons attempted to make use of the permission so obtained. Meanwhile, ownership changed hands. On 18 March, 1636/7, Gibbons and his wife's stepfather, Poole, sold their lease for £1300 to Sir Matthew Mennes, K.B., and four days later Mennes redemised the property to Gibbons for a term of twenty-seven years under a rent of £160 a year. On the latter date, Gibbons also entered into a recognizance or bond of £2100 to Sir Matthew. [83]

In and after 1647 the property was in litigation; [84] but, since the outcome did not shake Gibbons in his tenure, we need not go into the particulars here. It may be added, however, that, further to pleasure his patrons, in 1639 Gibbons planned to build coach-houses near his tennis courts.[85] About this time, too, Gibbons received a grant of a coat of arms; for he is entered as "Carolus Gibbons, Armiger," in the entry books of statutes staple.[86]

Sport and good eating were cut short by the outbreak of the

Civil War; and our next mention of Gibbons's establishment is after an interval of eleven years — in March, 1653. This is the unique record, already cited,[87] of a raid by the soldiery on a performance "at one *Mr. Gibbons* his *Tennis Court*" of *Claracilla*, a tragi-comedy by Tom Killigrew. We shall see that in 1660 the author of this play was to choose Gibbons's Tennis Court as the first Theatre Royal to house his newly created King's company.

But in 1653 plays were not yet by any means the chief entertainment at Gibbons's. The troublous times being past, tennis, bowls, and dinners once more attracted fashionable throngs. Prosperity increased, and in the autumn of 1654 our *arbiter sphaeristerii* busily set about putting into effect his license to build another covered court. We learn of this activity through the opposition it stirred up in the breast of one of his neighbors, who protested to Oliver Cromwell in the following terms:

> *To his Highness The Lord Protector*
> *and his Council.*
> The humble petition of John Tilson, gent., on
> the behalf of himself and divers others

Showeth unto your Highness, That one Charles Gibbons, a tennis court keeper near Lincoln's Inn Fields, who quietly enjoyeth his house and tennis court, to his best advantage (though thereby sometimes, by entertaining company at unseasonable hours, he giveth much offense to many): yet notwithstanding, the said Gibbons is now erecting one other house and tennis court adjoining to the same place, to the further disturbance of his neighbors, and ill example of others in this time of reformation; whereas formerly no person was known to undertake any such building without special authority.

He goes on to beseech Cromwell "to prohibit the building of the aforesaid new house and tennis court, which will be to the great quiet of the neighborhood and encouragement of many well-affected persons." [88] What action Cromwell took we do not know. Yet it is certain that Gibbons, whether hindered by prohibition or by lack of funds, never completed his second court.

Davenant, as will appear from a discovery in the chapter on his Opera, made use of Gibbons's court for sumptuous per-

REMAINS OF GIBBONS'S TENNIS COURT

As it appeared after the fire of September, 1809

(From Wilkinson's *Londina Illustrata*, vol. ii.)

formances in the early months of 1656. When therefore Killigrew in 1660 chose the court for a playhouse, he was taking advantage of an establishment which had been a fashionable centre of delightful exercise and entertainment of various kinds for a quarter of a century, and one which had already sheltered plays and players more than once. Certainly it is clear that such a house was far better fitted for the King's company than was the large, noisy, old, and open-air Red Bull, from which Killigrew and his players came to Gibbons's.

No view of this playhouse, the last of the Elizabethan kind, has been known until now, except the accompanying picturesque representation of its blackened ruins in 1809, after a destructive fire.[89] The print is accompanied by a plan, which indicates the inner dimensions of the court as some 23 by 64 feet. Such a size is very small for a playhouse and makes me doubt the accuracy of the scale. Interesting as this view is, it dates from an epoch more than a century after the house had been abandoned by the players. Thanks to my new information, I am able to identify two hitherto unrecognized contemporary views of Gibbons's. I find the first included in a curious plan of Lincoln's Inn Fields drawn on the back of a deed executed just prior to 10 November, 1657.[90] Gibbons's Tennis Court is shown in the lower left-hand corner, between the end of "Princes Streete" and "Lowches Howses." The artist has pictured three upper windows on the northern end of the building. This representation is, however, considerably less interesting than the bird's-eye view by Hollar, already mentioned.[91] Here we can recognize Gibbons's almost in the centre of the irregular block which occupies most of the left-hand portion of the plate, with its long roof approximately on a line with the file of soldiers in the Fields. The form as a tennis court is obvious, and the row of windows is plainly discernible. Since Gibbons's license allowed him to build a house at the end of the court, we may conclude that his dwelling is the house at the southern end of the tennis court, fronting south on Vere Street. The low buildings on the right at the upper end of the court probably represent the coach-houses mentioned above.

Gibbons's Tennis Court has been described in a variety of ways, first as being "in Lincoln's Inn Fields," a loose description, which obviously arose from its proximity to the Fields, and from the fact that the yard (later called Bear Yard [92]) in which the court stood had from earliest times an entrance from Lincoln's Inn Fields. By others it has been put "in Vere Street," which is more correct, since the main entrance was probably from this side. To say that it was "in Clare Market" is inexact but allusive, as Vere Street ran into Clare (or New) Market on the southeast. "Vere Street" is, I think, the most accurate designation.

To-day all trace is gone of this famous tennis court, which housed the first Theatre Royal. But Thalia has not lost her hold over the minds of Londoners in this neighborhood. On the site of Gibbons's arose the London Opera House, now converted into the Stoll Picture Theatre.

V. LISLE'S TENNIS COURT

Another tennis court, also near Lincoln's Inn Fields and not two hundred yards from Gibbons's, was destined to eclipse the latter in importance and fame as a playhouse. As Gibbons's was the last of the old order, so Lisle's was the first of the new — the first regular theatre to use movable scenery.[93] Davenant's opening of Lisle's Tennis Court late in June, 1661, as the Duke's Playhouse, was, in Mr. Lawrence's phrase, an event truly epoch-marking.[94]

Strange that our students of the theatre have discovered neither the beginnings nor yet the physical arrangement of a playhouse which stood as the first chapter in the history of the modern stage! A hope of filling part of such a reproachful gap impelled me to a rather laborious search, the fruits of which are here brought together for the first time.

The story [95] begins on 14 June, 1656, when Sir David Cunningham, Bart., of London, for £120 sold to Horatio Moore, Esq., of Lincoln's Inn a half-interest in a piece of ground in Lincoln's Inn Fields. It is described as

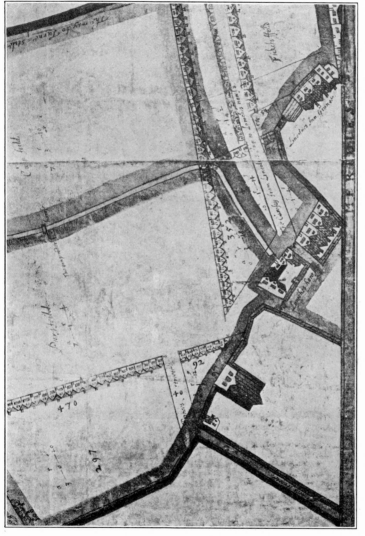

A PLAN OF LINCOLN'S INN FIELDS SHOWING GIBBONS'S TENNIS COURT

Gibbons's is represented in the lower left hand corner.

(From *The Black Books of Lincoln's Inn*, edited by W. P. Baildon, vol. ii.)

part and parcel of the said fields called Fickett's, Purse Field, and Cup Field, or one of them, adjoining on the east side to a great messuage or tenement, stables or other buildings there, then or then late of Sir Basil Brooke's, knight, wherein Thomas, Lord Brudenell then inhabited or dwelt . . . which . . . contains in breadth from west to east on the south side of the said great messuage and building seventy-three foot of assize or thereabouts all along from the said great house, stables, and buildings by the verge or edge of the causeway leading from the New Market place towards Lincoln's Inn; and ranging from west to east on the north side from the front of the said great messuage towards Lincoln's Inn Wall, seventy-three foot also of assize or thereabouts, and extending in length or depth from the edge or verge of the aforesaid causeway to the front or range of the said Sir Basil Brooke's house.

Six weeks later Cunningham sold Moore half of another plot, next to the foregoing and extending another 45 feet eastward toward Lincoln's Inn Wall. The other half-estates in these two pieces of ground were sold to one James Hooker, gentleman, of St. Clement Danes.

On the surface these transactions are simple enough. But it comes out that the real purchasers behind Horatio Moore were his mother-in-law, Anne Tyler of Fetter Lane, and her new husband, Thomas Lisle, Esq. Lisle's name appeared nowhere in the business, and even his marriage with Anne Tyler was concealed for some years, we are told, because he was "obnoxious to the powers" (that is, Cromwell's government) as a former servant to the King.

Shortly after the sale was completed, Anne Tyler and James Hooker began to build on their ground "all that tennis court . . . afterwards converted into a playhouse and commonly called the Duke's Playhouse . . . and two little tenements adjoining on the north part, and several little shops on the south part."

Their operations elicited a protest from the Council of the Society of Lincoln's Inn, in the shape of an order, 5 November, 1656, "to have an informacion drawne against James Hooker and Anne Tyler for the newe buildings in Lincolne's Inne Fieldes, intended for a rackett courte." [96] Yet we read that on 4 February, 1657, the Council was ready to receive "proposicions . . . from James Hooker and Anne Tyler concerninge the new building in Lincoln's Inne Fields, intended for a tennis Court." [97] Whatever the propositions may have been, no prohibitive action was taken by the society, and construction went forward, so far as we know, without serious interruption. We may suppose that the building was completed late in 1656 or early in 1657.

Moore made a written declaration on 27 June, 1657, that all the money he spent for the land and the buildings was Lisle's, and that his (Moore's) name was used in trust for Lisle. Up to this time Moore was only a lay figure. He entered actively into the business, however, when he bought out Hooker's half-interest in the ground and buildings on 28 March, 1658, for £500. A month later he granted a lease of 1000 years in this half-interest to Lisle, at a rent of £20 a year. Lisle, already owner of half the property, thus obtained a long-term lease of the remainder.

The tennis court was built along the south side of the ground and stood next to Lord Brudenell's coach-houses. The northern part of the ground abutted west on Lord Brudenell's dwelling, which stood at the eastern end of the half-finished Portugal Row. All this is made perfectly clear by a glance at the plate facing page 128. This is the splendid view by Hollar, containing a representation, hitherto unidentified, of Lisle's Tennis Court, as it was in 1657. There it stands, with open ground on three sides, between Lincoln's Inn Fields and Lesser (or Little) Lincoln's Inn Fields. People are rambling in the fields; clothes are being spread on the grass to dry. A few yards to the south of the court, a coach has pulled up at the door of the Grange Inn, where Davenant's players used to come and drink after the performance. The scene would be completely peaceful if one of London's trained bands were not using the Fields as a drill ground. Couples are strolling by the Tennis Court along what was first called the Causeway, which leads between the coach-houses and the burying ground of St. Clement Danes parish to New or Clare Market. Strype described this street as follows: "On the Back side of Portugal Row, is a Street which runneth to *Lincoln's Inn Gate*, which

LISLE'S TENNIS COURT

Enlarged from Hollar's View of West-Central London.

used to pass without a Name, but since the Place is increased by the new Buildings in Little Lincoln's Inn Fields, and the Settling of the Play House, it may have a Name given it, and not improperly, *Play-house Street*." [98] This quotation is from the 1720 edition of Strype's Stow. By 1755 the name had been settled as Portugal Street,[99] which it is to-day.

To return to Lisle's, the "two houses that adjoin and lean upon the north wall of the new tennis court" are plainly shown in the view, by the gables projecting beyond the roof of the court. I shall have more to say of these later. The shops on the south side are not represented in the engraving.

As to the dimensions of the court, a clue to its length is found in the assignment by Anne Tyler and Horatio Moore of a "parcel of ground in Fickett's Field containing 180 feet in length from the house then in the occupation of Lord Brudenell eastward and from the utmost south bounds of Cup Field aforesaid to the pales then before the said Tennis Court, and from the east end of the said Tennis Court, 100 feet." Subtraction gives 80 feet as the distance from Lord Brudenell's buildings to the end of the court. If we allow five feet for the passage between, indicated in Hollar's view, we then have 75 feet as the length of the building; which is shorter than the average length for a standard court. Julian Marshall [100] gives 100 English feet as the usual length of a *quarrée* court. Our conclusion that Lisle's is shorter than this is corroborated by Cibber's remark, referring to Lisle's as "a Tennis *Quaree* Court, which is of the lesser sort." [101] The width must have been about 30 feet. I have tried to indicate these matters in the sketch plan facing page 124.

To be able to follow the later history of the court, we must turn for a moment to consider the building of houses which now took place in Portugal Row, north of the court.

Acting for Lisle, Horatio Moore on 26 February, 1657/8, bought from Sir William Cowper and two others a part of Cup Field

. . . extending on the west part from the outermost eastern post of the rails before the brick house then . . . in the tenure . . . of the Lord Brudenell, standing at the west end of the southern long row or range of building in the Fields called Lincoln's Inn Fields and from thence in front extending seventy-two foot of assize straight on eastward from the said post . . . towards Lincoln's Inn . . . and from the said front running southward hence into the said field called Fickett's Field, containing by estimation one hundred and thirteen foot.

This 72-foot frontage was divided into three lots of 24 feet each. For a knowledge of the houses built here, I am indebted to the recent penetrating researches of Mr. W. W. Braines, carried out for the *London County Council Survey of London*.[102] Following Mr. Braines, I have numbered the lots on the sketch plan according to the present numbering of the houses on their sites. Upon Number 40, next to Lord Brudenell's, Moore built a house with Lisle's money before 12 November, 1658. On the latter date he sold to John Emline of "St. Martin's in the Fields . . . Brickmaker," the site of Number 39, measuring 24 by 127 feet, abutting east on the site of Number 38 (sold to one Adams), and south "upon the blue pale within four foot of the house on the north side of the Tennis Court." [103] A reservation was made to Moore and his assigns and the tenants of the Tennis Court of the use of a passage to be left at the east or west end of the plot, at least 3 feet, 3 inches in width and one story high, to go through the building as far as the "blue pale." This passage had an extraordinarily long life. It is found in exactly the same position on Rocque's map of London (1746), connecting the theatre with Lincoln's Inn Fields. Emline, in the course of 1659, erected a house on the site of Number 39, and sold the premises 3 December, 1659 [104] to William Witherings, Esq. In the deed he explains that the passage aforesaid had been formed on the "west end . . . as an alley to pass into and from Lincoln's Inn Fields." He also tells us that by this time Richard Adams had made over the next plot on the east (Number 38) to one Edward Greene, who had built a dwelling on it.

Affairs were in this posture when Davenant came on the scene. At the end of March, 1660, he contracted with Lisle for a lease of the Tennis Court,[105] to be converted into a theatre; and by the following winter he had made good progress in

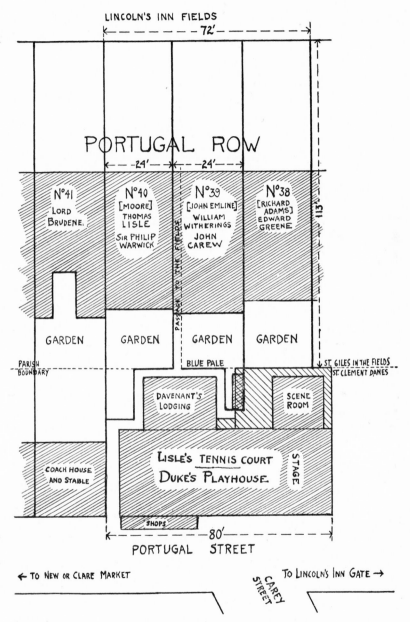

A PLAN OF THE FIRST DUKE'S THEATRE
(LISLE'S TENNIS COURT)

(Drawn by the author.)

altering the building. But he found the necessary enlargement on the north side cramped by the wall and ground of Number 39, which, meanwhile, Witherings had leased to one John Carew in July, 1660. As Davenant puts it, "there wanted room for the depth of scenes in the ground belonging to the said Tennis Court; and therefore for accommodation for the said scenes your Orator did take a lease of John Carew, gent., of certain ground which he . . . held in lease adjoining to the said Tennis Court." Dated 16 January, 1660/1, Carew's lease granted to Davenant

all that part of the brick wall . . . on the east end of the then garden and backside of the said John Carew in Portugal Row . . . and four foot of ground from the said wall westwards into and part of the said garden or backside, with free ingress, egress, and regress for . . . [Davenant] . . . his workmen and assigns to enter into the same garden or backside to build upon the same wall and four foot of ground; and at the end of the said lease (which was to continue for twenty years) again to pull down the same to the intent to re-erect the said wall and to make it as it was . . . yielding and paying every year . . . [Davenant] should use Representations [that is, present plays] in the said theatre to the said John Carew . . . £4 per annum.

I have indicated on the sketch plan this encroachment of Davenant's on Carew's wall and garden. Obviously the little house at the eastern end of the court must have been chosen for this enlargement to give space for scenery, since Davenant's invasion was from east to west. Furthermore, this fixes the location of the Duke's Theatre stage at the eastern end of the building. In the process of enlargement, the little house was sacrificed. From an indenture of 7 March, 1660/1,[106] I extract the following passage:

Sir William Davenant hath taken a lease of . . . Lisle's Tennis Court . . . and of two houses or tenements thereunto next adjoining . . . one of the which said houses is since demolished for the better enlarging and convenient preparing of the said theatre there and in the Tennis Court.

After Carew had agreed to let Davenant break down the wall and encroach on the garden, he found that he had thereby thrown himself open to an action of waste on the part of Witherings, the owner. To avoid difficulty, Carew brought

about an agreement, 14 February, 1660/1, between Witherings, Davenant, and himself, by which Witherings agreed not
to sue them on condition that Davenant within three years
after date "should throw down and remove the said wall so
by him erected, and erect and build a new house of office in
the same place where the house of office formerly stood, in
such manner and as substantially as they were." Davenant
was under bond of £200 to carry out this agreement.

All went well until the autumn of 1663, when Sir William
was making preparations to throw down the wall and retire from the encroachment. Unfortunately, it appears that
Carew had meanwhile sold his lease to William Walker, a goldsmith, who asserted that when he bought the lease he had "a
peculiar respect" to the annual £4 which Davenant had agreed
to pay Carew for the bit of garden. Still having an eye to the
£4, he therefore wished Davenant's scene-house to stay partly
in his garden, and even threatened action of trespass, and suit
for the rent, if Davenant attempted to take it away. Witherings, however, insisted on his agreement to restore the *status
quo prius*. Davenant was willing to fulfill it, but had no wish
to be sued by Walker. Such was the muddle presented to the
Court of Chancery. On 19 February, 1663/4, the court held
that things should stand as they were until the following term,
Davenant agreeing to indemnify Witherings for any damages
he might sustain by Davenant's not "demolishing and new
building" according to agreement. I have been unable to discover any further proceedings in the cause, and cannot tell
whether Davenant ultimately narrowed his scene-house or left
it as it was.

On the plan, I have represented a passage from the scene-
house to the other of the two houses: a passage which I suppose must have been made, since the other house was Davenant's lodging as master of the theatre. Here he died in 1668,
and of his funeral Pepys writes: "I up, and down to the Duke
of York's playhouse, there to see, which I did, Sir W. Davenant's corpse carried out towards Westminster, there to be
buried." [107] Aubrey (i, 208) notes that "the tennis court in

Little Lincoln's-Inne fields was turn'd into a play-house . . . where Sir William had lodgeings, and where he died. . . . His body was carried in a herse from the play-house to Westminster-Abbey."

Three years and a half after Davenant's death, his Duke's company moved to their sumptuous new theatre in Dorset Garden, opening 9 November, 1671. In the January following, the King's company, driven from their theatre in Bridges Street, Drury Lane, by a disastrous fire, took quarters in Lisle's Tennis Court, where they played for two years. On their departure, the building had to revert to its first use as a tennis court. To raise money for putting the court back into its old shape, Lisle made over half of his estate to his son-in-law, Richard Reeve. Before 1676 the latter had put £500 into "melioration" and repairs. He rebuilt "one of the said two tenements adjoining to the same Northwards [that is, the former scene-house] and the sheds or shops adjoining to the said tennis court southwards."

Tennis court it remained until Betterton's seceding company metamorphosed it once more into a playhouse in the spring of 1695. For a decade the old house again sheltered the drama. In 1714, after another considerable interval, Christopher Rich, who had been forced out of the control of Drury Lane, hired Lisle's at a low rent, and set about rebuilding it as a theatre. Although he died before the opening, his son John Rich took over the management; and it was this house which in 1728 saw the historic first production by Rich of John Gay's *Beggar's Opera*. The very success of the piece, however, doomed the playhouse; for Gay, newly rich, and Rich, newly gay, moved to a new and more capacious theatre in Covent Garden.

The old building was still standing in 1813, in use as a china warehouse. But during the last century it was swept away with others to make room for the present Museum of the College of Surgeons.[108] It is somewhat lugubrious to reflect that on the spot where Betterton once delivered the lines of Hamlet, which anatomize the human soul, we now have exhibitions of dissected human bodies.

NOTES FOR CHAPTER II

1 (82). Chambers (*Eliz. Stage*, ii, 445) gives the following bibliographical note: "The records of the suit of *Woodford v. Holland* (1613) were printed by J. Greenstreet in the *Athenaeum* for 28 Nov. 1885 from *Court of Requests Books*, xxvi, ff. 780, 890, and cxxviii, and therefrom by Fleay, p. 194; and more fully with those of the later suit of 1619 (misdated 1620) by C. W. Wallace in *Nebraska University Studies*, ix, 291 (cited as *W. v. H.*). Collier, i, 374, mentions evidence on the same transactions as 'in the Audit Office,' and misnames the complainant John Woodward."

2 (83). *Nebraska Univ. Studies*, ix, 304.

3 (83). *Ibid.*, p. 299.

4 (84). *Eliz. Stage*, ii, 446 n.

5 (85). Professor T. W. Baldwin (*Jour. Eng. & Germ. Philol.*, xxvi [Jan., 1927], 60 ff.), in considering the question of gatherers at the Red Bull, has been misled by the false assumption that the share was a seventh and not an eighteenth.

6 (85). *Nebraska Univ. Studies*, ix, 299.

7 (86). W. C., *London's Lamentation for her Sins* (1625): "Yet even then, Oh Lord, were the theatres magnified and enlarged."

8 (86). *Epistle to Histriomastix.*

9 (86). *Fortnightly Review* (May, 1916), pp. 820–829. See also his *Physical Conditions of the Elizabethan Public Playhouse* (1927), p. 129.

10 (86). B. M., E809.11.

11 (86). B. M., E809.23.

12 (86). B. M., E812.14.

13 (86). B. M., E835.4.

14 (87). Cf. Pepys, *Diary*, 14 Aug., 1666.

15 (87). *The Physical Conditions of the Elizabethan Public Playhouse*, pp. 4, 8, 9, 14, 80, 87, 90. Mr. Lawrence speaks here of the Red Bull "as it was in Commonwealth days, after it had been dismantled by the Puritans." It would be interesting to know on what evidence he bases his statement that the Red Bull was dismantled by the Puritans. So far as I am aware, it was only the Fortune, the Cockpit in Drury Lane, and the Salisbury Court which suffered in this fashion; the Red Bull was a conspicuous exception. See above, p. 43.

16 (88). *Shakespearean Playhouses*, pp. 348–367. Chambers's *Elizabethan Stage* does not cover the lifetime of the Phoenix.

17 (88). Stow's *Annales* (1631), p. 1004.

18 (88). Commendatory verses to James Shirley's *The Gratefull Servant. A Comedie. As it was lately presented with good applause at the private House in Drury-Lane, By his Majesties Servants*, 1630.

19 (88). For further description of Aldwich Close see *London County Council Survey of London*, v ("St. Giles-in-the-Fields"; ed. Sir Laurence Gomme, 1914), 34–37.

20 (88). No. 8.

21 (89). For Beeston's earlier history, see Chambers, *op. cit.*, ii, 302.

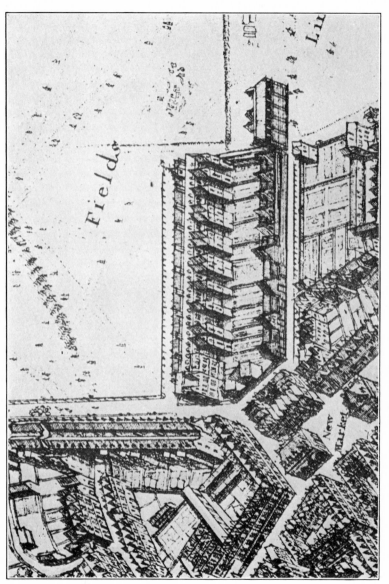

GIBBONS'S TENNIS COURT AND LISLE'S TENNIS COURT

Lincoln's Inn Fields. Gibbons's is in the left centre of the picture, set back from the street, its long narrow roof pointing in the direction of the file of soldiers in the Fields. Lisle's is in the lower right corner, and extends into the Fields where couples are strolling.

(From the London Topographical Society's facsimile of the unique copy of Hollar's engraving of West-Central London, *ca. 1657*.)

22 (89). No. 9.

23 (90). *The Black Books of Lincoln's Inn* (ed. W. P. Baildon, 1898), ii, 186.

24 (90). New Shakespeare Society's *Transactions* (1880–1886), p. 504.

25 (90). *Shakespearean Playhouses*, pp. 353 ff.

26 (90). Adams, *Dramatic Records*, p. 63.

27 (90). Lawrence, *The Elizabethan Playhouse* (First Ser.), pp. 230–233.

28 (91). Privy Council order of 8 June, 1632: " . . . the highway leading along the backside of the Cockpit Playhouse near Lincoln's Inn Fields, and the street called Queens Street adjoining to the same, are become very foul." Cf. Malone Society, *Collections*, i, 383.

29 (91). *Cal. State Papers, Dom., 1639*, p. 358. Cited in Thaler's *Shakspere to Sheridan*, p. 218.

30 (91). *Hist. MSS Comm., Rep. VII*, App., p. 480a.

31 (92). The will, hitherto unpublished, is printed at large in the Appendix.

32 (92). C7 127/52, Farnham v. Beeston (1666).

33 (92). *Shakespearean Playhouses*, pp. 75 ff.

34 (92). *Middlesex County Records*, iii, 164. Cf. Adams, p. 90.

35 (92). *The / Wandering whore / Continued / A Dialogue / With a more perfect List of the names of the / Crafty Bawds*, etc., London, 1660 (Thomason's note, "Dec. 5"). B. M., E1053.3. The same entry is repeated in B. M., E1053.8.

36 (93). It is instructive to note that this division, two thirds to the manager who hired the house, furnished the properties and costumes, and directed the company, and one third to the actors, is substantially that adopted by Davenant and his Duke's company of young actors in Nov., 1660. Davenant had had some previous experience as governor of the company at the Cockpit. He supplanted William Beeston (Christopher's son) there from 27 June, 1640, to the first week of May, 1641, when he fled to avoid arrest for complicity in a plot against Parliament. I find that, five weeks before Davenant's flight, William Beeston entered into a bond of £400 penalty to Michael Bowyer, one of the leading actors of the Blackfriars company (L. C. 4/66. 25 Feb., 1640/1). While we know nothing of the purpose of this bond, it may possibly have had something to do with Beeston's reinstatement in 1641 as governor of the Cockpit players.

37 (94). Richard Symonds, *Diary of the Marches of the Royal Army* (Camden Society), pp. 172, 219, 248, 252. After the loss of Hereford in 1646, Sir Jacob Astley, the last leader of the Cavaliers, found that "Sir Lewis Kirke had abandoned his command at Bridgenorth, and left everything in disorder." *Military Memoir of Col. John Birch* (Camden Society, 1873), p. 128.

38 (94). No. 10.

39 (95). No. 12.

40 (96). No. 17.

41 (96). No. 15.

42 (97). No. 16.

43 (97). C24 798/82.

44 (98). Chancery Decrees and Orders, Entry Book B1656, p. 675*b*.

45 (98). No. 17.

46 (99). C7 475/53, Rhodes *v.* Vaughan.

47 (99). Rev. A. H. Johnson, *History of the Worshipful Company of the Drapers of London* (1922), iv, 155.

48 (100). *The Shakespeare Society's Papers*, iv, 89 ff.

49 (100). No. 20.

50 (100). See the description and plan of the property in Adams, *Shakespearean Playhouse*, pp. 370–372.

51 (100). Sir George Gresley wrote on 24 Oct., 1629, of the Earl of Dorset's lease: ". . . the rest of his stables and outhouses towards the water side, he hath let for 1000 *l.* fine and 100 *l.* by the year rent, unto the master of the revels, to make a playhouse for the children of the revels" (quoted by E. F. Rimbault, in *Notes and Queries*, Second Ser., ii, 145). No mention is made of £1000 fine in either Cunningham's documents or mine. On the other hand, we read that the basis of the lease is "in consideration that Richard Gunnell and William Blagrove should at their costs and charges erect a playhouse and other buildings at the lower end of Salisbury Court." Furthermore, William Blagrove was not Master of the Revels, but Master of the Children of the Revels, and Deputy to the Master of the Revels. Gresley is therefore perhaps not an impeccable witness.

52 (101). That is, John Herne, Senior; not John Herne, Jr., as Professor Adams says (*Shakespearean Playhouses*, p. 380).

53 (101). Cunningham says (*The Shakespeare Society's Papers*, iv, 100) that the deed of sale was drawn in 1649 for £600, but was not executed.

54 (101). Above, p. 43.

55 (101). At this low ebb of the history of the Salisbury Court Theatre, Beeston put his hopes on the Phoenix, or Cockpit in Drury Lane. See above, pp. 95–96.

56 (102). Edward, Earl of Dorset, after the execution of Charles I in Jan., 1649, is said never to have stirred out of his house in Salisbury Court.

57 (103). Beeston's story here does not agree with accepted chronology. The *Dictionary of National Biography* gives Earl Edward's death as 17 July, 1652; that is, *after* the sale on 25 March, 1652, mentioned below, and not before it, as Beeston would have us believe.

58 (103). Cunningham's document gives the date as 25 March, 1652, and the total purchase price as £408 (*op. cit.*, iv, 101).

59 (103). See above, p. 92.

60 (104). No. 53.

61 (106). Chancery Decrees and Orders, Entry Book A1658, Saturday, 6 Nov., 1658.

62 (107). B. M., MS. Add. 5064, fol. 225, published in *The Shakespeare Society's Papers*, iv, 102.

63 (107). No. 21.

64 (107). See pp. 49–50.

65 (110). For convenience I have abbreviated the dimensions from words into figures.

66 (112). Chancery Decrees and Orders, Entry Book A1665, p. 335.

67 (112). Adams (*Shakespearean Playhouses*, p. 383) is wrong in assuming that Fisher and Silver erected the Duke's Theatre in Dorset Garden.

68 (112). In this it was like the Cockpit in Drury Lane. See Middleton's *Inner Temple Masque* (1618).

69 (113). *The Elizabethan Playhouse* (Second Ser.), p. 52.

70 (113). *Restoration Drama*, p. 277.

71 (114). Nicoll's suggestion that "Cockpit" was a clerk's error for Salisbury Court is beside the mark.

72 (114). Nicoll, *op. cit.*, pp. 277, 278.

73 (114). 20 Nov., 1660.

74 (115). Lawrence, *The Elizabethan Playhouse* (Second Ser.), p. 141.

75 (115). *The London Spy*, (Casanova Society), p. 196.

76 (115). No. 2.

77 (116). Common Pleas, 25/457.

78 (116). Patent Roll, 2740/10.

79 (116). No. 3.

80 (116). S. P. Dom., Chas. I, cccxii, 22 (23 Jan., 1635/6). Cf. Julian Marshall's *Annals of Tennis*, p. 81.

81 (117). C5 486/50.

82 (117). Patent Roll, 2740/10.

83 (117). L. C. 4/202, p. 6.

84 (117). No. 3.

85 (117). *C. S. P. Dom.*, Chas. I, *1638–39*, p. 551. Mar. 10, Docquet.

86 (117). L. C. 4, 19 Chas. I, 13 July. Joseph Haslewood says that he is down in the parish books of St. Clement Danes as "Charles Gibbons, esq." "Eu. Hood," in *The Gentleman's Magazine* (1813), lxxxiii, pt. 2, p. 333.

87 (118). See above, pp. 49–50.

88 (118). S. P. Dom., Interregnum, lxxvi, 56.

89 (119). Wilkinson's *Londina Illustrata*, vol. ii.

90 (119). *The Black Books of Lincoln's Inn*, (ed. W. P. Baildon, 1898), ii, frontispiece. Cf. *ibid.*, p. 418 and note.

91 (119). See above, p. 91, and compare the plate facing p. 128.

92 (120). "On the East side [of Vere Street] is a Passage into *Bear Yard*, which is a broad Place with Shambles and Stalls built, as designed for a Market Place to join to *Clare Market*, but the Project did not take; so of no Use, and but ordinarily inhabited. Out of this Yard is an Alley which leadeth into *Lincolns Inn Fields* against *Portugal Row*." Strype's Stow (1720), ii, 119*a*.

93 (120). The Cockpit in Drury Lane, which housed Davenant's Opera in 1658, was not licensed, but connived at by the authorities.

94 (120). *The Elizabethan Playhouse* (Second Ser.), p. 138.

95 (120). The following data are drawn from No. 26.

96 (121). *The Black Books of Lincoln's Inn*, ii, 414.

97 (122). *Ibid.*, p. 415. See also pp. 416, 417.

98 (123). Strype's Stow (1720), ii, 119*b*.
99 (123). *Ibid.* (1755), ii, 113*b*.
100 (123). *Annals of Tennis*, p. 35.
101 (123). *Apology* (ed. Lowe), i, 314, 315.
102 (124). Vol. iii, Parish of St. Giles-in-the-Fields; Pt. 1, Lincoln's Inn
      Fields, pp. 38, 48, 49, 52, 53.
103 (124). Close Roll, 3988/17, *Anno* 1658.
104 (124). Close Roll 4038/42, *Anno* 1659.
105 (124). The data which follow are from No. 25.
106 (125). Add. Charters 9296.   See Appendix.
107 (126). 9 April, 1668.
108 (127). Lowe's Cibber, ii, 101, n. 1.

CHAPTER III

DAVENANT'S "OPERA," 1655–1660

SIR WILLIAM DAVENANT has always commanded admiration for the remarkable adroitness with which he set up a pseudo-legitimate theatre in the face of the strict laws against playhouses, and under Cromwell's very nose. But although such a feat undoubtedly required courage as well as address, and energy as well as influence, it has been treated too often as an extraordinary and isolated phenomenon. In reality there were strong causes which led up to Davenant's achievement in a most natural fashion.

To begin with, the number of Cavaliers who remained in exile after the wars has usually been exaggerated. In the years after 1647, a good proportion of the nobility returned to London. These nobles, lacking a Stuart court to occupy and divert them with plays and masques, used to attend surreptitious performances given by the old regular actors at private residences; often, too, they risked arrest and fines by patronizing such public theatres as dared to give plays. But the taste of the nobility had been altered and "refined" by the court masques, with their music, dancing, and sumptuous scenery. It is natural, then, to see a growing dislike for the rough, out-of-door Red Bull, with its "low" audience, and a new desire for a small, select theatre, with all possible refinements.

In the early days after the war, however, when popular feeling was still strong against the late extravagances of the court masques, such a theatre was not possible. But we shall see that a way was found to obtain practically the same end under the guise of refined *education*.

The institution of which I am about to speak has until now escaped the notice of students: certainly its bearing upon the history of the stage has been entirely overlooked.

A new burst of patriotism at the close of the Civil War moved the English gentry to create in England an academy to teach the arts and sciences for which their youth had been going to France, Italy, and Spain. *Mercurius Pragmaticus* [1] for 12–19 September, 1648, published a prospectus of this academy, with an astonishing list of subjects of instruction, "much more then is taught in the *French Academies.*" Six languages are offered; history, ancient and modern, and government; "*experimentall naturall philosophy*"; and several mathematical sciences. Under the latter come perspective and architecture, "both that for *Building,* and that for Magnificent *Houses,* and in particular the *Secret Motions of Sceanes.*" The young nobles study scene design, while the soldiers arrest the actors of the Red Bull! Military sciences fill a large part of the curriculum of the academy; but then come "*Musick, Playing on Instrument, Dancing, Fencing, Riding the Great Horse . . .* As also *Drawing, Painting, Limning.*"

Of this academy the founder, organizer, and chief instructor was Sir Balthazar Gerbier, formerly special ambassador for Charles I, and Assistant Master of Ceremonies at his court. In spite of these courtly qualifications, however, he found means to make himself acceptable to the Parliament, and set up his temple of culture in the summer of 1649, at Bethnal Green, at this period a pleasant hamlet a mile northeast of London. The first public exercises of the academy were held on 30 July, 1649. *Perfect Occurrences* [2] gives an account of the entertainment, at which "many Knights, Ladies and Gentry" were present:

They were first entertained with a short Latin Oratory by Dr. *Dink,* and by an invitation (in English) by Mr. *Charles Gether,* holding forth the grounds and orders of the Academy. Secondly, with a Spanish ancient *Biezillian* course called *Iuego de cannas,* the throwing of darts against the defendants with shields (the ground *white,* covered with *flaming stars,* the Motto, *Sans vouloir mal faire.*) Thirdly, with an intermixt course of horsemen discharging their pistolls. Fourthly, by an intermixt fained fight with the sword. And lastly, with the running of the Ring.

Since the announcement of this sham tournament was made in a public newspaper, there was "an extraordinary concourse of unruly people"; and Sir Balthazar's house was robbed while he was conducting the ceremonies. To prevent such annoyances in the future, private invitations were henceforth circulated.[3]

In the week following these exercises, Sir Balthazar advertised his first public lecture; and added that at his academy,

All persons may learn any particular Language or Science. And those that will may be boorded, a great benefit to prevent the sending of Youth beyond Seas, to ruine them, as many have been.[4]

In the state newsbooks, notices are printed at intervals of similar public lectures on Saturdays. In November, the institution was moved to London, to "the *White Fryers*, at the house where Mr. Doctor *Chamberlaine* was used to dwell, near the Water side."[5] Later, to correct a misapprehension, Sir Balthazar informed the public

. . . that all Gentlemen are boarded therein for three pound a Moneth, Lodging, common fire, and Candell light included. . . . For Musick, Dancing, and Fencing, thirty shillings a Moneth, For riding the great Horse three pound a moneth.[6]

Of course this "select academy" did not escape the ridicule of the outlaw pamphlets. The government's sanction of it was enough to damn it for *The Man in the Moon*,[7] who printed an amusing mock advertisement:

He desires you to take notice hee is to play *Jack Puddings* part in Sir *Balthazars* Puppet-Play, and those that desire to see him eat his Custard, would send before hand, that room may be kept for them; provided they com before 3 afternoon. *Vivat Bradshaw.*

Gerbier's music and dancing smacked of royalty and the court, and as such must at length have offended the Puritans; for suddenly his announcements of lectures take on a pious cast: "the next after shall bee, God willing, on the Art of Musick, with that Ornament as may befit such a Lecture for godly persons and tender Consciences."[8] And a special vindication of dancing was required:

Of dancing among the other exercises of the body, the Academy is not desirous to say any more then what is warranted by the holy Writ, That

King *David* and *Miriam Aarons* sister, were moved by a pious zeale to dance before the Lord.[9]

And, "by special request" a lecture was given for ladies,

. . . Concerning the *Art of Well Speaking*, (being that whereby the rationall Soule doth Piously manifest it self to others).[10] . . . After which the Academy will indeavor to represent in severall Scenes . . . the opperations of several Sciences.[11]

Declamation, music, dancing, and "representation in scenes" — here are all the elements of Davenant's first performances (except a charge for admission!), practised with the tacit approval of the authorities.

Another important source which contributed to the interest of the gentry in masques, and so prepared the field for Davenant, was the literature of the time. Dramatists whose plays could not be produced nevertheless published them. And other writings contained descriptions of dramatic performances. For example, a very free translation of Assarino's *La Stratonica* [12] (published in 1651) contains an embellished account of a masque at an imaginary court. A few lines of it will suffice:

They were busie about the Theatre. It suited not with every capacity, for those Heroical Delights are unfit for common people. A moderate Hall was therefore made choice of, and immediately filled with innumerable Workmen, and abundance of Materials under the conduct of a famous Engineer, without limiting the Expences. They distributed Billets to a limited number, which were a Wedding Garment to him, who was for the space of four hours to be in an extasie of Pleasure.[13]

The state newsbooks, too, give striking evidence of the interest of the English upper classes in masques, in their accounts of the magnificent masques and ballets performed across the Channel at the court of Louis XIV, in which Charles II was taking part. At first the reports incline to mild censure of the extravagance of the French court; but as time passes, their praise of the beauty and splendor becomes unalloyed. It is possible here to give only a few examples of such accounts. *The Weekly Intelligencer* [14] for 16–23 May, 1654, says:

The *Italian Comedy* hath been often acted with much Ceremony. . . . At the last acting of the Comedy at *Paris* . . . there was present the late Queen of *England*, the titular King of *Scotland*, and the titular Dukes of *York*, and Glocester.

From Paris (13 September, 1655), *A Perfect Account* [15] describes

. . . a Mask at Court, in the Great Hall of the Guards, where appeared all the choice of our Nobility of both sexes, all of them richly cloathed, the Hall being made light by means of 52 stately Candlesticks, which bright lights, and the luster of the many jewels that were then seen, made the spectators admire at so beautiful an object.

Mercurius Politicus [16] for 14–21 February, 1656, after telling how the daughter of Charles I (the Princess of Orange) spends her week, namely, "in Visits, Bals, Balets and comedies," relates that

On the 16 the grand Balet, called Plyche [that is, *Psyche*] or the Power of Love, was danced at the Louvre, in presence of the Queen, the Princesse of Orange, her brother the Titular Duke of York . . . with many other great Lords and Ladies.

The same newsbook, on 18 January, 1655,[17] had reported from Brussels:

The Theatre which is cald Incomparable for the greatness, and fine inventions of Architecture and Painting, being prepared in the great Hall at the Court, will be soon perfected and finished: upon which Theatre is to be represented the same Comedie and Musick in the Italian tongue, which was acted some years since with very much praise and commendation to the Author and Actors.

The mind and disposition of the English nobility were by these means whetted for the refined entertainments with music and scenes which were to be presented by Sir William Davenant, the former poet laureate and distinguished author of masques and plays.

No light on the preparations of Davenant for his adroit achievement in putting on musical dramas under the Puritan régime was forthcoming until the records of the Chancery gave me up some of their secrets. Two suits especially were rich in new details — the one between Davenant's widow and her stepsons,[18] and the other between Davenant and some trusting citizens who had put money into his theatrical project.[19]

In the former we find first-hand material both to increase and to correct our knowledge of Davenant's life. I summarize it as follows. In October, 1652, when the Cavalier poet was released from his close imprisonment in the Tower for having taken up arms against Parliament, he was a widower, and had then but one child surviving — a girl — by Mary, his first wife. (This first wife of Davenant's seems to have been unknown to his biographers.) The capture by a Parliament frigate, two years before, of the barque in which he had set sail from Jersey, with all his worldly goods, for Maryland, had not only lodged Davenant in the Tower, but left him penniless and in debt. For him, as for many another, the quickest way to recoup lost fortune was a prudent marriage. No time was lost in finding the *bon parti* — Dame Anne Cademan, whose second husband, a Royalist physician named Sir Thomas Cademan, had died in 1651.[20] At their marriage in October, 1652, Dame Anne brought Davenant three sons by Thomas Cross, her first husband: Thomas, aged 22, Paul, 16, and John, 11; and one son by Sir Thomas Cademan — Philip, aged nine. She also brought him — which was more to the point — the best part of £800 left from her first husband's estate. With this sum Davenant was able to satisfy his most pressing obligations. The stepsons later accused him of being careless of their maintenance in these hard days, although Dame Anne had got the indigent knight to enter bond of £800 to provide them with "meat, drink, lodging, washing, linen and woolen and all other necessaries whatsoever" until (on or before 7 February, 1654/5) he should pay each of the four boys £100.

Instead, however, of paying them — which he fuond quite impossible — their stepfather promised them employment in his theatrical venture. And, as a matter of fact, the eldest, Thomas Cross, was to serve for many years as treasurer of the Duke's company, and Philip Cademan was trained and employed as one of the actors. Meanwhile Dame Anne died — in March, 1655.[21] Three months later Davenant made a "cer-

tain proposition" to Secretary Thurloe, which involved his
going into France.²² Had this proposition anything to do with
his operatic plans? At all events, he sailed for France in August,²³ and there married his third wife, "Henrietta-Maria du
Tremblay, widow, of an ancient family in St. Germain Beau-
pré" (Anjou).²⁴ This Angevin widow was to be the Lady Mary
Davenant who bore the poet numerous sons, and who figures
importantly in the annals of the Restoration stage. We know
enough of Davenant to feel sure that the du Tremblay match
brought him a dowry sufficient to underprop the superstruc-
ture of his theatrical schemes. On returning, the Davenants
moved from Tothill Street, Westminster, to Rutland House
in Charterhouse Yard; and by winter the knight had matured
his plan for introducing public plays under the specious title of
"moral representations."

It has always been supposed that *The First Day's Entertainment at Rutland House*, a representation with declamation and
music, given on Friday, 23 May, 1656, was the first of Davenant's performances during the Interregnum. I have new evidence to show that he had been giving entertainments before
April, 1656.

To introduce this subject, we may consider his preparatory
activities in raising money, which we find in the second Chancery document already mentioned.²⁵ We now learn that
Davenant, associating himself with a certain William Cutler,
interested several well-to-do citizens in his project to such an
extent that they signed an agreement with him 16 February,
1655/6, to go in as "adventurers." The company was to be
capitalized at £4400, divided into 16 shares at £275 a share.
The money was to be used "to build a structure for representations and shows"; and "Sir William Davenant was to be Poet
for composing such matters as should be represented." Cutler
and Davenant were to "buy a piece of ground near the Charter
house and build a Theatre for performing the said representations." We are told that, of these "adventurers," Jeremiah
Copping and Thomas Harper each paid his £275 in full;
George Blake put in £200, and John Wilcox £175, as part pay-

ment of their sixteenth shares. This makes £925; but they alleged later that, in all, the managers had obtained between £2000 and £3000. In return for their money, the investors were severally presented with a parchment writing which gave them each a sixteenth share in the clear profits of the proposed theatre, payable "on every Tuesday so long as the said representations should be made and exercised in the place aforesaid"; more than that, an assurance that Davenant and Cutler would

. . . not consent to allow the said company of representers to be removed to any other house or theatre without the agreement of the adventurers; and that in case the said representations should cease before [they] were reimbursed, that [the managers] should account unto [them] for their shares of the vestures, goods, chattels, and ornaments which should be in their custody.

According to the adventurers' story, the theatre was begun but not finished; the managers caused the representations to be shown "in another place which did not concern them"; and shortly afterwards "pretended that they were prohibited by authority to show the said representations." Complaining in Chancery in 1661, the four adventurers charged fraud. In answer, Davenant demurred; if he had broken the contract, they might sue him at law, not in Chancery. Moreover, he was answerable to each of them only for a sixteenth part of the stock that was left when the representations ceased. Davenant's demurrer was upheld by the court, but he was ordered, in case the complainants were not satisfied with his first answer, to reply to the charge of fraud.[26] Here the thread of the story is lost, and I can find no further proceedings. Whether or not the "adventurers" got any satisfaction does not appear.

But we have followed this dispute out of chronology. Let us go back to the winter and spring of 1656, when the managers, with the money they had raised, were beginning to build their theatre near the Charterhouse. What it was that discouraged them from completing it, we cannot learn. Puritan opposition? Lack of funds?

But, new theatre or no new theatre, Davenant was all this

time training the players whom he had collected for his venture. And now we come to a versified proof of the poet's activities, even more interesting than that couched in legal phraseology.

Gerard Langbaine, in his *Account of the English Dramatic Poets* (1691), mentions, as one of the "railleries" against Davenant, a certain "Ballad entitled 'How Daphne pays his Debts'"; [27] and says (though he does not quote it) that it was included in a book called *Wits Merriment*.[28] The importance of this ballad was never appreciated by modern students of the stage until Professor Rollins found it again in the collection called *Sportive Wit: The Muses Merriment*, and reprinted it.[29] *Sportive Wit* was published in London in 1656; but Rollins had no means of determining its date within the year. It was impossible to say whether Davenant's performances, referred to by the author of "How Daphne pays his Debts," were before or after *The First Day's Entertainment*. Fortunately, however, I have found that *Sportive Wit* was so scurrilous that it attracted the unfavorable notice of the Council; and therefore *The Publick Intelligencer* [30] for 21–28 April, 1656, prints the following:

A report was made from a Committee of the Council . . . that . . . *Sportive Wit* or *The Muses Merriment*, &c. . . . contains in it much Scandalous, Lascivious, Scurrilous, and profane Matter.

Allowing time, then, for the ballad to be composed, the book to be compiled, printed, circulated, seized, and condemned by the Council, and the report to appear in a weekly newsbook, we are safe in saying that the events described in the ballad "How Daphne pays his Debts" could not have occurred later than 1 April, 1656. Perhaps, indeed, they occurred much earlier. The contents of the ballad, delimited by the date, give us new facts of capital importance for the history of the English theatre.

We know from Davenant's petition on 22 March, 1654, for release from surveillance by the Lieutenant of the Tower, that he was at that time embarrassed by creditors who were serving writs upon him for debt. The ballad, after a few amusing

verses which recount Davenant's life until his release from the
Tower in the summer of 1654, continues:

6. But city *Dun* disturb'd him then,
       And cries, *Discharge your debt sir*,
    But he reply'd with cap in hand,
       I beg your patience yet sir.

7. *My patience yet*, quoth he again,
       Why how long shall ye stay?
    But unto this months end, quoth he,
       But he meant untill dooms day.

8. From Country then another came,
       And payment him beseeches,
    But *Daphne* onely makes a leg,
       And gives him some fair speeches.

9. Quoth he, *I now have made my book,*
       A fam'd Heroic Poem,
    For which I'm promis'd so many pounds,
       That I know not where to bestow em.

10. But when this *book* it did come forth
       As some have given a hinting,
    The gains of his pitifull *Poetry*
       Scarce paid for paper & printing.

11. At the months end they come again,
       Molesting him like Devils.
    Well now Ile pay ye all, quoth he,
       I must be master o' th' Revels.

12. *The State hath promis'd this to me,*
       As the Clerk of the Parliament saith,
    And I hope that you will do as I do,
       Believe the PVBLIQUE FAITH.

13. *Already I have hir'd a house,*
       Wherein to sing and dance;
    And now the Ladies shall have Masques
       Made a la mode de France.

14. This house was Pothecaries Hall,
       I tell to him that asks;
    Because of a meeting that was there,
       Which he said was one of his Masques.

15. If there you finde him not come to *S. Jones's,*
    Where his next house is hiring,
And if you come quickly, you shall see
    The Players themselves attiring.

16. For surely he doth play, but must
    Be watched like *Bacons* head,
Time is, Time was, but still you come
    When the *Time past* is said.

17. I can tell y' of more of 's houses, one
    In *fields* of *Lincolns Inne,*
Another in *Drury Lane:* and thus
    Daphne will never lin ——.[31]

18. Thus little you think that *Daphne* hath
    A Play with you begun,
Which is the cause you interrupt him,
    Ere the fifth Act be done.

19. Now the fifth Act is never done,
    Till th' *Exit* all fulfill;
Let him but make his *Exit* first,
    And then do what you will.

20. Yet *Daphne*, if they still molest thee,
    Faith, in the minde I'm in,
I'd do as Players use to do,
    Pay my great summes in tin.

21. Or as that you do play with them,
    Think that they play with you,
Conceit you owe them nought, you know
    How much Conceit will do.

22. Now in these houses he hath men,
    And cloathes to make them trim;
For six good friends of his laid out
    Six thousand pounds for him.

23. Then *Daphne* he will get at least
    A hundred pounds a day:
Why I think the Devil's in you all,
    Cann't you one minute stay?

24. If this won't do, but ye resolve
    With Bayliffs for to founder him,
Yet let this blunt your cholers edge,
    Ye shall have places under him;

25. His Landlord he shall have a copy
    Of some new Masque, or so,
    For which though he may largely crave,
    Let him use conscience though.

26. The taylor shall the wardrobe keep,
    And now and then steale a suit,
    Draper shall keep the half Crown boxes
    For Gentlemen of repute.

27. His Landress, 'cause she washes well,
    And kisses with a good smack o,
    Shall have a Shedd wherein to sell
    Strong Ale and foule Tobacco.

28. Nor ben't such Infidells to think
    This time will nere be found;
    For he that builds castles in the aire
    Can build a house o' th' ground.

29. Therefore pray set your hearts at rest,
    And do not wrack the poore,
    But if he pay not in two yeares time,
    Ile nere speak for him more.

Davenant, then, had already by April, 1656, made great beginnings toward reëstablishing the stage in London, and had "houses" in Lincoln's Inn Fields, Drury Lane, and other places. And although the performances of the Roscians of the Red Bull were still treated as illegal, under Davenant's direction the shows in private theatres and halls were not interfered with. But this astonishing poem asserts or implies so much that one must consider its statements in detail.

Stanzas 11 and 12 announce that Davenant had been promised the office of Master of the Revels, and that the Clerk of the Parliament had told him of it. In the first place, no Parliament was sitting at this time; strictly speaking, therefore, there was no Clerk.[32] Secondly, the Mastership of the Revels (if such an office existed in a Roundhead government) would be in the gift of the Lord Protector in Council, and not of Parliament. We shall see, however, that Davenant at some time in 1656 or 1657 addressed a memorandum to Secretary of

State Thurloe which contained persuasive arguments for the reëstablishing of plays.[33] Furthermore, it is well known that Oliver Cromwell loved ceremony and music; and that Sir Henry Herbert complained after the Restoration that Davenant "exercised the office of Master of the Reuells to Oliuer the Tyrant."[34] It is quite possible that Davenant hoped for an appointment as Master of the Revels under Oliver, and that Thurloe and Bulstrode Whitelocke, who were high in power, had given his hope some encouragement. Probably there is a modicum of truth in what the ballad writer represents Davenant as saying on this head.

Stanzas 13–17 and 22 are most important. They assert that, at the time the ballad was written, Davenant was giving performances in at least four different houses. Let us consider these in order.

It is said that he had hired Apothecaries Hall, and had presented a masque there with music and dancing. This statement is highly probable, for we know that after the Restoration Davenant used Apothecaries Hall (before the opening of his theatre in Lincoln's Inn Fields) as a house in which to rehearse the first and second parts of *The Siege of Rhodes*.[35] The hall was evidently suited for plays.

"*S. Jones's*" means, of course, the precinct of the dissolved priory of St. John at Clerkenwell. Dr. Rollins thinks that the house referred to is the Red Bull in St. John's Street. To me this explanation seems out of the question, in view of the fact that the Red Bull was a large unroofed house, and Davenant's shows were small, and for gentlefolk, making use of music and dancing, after the manner of indoor masques. As I see it, two possibilities remain. First, "*S. Jones's*" may refer to the ancient mansion at St. John's, long associated with actors and acting. Thomas Heywood tells us[36] that Edward IV

repaired to his palace at St. *Johns*, where he accustomed to see the City Actors. And since then, that house by the Princes free gift; hath belonged to the Office of the Revels, where our Court plaies have been in late dayes yearly rehearsed, perfected, and corrected before they come to the publick view of the Prince and the Nobility.

Sir Henry Herbert affords further details in 1662:

. . . the Great house at Saint Johnes's where the Earle of Elgyn [that is, Thomas Bruce, first Earl] liueth did anciently belong to the Office of the Reuells, and was giuen Away by King James to the Lord Aubigny.[37]

It is not at all impossible that Davenant hired this ancient rehearsal room from the earl or his assigns for surreptitious performances.

The alternative explanation is that "S. Jones's" refers to Rutland House, hard by in Charterhouse Yard, which we now know that Davenant occupied as his own residence.[38] Charterhouse Yard was very fashionable. Among the nobles who had houses there were Francis, Lord Willoughby of Parham, and Lady De La Warr. Rutland House was the mansion of Cicely Manners, Countess Dowager of Rutland. But as the countess was a Roman Catholic, her estate was sequestered for recusancy; and after her death in September, 1654, the state handed her house over to two men, George Thorn and John Hopkins, who had purchased the reversion.[39] Before Davenant moved in, however, the noble lady's household effects had been seized to be sold by the state, and Oliver Cromwell had claimed the proceeds as Lord Protector.[40]

This, then, was the house into which Sir William Davenant publicly invited, in May, 1656, a paying audience, to see *The First Day's Entertainment.* From the ballad it now seems possible that he had preceded the public opening by some private performances there. However that may be, it is certain that, prevented from completing his projected public theatre on a piece of ground near the Charterhouse, the knight had set up his "cupboard stage" in a large room in his own mansion of Rutland House.

So much for "S. Jones's." The ballad continues,

> I can tell y' of more of 's houses, one
> In *fields* of *Lincolns Inne.*

In the light of new evidence brought forward in a preceding chapter, this reference is perfectly clear. The house in question is Gibbons's Tennis Court, Lincoln's Inn Fields, later

THE ENGLISH ROPEDANCER

"Den Engelschen Koort-Dansser." A Dutch satire on Cromwell (1653). The Protector Oliver,
"A," dancing upon the tight-rope. Fairfax, "B," acts as his clown.

(From the extremely rare engraving by R. Stoop, preserved in the British Museum.)

used by Killigrew's company, from 1660 to 1663, as the first Theatre Royal.

It might hastily be supposed that the house referred to in the ballad was not Gibbons's, but the better-known Lisle's Tennis Court, also near Lincoln's Inn Fields, which was later converted by Davenant into the Duke's Theatre. But chronology puts this out of the question. The ballad refers to a time before 1 April, 1656, whereas Lisle's Tennis Court was not erected before the autumn of the same year.[41] Gibbons's, we remember, had already sheltered players under the rose, and had undergone the raid on *Claracilla* engineered by the treacherous "ill *Beest*." Now Davenant was regaling Gibbons's patrons with music, declamation, and dancing, which made of the Tennis Court an *odeum* rather than a theatre. At the Restoration, however, under Killigrew, the court changed again into an old-line Elizabethan private playhouse.

To the ballad again; and we find the author publishing the address of a fourth house hired by the astonishing Davenant:

> Another in *Drury Lane:* and thus
> *Daphne* will never lin ——.

It is hardly possible that this house is any other than the Phoenix or Cockpit in Drury Lane: Davenant's own theatre in 1640 and 1641.

Here, *vice* William Beeston, he had governed the King's and Queen's Company.[42] In 1658, as is well known, Davenant used the Cockpit again to house his opera. The interior, dismantled by soldiers in March, 1649,[43] was, as we have seen,[44] refitted early in 1651 by William Beeston in his abortive attempt to gain control of the building. Thus it was ready to be used again as a theatre by Davenant, before 1 April, 1656.

From the evidence in the stanzas of the ballad at which we have been looking, one would reasonably suppose that Davenant had collected one company, which acted now here, now there, surreptitiously, as the following implies:

> For surely he doth play, but must
> Be watched like *Bacons* head,
> *Time is, Time was*, but still you come
> When the *Time past* is said.

A later stanza, however, suggests that *he had actors and costumes in each of these houses:*

> Now in these houses he hath men,
>   And cloathes to make them trim;
> For six good friends of his laid out
>   Six thousand pounds for him.

Here we are called on to believe in a very large undertaking on the part of Davenant — larger, I think, than the facts warrant. We may well doubt that Davenant had four different companies acting at once. The description earlier in the ballad tends all the other way. "*S. Jones's* . . . Where his next house is hiring" shows that the performances were successive rather than simultaneous. As to the money laid out for Davenant's projects, we have proof of only £925. Even the £2000 or £3000 (which was the estimate given by the luckless "adventurers" to the Chancellor) comes far short of this alleged £6000.

We must beware, on the other hand, of belittling Davenant's achievements. Certainly he was in a far stronger position than the old actors, who, after the government's wrecking of the stages of the Cockpit, Fortune, and Salisbury Court in 1649, played at the Red Bull, in private houses, and at Gibbons's Tennis Court. Lack of *esprit de corps* was often disastrous to their success. Jealous actors frequently betrayed their own companies to the soldiers. The "ill *Beest*" was not an isolated criminal. In 1655, as we have seen, [45] *Fumigosus* reflected upon the dissensions of the players: "A . . . *Comedy* is next Week to be Acted at the Red-*Bull*, if the *Players* can but agree and be honest amongst themselves; which will be the best, though hardest Sceane they can Act."

Davenant was not only able to raise money and control a company, but he was also equipped with good friends in high positions under Cromwell — Bulstrode Whitelocke, Serjeant Maynard,[46] and others who are known to have been interested in him and his operas. No doubt it was their influence that protected his performances after 1656.

The ballad, moreover, has many earmarks of approximate truth. We shall see that it was manifestly not written by a city scribbler like *Fumigosus*, or by an ordinary balladeer, but by a member of the same "club of wits" which was responsible for the two little volumes of squibs on Davenant's *Gondibert*, composed in the same airy style as the ballad. Langbaine puts the "Daphne" ballad in the same class with Suckling's verses in *A Sessions of the Poets*, as "Railleries . . . broacht against Davenant by his Enemies" ("enemies" meaning "satirical friends"). Strength is lent to this surmise of the authorship by the presence of the name "Daphne" in the ballad. This clever sobriquet for Davenant originated in those little volumes already mentioned. Furthermore, the title-page announces that this poem is rather a courtier's lampoon than a typical satirical street ballad: "*A la mode Lamponnes . . . Never before exposed to the publick view. Collected . . . by a Club of sparkling Wits.*"

It seems apparent, therefore, that the author was quite familiar with Davenant's doings and, after discounting the exaggerated estimates of actors and capital, I am inclined to believe that the author of "How Daphne pays his Debts" told substantial truth about the knight, with a view to embroiling him with the authorities.

On 23 May, 1656, Davenant brought his arguments for the usefulness and lawfulness of "representations" more into the public eye by means of a musical and oratorical performance, for which he distributed bills entitled: "The Entertainment by Musick and Declamations after the manner of the Ancients." This was in the nature of an exordium or propitiatory prelude to the opera which was to follow at a later date. The performance was given in a narrow hall in the back part of Davenant's mansion, Rutland House. Before we look closer into the nature of this *First Day's Entertainment at Rutland House*, it is interesting to hear a contemporary account of it.[47] Although the anonymous writer refers to the piece as an "opera," it is evidently not that, but *an argument for the opera:*

The Bills for Sr Will: Dauenants
Opera are thus Intitled ./.

The Entertainment by Musick and Declarations [*sic*] after the manner of the Ancients./.

The Scene Athens

Vpon friday the 23 of May 1656 These foresaid Declarations began att the Charterhouse and 5$^{s.}$ a head for the entrance. The expectation was of 400 persons, but there appeared not aboue 150 auditors. The roome was narrow, at the end of which was a stage and on ether side two places railed in, Purpled and Guilt, The Curtayne also that drew before them was of cloth of gold and Purple./.

After the Prologue (wch told them this was but the Narrow passage to the Elizium theire Opera) Vp came Diogenes and Aristophanes, the first against the Opera, the other for it. Then came up A Citizen of Paris speaking broken English — and a Citizen of London and reproached one a nother wth the Defects of each Citty in theire Buildings, Manners, Customes, Diet &c: And in fine the Londoner had the better of itt, who concluded that hee had seene two Crocheteurs in Paris both wth heavy burdens on theire backs stand complementing for ye way wth, ceste a vous Monsr: Monsr: uous uous Mocquies de Moy &c: which lasted till they both fell down under their burden./.

The Musick was aboue in a loouer hole railed about and couered wth Sarcenetts to conceale them, before each speech was consort Musick. At the end were songs relating to the Victor (the Protector) The last song ended wth deriding Paris and the french, and concluded.

And though a shipp her scutchen bee
yet Paris hath noe shipp at sea./.

The first song was made by Hen: Lawes, y^e other by D$^{r.}$ Coleman who were the Composers. The Singers were Cap$^{t.}$ Cooke, Ned Coleman and his wife, a nother wooman and other inconsiderable voyces. It lasted an howre and a haulfe and is to continue for 10 dayes by wch time other Declamations wilbee ready./.

It is worth noting that this account mentions songs at the end "relating to the Victor (the Protector)." Although no such songs are to be found in the printed version, yet undoubtedly they were sung. Davenant is ever the trained courtier, propitiating the powers.

The harangues of Diogenes, while ostensibly against opera, actually argue for it; so that Aristophanes finds it easy to drive home his own arguments with ridicule of Diogenes. He ends:

Therefore instead of defending poetry, whose several beauties make up the shape of the opera, I will conclude in excuse and defence of her enemy, who hath much reason to dissuade you from moral representations, because he is himself the worst representation of morality; and is justly afraid to be represented in the theatre.[48]

After the amusing controversy between the Londoner and the Parisian, which flatters the government by contemning the French who harbor the exiled Stuart court, the epilogue ends with a clever exhortation to the audience to help lift the ban from the drama, and to get public plays again:

> Perhaps, some were so cozen'd as to come
> To see us weave in the dramatic loom:
> To trace the winding scenes, like subtle spies
> Bred in the Muses' camp, safe from surprise:
> Where you by art learn joy, and when to mourn:
> To watch the plot's swift change, and counterturn:
> When Time moves swifter than by nature taught,
> And by a *Chorus* miracles are wrought,
> Making an infant instantly a man:
> These were your plays, but get them if you can.[49]

We have no record of the "other declamations," to be ready later, mentioned above by our unknown auditor; the books called *Satyrical Declamations, by Sir William Davenant Knight*,[50] and *Satyricall declamations at the Opera*,[51] which I find advertised in 1658 and 1660, are probably texts of this very *Entertainment at Rutland House*.

The next performance at Rutland House was the first English opera, the epoch-making *Siege of Rhodes*. This was not produced until the autumn of 1656. Several weeks before the opening night, Davenant had sent the text of *The Siege of Rhodes* to the printer, as is shown by the Preface to the Reader, dated 17 August, 1656. And by 3 September he was able to send a copy to his influential friend, Bulstrode Whitelocke, with the following letter: [52]

My Lord,
    When I consider the nicety of the Times, I fear it may draw a Curtain between your Lordship and our Opera; therefore I have presumed to send your Lordship, hot from the Press, what we mean to represent; making your Lordship my supreme Judge, though I despair to have the Honour of inviting you to be a Spectator. I do not conceive the perusal of it worthy

any part of your Lordship's leisure, unless your antient relation to the Muses make you not unwilling to give a little entertainment to Poetry; though in so mean a dress as this and coming from, my Lord,

Your Lordship's,

most obedient Servant,

WILLIAM DAVENANT.

This was not mere compliment, for Whitelocke was experienced in poetical and musical entertainments. In 1628 he had been Master of the Revels for the Society of the Middle Temple,[53] when Davenant had lodgings there with Edward Hyde, the future Clarendon; and in 1633, when the four inns of court united to perform Shirley's masque, *The Triumph of Peace*, before the King and Queen, to Whitelocke "was committed the whole care and charge of all the Musick for this great Masque, which was so performed, that it excelled any Musick that ever before that time had been heard in *England*."[54]

Davenant, therefore, obviously freed from any interference from the authorities, hoped for Whitelocke's approval of his opera, but could not expect his presence at a performance on account of the "nicety of the times"; for the crucial point in the life of the Protectorate, the meeting of Cromwell's second Parliament, was at hand. Charles Stuart, helped by the King of Spain, was preparing to invade England, and the Royalists were ready to rise.[55] Whitelocke, as Lord Commissioner of the Treasury and future acting Speaker of the House of Commons, could hardly allow himself to attend a carefree entertainment while he was occupied with such anxious affairs of state.

The exact date of the opening performance of the *Siege* escapes us; but it was probably in September, to take advantage of the confluence of gentry to London for the opening of Parliament, and for Michaelmas term at the law courts.

Referring to the *mise-en-scène* of his opera, Davenant prefaces his published *Siege* with an apology to the prospective auditor:

We conceive it will not be unacceptable to you if we recompense the narrowness of the Room, by containing in it so much as could be conveniently accomplisht by Art and Industry: which will not be doubted in the Scenes by those who can judge that kind of Illustration, and know the excellency of Mr John Web, who design'd and order'd it.[56]

Just how masterly was this example of the art and industry of John Webb, nephew, son-in-law, pupil, and executor of Inigo Jones, was not known until the signal discovery of Mr. W. G. Keith at Chatsworth.[57] Mr. Keith has identified six drawings (which had been supposed to be Webb's designs for the Earl of Orrery's *Mustapha*) as the proscenium and five scenes for the first performance of *The Siege of Rhodes*. A comparison of these drawings with Davenant's own description of his stage and scenes puts the identification beyond the shadow of a doubt. Davenant says that his scenes are "confin'd to eleven foot in height" — which is exactly the height noted in Webb's section-drawing of the stage.[58] Further, Davenant's written details of the ornamental proscenium, with the cognizance of the Rhodian Knights and the Ottoman crescent, can be recognized, point for point, in Webb's drawings. The design for Act I, scene 1, which is "afar off, the true prospect of the City of *Rhodes*" and a "Turkish fleet making towards a promontory," combines topographical accuracy with the spirit of the opera in a fashion truly remarkable. The same is true of the rest of the settings, depicted on the movable back flats or "shutters."

The Siege of Rhodes, as Mr. Lawrence points out,[59] differed widely from the Italian operas of the period. For lack of space and funds, Davenant's opera had none of the machines or engines which on the Continental stages made possible an amazing succession of descending gods and opening paradises. The plot or story, which in the masques at Whitehall before the wars and in the Italian *dramme per musica* was highly complicated and mythological, in Davenant's opera was brought down to an historical plot of courage and love, shrunk "to a small narration"; because, as the hampered author says, "we could not convey it by more than seven Persons; being constrain'd to prevent the length of Recitative Musick, as well as to conserve, without encumbrance, the narrowness of the place."

On account of this restriction in funds and space, Davenant was also unable to use dancing, which was one of the staples of formal masquing and opera. As a result of concentration on the vocal and instrumental music, therefore, Davenant was able to secure the very best, written by the most eminent composers of the day. Furthermore, the dramatic action of his piece benefited by the absence of acrobatic tricks and mechanical legerdemain.

More important than these necessary and salutary alterations in the action of his opera is the fact that the mounting of *The Siege of Rhodes* carries on, in simplified form, the most developed masque stage of Inigo Jones, the collaborator of Jonson and Davenant at the Court of Charles I. A glance at the plan for Davenant's masque *Salmacida Spolia* (1640),[60] in the mounting of which Jones had been assisted by Webb, is enough to make the similarity clear. In 1656, Webb and Davenant, now restricted in space and in purse, were repeating as well as they could for the setting of *Rhodes* what they had done with Jones in the masque sixteen years before.

One idea used in the setting of *The Siege of Rhodes*, to wit, the representation of crowds and armies on canvas,[61] was new to the English stage. It is quite possible that Davenant, after his long sojourn in France during the wars, borrowed this feature from the French masques and ballets, where its use was well known.

It is interesting to see how gradually and tactfully Davenant introduced his wedge into the wall of Puritan opposition. These first performances, taking place in his private house, were no doubt regarded as *semi-private*. Although he distributed bills to those whom he expected to attend, doubtless he did not scatter them about too openly. He showed caution also in using for his players, not the regular actors, but former court musicians (who had never been suppressed by law!).

Upon the success of these semi-private performances, his next step should be to give his operas in a recognized public theatre in a more central position in London, though osten-

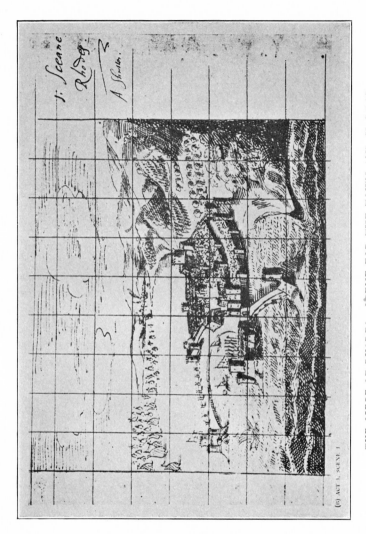

THE SIEGE OF RHODES. SCENE FOR THE TOWN AND HARBOR

(From *The Burlington Magazine*, xxv (1914), p. 86.)

sibly treating it more as an *odeum* than as a playhouse. This is actually what happened; but his step from private to public entertainment was greater than has been realized. One may say that there is very little difference between giving *The Siege of Rhodes* at Rutland House and giving it at the Cockpit. But from the point of view of the godly party, the difference was crucial; Davenant's players might act surreptitiously at the Cockpit, at Gibbons's, or in private houses; but that the government should connive at a public play, publicly advertised, given in a public theatre — monstrous! It was against an attitude such as this that Davenant had to contend.

It is not surprising, then, to find him using all his powers to persuade the influential officials to countenance his plays under the inoffensive description, "moral representations." To this end, in January, 1657, he addressed the memorandum [62] already mentioned to Secretary Thurloe, in which, on the grounds of both state policy and public economy, he argued the usefulness of entertainments: first, because they divert the minds of the people from "that melancholy that breeds sedition"; and second, because they would keep the wealthy (who were deserting the metropolis) in London, where they would spend their money and so give employment to "Mechanicks and retaylers."

So much Davenant has to say for plays in the abstract; but as an additional persuasive, he offers (thus avoiding any imputation of levity) to compose his "moral representations" on subjects which might be used as propaganda for the government's policy. Since Parliament was about to vote £400,000 for the prosecution of the war against Spain, Davenant proposes, if he may be permitted to do so, to write his first entertainment on "the Spaniards' barbarous conquests in the West Indies and . . . their severall cruelties there exercis'd upon the subjects of this nation." Thurloe was an excellent man to approach in such a matter as this, for his personal relations with Cromwell were very close, and the Protector valued no one's advice more highly than that of his secretary of state.

There was also a more indirect, but perhaps more efficacious, approach which Davenant did not scorn to use, and that was flattery. He who had been poet to Queen Henrietta Maria had little to learn in this art. We have it on two authorities that Sir William now composed an Epithalamium on the wedding of one of Cromwell's daughters: the only question is, *which* daughter. Professor Masson says that Davenant wrote and published, in the latter part of 1657, an "Epithalamium upon the Marriage of the Lady Mary, daughter of his Highness, with the Lord Viscount Falconbridge, to be sung to Recitative Music." [63] Sir Henry Herbert, in complaining of Davenant after the Restoration, remarks that the poet "published . . . an Epithalamium in praise of Olivers daughter Ms. Rich; — as credibly informed." [64]

As the girls were married within eight days of each other, it hardly matters whether Davenant wrote poems to one or to both. The important thing to note in connection with the whole affair is that the Puritan grip was loosening. The day after Frances Cromwell's marriage to Robert Rich,[65] the wedding feast was "kept at Whitehall, where they had forty-eight violins and fifty trumpets and much mirth with frolics, besides mixt dancing (a thing hitherto counted profane) till five of the clock" of the following morning.[66]

It is evident that by one means or another Davenant ultimately got permission to act his operas openly on the public stage. Accordingly we find him presenting the dramatized form of the idea which he outlined to Secretary Thurloe:

The Cruelty of the Spaniards in Peru. Exprest by Instrumentall and Vocall Musick, and by the Art of Perspective in Scenes, &c.

The title-page of the first edition tells us further that the opera is "Represented daily at the *Cockpit* in *Drury-Lane*, At Three after noone punctually." Performances must have begun at some time before 25 July, 1658, when Thomason purchased his copy of the above-mentioned text.

Davenant's dexterity in putting into his piece enough propaganda to satisfy the government, and enough drama to draw an audience, but yet not enough to outrage the Presbyterians, was astonishing. He took most of the incidents for *Peru* from a recent translation of Las Casas, dedicated to Oliver, entitled *The Tears of the Indians*.[67] He developed the idea of the Indian songs and dances which he found there, and dramatized the terrible scenes of torture.

At the Cockpit Davenant found himself much less restricted in space and facilities than he had been at Rutland House. And since we know from the "Daphne" ballad that he had acted here early in 1656, probably no great alterations were required. When, therefore, he opened the Cockpit in 1658, he was able to put his capital into new scenes, costumes, and certain "engines" or stage machines for startling effects. Mr. Lawrence is mistaken in saying that Davenant employed at the Cockpit the same proscenium which had served at Rutland House.[68] This would have been manifestly impossible; for the Cockpit stage must have been almost twice as large as the "cupboard scene" at Rutland House. Furthermore, Davenant himself describes the two "frontispieces," which were quite different from each other. The proscenium for *Rhodes* at Rutland House consists of " . . . columns of gross rustic work which bore up a large freese. In the middle of the freese was a compartiment, wherein was written RHODES." The frontispiece for *Peru* at the Cockpit, on the other hand, is "An Arch . . . rais'd upon stone of Rustick work; upon the top of which is written, in an Antique Shield, *Peru;* and two Antique Shields are fixt a little lower, on the sides." These two proscenia are evidently different in construction. One is a frieze, or horizontal border,[69] supported by columns, while the other is an *arch* with a top and descending sides. The proscenium, then, and all the scenery for *Peru*, being made for a much larger stage, were new constructions.

The Cruelty of the Spaniards, written for public performance, was, however, much less of a *drama* than the privately produced *Siege of Rhodes* had been. *Peru* was merely a series of pictures with illustrative songs, dances, and intercalated acrobatic feats. For example, at the end of the first speech spoken by the Priest of the Sun,

. . the Priest waves his Verge, and his Attendant, with extraordinary
Activity, performs the *Somerset:* and afterwards, waving his Verge towards
the Room where the Musick are plac'd behind the Curtain, this Song is
sung. . . . After this Song, a Rope descends out of the Clowds, and is
stretcht to a stifness by an Engine, whilst a Rustick Ayre is play'd, to
which two Apes from opposite sides of the Wood come out, listen, return;
and, comming out again, begin to dance, then, after a while, one of them
leaps up to the Rope, and there dances to the same Ayre, whilst the other
moves to his measures below. Then both retire into the Wood. The Rope
ascends.

It is worth noting that when *Peru* was revived after the Restoration, as a part of *The Playhouse to be Let*, the acrobatic
Attendant, with his "Sea-Horse," "Spring," "self-Spring,"
"Porpoise," and "double Somerset," was left out as undrama-
tic and extraneous.

Since this opera (as we have seen from Davenant's letter to
Thurloe) was written in praise of Oliver's present war against
the Spaniards, on whom Charles II counted for help to invade
England, it could not have been very palatable to the many
Cavaliers in London. It was probably one of these gentlemen
who wrote the little-known *Peru: Or, a new Ballad*.[70] The first
three stanzas of this amusing satire run:

> Now God preserue *the* Realme
> And Him that sits at Helme!
>   I will tell you of a new Story,
> Of *Sir* William & his Apes,
> With full many merry Japes,
>   Much after the rate of "John Dory."
>
> This sight is to be seene
> Neere the streete that's called Queene,
>   And the people haue nam'd it the Opera;
> But the devill take my wife
> If all the dayes of my lyfe
>   I did ever see such a Foppery.
>
> Where first there's one begins,
> With a Trip & a Cringe,
>   And a face set in Starch, to Accost 'um;
> I, and with a Speech to boote,
> That hath neith*er* head nor foote,
>   Might haue serv'd for a Charterhouse Rostrum.

The last three lines sneer at the windy harangues in *Peru*, and suggest that they might better have been included with the interminable "declamations" at Rutland House. But in spite of these Cavalier scoffings, Davenant was apparently able to attract a profitable audience.

The Cruelty of the Spaniards was followed, probably in the winter of 1658–1659, by *The History of Sir Francis Drake*. As Mr. Lawrence pointed out, the latter opera should logically have come first, since it relates an earlier part of the *Peru* story; and when the two were later joined together in *The Playhouse to be Let* (1663), *Drake* was placed before *The Cruelty of the Spaniards*. But this order of composition does not necessarily show, as Lawrence thinks, that *Drake* was a pure afterthought. The difference between the styles of the two pieces gives us a better explanation. *Peru*, being mostly panorama and dancing with music, was used as an entering wedge, being a "representation" rather than a play; *Drake*, being musical drama with plenty of action and some plot, was another long stride toward reëstablishing public plays. With *Drake*, Davenant was beginning to "weave in the dramatic loom," hiding his work with a covering of music, dancing, and anti-Spanish propaganda. The scene of *Drake* was also laid in Peru and the West Indies; and the old *Peru* frontispiece was used again, with the excuse, "it was convenient to continue it, our Argument being in the same country"; but behind the same proscenium arch, Davenant had consciously gone one step further toward the legitimate drama.

That very legitimacy, however, began to be loudly questioned in the winter of 1658–1659. The fact that no complaints of Davenant's opera made before Cromwell's death have come down to us makes it seem that Oliver's influence sheltered the poet. At any rate, we know that, before the great Protector had been a month buried, Presbyterian censure of the Cockpit performances grew insistent. On 14 December, 1658, Rachell Newport wrote to her brother: "It is thought the Opera will speedily go down; the godly party are so much discontented with it." [71] By Christmas the opposition had gained such strength that the following order was passed on 23 December by Richard Cromwell and the Council of State:

> A course is ordered for taking into consideration the *Opera* shewed at the *Cockpit* in *Drury*-lane, and the persons to whom it stands referr'd are to send for the Poet and Actors, and to inform themselves of the nature of the work, and to examine by what authority the same is exposed to publick view; and they are also to take the best information they can concerning the acting of Stage-playes, and upon the whole to make report, &c.[72]

The first part of this order is clear enough: we can see Davenant and his henchmen giving the committee every possible argument for allowing "moral representations," and leaning heavily on Whitelocke and other powerful officials who favored the drama. The second part of the order, while not so clear as the first, evidently does not mean "find out whether opera comes under the anti-stage laws," or yet, "look up the laws against the acting of plays"; rather it means "learn all you can about the surreptitious acting of plays now in London." We may conclude, therefore, that during the time that Davenant was exploiting the "opera" as a preliminary to bringing back public stage plays, the old actors continued to give their sporadic performances surreptitiously at the Red Bull and elsewhere. By 1658–1659, as we now see, these performances *sub rosa* had grown so obnoxious to the godly that the latter stirred the Council of State to look into them.

Yet even now nothing serious was done to check the players; for on 5 February, 1659, more complaints came in, this time to the House of Lords. In a manuscript journal of the House appears the following:

> The Lords being acquainted that, notwithstanding the Laws against stage-plays and interludes, yet there are stage-plays, interludes, and things of the like nature, called Opera, acted, to the scandal of Religion and the Government, — Ordered a Committee.[73]

This order is unequivocal in its recognition of the presence of stage plays as well as opera. Another committee — but as yet no repressive ordinances. Evidently the players had influential friends as well as determined enemies.

After the two committees had investigated stage plays and

the opera, the matter was brought into Parliament. But strong sentiment for the restoration of Charles was now abroad, and in the first week of April, 1659, Parliament had to choose whether to debate on the opera, or on a bill calling for the banishing of some 3000 Royalists who had been gathering in London. This dilemma of Parliament appears in an interesting letter to Secretary Nicholas from a correspondent who wrote under the name "R. Greene":

March ye last, 1659.

. . . and yet for all the mildnes and sweetnes of this good Prince [Richard Cromwell], we doubt the implacable humor of the Cavaliers wilbe stirring again this spring, else what should soe many of them doe in London, Mr. Secretary Thurlow having assured the Parliament that he hath a list of near 3000. And though for the present the howse waved the mocion for their banishment 20 miles from this citty, yet it will vndoubtedly be put in execucion are long, vnles the consideracion of Sir Wm. Davenant and his opera (which goes vp agen next weeke) prevaile to the contrary.[74]

Davenant himself must have been under consideration as a Royalist as well as an impresario, and his name entered on Mr. Secretary Thurloe's "little list." For while there is no record of his opera's being suppressed, he was suddenly imprisoned for complicity in the abortive rising of the New Royalists, which was set for 5 August. Thurloe, having learned all the plans of the conspiracy through his secret police, forestalled most of the trouble by imprisoning a large number of the conspirators, including Sir William Davenant. After a short confinement, however, the poet was released on 16 August.[75] It is probable that his friend Whitelocke was instrumental in obtaining his release, for Whitelocke was one of the Council of State which passed the following order on 17 August, 1659: "That it be referred to the Comitee of the Councell for Examinations to take security of Mr. Davenant upon the Act of Parlt agt. Delinqts, whereupon he is to have liberty to reside in England."[76]

The investigation mentioned above, by Parliamentary committee, of stage plays and opera in April, before the Royalist plot had matured, may have resulted in allowing Davenant to continue, while ordering the more daring of the surreptitious players to be suppressed. Such a state of things is implied in the cryptic and satirical *Endlesse Queries: or An End to Queries* (13 June, 1659): [77]

> Whether the Stage-players being turned out of dores, cannot, to get their livings, in imitation of the Opera, set up dumb Musick, and instead of black patches smut Ladies in their faces that shall not observe their part they are to play, according to the wisdome of the Ancients.

We know that the opera was playing (either *The Siege of Rhodes* or *The History of Sir Francis Drake*) on 6 May, 1659, for on that day John Evelyn, although, as he says, his conscience reproached him for witnessing such a vanity, went to "see a new opera, after the Italian way, in recitative music and sceanes." [78]

But Edmund Gayton, in his *Art of Longevity*, written in the same year, makes a gloomy comment:

> For Playes are down, unless the puppet-play,
> Sir *William's* lost, both *Oyle* and *Opera*.

"*Oyle* and *Opera*" is a pun on the proverb, *oleum et operam* [that is, lucubrations] *perdere* — to labor in vain.[79] Although we do not know at what time in 1659 this was written, it is possible that Gayton set down these lines while Sir William was in prison, in disgrace with the government. Probably Davenant had allowed illegal performances at his own Cockpit; for there is a record of fines received in 1659 "at the Cockpitt playehouse, of severall offenders, by order of the justices," amounting to three pounds, eight shillings, and six pence." [80]

At the beginning of March, 1660, Davenant, having been released from prison some seven months before, hailed the arrival of Monk in London with "A Panegyrick to his Excellency the Lord General *Monk*," [81] and in the same month he made up his mind to go to the Continent and look after his interest with Charles, whose restoration was now only a matter of months. Accordingly, he obtained a pass for France on 17 March, 1660.[82] We have seen, too, that in this month he secured a lease of Lisle's Tennis Court, with an eye to converting it into a theatre for his operas.

This brings us to the end of the poet's subtle and ingenious attempts to set up public drama in the face of the Puritan laws. We have witnessed the cleverness with which he graded his approaches, and have seen him using his influence with certain of Cromwell's chief officers to its utmost limits. It is useless to wonder how far he would have gone if the Restoration had not supervened. Already he had given regular public performances in a regular theatre; and although the opera leaned heavily on tableau, music, and acrobatics, the essence of drama was there. As for his audience, the high prices charged for admission and the elaborate embellishments make it evident that he was catering for "society." And yet we have some ground for thinking that his performances appealed to the common man. There is an undoubted ring of hearty approval in the *Farewell* of Phil. Porter, a notorious hector of the town:[83]

> Now God bless all that will be blest,
>   God bless the Inns of Court,
> And God bless D'Avenant's Opera,
>   Which is the Sport of Sports.

NOTES FOR CHAPTER III

1 (134). B. M., E464.12.
2 (134). 27 July to 3 Aug., 1649. B. M., E532.7.
3 (135). *The Tuesdaies Journall*, 7–14 Aug., 1649. B. M., E532.17.
4 (135). *Perfect Occurr.*, 17–24 Aug., 1649. B. M., E532.24.
5 (135). *Severall Proceedings*, 9–16 Nov., 1649. B. M., E533.24.
6 (135). *A Perfect Diurnall*, 11–18 Feb., 1650. B. M., E534.10.
7 (135). 2–9 Jan., 1650. B. M., E589.8.
8 (135). *Severall Proceedings*, 11–18 Jan., 1650. B. M., E533.38.
9 (136). *A Publique Lecture on the Languages*, 1650. B. M., E595.3.
10 (136). *Severall Proceedings*, 21–28 Dec., 1649. B. M., E533.32.
11 (136). *Ibid.*, 14–21 Dec., 1649. B. M., E533.30.
12 (136). *La Stratonica; or The Unfortunate Queen. Written in Italian by Luke Assarino, and now Englished. London, Printed by John Field. 1651.* B. M., E621.1.
13 (136). Pages 153 ff.
14 (136). B. M., E735.19.
15 (137). B. M., E853.18.
16 (137). B. M., E492.7.
17 (137). B. M., E825.4.
18 (138). No. 36. See Appendix.
19 (138). No. 24.
20 (138). B. M., MS. Sloane 2149.
21 (138). *Registers of Westminster Abbey* (ed. Chester), Harleian Society, x, 168.
22 (139). 15 June, 1655. Bodleian, Rawlinson, A27.345.
23 (139). A pass was granted him on 10 Aug. S. P. Dom. Interregnum, I. 76, p. 230.
24 (139). *Reg. of Westm. Abbey, loc. cit.*
25 (139). No. 24.
26 (140). Chancery Decrees and Orders, Entry Book A1661. Monday, 9 Dec.
27 (141). Page 114. The word "Daphne" embodies a rather clever double play on the Laureate: once on his name, and once on his office (δάφνη, laurel).
28 (141). This book may be identical with *Sportive Wit* mentioned below; for "Wits Merriment: or Lusty Drollery" appears as a running title to the pages of *Sportive Wit*.
29 (141). The complete title is: *Sportive Wit: The Muses Merriment. A New Spring of Lusty Drollery, Joviall Fancies, And A la mode Lamponnes, On some Heroick persons of these late Times, Never before exposed to the publick view. Collected for the Publick god, by a Club of sparkling Wits, viz. C. J. B. J. L. M. W. T. Cum multis aliis—. Semel in anno ridet Apollo. London, Printed for Nath: Brook, to be sold at the Angel in Cornhill, and at the New Exchange and other places. 1656.* Bodleian, Malone 391. Reprinted in part by Professor Rollins, *Studies in Philol.*, 1921, p. 322.

30 (141). B. M., E493.9.

31 (143). *Sic* in the original.

32 (144). The first Parliament summoned by writ under the Protectorate sat from 3 Sept., 1654, to 22 Jan., 1655; the second, from 17 Sept., 1656, to 4 Feb., 1658. Henry Scobell was Clerk to both these Parliaments. (*Journals, House of Commons*, vol. vii.)

33 (145). See below, p. 155.

34 (145). Adams, *Dramatic Records of Sir Henry Herbert*, p. 122.

35 (145). Downes, *Roscius Anglicanus* (ed. Knight), xxiv, 20. The building was originally Cobham House, purchased in 1632 by the Society of Apothecaries. Cf. C. R. B. Barrett, *History of the Society of Apothecaries*, pp. 42, 43.

36 (145). *The Actors Vindication* (1658), a reissue of *An Apology for Actors* (1612).

37 (146). *Dramatic Records of Sir Henry Herbert*, p. 112.

38 (146). See above, p. 139.

39 (146). *Calendar of Proceedings of the Committee for Compounding, 1643–1660*, p. 2735.

40 (146). *Ibid.*, p. 2189.

41 (147). See above, pp. 121–122.

42 (147). Adams, *Shakespearean Playhouses*, pp. 361, 362.

43 (147). See above, p. 43.

44 (147). See above, p. 96.

45 (148). See above, p. 56.

46 (148). Aubrey, i, 208.

47 (149). State Papers, Dom., Interregnum, cxxviii, 108. Reprinted also by Reyher, *Les Masques anglais*, p. 515.

48 (151). Davenant, *Dramatic Works*, ed. Logan and Maidment, iii, 213.

49 (151). *Ibid.*, iii, 229, 230.

50 (151). *Mercurius Politicus*, 13–20 May, 1658. B. M., E750.16.

51 (151). *A Catalogue of New Books*, London, 1660. B. M., E1025.17.

52 (151). Whitelocke, *Memorials*, 1732, p. 650b.

53 (152). *Ibid.*, p. 11a.

54 (152). *Ibid.*, p. 19a.

55 (152). C. H. Firth, *The Last Years of the Protectorate*, i, 1, 2.

56 (153). *Works*, ed. Logan and Maidment, iii, 234.

57 (153). "The Designs for the First Movable Scenery on the English Public Stage," *Burlington Magazine*, xxv (1914), 29, 85 ff.

58 (153). B. M., MS Lansdowne 1171, fol. 11, 12.

59 (153). *The Elizabethan Playhouse* (Second Ser.), p. 130.

60 (154). MS Lansdowne 1171. Reproduced by Reyher, *Les Masques anglais*, p. 369.

61 (154). Lawrence, *op. cit.*, p. 131 and note.

62 (155). Bodleian, Rawlinson, A46.293. Identified and printed by Professor C. H. Firth, *English Historical Review*, xviii (1903), 319. Professor Firth takes it to be an earlier document, written before *The First Day's Entertainment*, although it is bound up with papers dated Jan., 1657.

63 (156). Masson's *Milton*, vi, 274 n. I am ignorant of Masson's source for this statement; of course, Davenant did not care to recall the Cromwell poem when he published his *Works* after the Restoration (1673).

64 (156). *Dramatic Records of Sir Henry Herbert*, p. 123.

65 (156). The wedding was on Wednesday, 11 Nov., 1657.

66 (156). Dugdale to a friend, 14 Nov., 1657. *Hist. MSS Comm., Rep. V*, App., p. 177.

67 (157). *The Tears of the Indians: Being An Historical and true Account Of the Cruel Massacres and Slaughters of above Twenty Millions of innocent People; Committed by the Spaniards*. . . . *Written in Spanish by Casanus, an Eye-witness of those things; And made English by J. P[hillips]. London: 1656* [9 Jan.]. B. M., E1586.501.

68 (157). Lawrence, *Elizabethan Playhouse* (Second Ser.), p. 134.

69 (157). Compare the design and description of the proscenium for Davenant's masque, *The Temple of Love*. Lawrence, *op. cit.* (First Ser.), p. 105.

70 (158). Printed by Rollins, *Studies in Philology*, 1921, pp. 326 ff. Rollins takes his text from Bodleian, MS Ashmole 36, fols. 163, 164, and mentions a late printed copy in Dryden's *Miscellany Poems*, Third Part, 1716, pp. 323-325. It may be added that the latter is in all likelihood taken bodily from *Choyce Poems, Being Songs, Sonnets, Satyrs and Elegies. By the Wits of both Universities.* London, 1661. B. M., 238 *b*.35, pp. 1, 2.

71 (159). *Hist. MSS Comm., Rep. V*, App., p. 146*a*.

72 (160). *Publick Intelligencer*, 20–27 Dec., 1658. First quoted by Malone, *Prolegomena* (1813), p. 97.

73 (160). Printed by W. L. Bowles in his *Life of Ken* (1830–1831), i, 244, from "a MS Diurnal of the Parliament, 1658, in the possession of the descendant of Clement Walker, John Walker Heneage." Bowles gives the date as 5 Feb., 1658; this is evidently Old Style, for Parliament had risen on 4 Feb., 1658. The reference is undoubtedly to 1659.

74 (161). *Nicholas Papers* (Camden Society), iv, 83.

75 (161). "Aug. 16, 1659. Sir *William Davenant* was released out of Prison." Whitelocke, *Memorials*, 1732, p. 682.

76 (161). State Papers, Dom., Interregnum, I. 79, p. 453.

77 (162). B. M., E986.10.   R.

78 (162). *Diary*, ed. Wheatley, ii, 106.

79 (162). Cf. Plautus, *Poenulus*, I, II, 119.

80 (162). John Parton, *Some Account of the Hospital and Parish of St. Giles in the Fields*, p. 236.

81 (162). Kennet, p. 246.

82 (162). State Papers, Dom., Interregnum, I. 116, p. 7*a*.

83 (163). *Pills to Purge Melancholy* (1714), ii, 9. Cf. Chapter I, note 198.

CHAPTER IV

GEORGE JOLLY AND THE NURSERY

I. A Stroller in Germany

IN the tangle of Restoration stage history there is at least one bright thread which seems to have neither beginning nor end. This thread is the story of the life and activities of George Jolly. He appears in 1660 as a dangerous rival of Davenant and Killigrew, — the two courtiers who were doing their best to secure a monopoly of the drama in London, — and continues for a number of years as a thorn in their flesh.

The new light which will be shed on Jolly in the course of this chapter emanates from two sources: first, from German studies of Jolly's wanderings on the Continent during the Commonwealth; and second, from new English documents of importance for the history of the Restoration theatre.

For the lovers of the stage in Germany, George Jolly has a peculiar interest, since under the names of Joris Jollifus, George Jeliphus, and Joseph Jori, he appears in German town archives as the last of the great English strolling players who exercised such a powerful influence upon the German drama. But his story must be told from the beginning.

In 1648, when Davenant was writing his *Gondibert* at the Royalist headquarters in Paris, and while the Draconian laws against stage players were coming out in England, George Jolly sprang into view on the Continent full-fledged as one of the most capable and progressive of the English actor-managers. But at the outset we are confronted with a dilemma. It is certainly possible that Jolly had left England several years before 1648, to avoid the war and to try his fortune on the Continent. He may well have been one of the Prince of Wales's company of English actors in Paris which, in November, 1646, was reported dissolved for want of pay. This

I think the likeliest explanation. On the other hand, he may have been one of the actors whom Parliament suppressed in 1648. After the wars, in the autumn and winter of 1647–1648, as we have seen, the London companies had begun to open their houses and to present their plays with an almost *ante-bellum* vigor. Parliament viewed this renaissance of the theatre with alarm. Something drastic had to be done; and seeing that the former repressive ordinances were not enough to deter the bold actors, both Houses passed the harsh order of 9 February, 1648. Branding the stage players as rogues, it provided fines and imprisonment for the first offence, and for the second, public flogging.[1]

Though some of the players braved even these dangers, others felt that England was either too hot or too cold for them. A body of the latter got together, and on 8 March, 1648, we found them presenting a petition to the House of Lords. They desired "to have something to be bestowed upon them from the State, and to have passes to goe beyond the Seas." "But this Petition," says the state newsbook triumphantly, "was utterly rejected." [2]

Perhaps George Jolly was a leading spirit among these petitioners, and took a band of them out of England, in spite of being refused "passes to goe beyond the Seas." Or, what is more probable, he may have come from France to Holland on 24 February, 1648, at the head of the "pack of Players from France, who are to help away the time spent formerly in Martiall actions." At any rate, whether he came from France or from England, the evidence collated by Dr. Herz in his study of the strolling English players in Germany,[3] shows that it was Jolly's band of fourteen actors that arrived in Cologne at the end of April, 1648. They had come by way of the Netherlands, stopping at Bruges; and on Sunday, 26 April (N.S.), in the tennis court in the St. Apostelnstrasse, Cologne, they performed "with all propriety and decency" certain chronicles, histories, and comedies. On Monday they petitioned the town council for permission to play for five or six weeks. The permission was granted for fourteen days, on condition that the actors would charge no more than four pieces of silver for admission to the benches, and twelve pieces for seats on the stage ("auf das Theatrum"), and that they would give a handsome contribution for the benefit of the poor and the foundlings of Cologne.[4]

Jolly's acting pleased the burghers of that city so well, however, that his stay was prolonged until the end of July. In August the company went off to Frankfort for the great autumn fair. Returning to Cologne early in 1649 (but after the execution of Charles I in England), George Jolly informed the town councillor that his troupe had played in England, the Low Countries, and Germany; that (and here he stretched the truth) he could not go back to England because a bloody war had broken out there. Jolly may have been referring to Cromwell's 1649 campaign in Ireland. He asked again, therefore, permission to act in Cologne.[5]

It would take us too far to follow the complete itinerary of Jolly's band in Germany. Herz gives an excellent map [6] which traces all his known journeyings on the Continent. Our purpose is rather to study the man and his work: to see at closer range this last member of the great line of Elizabethan strollers.

The English travelling actors had made such an enviable reputation in Germany that many of the later German and Dutch companies advertised themselves as English. Jolly, for lack of English players, was forced to accept a certain admixture of Germans in his company,[7] but he usually announced his band as composed of "Englische commödianten," [8] although they acted in German.

From all the records we can gather about Jolly we get a picture of the typical violent and rapacious actor-manager of those troubled days. Germany had been ravaged by the Thirty Years' War; and in such a poor country no idealistic or gentle-natured man could possibly succeed with a travelling company. Boldness, rough authority, and unscrupulous dealing were required, and Jolly had these qualities to the full. If a rival actor showed himself in the town, Jolly was quite capable of attacking him with his fists in order to discourage competition. Numerous complaints of him have come down to us. One Johann Janicke, a stroller, complained to the authorities of Nürnberg of the blows and evil treatment he had received at Jolly's hands.[9] From Dresden came a complaint by letter that Jolly had left debts behind him there.[10] In 1655 he struck and wounded one of his leading actors, Christoph Blümels, who thereupon sued him for damages.[11] Two years later this same Blümels was committed to jail for having seduced an innkeeper's daughter; but he was soon released with no more than a caution, because Jolly could not act his "excellent comedies" without him![12] Besides a quick temper and a ready fist, Jolly had a rude tongue — which could nevertheless be very smooth when it was necessary to propitiate a town council.[13]

The year 1651 was an unlucky year for Jolly. Bringing his company up to Frankfort in August for the fair, he found to his dismay another troupe already installed there. He learned that his rivals were the Court Players of the late Prince of Orange, and that they were prepared to present "new and delightful histories, comedies, tragedies, and pastorals, embellished with lovely music and voices and many wonderful changes of scene, all according to the elegant French manner."[14] This was the first taste that the honest burghers of Frankfort had had of "pastorals" — that is, plays with music and movable scenery. Still, nothing daunted, Jolly set up his show; but as he was acting without scenes, on the old style of stage, it is no wonder that the extraordinary splendor of the Netherlandish company drew away all the public from Jolly's tennis-court theatre at the Krachbein Inn. The unfortunate manager could neither pay the theatre tax for the poor, nor satisfy mine host of the Krachbein. He was forced to pawn all the best costumes and properties of his company to the value of 1000 thalers, and to creep out of Frankfort with only the barest necessities.

By the next year, however, he returned to the same city, having gathered a new company composed largely of Germans and advertised as "hochteutschen Personen." While he had not yet recouped his losses, he had evidently learned a lesson.

He now knew that the popular taste was turning toward the music, decorations, and machines of the Italian opera, and he had made up his mind to meet and even to anticipate the demand. By May, 1653, he had developed such an up-to-date company that he was able to perform with success before His Imperial Majesty in Vienna; and in 1654 we find that he had become prosperous and had surpassed his old rivals, the Netherlanders, by including actresses in his company. In a letter to the Council of Basle he now offers to delight all who love plays "with his well-practised company, not only by means of good instructive stories, but also with repeated changes of expensive costumes, and a theatre decorated in the Italian manner, with beautiful English music and skilful women." [15] For some unknown reason Basle refused his offer, and Jolly returned to his old quarters in Frankfort.

According to Frau Mentzel (the historian of the theatre in Frankfort), George Jolly "is an important personality in the history of the Frankfort stage, for he first brought women upon the boards." [16] For English theatrical history Jolly is even more important, since his development of music, scenery, and the use of actresses preceded Davenant's opera by several years. Jolly is in reality the first English producer to use the modern stage.

With all the new improvements, Jolly's theatre in the Frankfort tennis court prospered. He made so much money in 1654 that he proposed to erect a theatre of his own. With the purpose of making it over into a theatre he hired the Golden Rose Tavern in the Karpfengasse; but the project was halted by an immediate revolt of the whole neighborhood. Angry citizens objected to having their houses threatened with fire by "such low fellows who go about with tobacco and drink." After a short absence in the winter, Jolly's company returned to Frankfort in 1655, to stay for the whole year.

We come now to a most interesting and gratifying confirmation of Mr. W. J. Lawrence's guess that George Jolly made the acquaintance of Charles II on the Continent. [17]

In September, 1655, a small royal party had resolved to go

on a lark. "Next week," wrote Secretary Nicholas from
Cologne on 17 September, "the King, Duke of Gloucester,
Princess Royal, and Lady Stanhope are going incognito to
Frankfort Fair; a strange journey, all things considered, but
young princes think of nothing but pleasure." [18] The plan was
carried out, and on 25 September the Marquis of Ormonde reported to Nicholas from Frankfort: " . . . wee arriued here
last night. . . . We haue allready seene the Jews sinagogue, the
Faire, and a play, and tomorrow wee shall bee at a Lutheran
service." [19] It was impossible, of course, to maintain the incognito long. The royal party met the Elector of Mainz and was
publicly honored by the town of Frankfort. *Mercurius Politicus*, the Parliament newsbook, says: "At their departure the
Souldiers were in arms, and gave them two Vollies of shot,
and some Canon was fired from the walls. I find not that their
conversation here hath *made them commendable to any so much
as to the English Stage-players, who stile themselves to be his*." [20]

From the above outlines it is not difficult to picture what
happened to the young princes who thought "of nothing but
pleasure." They came as private citizens to the fair and witnessed a performance by the only actors in town (that is,
George Jolly's company) at the Krachbein tennis court. Being
on a lark, the princes undoubtedly condescended to strike up
an acquaintance with their fellow countrymen, the English
players. Perhaps Charles even put up at the Krachbein Inn:
for its name to-day is no longer "am Krachbein," but "König
von England." [21] As soon as Jolly and his company learned the
identity of the newcomers, they promptly styled themselves
"The King's Servants," and doubtless gave them several performances *de luxe*. Jolly's alacrity in assuming this title makes
it seem more likely that he had been of Charles's company of
English actors in Paris in 1646. It is highly probable that
one of the plays given before the exiled Stuart was *Ermordete
Majestät, oder Carolus Stuardus, König von Grossbritannien;* a
tragedy or *trauerspiel* by Andreas Gryphius. [22] With the combined paraphernalia of ancient and modern tragedy, chorus,
strophe, antistrophe, ghosts, and allegorical figures, this play

sets forth the terrible end of Charles I. It begins with an ominous dialogue between the ghosts of Strafford and Laud, and ends after the execution with a blood-curdling imprecation on guilty Albion by the figure of Revenge. We know that this tragedy was presented in the following March (1656) at a town near Frankfort by "foreign comedians."²³ In all likelihood these were Jolly's actors, who frequently did the towns in the neighborhood of Frankfort.

It is no wonder, then, after being fêted by the highly-skilled English actor-manager in Frankfort, that Charles II, when he came to the throne in 1660, should have been kindly disposed toward George Jolly. But, not to anticipate our story, we must see what befell the stroller in the five years remaining before the Restoration.

Frau Mentzel has traced this part of Jolly's stormy life in great detail.²⁴ Just before the Easter fair at Frankfort in 1656, Hoffmann and Schwartz, two of his chief actors, deserted him and formed a company of their own. Hiring the Krachbein tennis court in September for their own use, they forced Jolly to find a poor place, where he could not properly act and where he got barely enough to keep him alive. In the following winter the seceding actors and their company were employed at the Heidelberg court of Elector Karl Ludwig von der Pfalz; but when the spring came, Jolly took revenge upon them by hiring the Krachbein tennis court first. The Hoffmann–Schwartz troupe, being obliged to set up their theatre in the unwieldy Pfuhlhof, and hampered by the illness of their best actress, Schwartz's wife, did very poor business.

They were resolved to turn the tables on Jolly for the autumn fair, and on 14 July ensconced themselves in the Krachbein two days before the Englishman appeared in town. Jolly was put to it to find a place to act. No one would rent him a suitable house, and at length he was reduced to building a temporary booth out of boards. Meanwhile, the other actors had for some reason been ejected from the tennis court. They used a house called the Nürnberger Hof until they were likewise driven thence; whereupon they tried to follow Jolly's example and build a temple to Thalia out of pine boards. But the citizens of the neighborhood protested against "such a wicked and dangerous design," and the Hoffmann–Schwartz band found itself again in the huge Pfuhlhof.

Between the two companies there now developed a bitter feud. They undercut each other's prices, printed uncomplimentary bills about each other's performances, and when their opposing members met by chance in taverns, they fell into fierce brawls. By 29 September, 1657, the rivalry reached a crisis. Each company, hoping to obtain a longer permission to act in Frankfort, and, as if to settle once for all the question as to which company the authorities favored, invited the elders of the town to attend a free performance. The performances at the two houses were set for the same day, from three to six in the afternoon. The authorities, however, cleverly evaded the invidious position of dramatic judge by accepting *both* invitations, and by informing the two companies that on a certain day both would have to cease their performances.

This order had a prompt effect. Jolly and the Hoffmann–Schwartz combination immediately announced that they had sunk their differences and had joined together, and that now they looked forward in their new unity to presenting "something gallant and renowned." But alas for good intentions! There was a certain difficulty about Jolly's temper: for shortly after the first united performance the leaders of the two companies fell into another quarrel, which spread into a general fight between the devoted followers. The old enmity was back with a vengeance, and the councillor now prohibited both companies from playing.

Hoffmann and Schwartz left town at once; but Jolly was not able to go, and begged an opportunity to earn money for his ailing wife, for whom, he said, he had to employ two physicians every day. It does not look as if Jolly deserved much mercy, but his appeal touched the apparently hard-hearted councillor, who not only granted Jolly permission to act twice or thrice a week for a certain time, but also accepted him as an "inhabitant," thus allowing him to remain in Frankfort over the winter.

Donnerstags / den 23. Octobr.
Wird denen Gnädigen und Gönstigen Herren Zuschauern auffgewartet werden /
mit einer gantz Neuen Action / dergleichen sie an angenehmer Vollkommenheit und Lustigkeit
noch niemahls gesehen haben /
Genannt /
Die

Standhaffte Mutter der MACHABÆER,

Wie dieselbe mit ihren sieben Söhnen hingerichtet wird.

Personen der Action /

1. Salome die Mutter der Machabæer.	9. Antiochus König in Aegypten.
2. Machabæus.	10. Bachides deß Königs geheimer Rath.
3. Aberet.	11. Sosander deß Königs Feld-Hauptmann.
4. Machir.	12. Eleasar } Zwey Juden.
5. Judas. } Ihre sieben Söhne.	13. Barachias }
6. Areth.	14. Menelaus Heydnischer Priester / ein abgefallener Jude.
7. Achas.	15. Sara eine abgefallene Jüdin.
8. Jacob.	16. Javan ein närrischer Diener.

PROLOGUS.

Die Kirche wird vorgestellet als eine Jungfrau mit einer Krohne von 12. Sternen / den Mond unter
den Füssen mit hellen Schein bekleidet / der Satan in Gestalt eines Drachen sucht sie zu unterdrücken /
wird aber von dem Ertz-Engel Michael in den Abgrund gestürtzet.

Kurtzer Summarischer Inhalt / Der Ersten Handlung.

Eleasar , und Barachias kommen mit etlichen Juden auß einer Höle gekrochen / darein sie sich auß Furcht versteckt hatten / sie beklagen die grosse Verfolgung / so sie und ihres Gesetzes halben außstehen müssen / Salome kombt mit ihren Kindern zu ihnen / und vermeinet alda sicher zu sein / Javan kombt gelauffen / und ermahnet sie zur Flucht / Eleasar und Barachias, wie auch Machabæus verkriechen sich in die Höle / Sosander , kombt mit etlichen Soldaten / und nimbt die Salome mit ihren 6. Söhnen gefangen / Machabæus kombt auß der Höle hervor und beklagt seiner Mutter und seiner Brüder Unglück / Eleasar bemüht sich ihn zu trösten / worbey Javan seltzame Possen treibt / darauff sie sich endlich entschliessen nach Hoffe zu gehen / und sich als gefangene dem König darzustellen / Menelaus stellt sich ein des Bachi Fest helffen zu begehen / zu ihm kombt Eleasar , Machabæus , Bachides , fragt was ihr begehren sey / und ob sie ihren Göttern ein Opffer bringen wolle / darauff sie sich erklären alle Marter außzustehen ehe sie ihre Götter verehren wollen / Antiochus will dem Bacho opffern / Sosander bringt ein hauffen gefangene Juden / welche dem Bacho zu Ehren sind gekrohnet worden / der König verrichtet das Opffer / sie sollen den Eleasar darzu zwingen daß er auch dem Bacho opffern soll / Er aber bringt es durch sein andächtiges Gebet dahin / daß des Bachi Bild / von dem Donner wird niedergeschlagen.

Der Andern Handlung.

Machabæus entschliesset sich / daß er will hingehen / und sich bey seiner Mutter und Brüdern lassen gefangen setzen / Javan vermeint ihn davon abzuhalten / Sosander erzehlet Bachides daß er in die Salome verliebt sey / Salome kombt zu Sosander , welcher bey ihr umb Liebe anhält /

Sie aber will ihm kein gehör geben / Machabæus welcher auff der Seite gestanden / und alle ihre reden angehört / vermahnet seine Mutter / daß sie in ihrer Beständigkeit fortfahren soll / und sich durch keine schmeichelnde oder liebreigende Reden verführen lassen / Bachides fragt Sosandern ob Er in seiner Liebe glückselig gemacht worden sey / die Söhne kommen und klagen ihrer Mutter daß man sie mit Gewalt zum Opffer zwingen will / der Mutter aber erinnert sie ihres Gesetzes / daß sie unverrückt darbey verbleiben sollen / darauff werden sie alle wieder in das Gefängnüß geführet / Antiochus fragt Bachides ob die Salome noch nicht zu andern gedancken gebracht worden / darauff läst er Eleasar vor sich kommen / denen wollen sie nun der Güte bereden / daß er ihren Göttern opffern soll / weil er aber nicht drein willigen will / so wird er zu rode gegeisselt / die 7. Machabeer werden vor den König gebracht / Eleasar wird ihnen gezeiget / und weil sie von ihren Gesetz nicht wollen abweichen / so wird man eben auff solche weise mit ihnen verfahren / und sie durch allerhand Marter zu dem Opffer ihrer Götter zwingen.

Der Dritten Handlung.

Salome liegt im Gefängnüß / und beklagt ihr grosses hertzleid wegen ihrer Kinder / Javan erzehlt daß es ihm anietzo viel besser gehe da er im Heyde worden als da er noch ein Jude gewesen / Sara kombt zu ihm / und haben artliche Possen miteinander / Menelaus trifft sie beysammen an / und weil er sie vor Juden hält / will er sie lassen in das Gefängnüß werffen / Sie aber machen sich durch eine sonderliche List von ihm los / Machabæus im Gefängnüß beklagt sich über die Marter so ihnen wird angethan / Bachides bietet der Salome nochmahls der Königliche Gnade an wofern sie ihren Göttern opffern wollen / weil sie aber solches nicht thun will / läst er ihre Kinder holen / und beschicht sie auff das ärgste zu greissen / Menelaus will daß Javan zum Opffer gehen soll / Er aber macht sich durch seine lustige Possen wieder von ihm frey / Antiochus mit Bachides befiehlt Sosandern / daß er die Salome mit ihren 7. Söhnen soll lassen vor ihm kommen / der König läst ihnen allen noch einmahl seine Gnade anbieten / weil sie aber gantz nicht abweichen kein / sondern bey ihrem Gesetz beständig verbleiben wollen / So werden die Kinder / und zwar von den ältesten an biß zu dem jüngsten hingerichtet / und zu letzt läst der König die Mutter auch enthaupten.

Nach der Action soll ein lustiges neues Nach-Spiel beschliessen.
Und werden im Krachbein præcisè umb 2. Uhr anfangen.

A FRANKFORT PLAYBILL, *circa* 1656

If this bill of a performance of *Die Standhaffte Mutter der Machabæer* is correctly assigned
to 1656, the actors who gave the play were Hoffmann and Schwartz, the seceders from
George Jolly's company.

(After E. Mentzel in *Archiv für Frankfurts Geschichte und Kunst*, 1896, pp. 172 ff.)

The next year, 1658, saw the coronation of Emperor Leopold I at Frankfort. So great was the confluence of people to that city that Jolly was enabled not only to pay his debts but also to reëstablish his company in its former magnificence, and to plan a theatrical visit to Vienna. In the course of 1658, however, Jolly's relations with his old companions, Hoffmann and Schwartz, underwent several vicissitudes. Elector Karl Ludwig von der Pfalz, who knew Jolly very well, and had employed Hoffmann and Schwartz's company at his court at Heidelberg, gives us some interesting facts in his letters. In May, 1658, the Elector says that the two companies had reunited; for he saw their combined performance of *The Prodigal Son* at Frankfort, where he had come for the coronation. At the same time he gives his opinion of the bad lighting of the tennis court at the Krachbein. It was so dark that, although he could see the actors, he could make out none of the other people in the hall. Yet in spite of this drawback, the performances of "Master George," as he calls Jolly (using the English words), were very well attended by the nobility.

The companies acted together for nearly two months; but by July they had split again. The Elector puts the blame on Jolly's temper. "Sein colera," he says, drove even the actresses from him, and left him with only eight players. Forced out of the tennis-court theatre, Master George was reduced to wretched straits. He was obliged to humble himself to make peace with all his former associates before the group could carry out the plan which they had made to play in Vienna. When he had done this to their satisfaction, they all set off together. Upon the travelling actors' arrival at their destination, however, we learn that their performances shocked the Viennese, who complained that their comedies were "spiced with the most scandalous obscenities."

Here we lose track of Jolly for a time, and the last records of his activities in Germany come from Nürnberg, where he held the stage during May and June, 1659. He was twice refused permission to act here, in September and October, but was successful in his petition of 14 November. In the baptismal books of St. Sebald, Nürnberg, appears the following entry: "29. Dez. 1659. *Georgius Jeliphus* von Chelse in Midllsex bey London ein *Comoediant. Maria di Roy* von Utrecht in Holland."[25] The name of the child follows.

On 31 January, 1660, Jolly was expelled from the town because of a passionate quarrel. So Master George ended his theatrical career in Germany — going out in a warm red mist of fiery temper.

A few months later the Restoration was in sight in England, and Jolly made up his mind to return to the land which he had left twelve years before, and take part in the revival of the drama.

II. Stage Nurseries in London

Shortly after Charles II came to the throne George Jolly landed in England, where he was destined to play an important rôle in the history of the early Restoration stage. Just how important his part was has never been clearly ascertained. The patient research and keen thinking of Mr. W. J. Lawrence have put before us all that has hitherto been known about Master George's life in England after the Restoration, and all that could properly be surmised on the basis of the obtainable evidence. These results Mr. Lawrence has embodied in two important papers: "A Forgotten Restoration Playhouse"[26] (1904), and "Restoration Stage Nurseries" (1914).[27]

A close search, however, among the manuscripts of the British Museum has enabled me to uncover new facts which greatly increase our knowledge of George Jolly and which necessitate a new interpretation of the old evidence. Before introducing the new documents in their proper places, it is desirable to survey the theatrical situation at the time of Jolly's arrival in London.

Davenant and Killigrew, on 21 August, 1660, had obtained a joint grant for two companies which gave them (on parchment) a monopoly of the stage in London. Though it was some time before their monopoly became real, they made use of their grant to select one company from among those who were acting in London.[28] This arrangement lasted no longer than a month, after which each of the two managers took a company of his own. Killigrew chose the Mohun company of pre-war actors. Playing for only three days at the Red Bull, he promptly moved them to Gibbons's Tennis Court, which thereupon became the first Theatre Royal. This was in November, 1660; and in the same month Rhodes's company, of which Betterton was the leading actor, entered into articles with Sir William Davenant and began to act under the knight's direction in the Salisbury Court, newly fitted up by William Beeston.

At this point, some time in November, 1660, George Jolly appeared upon the scene and desired to take up his profession. In his petition to Charles II for a license to act, he undoubtedly reminded him of the royal entertainment which he had given to the exiled Stuart at Frankfort Fair in 1655. Now, although we have seen that the Davenant–Killigrew grant prohibited all other theatres, Charles had been so eager to have Italian opera, with its scenery and music, in London that on 22 October, 1660 (about a month before Jolly's appearance), he had issued a grant to Giulio Gentileschi "to build a theatre for an Italian band of Musicians whom he is bringing into England." [29] Nothing, however, was done by the Italian on this permission. The great difficulty, of course, was the expense of the undertaking.

Davenant was beginning to make his preparations for opera at Lisle's Tennis Court in Lincoln's Inn Fields, but it was to be half a year or more before he would be ready to put on productions. When Jolly arrived and asked for permission to give performances, Charles no doubt remembered the delightful plays with music, actresses, and scenes "in the Italian manner," which he had seen Master George present in Frankfort; and in the hope that he might do the like in London the King issued to Jolly the following grant, dated 24 December, 1660: [30]

CHARLES R

. . . Whereas we have thought fitt to allow . . . publique Presentations of Tragedies and Comedies . . . and being well informed of the art and skill of George Jolly Gentleman for the purpose aforesaid, doe hereby grant . . . unto the said George Jolly full power and authority to erect one company . . . and to purchase, build or hire . . . One House or Theatre with all convenient Roomes . . . and in regard of the extraordinary Licentiousness that has bin lately used in things of this nature, Our pleasure is that you doe not at any time hereafter cause to be acted or represented any Play, Enterlude or Opera containing any matter of profanation, scurrility or obscenity, and this our Grant and Authority made to the said George Jolly shall be effectual notwithstanding any former grant made by us to our trusty and well beloved Servant Thomas Killegrew Esq[r] and Sir William Davenant K[nt]. or any other person or persons whatsoever to the contrary. Given under our Signet at the Court at Whitehall the 24th day of December 1660 in the 12th yeare of our Reigne

By his Majesties command
Edw. Nicholas

In regard to this grant, of which he had evidently not seen the original, Mr. Lawrence says, "It is a moot point whether this license gave Jolly permission to build a new theatre." [31] The original document here given leaves no doubt upon this point. Mr. Lawrence, indeed, might have settled the question from another source by examining more closely the grant made in 1664 to William Legge,[32] which he himself reprinted.[33] Legge's patent recites the terms of the grant to Jolly: ". . . to purchase, build, or hyre, att his cost and charges, one house or theatre."

On the strength of his new license, Master George collected a company of actors and hired the Cockpit either from the Kirks or from Rhodes — whichever of the two held the lease. After the following summer, when Davenant's company had finally moved from the Salisbury Court, as we have seen in the chapter on that theatre, Beeston persuaded Jolly to move from the Cockpit to his theatre in Salisbury Court. That Jolly was not satisfied with the internal arrangement of the latter, however, appears from Beeston's statement, and from the fact that it was necessary for the King to order Jolly, who had returned to the Cockpit, to come back and use Beeston's house.[34] Nevertheless, Jolly's troupe used the Cockpit for at least part of 1662. Evidence for this statement is provided by a note in the memorandum book of Dr. Edward Browne.[35] This book records the plays which Browne saw at the various theatres in London, most probably at the end of 1662. By 1662, Davenant's and Killigrew's tennis-court playhouses in Lincoln's Inn Fields were in full career. Opposite his entry of *Beggar's Bush*, seen at Killigrew's "new Theatre in Lincolnes Inne fields," Dr. Browne notes in the margin, "Kings players"; and, lower, opposite *The Alchymist*, he writes the abbreviation "K. P." Now it seems that Killigrew's company (the King's players) about this time performed also at the "Cock Pit in Drewry Lane"; for opposite *The Silent Woman*, seen at the latter playhouse, he notes likewise "K. P." Farther down the same list, however, we come upon the important entry which undoubtedly refers to Jolly's company at the same theatre: "*Dr. Fostus* . . . . . . Licens: Players."[36] The epithet "licensed" serves to distinguish this company from Killigrew's (the King's) players, and from Davenant's actors at the Duke's theatre. Besides these two companies, Jolly's were the only "licensed players" in London.

In January, 1663, Jolly received a license from Sir Henry Herbert to raise a strolling company to act plays in the country. From this fact Mr. Lawrence surmises that Killigrew, as yet unsuccessful in his efforts to have Jolly's London warrant utterly revoked, was obliged to agree to letting him have this country license as a compromise. We shall see that the fact of the matter was quite different. Killigrew and Davenant had rented Jolly's grant from him for four pounds a week; and now, when he had left London to act in the country, they took advantage of his absence to try to cheat him of his rights by misrepresenting the state of affairs to the King. The steps of their chicanery can best be traced from the beginning by a careful reading of the following documents.

The first of these new documents is an agreement, made on 30 December, 1662, between Jolly of the one part and Killigrew and Davenant of the other, by which it is agreed that

1. Davenant and Killigrew, in return for the use of Jolly's warrant, shall pay Jolly four pounds a week during his life, beginning 27 December, 1662.

2. When Davenant and Killigrew shall set up a company by virtue of the same, the four pounds a week is to continue except when the said company is prohibited from acting by reason of the plague.

3. If Davenant and Killigrew shall fail to pay Jolly the weekly stipend of four pounds, within ten days after such failure they shall redeliver to him his warrant.

To make this agreement the firmer, Jolly obliged Davenant and Killigrew to enter into a bond of two thousand pounds to hold to its conditions.

It is worth while to append the complete text of the document [37] and the important parts of the bond:

ARTICLES of Agreement had made concluded Betweene George Jolly of London gent of the one part, Thomas Killigrew Esqr, one of the Groomes of his ma*jes*ties Bedchamber And S*ir* William Davenant of London Knight, are as doe followe:

WHEREAS his sacred Ma*jes*tie by his Royall Grant or Warrant under his privy Signet . . . at Whitehall the Twenty fourth day of December in the yeare of our Lord one Thousand Six hundred & Sixty did give and grant unto the said George Jolly ffull power & authorety to Erect a Company of players for the representat*i*on of Tragedyes Comedyes Playes Operas & ffarces in such manner as by the same may appeare And the said George Jolly did for som tyme exercise *the* Authority thereby Given And now it is Agreed between the p*a*rtyes before ment*i*oned in this manner that is to say

FFirst the said George Jolly hath actually delivered the said Warrant or Grant to the said Thomas Killigrew & S*ir* William Davenant And doth hereby Acquitt all pretences to the same And is contented & willing, That the said Thomas Killigrew & S*ir* William Davenant, them or either of them shall make use thereof for their or eyther of theire owne purposes and for their or eyther of theire owne benefitts, as they or eyther of them shall think fitt order and Agree.

Then the said Thomas Killigrew and S*ir* William Davenant in consideration hereof doe for them and eyther of them, their & eyther of their heires executors admin*i*strators & Assignes covenant promise & Agree to and with the said George Jolly & his Assignes to pay unto the said George Jolly & his Assignes during the naturall life of the said George Jolly the sum*m*e of ffower pounds of lawfull money of England [every] week weekly during the Tearme aforesaid The first payment thereof to begin upon Satterday the Seaven and Twentieth of this month December . . . thenceforth to be contynued from Satterday to Satterday in every week weekly & successively ontill the said Thomas Killegrew & S*ir* William Davenant them or eyther of them shall Erect a Company of players by vertue of the said

Warrant or Grant And after the said Company Erected Itt is Agreed that the said payment of the sume aforesaid shall bee contynued & paid uppon every Satterday ensuinge in every week weekly & successively duringe the tearme aforesaid unles by reason of publique prohibition in tyme of plague or pestilence, the said company or those that are to succeed them shall not play. And during such prohibition in such time of plague or pestilence as aforesaid the said payments are to cease, and noe longer. And uppon their new Acting or playinge, the said payments are to be revived & contynued in such a manner & forme, & for such time & tearme as in this present Article Aforementioned & expressed

Lastly the said Thomas Killigrew & Sir William Davenant doe for them and eyther of them, their or either of their heires executors administrators & assignes covenant, grant & Agree to and with the said George Jolly & his Assignes, That in case if any default shall happen to bee by the said Thomas Killegrew & Sir William Davenant, them or eyther of them, their or eyther of their heires executors administrators or assignes of the summe or summes aforesaid at such time & times of payment as the same are hereby lymited & appointed That then within tenn daies after such default by Thomas Killegrew & Sir William Davenant, them or eyther of them their or either of their executors administrators or assignes shall deliver & yeild upp unto the said George Jolly or his assignes the aforesaid warrant or Grant Acquitting all future pretences to the same being contented & willinge, that the aforesaid George Jolly or his Assignes shall make use thereof for his or theire owne purposes and for his or their owne benefitt as hee or they shall think fitt and Determine. *In Witnes* whereof the parties first above named to theis present Articles of Agreement have set their hands & Seales this Thirtieth Day of December in the ffowerteenth yeare of the Raigne of our Soveraigne Lord Charles the second by the grace of God of England Scotland ffrance and Ireland king Defender of the faith etc. And in the yeare of our Lord God According to the Computation of the Church of England One Thousand Six Hundred Sixty and Two.

[*Endorsed:*]

[*signed*]   georg jolly

Sealed and delivered in the presence of

[*signed*]   John Craven[?]

Joh Wrightinton at Grayes Inn

[*below:*]   30 Decimber: 14: Char. 2d 1662./

Mr. Jollyes Articles of Agreement with Tom. Killigrew Esq & Sir William Davenant about his Grant from the King concerning players.

[*Second membrane:*]

Noverint omnes psentes Nos Thoma Killegrew . . . Valett Cubicili Dni Regis et Willm Davenant de London mil. . . . teneri et firmiter obligari

Georgio Jolly de London gen in Duabus mille Libris bone et legalis monet
Angl. . . . etc.
    Dec. 30, 1662.
Sigillat et delibat in prtia
    [*signed*]   John Craven   [*signed*]   Tho Killegreue
                  Joh Wrightinton   Will D'avenant

[*endorsed:*]

The Condition of the within written obligation is such that if the within
bounden Thomas Killegrew & Sir William Davenant, or eyther of them,
their or either of their heires executors Administrators and Assignes doe
& shall well & truly observe fulfill & keepe All & singuler the Covenants
Grants Articles, Clauses payments & Agreements, contayned specifyed or
declared in certein Articles of Agreement bearing the date within, made
betweene the within-named George Jolly of the one part And the said
Thomas Killegrew & Sir William Davenant, their heires, executors, administrators & assignes, are to be observed done paid performed fulfilled
& kept, & that in & by all things according to the purport effect bearing
intent & meaning of the said Articles Then the within written obligations
to be frustrate voyd & of none effect, or els the same to remayne & con-
tynue in full force & vertue. . . .

                                                    vera Copia

Two days after this instrument was executed, the Master of
the Revels issued (1 January, 1663) letters of authorization to
Jolly "to raise a company of Stage players or less to act Comedies &c throughout England with exception onely to the Cities
of London and Westm: and the suburbs of each respectiue
city." [38] And on 29 January, as if the above were not authority enough, the King granted permission to Jolly to act
plays in the country, reinforcing his grant with instructions
"to all Mayors, Sheriffs, Justices of the peace, Bayliffs, Constables, and head boroughs" to assist and protect the said
George Jolly in exercising his profession. [39]

We come now to the carrying out of the dishonorable plan
which Killigrew and Davenant had concocted. Having obtained possession of Jolly's grant, they waited until Master
George had departed from London. Then, instead of raising a
company as agreed, on the strength of it, on 23 July, 1663, they
approached the King with the warrant, and represented that
they had *bought* it from Jolly outright. Therefore they asked

that now, by virtue of Jolly's grant, they might have another license made out in their own names, declaring their complete monopoly of the theatres in London, and giving them permission to erect a third playhouse in addition to the two they were already allowed. It was understood that this new playhouse was to be a nursery for training actors for the two regular theatres.

This petition was favorably received by the King, who believed that what they said was true; and thereupon a warrant for the new license was drafted and Jolly's grant was declared revoked.[40] The license, however, which carried out the terms of the warrant, did not pass the privy seal until eight months later.

In the meantime, Davenant and Killigrew had made an arrangement with Colonel William Legge, a Groom of the King's Bedchamber, by which the license should be made out in his name, with an inserted clause giving Davenant and Killigrew supervision and control of the Nursery company. In other words, Legge should be a lay-figure or sleeping partner, while the actual director of the Nursery was to be an employee of Killigrew and Davenant. With this plan in mind, the astute managers petitioned the King to make William Legge the nominal licensee, rather than themselves.

Accordingly, the license was issued on 30 March, 1664. In referring to it, Mr. Lawrence says that as part of its preamble this document recites "the revocation of Jolly's patent."[41] This is hardly accurate. It *does* mention Jolly's warrant, not as revoked, however, but as having been given up to Davenant and Killigrew by the agreement of 30 December, 1662, "with the full use and benefit thereof." Here the trickery is manifest: the reader is intended to suppose that Jolly had given up all his rights, and that the new (Legge) license was to supersede the old one. Moreover, it is evident that the new authority was obtained by further misrepresentation; for the document, after reciting the terms of Jolly's license, adds that of this "said warrant the said George Jolly had made noe use." This is a lie, inserted probably by Killigrew. The articles of agreement of

30 December had expressly said that Jolly "did for som tyme exercise *the* Authority thereby Given"; and the Lord Chamberlain's order already mentioned,[42] commanding Jolly and his company to cease acting for a time, is proof sufficient that Jolly *had* made use of his license.

At this point it is necessary to bring forth additional evidence to prove the charge of dishonest dealing on the part of Davenant and Killigrew. This is now at hand in a circumstantial complaint made much later by George Jolly, which categorically recites his grievances. It is strange that this document, which throws so much new light, has been unnoticed by historians of the stage. Written in the nervous language of the choleric Master George, it tells its own story:

Whereas by a Warrant Granted unto George Jolly Confirmed by his Sacred Majesty's hand and Privy Signett, the said George Jolly had full Power and Authority to Erect a Play house and Company of Actors, which ffor some Time he did Excercise. Now uppon an Agreemnt made betweene Mr Tho: Killegrew, Sr William Davenant, and the said George Jolly the afforesaid Warrant was Rented ffor 4 Pounds a week, and uppon the Nonpayment of the said 4 Pounds a Week the said Warrant to bee Resign'd into the hands of the aforesaid George Jolly againe, they the said Tho: Killegrew and Sr William Davenant, quitting all fformer Pretences to the same, Agreeing that he the said George Jolly should make use of itt ffor his owne Benefitt and Purpose, as he shoud [see] ffitt. In the meane time Mr Killegrew and Sir William Davenant unknown to the said George Jolly goe privatly to his Majesty, affirming that they had bought the Warrant, and desird his Majesty to give them a Pattent out of itt which his Sacred Majesty (beleiving it was as they said granted them) The said George Jolly according to Covenants went to demand his Money. They answerd that they coud pay it no longer but according to Covenant he must take the Warrant againe and make use of it as he did fformerly, which Accordingly the said George Jolly did, and after he had raisd a Company by Vertue of that Warrant, Mr Killegrew goes to my Lord Chamberlaine and getts a Warrant ffor the said George Jolly to Lay him by the Heeles if he durst Proceed any ffurther, saying they had a Pattent and the Warrant was no Longer Significant Whereas they were bound in a Bond of Two Thousand Pounds if they did not pay the said George Jolly according to Agreements to Lett him Proceed without Interruption. Whereuppon he the said George Jolly threatned to Complaine to the King and Privy Councell of theire unjust Dealings, They ffearing that Profferd the said George Jolly if hee woud raise a Company, build and Provide all necessaryes as a Deputie under them, he and his Actors shoud enjoy two Thirds and they one cleere to themselves; To which the said George Jolly being necessitated (not at all quitting his ffirst pretences), was fforst to Agree too————————

Articles being drawn it was Agreed that the said George Jolly shoud enjoy this Power ffor his Natural Life, and in Case they shoud take it ffrom him (giveing him a Months Warning) then to allow him Six and Eight-pence a Day every Day the Nursery shoud Play

Now Mr Killegrew since he hath beene Mr of the Revells has taken quite away all ffrom the said George Jolly, and denyes to Pay him the Money due by Covenant, Notwithstanding my Lady Davenants Concern in the Pattent, togeather with the Interest of the said George Jolly comes to more then Mr. Killegrews halfe, yett he still unjustly opposes the said George Jolly to the Ruine of himselfe his Wife & Children.

My Lady Davenant has wrott in the behalfe of the said George Jolly 3 or 4 Letters pleading his Cause, and Condemning the unjust Crueltyes of Mr Killegrew who will not suffer him to Play even at this Time when both the theatres Lye still, which were so ffarr ffrom mollifiing his Nature, that he the said Mr Killegrew has declard, his Designs are utterly to Ruine the said George Jolly————————

And which is worst of all Mr Killegrew has Inform'd his Majesty many untruths of the said George Jolly, hopeing thereby to Cloak his owne In-justice, and Incurr the displeasure of his Sacred Majesty uppon the said George Jolly. [43]

Although this extraordinary document is undated, the refer-ence to Lady Davenant's owning the patent shows that it came between Sir William's death, in 1668, and Charles Dave-nant's majority in 1677 or 1678. The mention of Killigrew as Master of the Revels further serves to limit the document to the period between 27 April, 1673, when Sir Henry Herbert died and Killigrew succeeded him in office,[44] and 24 February, 1676/7, when Killigrew resigned in favor of his son Charles. Jolly's complaint, then, came at some time after April, 1673, and before February, 1677.

There is little doubt that Jolly was here telling the truth. It is a pity, however, that he did not specify more exactly just when the various events he describes took place. We know when Davenant and Killigrew got the Legge patent by means of Jolly's warrant; but we cannot say with any certainty just when they defaulted on the four pounds a week and were forced to return the original warrant to Jolly. (It is to be noted that they had kept this grant even after obtaining the Legge patent "out of " it.)

All these new details make it necessary to outline afresh the story of Jolly's activities on the Restoration stage.

In the first place, we do not know how long Jolly's company remained on the road after it left London early in 1663. Presumably Davenant and Killigrew lived up to their bargain with Jolly until after they had secured the Legge patent at the end of March, 1664. When they then refused to pay, Jolly returned to London, received his warrant again at their hands, and set about raising a company. Probably he had begun to act when Killigrew, armed with a warrant from the Lord Chamberlain, tried to "Lay him by the Heeles." As we know from his history in Germany, Jolly was a difficult man to deal with in an altercation, especially when he thought that he had the right on his side. Undoubtedly there was a stormy scene. Jolly raged, threatened to complain to the King of Killigrew's double dealing, and boldly went on giving performances. Only by supposing that he continued successfully to act in defiance of Killigrew and the Lord Chamberlain's warrant, can we understand the reference by Chappuzeau (who visited London about the year 1665) to *three* theatres—the King's, the Duke's, "et une troisième en Drury Lane qui a grand abord." [45] This must be Jolly's company at the Cockpit, which therefore was playing up to the spring of 1665, when the pestilence closed all the playhouses. Undaunted by this period of enforced idleness, Jolly made a prompt and vigorous opening in the winter of 1666–1667, when the stage was again allowed. One can tell that he began promptly; for the stern order which Killigrew brought to bear on him already in March, 1667, reminds the victim of several earlier orders which he had evidently disregarded:

Whereas Wee are informed that by virtue of a Patent by Vs granted unto you, you are now presuming to sett up a Play-house notwithstanding that you have been severall times commanded the contrary, Wee have thought fitt hereby to require you forthwith to deliver Your sd Patent into the hands of one of Our Principal Secretaryes of State, there to remaine untill Our further Pleasure in this behalfe, whereof you may not faile as you will answer the contrary. Given Att Whitehall the [*blank*] day of March 1666/7 in the 19th year of our Reigne.

to GEORGE JOLLY   By his Ma*jesties* Command [46]

Jolly, however, defied even this peremptory command; and Killigrew was forced to go one step further. On 2 April, 1667, he obtained a royal order, signed by Secretary of State Arlington, which officially revoked Jolly's license: " . . . Wee have thought fitt to revoke, determine, & annull *our* sd Grant of the 24 dec to *th*e sd Joly as aforsd, & every part, pow*er*, & clause therein contained."[47] The reason for the harsh nature of these last orders appears when we recall that only by this time — 1667 — did Killigrew, using the Legge patent, set up his Nursery under Captain Edward Bedford [48] in Hatton Garden. Naturally he now wished all the more to force Jolly out. But Master George held on, and at least for a time defied the King's Jester. No doubt he relied more or less on Davenant, since we know from his complaint later that, after the knight's death, Lady Davenant was favorable to him. That there were two nurseries in 1667 seems to be implied in a passage recently discovered by Mr. W. J. Lawrence and kindly communicated to me. The passage in question is taken from the Prologue to John Dover's unacted tragedy, *The Roman Generalls*, licensed for printing 7 November, 1667:

> The Poet had design'd His Play should be
> Bestow'd on both the Houses *Nursery*.
> His modest Judgement deemed it most fit,
> In Nurseries to plant young twiggs of Wit.
> Thinking to shun a Public Censure, since
> They count ten people there an audience.

I confess that, on reading this passage, the first meaning that I took was that there was *one* nursery for "both the Houses." Mr. Lawrence, however, reads "*Nursery*" as an adjective in the inverted position — that is, "both the *Nursery* Houses." I am still uncertain as to Dover's meaning; but if in 1667 there *were* two of them, I agree with Mr. Lawrence in thinking that this state of affairs could not have lasted long. The existence of two nurseries at once runs flatly counter to the principle laid down in the Legge patent: one nursery only for two houses, and Jolly's permission to be revoked.

But Jolly was not the man to submit easily. He knew that

Killigrew and Davenant had cheated him and deceived the
King in obtaining the Legge patent for the nursery playhouse.
If he informed the King of the rights of the matter, an investigation might make the two managers very uncomfortable. His
stubbornness and tenacity forced the managers to take him
into their employ. As we have learned from Jolly's complaint,
articles were drawn by which he was to be deputy under Davenant and Killigrew. Jolly was to raise a nursery company,
provide a theatre, and have charge of the same all his life. In
return, he and his young actors (composing the nursery) were
to have two thirds of the income of the house. In case he were
replaced by another manager, he was to receive six and eight-
pence for each day the nursery played; which (counting six
performances to the week) amounts to a weekly salary of two
pounds.

This is the most important piece of information yet discovered concerning the history and constitution of the well-
known but shadowy institution called the Nursery. We now
know the terms upon which it was set up; and we know that its
manager was the famous George Jolly.

But since the Hatton Garden Nursery set up by Killigrew
and led by Captain Bedford continued on into 1668, Jolly must
have disbanded his company upon making the agreement
with Davenant and Killigrew, and accepted the six and eight-
pence per acting day in lieu of his right to act. We learn from
the Lord Chamberlain's books that Bedford was associated
with Jolly in money matters.[49]

Exactly when in 1668 the Nursery moved from Hatton Garden, it would be hard to tell. What evidence exists is clearly
given by Mr. Lawrence.[50] He points out that in 1667 Shirley's
Constant Maid was reprinted "as acted at the New Playhouse
called the Nursery in Hatton Garden." Furthermore,
Thomas's *Life of Jo Hayns* (published in 1701) says that Jo
began at the Nursery, and "acted under Captain Bedford
whilst the playhouse in Hatton Garden lasted." And on
7 March, 1667/8, Pepys reports Jo at the King's playhouse,
"only lately come hither from the Nursery."

At all events, we know that the Nursery, at least before 23 April, 1669, had removed to Gibbons's Tennis Court, Killigrew's old theatre in Vere Street, Lincoln's Inn Fields. For on that date Mrs. Samuel Pepys told her husband that "she spent all day yesterday with M. Batelier and her sweetheart, and seeing a play at the New Nursery, which is set up at the house in Lincoln's Inn Fields, which was formerly the King's house." We may presume that in November of this year Bedford left the Nursery, for we find him setting up a strolling company and receiving a license to act in the country under the name of the Duke of Monmouth's Company.[51]

His place as leader of the Nursery under Jolly was taken by John Perin. This fact appears from one of my Chancery bills,[52] just discovered, which also proves that the Nursery left Gibbons's Tennis Court about May, 1671. I summarize the bill as follows:

John Perin of St. James's, Clerkenwell, in April, 1671, desiring to build "a booth or playhouse," applied to Thomas Duckworth, a young carpenter of Deadman's Place, Southwark. On 13 April, Duckworth came to an agreement with Perin and his company to build upon "a certain piece of ground of the said Perin's situate in Finsbury Fields, commonly called Bun hill, one booth or playhouse: to contain in length threescore foot, and in breadth forty foot from out to out." Perin agreed to pay him £300 for it by instalments, and to keep it in repair. At the end of six years the ownership of the building should revert to Duckworth — or before, if any default of payment should be made. Perin occupied the playhouse as soon as it was ready. His company "acted several plays and so continued acting as often, at his and their pleasure, as they pleased for the space of nine weeks, and until some difference did happen between the said Jno. Perin and the Lady Davenant[53] and several of the actors which withdrew themselves. And the house standing empty and no acting being therein for the space of half a year," Perin fell into arrears with his payments. Just after Christmas, 1671, Duckworth proceeded to take down and carry away most of the timber of the playhouse, but "left standing [part] of the said booth, being a place separate and apart where the said Perin and his company used to lay their acting clothes and dresses, and also one part of the stage." The timber so left, valued at between four and five pounds, Duckworth avers he "left in the presence of the said Perin and several other of the said Perin's companions and friends amongst others who were spectators and then present." The carpenter complains that Perin and one Buckston are suing him for damages on pretended trover and conversion of "some of their play clothes or fopperies." He wants them enjoined and ordered to appear and answer for the money they owe him. What the result was, I cannot learn.

For nine weeks, then, in the summer of 1671 the Nursery in Bunhill played, until the defection of some of the young actors from Lady Davenant and Perin.

In the autumn of the year, in the midst of the adult company's anxious preparations for opening the magnificent and ruinously expensive new theatre in Dorset Garden, Lady Davenant found time to begin another playhouse for the theatrical nurslings in London. I learned of her activities as the result of a search in the Mayor's Court Repertories at Guildhall. The matter, I find, is first noted on 19 October, 1671, under the heading, "Playhouse erecting in Barbican": [54]

A Peticōn being now presented by the Inhabitants of the parish of St. Giles without Cripplegate, shewing that the Lady Davenant is in hand to erect a Playhouse in Barbican within the said parish, and that the same if it proceed to effect, will tend to the great evill & inconveniency of the said peticōners and the Citty in generall in diverse respects, as is therein more fully sett forth, And this Court vpon debate of the matter conceiving also that manyfold evills would ensue to the Citty from a Playhouse there or in any other place soe neere the Bowells of the Citty Doth order that a copy of the said peticōn bee sent to the Lady Davenant with the intimation that vnlesse shee shall appear and give satisfacōn vnto this Court touching this matter, they shall hold themselves concerned to vse all Lawfull meanes & endeavour to prevent & hinder the erecting of the said Playhouse.

Popular petition and mayor's intimation had no effect on Lady Davenant or on her building work; and on 16 November the court gave order

... that Mr Sheriffes doe with all convenient speed represent to his Majesty the great evills and inconveniencies that will arise to the Citty by the new Playhouse now preparing in Barbican, and make suit to his Majesty for his favour and command for suppressing the s^d Playhouse.[55]

This order of the mayor's court bears out the statement that Lacy puts into the mouth of Alderman Buffoon: "Poets and Players are never useful but when a King is crown'd, or a Lord Maior is chosen; and 't is the opinion of the Court of Aldermen, and I'll stand in it." [56]

The mayor's representations were taken to Charles, who answered with cool insolence that "playhouses should be pulled down when the meeting houses were" — the Catholic King's offer to give the Nonconformists a *quid pro quo*. Williamson, the Secretary of State, alarmed at some recent disorders in London, urged the King to abolish the new Nursery, together with the old structure standing a third of a mile to the northeast in Bunhill. His notes for a conference with Charles on 23 November run: [57]

> The Nursery in London.
> Pull down that and coffee houses, and nothing can be more to the establishment of the government.
> The City government is too lax already.
> If the two Nurseries in Barbican and Bunhill be not taken away in a year, expect a disorder. Advised to take them away now upon the putting down meeting houses.
> The Apprentices are already grown too heady.
> The King's answer to My Lord Mayor, That Playhouses should be pulled down when the Meeting houses were, had an ill interpretation, and has done disadvantage.

After reading these urgent notes of Williamson's, who can question the profound importance of the nursery in the history of London? In 1671 it presented, together with the coffeehouses, a source of the greatest danger to government.

A passage in the *Reliquiæ Baxterianæ* [58] runs:

> This Year [that is, 1671] a new Play-House being built in *Salisbury-Court* in *Fleet-Street*, called the *Duke of York's*, the Lord Mayor (as is said) desired of the King, that it might not be; the Youth of the City being already so corrupted by Sensual Pleasures; but he obtained not his desire.

I have found, however, no objection noted by the Lord Mayor in his books except the one against the Nursery. And since Baxter reports by hearsay — "(as is said)" — it seems likely that his informant had confused the two theatres, both erected in the same year.

The Nursery waxed and flourished in Barbican, in spite of the Lord Mayor of London and the Secretary of State; and here it continued for at least eleven years — until 1682, when it figured in Dryden's *MacFlecknoe*. After glancing at the ancient barbican or tower which gave its name to the street, and at the brothels which now occupy it, the poet goes on:

> Near these a Nursery erects its head,
> Where Queens are formed, and future Hero's bred;
> Where unfledged Actors learn to laugh and cry,
> Where infant Punks their tender voices try,
> And little *Maximins* the Gods defy.

It is necessary here to find an answer to the puzzling question of the site of this Nursery in Barbican, the longest lived of all the nursery theatres. The question leads back to a picture, published by Robert Wilkinson in 1819, of the decorated façade of a mysterious brewery.[59] Wilkinson declared that this brewery was the remnant of the old Fortune theatre: an assertion which he attempted to bolster by adding that there was a sloping gallery in the house, with degrees for seats. These circumstantial statements of Wilkinson's, together with the royal arms flanked by two statues which are displayed on the façade, were sufficient to take in not only the credulous theatrical amateur, but even men like Percy Fitzgerald [60] who passed for experts. Mr. W. J. Lawrence, however, saw at once that the house could not possibly be the Fortune, for, as he demonstrated, the latter was completely demolished shortly after the Restoration.[61]

So far, good; all agree now that Wilkinson's questionable brewery is not and never was the Fortune. But Mr. Lawrence goes further, and would identify the building with the Barbican Nursery.[62] This shot, it can be shown, is equally wide of the mark. Whatever the Wilkinson house may have been in

THE SITE OF THE NURSERY THEATRE IN BARBICAN

From *A Large and Accurate Map of the City of London by John Ogilby
Esqre . . . 1677.*

its younger days, it was certainly never Lady Davenant's nursery for little Maximins in Barbican. A glance at the map is enough to show that the brewery was not in Barbican at all, but a sixth of a mile away to the north, in Golden Lane. Barbican, it should be repeated, is neither parish, district, neighborhood, nor region, but a short and definite thoroughfare extending only from Redcross Street to Aldersgate Street. After all, in hunting for a Barbican nursery the natural course to pursue is to look in Barbican. This I have done, and found the playhouse and its approximate dimensions clearly indicated on Ogilby's familiar *Large and Accurate Map of the City of London*, 1677. Southward out of Barbican, about half-way down its length, runs a narrow alley which, after about 100 feet, broadens out into a courtyard, whose legend, "b66," is interpreted by the key as "Play-house Yard." At the southern end of this yard stands the Nursery playhouse, an irregular oblong, with a curious small projection built on its front wall. Its dimensions, to judge by the scale given, are 45 feet in width by 90 in length — considerably more than those of the Bunhill Nursery, which, it will be recalled, were 40 feet in width by 60 in length. Lady Davenant's Barbican Nursery, then, occupied less than half as much area as the Duke's Theatre in Dorset Garden; on the other hand, it was perhaps a little larger than the first Duke's Theatre in Lisle's Tennis Court. On the so-called Morden and Lea map of 1682, the yard out of Barbican is numbered 251, for which the key once more gives "Playhouse Yard." When I had reached this point in my search, I consulted Harben's *Dictionary of London*, page 477, *s. v.* "Playhouse Yard." I was referred to Strype (1720), I, iii, 93, who in that year also described the place as "Play House Yard, long, with old Buildings; so called, for that here was a Play House in former Days." But if we recall the King's retort to the objecting Lord Mayor, that "playhouses should be pulled down when the meeting houses were," the cream of the story comes when we consult Rocque's map (1746) and find the Barbican Playhouse Yard now renamed Black Horse Alley, and the Nursery theatre labeled "Annabaptist M[eeting House]." [63]

We do not know when the Nursery passed out of existence, but it was not many years after 1682. George Jolly, as we learned from his complaint, was in charge of it as late as 1673 and perhaps later. Who can tell whether Lady Davenant's efforts in his behalf and Jolly's own appeals had any effect on the hard-hearted Tom Killigrew? Or whether the veteran Master George was pensioned in his old age, or ruined?

For the sake of Jolly's reputation for skill and excellence in dramatic production, however, a further word must be said. Why is it, the reader will ask, if Jolly was a proficient manager, that Pepys alludes to the performances of the Nursery only with the greatest contempt? The answer must be that Jolly was for many years replaced as immediate head of the Nursery players by Bedford and Perin. But in any case the managers of the Nursery were hampered by poor material. They had to train novices; and as soon as any pupils showed ability, such were taken to fill the ranks of the regular companies. Furthermore, if the King's and Duke's companies were not any too prosperous, what is to be said of the Nursery, which was suffered to keep only two thirds of its own earnings? It is evident that Davenant and Killigrew made the Nursery contribute to the financial support of their theatres; at the same time, they kept it so poor in both money and good actors that it could never aspire to any rivalry.

Such an end, that of a wretched underling at the mercy of tyrannical Tom Killigrew, is a sad one for Jolly — for Master George Jolly, the last of the famous English strollers in Germany; the first man to introduce actresses to the stage of Frankfurt-am-Main; the first English manager to develop the operatic form (preceding Davenant by several years); and, finally, the actor who had played "before the crowned heads of Europe."

NOTES FOR CHAPTER IV

1 (168). See Chapter I, note 135.

2 (168). *The Kingdomes Weekly Intelligencer*, B. M., E432.6.

3 (168). E. Herz, *Englische Schauspieler und englisches Schauspiel zur Zeit Shakespeares in Deutschland*, 1903, p. 59.

4 (169). J. Wolter, "Chronologie des Theaters der Reichstadt Köln," in *Zeitschrift des bergischen Geschichtsvereins*, 1896, p. 100.

5 (169). *Ibid.*, p. 101.

6 (169). Herz, *op. cit.*, Karte V.

7 (169). E. Mentzel, in *Archiv für Frankfurts Geschichte und Kunst*, 1896, p. 185n.

8 (169). Cohn, in *Shakespeare-Jahrbuch*, xxi, 272.

9 (170). Theodor Hampe, *Die Entwicklung des Theaterwesens in Nürnberg*, 1900, p. 284.

10 (170). *Ibid.*, p. 282.

11 (170). *Ibid.*, pp. 281, 282.

12 (170). *Ibid.*

13 (170). E. Mentzel, *Geschichte der Schauspielkunst in Frankfurt*, 1882, p. 79.

14 (170). *Ibid.*, p. 74.

15 (171). Cohn, *Shakespeare in Germany*, 1865, p. cii.

16 (171). *Archiv für Frankfurts Geschichte und Kunst*, 1896, p. 186.

17 (171). "A Forgotten Restoration Playhouse," *Englische Studien*, xxxv, 282.

18 (172). *Cal. State Papers, Dom., 1655*, p. 325.

19 (172). *Nicholas Papers* (Camden Society), iii, 60.

20 (172). 11–18 Oct., 1655. B. M., E489.5. The italics are mine.

21 (172). Mentzel, *Geschichte*, p. 75.

22 (172). *Dramatische Dichtungen von Andreas Gryphius*, ed. Julius Tittmann, Leipzig, 1870.

23 (173). *Archiv für Geschichte und Alterthumskunde des Ober-Main-Kreises*, vol. i, pt. i, p. 74.

24 (173). *Geschichte*, pp. 78–89.

25 (176). *Shakespeare-Jahrbuch*, xlvi (1910), 128.

26 (176). *Englische Studien*, xxxv, 279.

27 (176). Herrig's *Archiv für das Studium der neueren Sprachen und Litteraturen*, 1914, p. 301.

28 (176). See the chapter on the Duke's Company.

29 (177). *Cal. State Papers, Dom., 1660–1661*, p. 319.

30 (177). State Papers, Dom., Charles II, xxiv, 37, Public Record Office.

31 (178). *Studien*, p. 284.

32 (178). Printed in the *Shakespeare Society's Papers*, iii (1847), 163.

33 (178). Herrig's *Archiv*, p. 302.

34 (178). See above, p. 114.

35 (178). B. M., MS. Sloane, 1900.

36 (179). In his transcription of this entry (*Gentleman's Magazine,* July, 1906, pp. 69 ff.) Dr. Greg reads "Quenes Players." I think his reading is erroneous.

37 (180). B. M., Additional Charters, 9297.

38 (182). State Papers, Domestic, Entry Book, xlviii, 6a, Public Record Office.

39 (182). Ibid., Entry Book, ix, 247.

40 (183). *Cal. State Papers, Dom., 1663–1664,* p. 214.

41 (183). Herrig's *Archiv,* p. 302.

42 (184). See above, p. 113.

43 (185). B. M., Add. MS. 34,729, fols. 124, 125.

44 (185). *Dictionary of National Biography,* xi, 114a.

45 (186). *Europe Vivante,* 1667. Quoted by Lawrence, *Studien,* p. 279.

46 (186). State Papers, Dom., Charles II, cxcv, 109.

47 (187). Ibid., lxxvii, 39.

48 (187). In 1678 Bedford commanded a company of 120 foot in the Country or Last Regiment in Middlesex under the Earl of Craven. *Cal. State Papers, Dom., 1678,* p. 440.

49 (188). Nicoll, *Restoration Drama,* p. 279.

50 (188). Herrig's *Archiv,* p. 308.

51 (189). Nicoll, *loc. cit.*

52 (189). No. 28.

53 (189). Sir William Davenant had died in 1668, and Lady Davenant now controlled the Duke's company.

54 (190). Mayor's Court Repertories, 76/293b.

55 (191). Ibid., 77/12.

56 (191). *Sir Hercules Buffoon,* Act IV, scene 2.

57 (191). State Papers Dom., Charles II, ccxciv, 64.

58 (191). 1696; pt. 3, p. 89.

59 (192). *Londina Illustrata,* ii, 141.

60 (192). *A New History of the English Stage,* i, 66.

61 (192). In Jan., 1662/3, there were "matters in difference between the inhabitants of the liberties of Golding Lane and Whitecross Street . . . touching several houses which are lately erected upon the piece of ground where the Fortune Playhouse formerly stood." *Middlesex Sessions Books, Cal. January 1656–July 1664,* p. 156.

62 (192). Herrig's *Archiv,* p. 314. Montague Summers (Buckingham's *Rehearsal,* 1914, p. 96), and Allardyce Nicoll (*Restoration Drama,* p. 280) also mistakenly locate the Nursery in Golden Lane.

63 (193). To-day the alley is called Jacob's Well Passage. Harben, p. 318.

CHAPTER V

THE DUKE'S COMPANY, 1660–1682

THE Stuart Restoration, far from bringing back the good old days of London's theatrical enterprise and multiple theatres, produced a monopoly restricting the legitimate theatres to two. This result, which placed the courtiers Will Davenant and Tom Killigrew at the head of the world of the stage, was not brought about, however, without a protracted and interesting struggle. In making their monopoly *de facto* as well as *de jure*, they had to contend, not only with the reluctance of the existing companies to be limited and managed, but with the vigorous opposition of Sir Henry Herbert, the Master of the Revels. Complicated and obscure though this story has been, I hope by means of new documents to disentangle some parts and to illustrate others.

First we shall go back to the early months of 1660. When the Restoration was in sight, the players fell into their old dangerous habit of acting too openly. We have several accounts of arrests and trials of actors.

Downes's famous story in *Roscius Anglicanus* [1] about the license that John Rhodes obtained for a company "from the then Governing State" (that is, Monk) is very doubtful, although Rhodes certainly had a company that acted at the Cockpit during Davenant's absence in France. As Professor Rollins has pointed out, [2] General Monk and his Council, influenced probably by the Presbyterians, issued an order on 23 April, prohibiting stage plays. [3] Furthermore, already on 4 February (the day of Monk's entry), Thomas Lilleston, who was one of Rhodes's chief actors, had been brought before the Middlesex Sessions, "charged by Gervis Jones to act a publique stage-play this present 4th of February in the Cock-Pitt in Drury Lane . . . contrary to the law." [4] He was released on £80 bail to appear at the next Sessions. Also, on

12 May, Anthony Turner (later of Rhodes's company) and
Edward Shatterell (later of Killigrew's) were ordered to appear to answer "for the unlawfull mainteining of Stage-playes
and enterludes att the Redd Bull in St. John's Street." [5]
There is a record that on 28 July, 1660, Rhodes, for illegal acting at the Cockpit, had to pay a fine of £4 6s., representing,
it is said, "2d. for every day the[y] play'd till the 28th of
July, 1660." [6] On dividing, we find that this fine covers a
period of 516 days — which is preposterous. It seems to me
that the ridiculously small "2d." is an error for "2s." Two
shillings fine per diem would bring the total down to 43 acting
days, a more credible period, in the spring of 1660.

Shortly after Davenant's return to England — no doubt in
the train of Charles II — there were at least three independent
companies acting in London. Rhodes had a young company
at the Cockpit; the old actors, of which Major Michael Mohun
was leader, were at the Red Bull; and another band occupied
Beeston's Salisbury Court.

Over these Sir Henry Herbert was energetically reasserting
the authority of the Office of the Revels, in abeyance for the
eighteen years of Interregnum. He claimed "the allowance
of plays, the ordering of players, and the permitting of playhouses" — powers which had belonged to the office, as he
said, "time out of mind." The last of these three he exercised
in authorizing William Beeston

to Continue and Constitute the said . . . house called Salisbury Court
Play house into a Play house . . . Provided that no persons be admitted
to act in the said Play house but such as shall be allowed by the Master of
his Majesties Office of the Revells.[7]

Further, we have it from Sir Henry that Beeston agreed to
pay him £4 a week when the company acted, and that Rhodes
promised a like sum. The Mohun company at the Red Bull
also made an agreement with Herbert, as will appear from
what follows.[8]

Meanwhile Davenant was not idle. Joining forces with
Thomas Killigrew, playwright, and Groom of His Majesty's
Bedchamber, the Poet Laureate resolved to gain a monopoly of

theatres by royal grant — to select, with Killigrew, two companies from among the best of the city's actors, and then to use the royal authority in suppressing all rivals.

Sir William already had in his possession an old patent which he had never used, by which Charles I in 1639 had granted him permission to erect a company and a theatre. Killigrew promptly obtained, on 9 July, 1660, an order for a royal warrant,[9] which, besides giving him similar authority to raise a company and a theatre, provided that his company and Davenant's should be the only ones allowed to play in London. Davenant was, of course, not content with his 1639 patent, and ten days after Killigrew had secured his warrant, Sir William with his own hand drafted a further order which incorporated the other two, and gave Killigrew and himself a joint monopoly. Since this document has never been reproduced, and the fact that it is written in Davenant's hand has been unknown until now, I append it here:

Our will and pleasure is that you prepare a Bill for our signature to passe our Great Seale of England, containing a Grant unto our trusty and well beloved Thomas Killegrew Esquire, one of the Groomes of our Bed chamber and Sir William Davenant Knight, to give them full power and authoritie to erect Two Companys of Players consisting respectively of such persons as they shall chuse and apoint, and to purchase or build and erect at their charge as they shall thinke fitt Two Houses or Theaters with all convenient Roomes and other necessaries therto appertaining for the representations of Tragedys, Comedys, Playes, Operas, and all other entertainments of that nature in such convenient places as shall be thought fit by the Surveyor of our Workes; and likewise to setle and establish such payments to be payed by those that shall resort to see the sayed Representations performed as either have bin accustomarily given and taken in the like kinde or as shall now be thought reasonable by them in regard of the great expences of scenes, musick and new decorations as have not bin formerly used, With further power to make such allowances out of that which they shall so receive to the Actors and other persons imployed in the sayed Representations in both Houses respectively as they shall thinke fit. The sayd Companys to be under the jurisdiction, government and authoritie of them the sayed Thomas Killegrew and Sir William D'avenant. And in regard of the extraordinary lisence that hath bin lately used in things of this Nature our pleasure is that there shall be no more places of Representations or Companys of Actors or Representers of sceanes in the Cittys of London or Westminster or in the liberties of them then the Two

to be now erected by virtue of this authoritie, but that all others shall be absolutely suppressed. And our further pleasure is that for the better in-abling of the sayed Thomas Killegrew and Sir William D'avenant to per-forme what Wee intend hereby that you add to the sayed Grant such other ~~and further beneficiall~~ [*sic*] Clauses ~~and Grants~~ [*sic*] as you shall thinke fitt.
                    July 19th 1660. [*in another hand*]

To our trusty and well beloved ⎫
Sir Jeffery Palmer Knight   ⎬   [*In Davenant's hand*]
Our Attorney Generall   ⎭

                [*Endorsed, not in Davenant's hand*]
    Playhouses Mr Kyllegrew & Sʳ Wᵐ Davenant.[10]

This draft by Davenant is probably the model for the sign-manual later delivered to Attorney-General Palmer. When the matter came before him, Palmer demurred at the plan of passing a royal grant establishing a monopoly of stage plays; but when Davenant and Killigrew complained to the King, the Attorney-General acquiesced. Here follows Palmer's holo-graph note to Charles, written on 12 August, 1660: [11]

May it please yoʳ Maᵗⁱᵉ: the humble repʳsentation wᶜʰ I made to yoʳ highnes concerning the provided grant to Mʳ Killegrewe & Sʳ Wᵐ Davenant was onelie that the matter was more proper for A tolleration; then A Grant under the greate Seale of England; and did not interpose any other ob-stacle; nor doe find cause to obiect against the twoo warrants they haue now produced.

                                G. PALMER
                                12° Aug. 1660.

Within ten days after this letter, on 21 August, the warrant for which Davenant had prepared the order passed the privy signet.[12] In addition to establishing a monopoly of dramatic productions, this grant also infringed upon the powers of the Master of the Revels. Censorship had been one of this officer's chief sources of revenue; but a clause in the warrant authorizes and commands "Thomas Killigrew and Sir William Daue-nant to peruse all playes that haue been formerly written, and to expunge all prophanenesse and scurrility from the same, before they be represented or acted."

An order, dated 20 August (the day before the passing of the above grant), containing instructions to city officials to sup-press the actors at the Red Bull, Cockpit, Salisbury Court, and other theatres, is calendared in the State Papers.[13] Ostensibly, this order is from the King. An examination, however, of the original paper shows that in reality it is a draft in Davenant's own handwriting. The fact that the paper bears no official signature, and is not included in the Entry Books, which recorded such orders, is proof enough that this is not the King's order, but *an order which Davenant hoped that the King would issue.* The document, which has never been reproduced hitherto, runs as follows:

Forasmuch as wee are advertis'd, that divers persons, and Companies have assembled, and doe dayly assemble themselves together at the Play-Houses called the Red-Bull, in St. Johns Street, the Cockpit in Drury Lane, and a certaine Play-House in Salisbury Court, and at other places within our City of London and County of Middlesex, without the least Colour of Authority, and doe there act, performe and shew in publique, Comedies, Tragedies, and other Entertainments of the Stage, therein publishing much prophaneness, scurrility, obsceneness, and other abuses tending to the great Scandall of Religion, corruption of Manners, and ill example of our loving subjects: for the future prevention, therefore, of these and such like abuses and enormities. Wee doe hereby command, impower, authorise, and stricktly enjoine, you, and every of you, from time to time, from and after the date of this our Warrant, to forwarne and forbid all and ev'ry such person and persons, Assemblies in Publique, such or any other Entertainments of the Stage. To desist and forbeare the performing, acting and shewing any Comedies, Tragedies, Operas by Recitative Musick, or any Representation by Dancing, or Scenes, or any Plays, or other Entertainments of the Stage whatsoever, uppon paine of our high displeasure, and such other penaltie as shall fall thereon, And wee doe hereby further command and authorise you, and every of you to suppresse, and disperse, and cause to be suppressed and dispersed all and every such Assemblies, Companies and meetings; and for the better effecting hereof, Wee doe hereby enjoine, authorise and command all Constables, and other Officers of the Peace, and such and so many of our loving Subjects (fit for that purpose) as to you or any Two of you shall seeme meet, to be ayding and assisting to you and every of you (upon sight hereof) for the performance of this our will and pleasure herein. And for the doeing hereof this shall be your sufficient Warrant. Given at our Palace of Whitehall this 20th day of August in the Twelfth yeare of our Reigne

To our trusty and well beloved

[*The following paragraph is written in another hand:*]

Sr Wm Wild Recorder of our Citty of London Sr Richard Browne Knt Alderman of Or said citty of London John Denham esqre Surveyor Generall of or Works Doctor Baber one

of Our Physitians in ordinary Thomas Babs, Robert Jegon William Glas-
cock Esq[rs]

[*Davenant's hand continues:*]
and all other our Justices of the
Peace, and others whom this may
concerne.[14]

It is interesting to see Davenant over-reaching himself in
his efforts to kill competition. He submitted his plan for suppressing the other players before his own monopoly had been
passed.

While the grant was pending, Herbert had entered a strong
protest, on 4 August, against the proposed monopoly, calling it
an "vniust surprize, and distructiue to the powers graunted"
to the Office of the Revels.[15]

But, although he could not drive Davenant and Killigrew
entirely from the ground they had won, Herbert was by no
means defeated. Before the passing of the monopoly on 21
August, he had asserted his authority over the three companies. The most important of these, the Mohun company,
acting at the Red Bull, came to terms with him on 14 August.
I transcribe the agreement from the record of a subsequent
lawsuit:

> Wee whose names are here vnderwritten doe hereby promise & Covenant
> to pay or cause to be paid vnto S[r] Henry Herbert Kn[t] Master of his Ma-
> *jestie*s office of the Revells or to his deputy or agent the sume of tenn pounds
> on Saterday next after the date hereof and what playes soever wee shall act
> for the future to pay or cause to be paid to the said S[r] Henry Herbert his
> deputy or agent for eu*e*ry new play forty shillings & for eu*e*ry reviued play
> twenty shillings as fees aunciently belonging to the Master of the Revells
> and wee doe hereby furthermore promise & Covenant to pay or cause to be
> paid fower pounds to the said Master of the Revells his deputy or agent on
> eu*e*ry Saterday successiuely next after the date hereof In witnes whereof
> wee haue herevnto set our hands & seals the fowerteenth day of August one
> thousand six hundred & sixty These Covenants are to be made good dureing
> the time of acting vnder the said master of the Revells Mic Mohun Rob[t]
> Shatarall Willm Cartwright Willm Wint*e*rshall Walt*e*r Clunn Charles
> Hart & Nich Burt [16]

That postscript — "to be made good during the time of acting
under the said Master of the Revels" — is a sign that the play-

ers were not sure of the permanence of Herbert's authority over them.

I think it is obvious that this agreement of 14 August is identical with the covenant of "the 11th of August" referred to by Herbert on 4 June and 11 July, 1662, which was recently thought to be not extant.[17]

The passing of Killigrew's and Davenant's joint grant on 21 August, and their consequent attempts to subjugate the players, threw the latter into an uncomfortable position. It was clearly impossible for them to serve two masters. What happened we now learn for the first time from a record in the Court of Common Pleas.[18] Here it appears that the Mohun company's agreement with Herbert lasted less than a month. But it will be more interesting to summarize the case as it was argued more than a year later before Sir Orlando Bridgeman, Lord Chief Justice of the Common Pleas.

Herbert brings suit against the seven contracting parties of the Mohun company to force them to keep their agreement of 14 August (already quoted), saying that between 14 August and 16 October (when he obtained the court's writ) the Mohun company acted thirty revived plays — ten before 10 September, and twenty after — for which they owe him £30: that they still owe the first £10 agreed on, and also £4 each for the seven Saturdays between 14 August and 16 October. These £30, £10, and £28 come to £68 which they have not paid. Herbert asks £300 damages.

Mohun and his men ask to have the agreement read into the record. They insist that they paid Herbert his £10 on 18 August, the Saturday after the agreement, and that they acted no revived plays between 14 August and 10 September — the period in which they acted under Herbert. They paid him £4 on each of the four Saturdays in this period, and on 10 September they ceased to act under him. Herbert denies the £10 payment and the alleged payments on 1 September and 8 September, protesting that they did not cease to act under him on 10 September.

At the trial, the jury found that the thirty plays were acted as Herbert alleged; but that the Mohun company *had* really paid him the £10 on 18 August, and £4 on both 1 September and 8 September. Herbert was adjudged to recover £48 against them.

We notice that there was no decision made as to the continued authority of the Master of the Revels over the company. Plainly, the actors had felt after 10 September that Herbert's authority was weakening, and so neglected to pay his fees. Furthermore, they were being worried by the attacks of the joint patentees. Davenant and Killigrew, not finding the Mohun company eager to submit to their newly acquired power, brought to bear their influence with the King.[19] The courtiers complained to Charles that the company charged exorbitant prices, gave scandalous plays, and acknowledged no authority.[20] By this means Killigrew got a royal warrant which suppressed their acting, until they entered on an agreement with the patentees "to act with woemen, a new theatre, and habitts according to [their] sceanes." Furthermore, a company made up of the best actors from the several troupes was chosen and united under the new patent as His Majesty's Comedians. In the words of a petition signed by Burt, Wintershall, Hart, and Shatterell, "according to your Majesties approbation, from all the companies we made election of one company." The fact of this amalgamation of the best actors as a new company under the patent was surmised by Lowe, who discovered among the Lord Chamberlain's papers a list [21] of His Majesty's Comedians which includes not only Mohun and his fellow actors,—Burt, Hart, Robert and Edward Shatterell, Cartwright, Clun, Wintershall, Lacy, Baxter, and Loveday,—but also Betterton and Kynaston from Rhodes's company.[22] This list is dated Saturday, 6 October, 1660. The royal warrant suppressing the actors until they agreed to this united company, then, must have been obtained by Killigrew before 6 October.

We come now to conclusive proof of this united company, which fills out the story in most satisfactory style. Again it is the record of a lawsuit which furnishes the new light — a suit brought by Sir Henry Herbert and Simon Thelwall against Killigrew and Davenant on 16 October, 1660,[23] and tried before a jury on 3 February, 1661/2. The plaintiffs, after setting forth the ancient powers of the Office of the Revels, accuse Killigrew and Davenant of scheming unjustly to hinder and disturb them in the exercise of their office, and to deprive them of the fees, vails, regards, profits, and advantages to that office belonging. Specifically they say (I paraphrase the Latin) that on 8 October, 1660, Killigrew and Davenant, of their own authority, set up a company of public actors of plays to the number of twenty persons, and have maintained the same so erected from that time to this, and have had publicly performed divers plays on each day from that to 16 October, 1660, and received divers sums of money arising therefrom, and converted and disposed the same to their own proper use and commodity.

This declaration explains many things. To begin with, it shows that the united company, entered as His Majesty's Comedians on Saturday, 6 October, began to act under the authority of the patentees on Monday, 8 October. On this same Monday, Herbert addressed a peremptory warrant to Rhodes:

> These are therefore in his Maiesties name to require you to attende mee concerning your Playhouse called the Cockpitt Playhouse in Drury Lane, And to bring with you such Authority As you haue for Errecting of the said house Into a Playhouse, at your perill. [24]

Mr. Nicoll is confused by this warrant, which, he says, inquires about Rhodes's "license to act" at the Cockpit — whereas another warrant shows that the Mohun company was also at the Cockpit on 13 October. But the explanation is simple. Herbert's warrant asks Rhodes, not about his license to act at the Cockpit, but about his authority (that is, as lessee) for making it a playhouse. It is clear now that the united company began acting under Davenant and Killigrew on Monday, 8 October, at the Cockpit, of which Rhodes was the lessee, and continued at least until 16 October. Meanwhile, as we have seen, Herbert tried to assert his authority, first over Rhodes the lessee, and on 13 October over the company of players, insisting that they lower their rates and bring him their old plays to be censored.[25] Failing in his attempt, he sued out a writ at common law against Killigrew and Davenant on 16 October, and another on the same day against the Mohun company.

A situation which forced so many of the minor actors out of employment, however, could not last long. The obvious solution — the forming of two companies as allowed by the joint monopoly granted on 21 August — was reached at the beginning of November. Killigrew took as his company the band of elder actors — Mohun, Hart, and the rest. From Monday, 5 November, to Wednesday, 7 November, they acted once more at the Red Bull. On Thursday he moved them to Gibbons's Tennis Court, which had been fitted up as a theatre in the old Elizabethan style. But I shall save the particular history of this company for the succeeding chapter, and follow here the doings of Davenant's (the Duke's) players.

Davenant chose the younger actors — Rhodes's former Cockpit company, who now acted at Salisbury Court. On Monday, 5 November, he came to an agreement with the leading members of the troupe, and with another actor, Henry Harris. The articles are tripartite: Davenant of the first part; the actors Thomas Betterton, Thomas Sheppey, Robert Nokes, James Nokes, Thomas Lovell, John Moseley, Cave Underhill, Robert Turner, and Thomas Lilleston of the second part; and Henry Harris of the third part. It is immediately noticeable that several of Rhodes's actors mentioned by Downes are not included. Kynaston, one of the most talented, had gone over to Killigrew's company. James Dixon and Edward Angel we know were later employed in Davenant's company. The omission of their names from the agreement shows either that they came in shortly after the date of the articles, or that they were hirelings and not actor-sharers. Two others not mentioned are the boy actresses, William Betterton, drowned shortly after, and one Floid.

By these articles it is agreed that:

1. Davenant hereby constitutes the actors into a company, to act in London or Westminster until he provides a new theatre with scenes.

2. Before they open in the new theatre they are to act at the Salisbury Court or elsewhere only on the following terms:

   (a) Net profits are to be divided into 14 shares, of which Davenant is to have four;

   (b) Betterton, James Nokes, and Sheppey are to be Davenant's deputies, to receive his shares and oversee the accounts;

   (c) A band of musicians is to be provided out of the gross receipts at not more than 30s. a day;

   (d) At one week's notice the company is to come to the new theatre, and join with Harris and the other actors and actresses that Davenant will provide.

3. Thereupon profits are to be divided into 15 shares; two are to go to Davenant for house-rent, building, and scene-frames, and another one for costumes, properties, and scenes.

   (a) The remaining 12 are to be divided into seven and five; seven to Davenant for maintaining the actresses of the company, and in consideration of his authority and his "pains and expenses"; and five to the actors; Harris is to have as great a share as any.

   (b) Receipts are to be by *ballatine*, or tickets sold for all doors and boxes.

   (c) Davenant is to provide three receivers or treasurers. Two or three of the company are to act as a control. Davenant is to have his seven shares nightly.

   (d) Davenant is to appoint half the door-keepers, the wardrobe-keeper, and the barber, who are to be paid out of the gross receipts.

   (e) On the death of any actor-sharer, Davenant is to appoint his successor. Hirelings also are to be appointed by Davenant.

   (f) Davenant is not to supply hats, feathers, gloves, shoes, etc., out of the money for costumes.

   (g) Killigrew is to have free box holding six persons.

   (h) Sharing actors are to be bound in £5000 (that is, £500 each) to keep these covenants.

   (i) Harris is to join on a week's notice and enter bond.

4. Davenant is to be sole "Master and Superior," or governor, of the company.

It is a pity that the various proportions of the sharing actors are not particularized. The only scrap of evidence on this head that I have found is a statement of Cave Underhill, who recalled in 1705 that his original portion of the five had been three quarters of one share.[26]

Under its new régime, the company began playing immediately at Salisbury Court, while Davenant pushed on his
preparations at Lisle's Tennis Court.[27]

The first play given at court after the Restoration was in the
nature of an entertainment offered by George Monk, Duke of
Albemarle, to their Majesties on Monday evening, 19 November. It was presented in the Cockpit at Whitehall, adjoining
the apartments of the Duke. Although Killigrew's company
was elected to act the play—Ben Jonson's *The Silent Woman*[28]
—Davenant wrote the prologue to the King.[29] It was a fine
moment for the actors when one of their number — Mohun,
Hart, or Burt — stepped forward to welcome the Stuart to his
own again, in the words of the Poet Laureate:

> *Greatest of Monarchs, welcome to this place*
> *Which* Majesty *so oft was wont to grace*
> *Before our Exile, to divert the Court,*
> *And ballance weighty Cares with harmless sport.*
> *This truth we can to our advantage say,*
> *They that would have no* KING, *would have no* Play:
> *The* Laurel *and the* Crown *together went,*
> *Had the same* Foes, *and the same* Banishment:
> *The Ghosts of your great Ancestors they fear'd,*
> *Who by the art of conjuring Poets rear'd,*
> *Our HARRIES & our EDWARDS long since dead*
> *Still on the Stage a march of Glory tread:*
> *Those Monuments of Fame (they thought) would stain*
> *And teach the People to despise their Reign:*
> *Nor durst they look into the Muses Well,*
> *Least the cleer Spring their ugliness should tell;*
> *Affrighted with the shadow of their Rage,*
> *They broke the Mirror of the times, the Stage;*
> *The Stage against them still maintain'd the War,*
> *When they debauch'd the* Pulpit *and the* Bar.
> *Though to be* Hypocrites,* *be our Praise alone,*
> *'Tis our peculiar boast that we were none.*
> *What er'e they taught, we practis'd what was true,*
> *And something we had learn'd of honor too,*
> *When by Your Danger, and our Duty prest,*
> *We acted in the Field, and not in Jest;*
> *Then for the* Cause *our Tyring-house they sack't,*

* ὑποκρῐτής, a player, actor.

And silenc't us that they alone might act;
And (to our shame) most dext'rously they do it,
Out-act the Players, and out-ly the Poet;
But all the other Arts appear'd so scarce,
Ours were the Moral Lectures, *theirs the* Farse:
This spacious Land their Theater *became,*
And they Grave Counsellors, *and* Lords *in Name;*
Which these Mechanicks Personate so ill
That ev'n the Oppressed with contempt they fill,
But when the Lyons dreadful skin they took,
They roar'd so loud that the whole Forrest shook;
The noise kept all the Neighborhood in awe,
Who thought 'twas the true Lyon by his Pawe.
If feigned Vertue could such Wonders do,
What may we not expect from this that's true!
But this Great Theme must serve another Age,
To fill our Story, and adorne our Stage.

A week after this triumphant evening, I find Sir William using his influence with Charles in an unworthy manner. It looks as if he were forcing himself into another man's position. John Ogilby had been Master of the Revels in Ireland, and managed the Werburgh Street theatre (the first in Ireland) from 1635 to 1641. The house had been ruined by the Civil Wars, and we know that Ogilby, just after the Restoration, was preparing to launch a new venture. But here is Davenant, obtaining on 26 November, 1660, the following royal warrant:

CHARLES R.

Right trusty and right well beloued Councello^{rs} We greet you well. Wheras We have thought fitt and convenient to allow in Our City of London such Publique Presentations of Tragedies and Comedies as have been formerly permitted by Our Royall Predeceso^{rs} for ye harmelesse Recreation & divertisement of such of Our owne Subjects or fforregners as shall be disposed to resort to them with a strick Injunction that all such Tragedies & Comedies as have been formerly or shall be hereafter presented shall be purged and freed from all obsenenesse and profanes & soe become instructive to Morality in Our people. And Wheras Sir William Dauenant Knight hath had a Pattent under ye broad Seale of England from our Royall ffather of blessed memory to erect a Theater in Our City of London and hath been lately authorized by Us to exercise the said priviledge Therefore Our will and pleasure is (being willing to allow ye same harmelesse recreations to Our Subjects in Ireland) that you forthwith cause a Pattent to be drawne & passed wherby the said Sir William Dauenant may be authorised to erect or provide a Theater in Our Citty of Dublyn, confirming ye said priviledge to him for his life and his heyres.

And wheras We have lately authorised Two Howses or Theaters and noe more to be erected in Our Citty of London, soe in consideraĉon of the expences necessary to that work We doe enjoyne that noe more Theaters or Play Houses be permitted in Our Citty of Dublyn then that One Theater or Play house to be erected or prouided by the said Sir William Dauenant. And Our further Will and pleasure is That by the said Pattent the said Sir William Dauenant shall enjoy the authority and office of Master of Revells of Ireland during his life with such priviledges annext unto it as you shall thinke fitt; for which this shall be your Warrant. Given at Our Court at Whitehall this 26th day of November in the Twelfe yeere of Our Reigne.

By his Majesties Command
[*signed*] EDW. NICHOLAS

Sir Wm Dauenant Mr of ye Revills in Ireland.[30]

On the face of it this seems conclusive enough; but I am glad to find that Davenant did not succeed. Ogilby petitioned the King, mentioning his former grant of office of Master of the Revels in Ireland from Strafford, "which after his great preparations and disbursements in building a new theatre, stocking and bringing over a company of actors and musicians, and settling them in Dublin, fell to utter ruin by the calamities of those times." He estimates his loss at £2000, and, "notwithstanding Sir William Davenet's [*sic*] pretences," prays for a grant of the office.[31]

Charles must have seen the rights of the case, for in March, 1661, Ogilby obtained his warrant for the office, and authority to set up a theatre wherein "to represent Comedies, Tragedies and Operas and other Interludes decent and not obnoxious," with "a Revocation of all Grants made to other under ye Signet or Sign Manual for representing anything of ye same or like nature." [32] This grant was confirmed as a patent under the broad seal on 8 May following.

Routed in his contest with Ogilby over the Irish stage, Davenant had better fortune in his battles with Sir Henry Herbert. This persevering official had by no means abandoned his efforts to dislodge the intruding courtiers, and in the next year and a half he tried repeatedly to substantiate his former powers in the courts of law.

In Trinity term, 1661, he filed a suit in London against Killigrew and Davenant for damages arising by their united company's acting from 8 to 16 October, 1660.[33] No trial or judgment is entered, but in the following Michaelmas term Herbert brought a similar suit in Westminster. As we have seen, this case was tried 3 February, 1661/2. Davenant and Killigrew were acquitted.[34] There was considerable delay, however, before the judges were ready to give their judgment. Finally, on 26 May, 1662, they awarded Killigrew and Davenant £25 and costs. Meanwhile, Herbert had brought another suit in London against Davenant alone, for maintaining a company from 16 October, 1660, to 23 October, 1661, when the writ was issued. This case did not come up for trial until Friday, 20 June, 1662; but when it did, the jury at London Guildhall found for Herbert, and awarded him £25 damages.[35]

The outcome of this suit elicited a protest from Davenant to the King, which is worth quoting entire.

To the King's most Sacred Majesty
The humble Petition of Sir William Davenant, Knight,
Sheweth,

That your Petitioner has bin molested by Sir Henry Harbert with severall prosecutions at Law.

That those prosecutions have not proceeded by your Petitioners default of not paying the said Henry Harbert his pretended Fees, (he never having sent for any to your Petitioner,) but because your Petitioner hath publiquely presented Plaies; notwithstanding he is authoriz'd therevnto by Pattent from your Majesties most royall Father, and by severall Warrants vnder your Majesties royal hand and signet.

That your Petitioner (to prevent being out Lawd) has bin enforc'd to answer him in Two Tryals at Law, in one of which, at Westminster, your Petitioner hath had a Verdict against him, where it was declar'd that he hath no Jurisdiction over any Plaiers, nor any right to demand Fees of them. In the other, (by a London Jury,) the master of Revels was allow'd the correction of Plaies, and Fees for soe doeing; but not to give Plaiers any licence or authoritie to play, it being prov'd that no Plaiers were ever authoriz'd in London or Westminster, to play by the Commession of the Master of Revels, but by authoritie immediately from the Crowne. Neither was the proportion of Fees then determind, or made certaine; because severall witnesses affirm'd that Variety of paymentes had bin made; sometimes of a Noble, sometimes of Twenty, and afterwards of Forty shillings, for correcting a new Play; and that it was the custome to pay nothing for supervising reviv'd Plaies.

That without any authoritie given him by that last Verdict, he sent the day after the tryall a prohibition under his hand and seale (directed to the Plaiers in Litle Lincolnes Inn fields) to forbid them to act Plaies any more.

Therefore your Petitioner humbly praies that your Majesty will graciously please (Two Verdicts having pass'd at Common Law contradicting each other) to referre the Case to the examination of such honourable persons as may certify your Majesty of the just authoritie of the Master of Revells, that so his Fees, (if any be due to him) may be made certaine, to prevent extorsion; and time prescrib'd how long he shall keep plaies in his hands, in pretence of correcting them; and whether he can demand Fees for reviv'd Plaies; and lastly, how long Plaies may be layd asyde, ere he shall judge them to be reviv'd.

And your Petitioner (as in duty bound) shall ever pray, &c.[36]

Charles referred this petition, on 30 June, to the Chancellor and the Chamberlain. The former set 9 July for a hearing of the case. In the meantime, Herbert tried again to suppress the Duke's company. Already on 6 May he had obtained a writ against Betterton, to sue him for wrongfully acting "10 new and 100 revived" stage plays between 5 November, 1660, and 6 May, 1662.[37]

And now, on 4 July, it seems that Herbert sent Edward Thomas, one of the messengers of the Office of the Revels, with a warrant to stop their playing, and that Betterton and his fellows, annoyed by such treatment, took some pains to persuade him not to come again. For I find that on 18 July, 1662, a Middlesex jury brought in a true bill that on 4 July Thomas Betterton, James Nokes, Robert Nokes, Robert Turner, Thomas Lilleston, Matthew Medburne, Cave Underhill, Samuel Sandford, James Dixon, Joseph Price, Henry Harris, and Francis Pavy, all twelve late of St. Clement's Danes, gentlemen, with divers unknown disturbers of the peace, riotously assembled together and assaulted Edward Thomas, gentleman, and beat and maltreated him, and held him their prisoner for the space of two hours. Each of the twelve riotous gentlemen confessed the indictment, and was fined three shillings and fourpence.[38]

While we do not know the decision of the Chancellor in the Davenant–Herbert case, it is practically certain that the end was a compromise: Herbert had to relinquish his claim to the power of allowing theatres and companies, and Davenant had to pay him his play-licensing fees regularly. The fact that Herbert's suit against Betterton (entered for Michaelmas term, 1662) never came to trial indicates that by that time a settlement had been found. We shall see from the next chapter that Killigrew came to terms with the Master of the Revels somewhat sooner than Davenant.

The list of Duke's players given above is instructive for comparison with the rosters provided by Downes. The old prompter says that when Davenant opened his new theatre in Lisle's Tennis Court — which, as we know from Pepys, was late in June, 1661 — he completed his company by adding Harris, Price, Richards, and Blagden. The first two appear among the "riotous gentlemen" just mentioned. Richards about this time, as we learn from a warrant in Davenant's handwriting, signed by Secretary Nicholas, and dated 6 August, 1662, was lured away for a time from the Duke's company to Ogilby's Dublin theatre.[39] Blagden, who before November, 1662, had gone over to the King's company,[40] was not implicated in the riot. Downes tell us that another five actors — Smith, Sandford, Medburne, Young, and Norris — "came not in till almost a Year after they begun." Of these, Sandford and Medburne were among the gentlemen who maltreated the messenger of the Revels. The inclusion of Francis Pavy's name is interesting, as he is not spoken of by Downes, and the earliest mention of him seems to be in the list of James II's royal comedians for 12 January, 1687/8, discovered by Professor Nicoll.[41]

As we have seen, besides the two companies of Davenant and Killigrew, Jolly's was the only other company in the early years of the Restoration licensed to play in London and Westminster. What happened, it may be asked, to Beeston and Rhodes, the other two managers who had set up companies at the Restoration? Beeston for a time tried to act without authority. One warrant was issued for his arrest on this score on

29 August, 1663,[42] and another on 7 September, 1664. He must soon have capitulated, for Downes included him among those who came to Killigrew's company after the opening of the Theatre Royal in Bridges Street.

As for Rhodes, Professor Nicoll thinks that, after giving up his first company to Davenant, he set up and maintained a separate company in London up to the end of 1662. Mr. Nicoll's ground for this opinion is a warrant from the Lord Chamberlain to pay "vnto John Rhodes the sum*me* of Twenty pounds for acting of the play called Ignoramus or the Accademicall Lawyer at Court before his Ma*jes*tie the first of November 1662."[43] But evidence is now at hand to show that the company which gave this performance was not a new company collected by Rhodes, but the regular Duke's players. Rhodes must have been Davenant's deputy in the matter. I find the following notes of the performance among the manuscripts of the Marquis of Westminster:

Ignoramus, or the Academical Lawyer, acted at the Cockpit in Drury Lane, and also before the King and Queen's Majesty at Whitehall on Saturday night, 1 Nov. 1662, with great applause, paraphrastically from the Academic to the English Theatre, by Ferdinando Parkhurst, Φιλοδικαιολογος.

The Names of the Actors

Mr. Lillist[on]	Theodorus	An ancient Gentleman.
Mr. Smyth	Antonius	His son, in love with Rosabella.
Mr. Underhill	Ignoramus	An English Lawyer.
Williams	Dulman	
Will	Pecus	Ignoramus's three clerks.
R. Nokes	Musæus	
Mr. Norris	Torcal [that is, Torcol]	A Portugal and pander.
Mr[s]. Jennings	Rosabella	A young gentlewoman.
Mrs. Margaret	Surda	An old deaf woman.
Mr. Medb[urne]	Trico	Servant to Theodorus.
Mr. Crosby	Banacar	A black Moor boy.
[Mr.] Sandford	Cupes	A belly flatterer.
Mrs. Norris	Polla	Wife to Cupes, a shrew.
R. [that is, J.] Nokes	Cola	A fryer.
Mr. Angell	Pyropus	A phanatick broker.
Mrs. Brown	Dorothea	Wife to Theodorus.

Boy	Vince	Page to Dorothea.
Pegg	Nell	Her waiting maid.
Revet	Richard[us]	Servant to Theodorus.

A victualler.
A fidler.
Mutes.

Scene, Burdeaux.

A prologue to the King, spoken by Alexander Read, alludes to James I. having heard the play.

There are two copies of close [translation] and one copy of the paraphrastical translation. (Hawkins, in his preface to his edition of *Ignoramus*, does not mention this translation by Parkhurst).[44]

It is to be noted that this "paraphrastical" translation by Ferdinando Parkhurst of Ruggle's famous play has not been known to scholars,[45] and is of course not identical with the translation by "R. C.," attributed to Robert Codrington.[46] Although Betterton had no part in this performance, most of the other actors are mentioned. Cave Underhill, later famous as the First Gravedigger in *Hamlet*, took the title rôle. "Williams," who played Dulman, cannot be identical with Joseph Williams, Harris's boy, as the latter was not born until 1663. Robert Nokes, of whom our knowledge is very scanty, appeared as Musæus, the serious representative of the arts (who in Ruggle's comedy is remarkable for speaking good Latin). His brother, the great comedian James Nokes (here mistakenly also listed as "R." Nokes), — destined to fame in such parts as Sir Nicholas Cully, Sir Arthur Addle, and Sir David Dunce, — is down for Cola, the loose friar. Angel, another brilliant comic, appears as Pyropus, evidently a satire on the Puritan tradesman. And Sandford, who "acted strongly with his Face, — and (as King *Charles* said) was the best *Villain* in the World," walked on in the repulsive character of Cupes, the book-vending parasite. The beautiful Mrs. Jennings played the heroine to William Smith's Antonius, and Mrs. Norris, the mother of "Jubilee Dicky" Norris, was the shrew. Revet and Crosby had unimportant characters. Our only other knowledge of the former of these two is the negligible play he wrote, called *The Town-Shifts* (1671). Downes tells us (page 31) that

Crosby was taken into the company about 1670. As for Williams, Will, Mrs. Margaret, Mrs. Brown, Boy, and Pegg, I confess to ignorance. And who was Alexander Read, who gave the prologue? Certainly not old "Reed of the Friers." [47]

Besides Mrs. Jennings and Mrs. Norris, Downes mentions six other "Women Actresses," — Mrs. Davenport, Mrs. Saunderson (later Betterton), Mrs. Davies, Mrs. Long, Mrs. Ann Gibbs (later Shadwell), and Mrs. Holden, — the first four of whom Sir William boarded at his lodgings adjoining the Lincoln's Inn Fields Theatre.

To return to Rhodes, no one has yet shown that he had a company in London after the erection of the short-lived united company under the joint patentees on 6 October, 1660. The question of strolling companies, however, is a different matter. Rhodes received a license on 2 January, 1663/4, to take a company into the country, a troupe which, as Professor Nicoll suggests, was probably the one styled the Duchess of Portsmouth's Servants. Bedford, as we have seen, after giving up the Nursery under Jolly, on 25 November, 1669, also received a license for a strolling company called the Duke of Monmouth's Company.[48]

As a consequence of all this new light, Nicoll's estimate of the number of companies in London as three until July, 1660, four or five in 1660 and 1661, and three or four until the end of 1662, will have to be pared down. We must keep clearly in mind that the only London theatres licensed by the King were two for the patentees in July, 1660, and one for George Jolly in December, 1660. The Legge Nursery patent was intended by the patentees to supplant Jolly, not to add to the number of licensed theatres; but, as we have seen, their attempt to cheat Jolly was not wholly successful. Looking over the history again, I find in the summer of 1660 three companies — Mohun's, Beeston's, and Rhodes's. These were suppressed, and one company was chosen on 6 October, 1660. On 5 November we have the division into two separate companies — Davenant's (Rhodes's) and Killigrew's (Mohun's). Beeston, although not licensed, may possibly have found means to act from time to time. Jolly, however, appearing with a royal warrant, hired at first the Cockpit and then Beeston's Salisbury Court Theatre in the summer or autumn of 1661, for his players. Thus in the winter of 1660 and all through 1661 and 1662 we have three — and a highly problematical fourth in Beeston. The latter gave up his independent efforts in 1664 and joined Killigrew's company. The struggle over the Nursery license was not ended until 1667. It is just possible that there were two nurseries in that year, one under Jolly for Davenant's company, and one under Bedford for Killigrew's. But if two did exist simultaneously, they were shortly afterwards reduced again to one. At no time, then, were there more than three regular theatres, with the exception of Beeston's illegal and sporadic attempts before 1664. On 16 May, 1661, Davenant had received an exemplification of the patent granted to him by Charles I in 1639. For this new theatrical monopoly with Killigrew, however, he needed a new and specific grant. While Killigrew's particular patent passed the great seal on 25 April, 1662, Davenant's was issued nine months later.[49] The knight had more trouble in procuring the passing of his. First he had to obtain a sign-manual warrant for a separate license, which warrant was granted on 14 August, 1662;[50] the license itself passed the privy seal in November following,[51] and in December the patent was ordered [52] and marked "Imediate," whereupon followed the ultimate issue of his patent on 15 January, 1663.[53]

Reciting the former patent and exemplification, both of which are now surrendered, the King grants Davenant authority as follows:

1. To build a theatre and set up and govern a company to be called the Duke of York's players.

2. To receive customary prices for admission, or such as shall be "reasonable in regard of the great expense of scenes, music and such new decorations as have not formerly been used."

3. To pay actors and persons employed as he shall see fit, and to be sole governor: "All scandalous and mutinous persons shall from time to time be ejected, and disabled from playing in the said theatre."

Being informed that divers unauthorized companies are presuming to play publicly in London and Westminster, the King declares "his dislike of the same," and his will that the only two companies shall be those under Davenant and Killigrew; others to be suppressed.

No actor ejected from or deserting one company shall be received by the other, without the consent of the governor of the former company.

Plays formerly acted contained obscene and scurrilous passages, and women's parts have been acted by men, which has given offense. To prevent these abuses, plays shall be purged by the governors of offensive passages, and women shall be allowed to perform women's parts, to the end that plays may "be esteemed not only harmless delights, but useful and instructive representations of human life."

This patent and Killigrew's formed the basis of the principle of monopoly which was saddled on the London theatrical world for nearly two centuries.

Not long after the granting of his definitive license, Sir William Davenant took occasion to express his thanks in heroic couplets and to congratulate Charles on his patronage of the theatre. In phrases of courtly compliment the knight insists that not only the ingenious development of movable scenery, — through which the Restoration theatre far surpasses that of the ancients, — but also the reformation of morals on the stage was brought to pass by the King himself:

> The *Theatre* (the Poets Magick-Glass
> In which the Dead in vision by us pass;
> Where what the *Great* have done we do again,
> But with less loss of time and lesser pain)
> Is in the *Scene* so various now become,
> That the *Dramatick* Plots of *Greece*, and *Rome*,
> Compar'd to ours, do from their height decline,
> And shrink in all the compass of design.
> Where Poets did large Palaces intend,
> The spacious purpose narrowly did end
> In Houses, where great Monarchs had no more
> Removes then Two low Rooms upon a Floor:
> Whose *thorow lights* were so transparent made,
> That Expectation (which should be delai'd
> And kept a while from being satisfi'd)
> Saw, on a sodain, all that *Art* should hide;
> Whilst at the plain contrivance all did grieve;
> For it was there no *trespass* to *deceive*.
>   If we the antient *Drama* have refin'd,
> Yet no *intrigues*, like Lab'rinths, are design'd,

In Counterturns so subtle as but few,
When entred, can get forth without a Clue:
Where Expectation may *intangled* be,
But not so long, as never to *get free:*
Where *Love* throughout the *Character* does last;
And such unblemish'd love as all the chaste
May still endure with publick confidence,
And not at *vanquish'd Beauty* take offence;
Where *Valour* we so possible express,
That we should wrong the *Great* to make it less.
   If to reform the publick Mirrour (where
The Dead, to teach their living Race, appear)
May to the People useful prove, even this
(Which but the object of your leisure is
To respite Care, and which successivelie
Three of our last wise Monarchs wish'd to see,
And in a Century could not be wrought)
You, in Three years, have to perfection brought.
If 'tis to height of Art and Virtue grown,
The form and matter is as much your own
As is your Tribute with your Image coin'd:
You made the Art, the Virtue *You* enjoyn'd.[54]

Whatever the poet may have meant by the reformation of morals, whether public or private, by the libertine Charles Stuart, he had reason to be proud of the development of the art of the stage in his theatre, of which he proved to be a most capable and energetic manager. Unlike Killigrew, he lived at his theatre and governed in his own person until his death.

In order, however, to launch his theatrical project, which was to specialize in the new and expensive operatic form, he had to raise funds. To this end he began to sell off some of the ten shares allotted to him by the articles of 5 November, 1660. These brought £600, £700, or even £800 each, depending on the prosperity of the theatre at the time of sale. Weekly income from a share amounted as a rule to about £2 15s., or £3. Counting approximately 33 weeks to the year, this was an annual return on investment of from 11 to 16 per cent. Although this seems very good, the risks were great. There was always the chance of plague, the scourge which actually drove the theatres to close their doors in 1665 and 1666, and cost the

players and "adventurers" dear. Fire and embezzlement
were grave dangers. The Theatre Royal in Bridges Street was
burned in 1672, and in 1693 Alexander Davenant decamped
after defrauding the shareholders right and left. As a consequence of conditions such as these, investment in those days
was far more speculative than it is to-day.

To borrow the words of Skipwith and Rich in 1694, Sir William Davenant,

> ... Immediately after the King granted him his Patent not knowing other-
> wise how to carry on the Charge of Acting without great summs of Money
> to buy Apparell Habitts & propertys Machins & other decorations sold out
> to the Honorable Mr. Ashburnham late Cofferer of his Majesties Hous-
> hould the Honnorable John Harvey Esqr. the Lord Lonnolly [read Lum-
> ley] & severall other persons diverse parts & shares in the proffitts thereof. [55]

Just who these persons were, their proportions, and the dates
of sale, I have succeeded in finding out after sifting a large
number of Chancery records.

The first sales took place on 7 March, 1660/1, when Sir William sold a half-share to Richard Alchorne, Esq., of Crows-
hurst, Sussex,[56] and a whole share for £600 to Sir William
Russell, Bart., of Strensham, Worcestershire.[57] In the sale of
this share a special agreement was made that "the charges of
habitts and scaenes for the two first representations and of
fitting and preparing of the said theatre and the rent to be
payd for the same for the first yeare is to be soly defrayed by
the said Sr. William Davenant, and the said Sr. William Russell . . . to be quitt therof." On the eighteenth day of the
same month Davenant set over another half-share to Russell
in trust for Olive, the widow of his old friend and patron Endimion Porter.[58] In June, 1661, the month which saw the opening of Davenant's new theatre with scenes, in Lisle's Tennis
Court, the knight made several further sales to meet his heavy
expenses — three on Thursday, 6 June: a half-share to Robert
Garter,[59] another half-share to Richard, Viscount Lumley[60]
(mentioned above), and a third to Richard Cheston.[61]

The original selling prices of these half-shares are unfortunately not given. To George Porter, Endimion's eldest son,

Davenant sold a half-share on 21 June.[62] Three months later (16 September) William Ashburnham, His Majesty's Cofferer, bought a 1000-year interest in another whole share.[63] Also, we learn that at some period before Davenant's death Ashburnham purchased a life-interest in another share and two tenths, concerning which more later. On 13 June, 1662, for £700, the knight made over a 1000-year interest in a whole share to "Richard Bayly of Gray's Inn, Esq." Finally, Abraham Cowley, the poet and dramatist, had, I find, a half-share from Davenant. Years later, in 1687, Davenant's son Alexander tried to make it appear that Cowley's tenure of the half-share was in return for services done and for his life only; but the fact that Cowley's heirs had since been regularly receiving profits on account of it shows that Alexander Davenant was fabricating a specious tale. Still, his representations are of interest as to the part that Cowley played in Davenant's enterprise:

. . . the said Abraham Cowley being an Ingenious Man And well skilled in Poetry And A familiar Acquaintance with the said Sir William Davenant, [the latter] did take his Assistance & Judgment in Writing Correcting & providing Tragedies Comedies And other Poetic Entertainments for the stage; And in recompense for the said Mr. Cowley's pains therein did voluntarily permit and suffer him the said Mr. Cowley or such as he appointed (but only at the Will of him the said Sir William Davenant) to take such half share of the profits of the said stage during the life of the said Sir William Davenant.

Alexander, in a passage immediately following this, makes Cowley survive Sir William, a glaring misstatement which does not strengthen one's confidence in his veracity.

Some of these shares, of course, changed hands more than once in the space of a few years. But although a few such transactions escape me, the outlines are clear enough.

First, we have it on the evidence of Thomas Cross [64] that the knight at his death owned "Three fifths of Five shares and a half" — or, expressed decimally, 3.3 shares. Now, the sales enumerated above amount to 7.7 shares; and since Davenant had only ten to begin with, it is clear that one share must have reverted to him before his death, either by purchase or by some

other means. Which this was is uncertain, but I suspect that
it was Russell's whole share. However that may be, the 3.3
proportion as the legacy left by Davenant is corroborated by a
1674 list of builders' or renters' shares furnished by Harris.[65]
We must also bear in mind the 1.2 shares made over to Ashburnham for life, which therefore reverted to the Davenant
estate on the former's death in 1679.

Sir William, as I have said, managed his theatre himself,
and made of it a very good property for his family. The
shares increased in value, and after his death were said to be
worth £800 apiece. We have already seen that two of the
stepsons were given employment as "hirelings" about the
theatre: Thomas Cross, the eldest, as treasurer, and Philip
Cademan, the youngest, as actor. Davenant's numerous male
offspring by his last wife, Mary, were not yet old enough for
such occupations. Cross, who served as treasurer from the
theatre's inception to 1675, in the following words describes
his duties:

... delivering out Tickets to his fellow Treasurers (who had an equal power
with this Defendant both in Receipts of money, payment of charges, and
making up the Charge of the Theatre), and then to receive the Tickets in
again from all the Doorkeepers of the Pit, Galleries, and Boxkeepers'
moneys, as also making up the whole Receipts and expenses of the day,
comparing the number of Tickets with the money brought in, wherein the
Company had always a check upon this Defendant, and they might and
did almost daily view and examine this Defendant's Accounts, which one
or other of them did or might have done when they pleased; And also this
Defendant had the sole trouble of paying the whole charge of the House
weekly, that is to say, the Salaries of all hireling Players both men and
Women, Music Masters, Dancing Masters, Scene men, Barbers, Ward-
robekeepers, Doorkeepers, and Soldiers, besides Bills of all kinds, as for
Scenes, Habits, Properties, Candles, Oil, and other things, and in making
and paying (if called for) all the Dividends of the Sharers, dividing each
man his particular share according to his proportion, and often in the crowd
of this Defendant's [business], and all this done by this Defendant without
having any Receipts from any of the Company, or any of the Hirelings or
any others belonging to the Company for any one Sum paid them by this
Defendant. And also this Defendant had the paying the sharers of the Ten
Shares (being the Assignees of the said Sir William Davenant) who came
or sent for their moneys when they pleased, having free access by themselves, servants, or Agents, to the Books of Accounts of all the Receipts

and disbursements of the foregoing week with the several Dividends, this Defendant being ever ready when required to Satisfy them in every particular, and to deliver them their shares at every week's end. . . . [And for his labors] he did receive, for such weeks only as they acted, after the rate of Twenty Five Shillings *per* week; and some time after [Sir William's] decease was by the said Company advanced to Thirty shillings, in consideration (as he conceives) of his great pains and care, and no more.[66]

The orderly course of business, both dramatic and financial, at the Duke's playhouse was broken in April, 1668, by the death of its founder.

The passing of Sir William Davenant, who was not only the patentee but the master and moving spirit of the enterprise, marked an epoch in stage history. Through him more than any other the Restoration theatre was linked to its Elizabethan forerunner, and to the music, scenes, and machinery of the Caroline court masques. Flecknoe, amid the raillery of his squib on the departed poet, entitled *Sᵣ William D'avenant's Voyage To The Other World*,[67] inserts the following pregnant lines:

> *Now* Davenant's *dead, the Stage will mourn,*
> *And all to Barbarism turn:*
> *Since He it was this later Age,*
> *Who chiefly civiliz'd the Stage.*
>
> *Great was his Wit, his Fancy great,*
> *As e're was any Poets yet:*
> *And more Advantage none e're made*
> *O' th' Wit and Fancy which he had.*
>
> *Not onely* Dedalus *Art he knew,*
> *But even* Promethius's *too:*
> *And living Machins made of Men,*
> *As well as dead ones, for the Scene.*
>
> *And if the Stage, or Theatre be*
> *A little World, 'twas chiefly he,*
> *That* Atlas-*like supported it,*
> *By force of Industry and Wit.*
>
> *All this, and more, he did beside,*
> *Which having perfected, he dy'd:*
> *If he may properly be said*
> *To dy, whose Fame will ne'er be dead.*

Flecknoe represents the foregoing "Elogium" as the work of a poet "more Humane than the rest" — none of whom would afford Davenant's memory "so much as an Elegie; whether because he sought to make a Monopoly of the Art, or strove to become Rich in spight of Minerva." One other versifier, however, twelve days after the poet's death, published the following eulogy of Davenant as a folio-broadside: [68]

AN ELEGY / Upon the Death of / Sʳ WILLIAM DAVENANT

If those Great Heroes of the Stage, whose Wit
Swells to a wonder here, shall think it fit,
When Poet Lawreat's dead, that he should ly
Twelve days, or more, without an Elegie:
I that am less presume to undertake,
A short Memorial for their Credits sake.

Death in the shape of a thin Poet's come,
To summon *Davenant* to Elyzium:
Sent for by strict Express, for to appear
Upon the Stage of *Tempe*'s theatre.
His Voice compleats the Chorus among those
Who sing the Numbers they themselves compose.
 Now *Davenant* is arriv'd, the Fields and Plains
Resound unto his Welcome, Lofty Strains.
For every Poet there it shall be free
To raise his Joy unto an Extasie.
 Imagine him encircled in a Sphere
Of those Great Souls who once admir'd him here:
First, *Johnson* doth demand a share in him,
For both their Muses w[hip']d the Vice of time:
Then *Shakespear* next a brothers part doth claim,
Because their quick inventions were the same.
Beaumont and *Fletcher* their Petitions joyn,
This, for clear Style, that, for his deep Design:
Tom Randolph asks a Portion 'mongst the rest,
Because they both were apt to break a Jest.
Shirley and *Massinger* comes in for shares,
For that his Language was refin'd as theirs:
Laborious *Heywood*, witty *Brome*, and *Rowley*,
The learned *Chapman*, and ingenious *Cowley*,

Ask their proportions as they've gain'd applause,
By well observing the Drammatick Laws:
Last, Sir *John Sucklin* saith his Title lies,
Because they both (were Knights, and) writ concise.
    Thus the Experienc'd *Davenant* did ingross
A Soul of Wit divided among those,
Whose pregnant Muses have, from age to age,
Fix'd swelling Glories on the English Stage.
A Mirrour of the World, that it might see
Virtues sweet looks, Vices deformity.
And all is in one moment gone, since now
The Lawrels snatch'd from mighty *Davenant*'s brow,
For ever wither'd must neglected ly,
T'impale the head of Night's obscurity.
    But soft — yon black Chymæra sure doth bear
The Muse of *Davenant* through the yielding air;
Through clouds of Melancholy she is brought,
Clad in a weed of discomposed thought:
A pendent brow hath hid her smiles, as if
It were a sable Vail, and not a Grief:
Her arms (without Bracelets of mirth) across:
And thus she doth bewail her *Davenant*'s loss.
    "Engins of Fancie, crack, and now let loose
    "Spirits of Ignorance, that shall reduce
    "The World to its first Chaos, that not one
    "But shall drink Lethe 'stead of Helicon.
Down with Parnassus, and thou Great Apollo,
Patron of Arts, I need not wish thee follow
This wrack of Time; for when it shall be said
With one poor moments breath that *Davenant*'s dead
Thou wilt resign that happy place, and leave
Practise of Arts, and only learn to grieve.
See here Heroick Tragedie, hard fate!
None to assume her Crown or Robe of state.
Comedie wants a head, on which to place
Her worthy Wreath of almost fading Bayes.
    Now thou (Great Soul) art gone, who shall maintain
The Learned Issue of thy pregnant Brain?
Thy *Lovers* (now so different is their state)
Are both Platonick and Unfortunate.
Thy *Cruel Brothers* smooth designs shall be
Laid open to Times greater Cruelty.
Now Ignorance is loose, it is a wonder
If *Madagascar* do avoid a Plunder;

Since *Rhodes* it self will be besieg'd again,
Nor can great Numbers such a foe restrain.
How canst thou hope that any should escape,
When on thy *Witts* it will commit a rape?
    Since *Davenant*'s dead, I can forget my birth,
And in that rocky substance of the earth,
I'll cut my passage deeper than the Seas,
And whisper something to th' Antipodes
Shall raise Imagination to conceit
There are no Gods, but *Poets Lawreat*.

The *EPITAPH*.

Here lyes a Subject of Immortal praise,
Who did from *Phœbus* hand receive his Bayes:
Admir'd by all, envied alone by those
Who for his Glories made themselves his foes:
Such were his virtues that they could command
A General Applause from every hand:
His *Exit* then this on Record shall have,
A *Clap* did usher *Davenant* to his Grave.

FINIS.

The lofty tone and apparently real feeling of the greater part of this elegy make the ribald pun at the close an anticlimax almost impossible to believe. I cannot think that the whole piece was composed for the sole sake of the low jest in the last line. The latter rather seems to me an egregious example of Restoration bad taste.

Whatever the intention may have been, Davenant was beyond reach both of satire and of eulogy, in honorable repose in Westminster Abbey. He had been buried there on 9 April, 1668. As for his worldly goods, he died intestate; and we are told that, on 6 May, letters of administration were granted to "John Alway, principal creditor, the Lady Mary Davenant, his widow, having first renounced." [69] But there is more than appears on the surface. It is obvious, from the testimony of the eldest stepson, Thomas Cross, and others, that Lady Davenant was practising a ruse to prevent the stepsons, and perhaps other claimants, from getting hold of any part of the estate. Alway — of whom I can learn nothing — is held by Cross to be not the principal creditor at all, but "an absurd person of no residence." That is to say, Davenant's real creditors could not find Alway when they wished to sue him for their money. In his answer of 1684, Cross maintains that the administration granted to Alway was fraudulent; that

all things were so secretly transacted between the said Alway and [Lady Davenant] and her son Doctor Charles Davenant that till about the years 1677 or 1678 [he] could not discover what personal Estate of the said Sir William Davenant came to the hands of the said [Lady Davenant, and] till of late could not be satisfied that the shares of the clear profits of the Plays which the said Sir William left at his death were Assets, the said Complainant and her son Doctor Davenant till of late affirming that the said profits were only Inheritance and not Assets.

Whatever may have been the rights of the matter, Davenant's widow obtained Alway's alleged interest in the estate, kept the 3.3 shares intact, and controlled the Duke's company as patentee after Sir William's death.

At this point it is necessary to correct an error which has arisen from a loose statement concerning the government of the theatre, made by the old prompter, Downes. He says (page 31) that the "Company after Sir *William's* Death [was] under the Rule and Dominion of his Widow the Lady *Davenant*, Mr *Betterton*, and Mr *Harris*, (Mr. *Charles Davenant*) her Son *Acting* for her)." From this, Lowe concluded [70] that on his father's death Charles Davenant was his mother's agent in the control and business of the theatre. Such is not the case. At the knight's death in 1668 Charles was a child of eleven or twelve, under the guardianship of his mother. We now have it on Lady Davenant's own testimony, given in 1677,[71] that she

. . . had, used, or exercised the sole Government of the said Theaters one after the other, & the appointment of Treasurers and Receivers, making Dividends & ordering of affairs Relating thereunto during the Respective times that the said Company hath acted therein respectively, from the said Sir William Davenants Death until about June One thousand six hundred & seventy three, about which time she . . . Assigned and Transferred such Government thereof . . . unto the said Charles Davenant.

For five years, then, from April, 1668, to June, 1673, Lady Davenant as Charles's guardian was in control. She was not fitted, however, to take Sir William's place also in the artistic direction of the players. This duty was assigned to the chief actors, Betterton and Harris. In a certain Chancery deposition made by Harris in 1691, we find important evidence bearing on the status of the function of artistic director under Davenant's patent: [72]

> Sir William Davenant did to the time of his death manage the said Theatre as having the Patent thereof and had not any Salary allowed him for the same; But he dying, leaving his son the said Doctor Davenant a Child & so not capable of managing the said Theatre, this Deponent and Mr Betterton were chose by all Parties interested in the said Theatre to manage the same: which was the first time that any Person or Persons were chose or appointed to manage the said Theatre, the management thereof always before belonging to the Patentee without any salary or consideration for the same beside the share or shares he had therein. And this Deponent and the said Mr Betterton from that time till about 14 or 15 years since [that is, 1676 or 1677] continued the management thereof and had twenty shillings a week allowed to each of them for the same out of the Public receipts of the said Theatre; which was done out of kindness to the said Doctor Davenant or those that had the right of the Patent, for that it properly belonged to him or them to manage the said Theatre without any Salary, or otherwise to have paid for the management thereof out of his or their own proper share or shares. And . . . after this Deponent left the management of the said Theatre, Mr Smith and Mr Betterton (as he believes) managed the same in the same manner and for the same salary until this Deponent left the said Theatre which was about 10 or 11 years since [that is, 1681 or 1682]. And . . . he doth not other or otherwise than as aforesaid know of any such Officer . . . as a Governor of the said Theatre.

Much of Harris's deposition is here ahead of our story. We shall see the force of it later.

Although the Duke's players, under Sir William's management, had prospered in Lisle's Tennis Court, the edifice was felt to be much too small to house the audience comfortably and to mount elaborate operas. Shortly after the knight's demise, therefore, plans were set on foot for a new theatre. As Lady Davenant says, she

> . . . and the said Actors, and owners of the said . . . Ten shares, did Mutually Agree at their Respective Charges, proportionably to their Respective shares aforesaid, to Build a New Theatre or Playhouse wherein the said Company might (as was Conceived) with more Conveniency Act.

Late in 1669 or early in 1670, as we now learn for the first time, the owners and actors began to consider "the Garden Plot behind Salisbury House in the Strand to build a new Theatre." [73] Salisbury House and Dorset House are one and the same, and this "Garden Plot" is consequently part of Dorset Garden. Dorset Garden is not, however, the site of the former Salisbury Court Theatre. Salisbury Court and Dorset Garden were adjacent, but not identical, pieces of ground.[74] The "Garden Plot" aforesaid was held by a certain Laud Doyly. But in July, 1670, after some conferences with Doyly, Betterton and Richard Bayly (the counsel for the company and a part sharer in the theatre), changed their proposed site to a more southerly part of Dorset Garden, fronting the Thames, with a wharf next to Dorset Stairs. This second plot in Dorset Garden, I find, was then held on a long-term lease by one Roger Jerman or Jarman, a carpenter.[75] On 11 August, 1670, Jerman leased the "said piece and plot & Wharf and Angular piece of ground"[76] to Henry Harris and a certain John Roffey (who at this time held a share in the theatre), in trust for Lady Davenant, Betterton, and all the rest of the sharers, for thirty-nine years reckoned from the preceding 23 December (1669), at a yearly rent of £130. On the day following (12 August, 1670) the sharers agreed to raise among them £3000, each contributing in proportion to his share; and to contribute more in like manner if the £3000 were not sufficient to complete the theatre. Further, it was agreed that after the building should be finished, such income (or "rent") "should be proportionably paid to the said respective sharers . . . as in four years (to be computed from the first Public Acting in the same Theatre) should reimburse them their principal monies," deducting, of course, the days when there was no acting, and also deducting each sharer's part of the £130 ground rent, and taxes. This agreement calls for an annual return on investment of 25 per cent, since the "rent" or income to the sharers, as we shall see, was to continue indefinitely after the principal had been paid up.[77] Also it was on 12 August, 1670, agreed "that to the Intent that the Company then Actors in the said Theatre in Lincoln's Inn Fields might act in the said intended Theatre," Harris and Roffey should reassign the lease to Nicholas Davenant and Thomas Cross, "in trust for the said Lady Davenant, or such as should then have right to the Government of the said Company."

It will be recalled that, by the first agreement (5 November, 1660) made between Davenant and his actors, Davenant was to have ten shares, and the actors five. Now we find[78] that at some time shortly after 1668, Lady Davenant came to an agreement with "the Proprietors & the Company of Actors to divide the General Receipts of the said Theatres into ten equal shares . . . (all House rent, Hirelings, Charges of Women, Scenes, habits, and other Charges being first deducted)," of which five went to the proprietors, and five to the actors. These two sets of five were again split in two, so that there were now twenty shares, where originally there were only fifteen. At first glance it would seem that the proprietors, or "adventurers," were robbing themselves to reduce their shares to parity with those of the actor-sharers. But it is quickly obvious that what they actually did was to divest their shares of responsibility for the rent and charges for costumes and scenery, and for paying the hirelings and actresses,—all of which would now be pooled (that is, paid out of the gross receipts before the dividends were made up),—so that, in fact, the ten shares held by the "adventurers" were now disencumbered of the charges assumed by Sir William in 1660. As for the actors, who had formerly taken one third of all the receipts (after some "general expenses" had been deducted), they now received one half of the net profit, after all the charges for rent, actresses, hirelings, costumes, and scenes had been taken out. What real change this brought about in their income is not clear, but it could hardly have involved much reduction if they agreed to the new method.

When the Duke's theatre concern, both in Lisle's Tennis Court and afterwards in Dorset Garden, had been running for a dozen years or so, we find a tendency to concentration of the shares in a few hands. The wealthier "adventurers" and leading actor-sharers bought out some of the holdings of the little fellows. On 18 July, 1674, for example, it now appears that the shares were held as follows: [79]

1.	Ashburnham, Hon. William, of Chiswick, Cofferer of H. M. Household		2.2
2.	Hervey, Hon. John, of Ickworth, Suffolk, Treasurer to the Queen's Majesty		2.5
3.	Davenant, Dame Mary, of London, widow		3.3
4.	Bayly, Richard, Esq. of Gray's Inn		.5
5.	Garter, Robert, of St. Giles, Gent.		.5
6.	Harris, Henry, of London, Gent.		2.75
7.	Betterton, Thomas	" "	3.25
8.	Smith, William	" "	1.5
9.	Nokes, James	" "	1.5
10.	Underhill, Cave	" "	1.5
11.	Cross, Thomas	" "	.5
	Total		20

It will be seen that, of the ten actors who articled with Davenant in 1660, only four are left as sharers: Betterton, Harris, Nokes, and Underhill. The rest are either dead or retired. Another thing to notice is that these four, with the famous Smith, — five actors in all, — together own ten and one-half shares, or more than half the stock. Again, we can observe that five persons, Ashburnham, Hervey, Lady Davenant, Harris, and Betterton, own fourteen shares, or nearly three quarters of the concern. With the exception of Lady Davenant, Betterton is the largest single shareholder.

From this list of 1674 the names of several of the purchasers of shares from Sir William have disappeared. Abraham Cowley, the poet, has died and left his half-share to his patron, John Hervey. By mesne assignments, Hervey has also apparently got hold of the half-shares of Lord Lumley, Porter, and Cheston, as well as half of Bayly's whole share. Alchorne's half-share has been sold through Roffey to Betterton, and Russell's half-share has gone to Thomas Cross.

To go back to the raising of funds for building in 1670, the first estimate of £3000 (or £150 on each share) soon proved inadequate. To stage historians heretofore the ultimate total cost of the Dorset Garden Theatre has been a matter of doubt. On the basis of a petition of 1709 mentioned by Malone, the sum has been given by Lowe,[80] Lawrence, Thaler,[81] and Nicoll [82] as £5000 and upwards. Fitzgerald, who gives no authority, says the theatre cost £8000.[83] From my Chancery documents I am able to quote the true cost, given once by Thomas Cross, treasurer of the theatre, and again by Betterton, a chief shareholder. Cross, after mentioning the first "stock of three thousand pounds," says that "the remaining charge was about Six thousand pounds more." [84] Betterton avers that on one of his half-shares he paid (toward the building) £225.[85] Consequently, we may reckon the charge on a whole share at £450, and on twenty shares, £9000: which is the sum given by Cross. Betterton tells us further that, of this £225, he paid down £102 10s. in ready money, and £122 10s. "by allowance out of his proportion of the rent or rents of the same new Theatre and his share of several debts due for the said Company's Acting." As to the total daily "rent" or income to the building-investors on their outlay, Betterton tells us that it was fixed as follows: from the opening of the theatre, 9 November, 1671, to 16 March, 1671/2, £5; from then until 23 February, 1673/4, £6; after 23 February, 1673/4, £7. This sum was to be divided among the holders of the twenty shares for every acting day. Now, if we allow 200 acting days to the year (which, as we shall see, is a fair average), the total annual return to one share at 7s. a day (one twentieth of £7) is £70; and since the whole investment was £450, the income is 15½ per cent — which is far from equalling the expected 25 per cent. And if we are to judge by Betterton's case just mentioned, more than half of the investment was taken out of the daily income, and there was no return on the outlay for more than three years. I fancy that a self-seeking investor would have had a rather thin time with the Dorset Garden concern in its early years.

On 21 July, 1674, Harris and Roffey (in whose names the lease of the theatre had been taken), by agreement with the rest of the sharers, assigned the lease to two trustees, John

Baker and Thomas Franklin. The sharers agreed to pay the annual rent of £130, and all charges for repairs and taxes, and also to protect Harris and Roffey, and Baker and Franklin, against loss. Further, by another indenture tripartite on 22 July following, Baker and Franklin, at the sharers' direction, leased the theatre and ground for thirty-five years to Nicholas Davenant and John Atkinson. The latter were to pay Baker and Franklin £7 every acting day, in trust for the sharers. And the latter covenanted with Davenant and Atkinson to pay each his part of the £130 a year rent, and of charges for repairs. Why all this leasing and re-leasing to trustees was found necessary, I cannot say. It reminds one of the elaborate legal arrangements of the Elizabethan companies of players.

Let us escape from the labyrinth of playhouse finance for the moment, and look at the Dorset Garden theatre building itself. There is a tradition that it was designed by Sir Christopher Wren; certainly it was the most magnificent public theatre ever constructed in England before 1671. Its dimensions, to judge from Ogilby and Morgan's large-scale map of 1677, were: length over all, 140 feet; width, 57 feet. Fronting the river, its ornamented façade [86] was surmounted by the arms of its patron (until 1685 James, Duke of York) and the statues of Melpomene and Thalia. The two upper stories of the front are supported by columns, which form an arcade on the ground floor. I have found out what the upper stories of the front of the theatre were used for. They were divided into two apartments, or "houses," one of which was occupied by Richard Middlemore — a sharer in the theatre — and the other by Thomas Betterton, who, as we now learn, was not only manager of the acting, but also "keeper" of the playhouse.

Let us hear Betterton himself speaking in 1691 on the subject: [87]

One of the Front Houses adjoining to the Theatre in Dorset Garden is and hath been held and Enjoyed by this Defendant ever since It was built and finished. And this Defendant had the Consent of the persons Interested therein or the Major part of them to live and Inhabit in the said Messuage or Tenement gratis, By Reason of his vigilancy and great Care he should take in preserving the Theatre thereto adjoining. And moreover this Defendant saith that he had more than a Tenth part and One . . . Twentieth part in the Interest thereof, and that by his own Care & Management of the playhouse and by his nearness and diligence he hath several times preserved the Playhouse from being burnt. And besides this Defendant Saith that he hath laid out and expended about the said House more Money than any person would give for the purchase thereof, considering the great Inconveniencies it is Subject to; which House if it were now to be let, this Defendant believeth that it would not fetch above Sixteen pounds per annum. And this Defendant saith that the other Front House is Let to one Mr. Middlemore for Sixteen pounds per annum.

In this matter Alexander Davenant corroborates Betterton, and says that the "Lodgings or Apartments" belonged as of right to Davenant's patent; and moreover that

Sir William Davenant, as this Defendant hath been informed, had always Lodgings or Apartments at the said Theatre [should be "at the Theatre in Lincoln's Inn Fields," where the poet died]; and after his death this defendant's Mother, as Guardian or Trustee to the said Charles Davenant, lived in the said Lodgings or Apartment during his Minority & afterwards, and Moreover this Defendant saith that there has been laid out and Expended by them above two Hundred and Fifty pounds about Finishing and making the said Lodgings fit to live in; which Money so expended this Defendant Looks upon to be more than the said Lodgings or Apartments are worth to be Sold.

Betterton, then, lived at the Dorset Garden Theatre rent-free, as keeper or caretaker, from the time it was built, in 1671, at least until his secession in 1694/5.

As for the interior disposition of the theatre proper, I have discovered no more interesting account than that of François Brunet, who, in his unpublished *Voyage d'Angleterre*, 1676,[88] details a description which I think has been unknown to students of the stage. After telling us that on 6 October the lord mayor was occupied, and so could not see him and his friends, Brunet says that they visited

. . . la Comedie de la trouppe de M^r Le Duc Dyorcq ou nous n'entendismes que baragouines. Les habits des Comediens Sont a la françoise, La magnificence n'en est pas plus grande que celle des troupes qui vont dans nos Provinces, Le lieu ou l'on joue est incomparablement plus beau et plus propre que ceux de nos Comediens, on est assis dans le parterre qui est en Amphiteatre ou l'on entend jamais de bruit, il ny a que Sept Loges qui peuvent

THE DUKE'S THEATRE, DORSET GARDENS

This Theatre was built by Sir Christopher Wren, and first opened by the Duke of York's Company on their removal from the Play house in Little
the 9th Nov. 1671. — Betterton, there manager with Harrison, Mrs Mary Leigh, Lady Davnet, Mr Sanderson and other principal actors performed under
union of the Duke and the King's companies in 1682, most performances were exhibited occasionally until 1697. The whole fabrick was demolished
April 1709 and the present edifice at the New River Company have been erected on the site of the Theatre.

contenir chacun Vingt personnes. Il y a encore pareil nombre au dessus et un paradis plus haut.

On donne en tout temps quatre Chelins qui valent 54 sols pour chaque place des Premiers loges deux Chelins pour le parterre, et un Chelin et demy pour les secondes loges, Le paradis est pour les lacquais qui entrent gratuitement.

L'On joue Les françois dans la plus part des Comedies qui sont faittes pour Se mocquer de nos moeurs. La Composition en est bonne, et ils pretendent que leur poesie surpasse la nôtre à cause de la liberté de l'expression ils n'obseruent pas la regle des vingt quatre heures ny les autres qui nous contraignent dans les ouvrages du theatre françois. nous n'y demeurasmes que jusquâ la fin du second acte parceque nous n'y entendions rien. nous y vismes de tres belles personnes qui ne nous empescherent pas de nous en aller.

As might be expected, Brunet is struck by the cleanliness and relative quiet of the English seated pit, in contrast to the Parisian *parterre*, which was as dirty and noisy as a beargarden. For stage history, however, the most instructive part of this valuable passage is the account of the construction of the galleries. Mr. Lawrence has shown that the Restoration pit sloped upwards "en Amphiteatre" to the boxes; but here we learn for the first time how the latter were divided in the Dorset Garden Theatre. There were seven boxes, holding twenty persons each; above them, the middle gallery, similarly divided into boxes, and the upper gallery, or "paradis," higher still. If the Frenchman's estimate of the capacity of the lower and middle-gallery boxes be correct, these two together held 280 spectators. Brunet gives "deux Chelins" as the price of the pit. This must be a slip, since we know that the regular charge all through the period was half a crown. The other prices are as we expect — with the exception that Brunet represents the upper gallery as being free. It is true that, at the Theatre Royal in 1697, Cibber tells us that, to curry favor, the patentees opened the gallery gratis to footmen. But he represents this both as a disgraceful nuisance and as an innovation.[89] We have thought that, before this innovation of 1697, the charge for admission to the gallery at either theatre was a shilling, with the exception that footmen were admitted free at the end of the fourth act.[90] Perhaps Brunet was misinformed. As for his points of literary criticism, one can but admire the judicial lack of animosity which allows him to say of the English comedies, written to jeer at French customs, "La Composition en est bonne." So much for this temperate and observant Frenchman's impression of the Duke's Theatre.

Although, as I have said, Lady Davenant handed over the reins of the company to her son Charles in June, 1673, he was then still a minor, seventeen years of age. On coming, in 1677, into his inheritance of the patent and shares in the Dorset Garden Theatre, Charles lost little time in looking about for a suitable marriage to increase his fortune. He found the desired object in Frances, only daughter of Sir Leoline Walden. Before the wedding could take place, however, Davenant was obliged to buy himself a lucrative place in the Excise. On 22 August, 1678, after his purchase of office, we find him writing to Secretary Williamson, who had helped him into the good graces of Sir Leoline, "now there is no obstruction to my marriage, which will be at Michaelmas." [91] The marriage contract, as we shall see later, contained a settlement upon his wife Frances of some of his "adventurers'" shares in the Dorset Garden Theatre.

Charles's marriage is the last important transaction affecting the Duke's Theatre until the preparations for the amalgamation of the patents in 1682, which I shall take up under the King's company in the next chapter. Before we leave the Duke's company, however, there is a new source of light on its income to be considered. This is found in a "schedule," or account, subjoined to a certain answer in Chancery made by Dame Mary Davenant and her sons, Charles and Alexander. [92] Covering the period from 30 November, 1675, to 19 May, 1677, this document gives the dates on which dividends were declared, and the total amount to be divided among the ten "adventurers'" shares. I reproduce the account here in full:

The Account which the Annexed Answer Refers to

[From 30 November, 1675, to 6 March of the same year], no Dividend was made of the Profits of acting in the New Theatre . . . (those profits being for that time very small) but on the Sixth of the same Month & year

a Dividend was made of the Net profits of the Five shares in Ten shares
to be Divided

		£	s.	d.
1675	30 Nov to			
1675/6	6 Mar inclusively comes to.......	52	06	08
	10 "	20		
1676	12 May.........................	15		
	15 "	10		
	19 "	20		
	19 Jun.........................	2		
	26 "	12	10	
	3 Jul.........................	10		
"same year"	8 Jan.........................	7	15	
	19 Feb.........................	2	8	4
1676	1 Apr.........................	30		
	8 "	15		
	15 "	10		
	22 "	33	10	
	29 "	20		
	6 May.........................	50		
	13 "	55		
	20 "	50		
	26 "	20		
	3 Jun.........................	44		
	9 "	59		
	17 "	14		
	24 "	19		
	1 Jul.........................	19		
	8 "	25		
	15 "	14		
	22 "	14		
	29 "	25		
	23 Sep.........................	13		
	30 "	24		
	6 Oct.........................	19		
	14 "	24		
	21 "	24		
	28 "	49		
	4 Nov.........................	19		
	11 "	49		
	24 "	33		
	30 Dec.........................	18	13	4
1676/7	6 Jan.........................	29		
	20 "	8		
	3 Feb.........................	8	3	4

			£	s.	d.
1676/7	10 Feb		19		
	24 "		13		
	3 Mar		24		
1677	30 "		37	16	8
	28 Apr		50		
	19 May		100		

Why it is that two sets of dates are given for the first half of 1676 is not explained. Either there were separate accounts kept for some reason, or the shorter list may refer to performances at Court. At all events, the sums are intended to be lumped together. In order to find the average weekly income on one share for a year, I have taken the year from 1 January to 30 December, 1676. As to the £52 6s. 8d. earned from 30 November, 1675, to 6 March, 1676 (three months), I have allotted two thirds of it (£34) to 1676. The whole for 1676, therefore, amounts to some £920. A tenth of this, or one share, is £92. Reckoning 200 acting days, or 33 weeks to the year, the weekly profit on one share comes to about £2 16s. a week. If we regard 1676 as an average year, this represents a return on investment of 11½, 13, or 15 per cent, depending on whether the purchase price of a share was £800, £700, or £600. These percentages are not far from the 15½ per cent which, as we found, was the ultimate annual return on the Dorset Garden building investment.

In spite, then, of the enormous initial cost of the theatre, by 1676 the concern was making a substantial return. There is every reason for thinking that this prosperity continued down to the union of the Duke's company with the King's in 1682; for in the words of William Smith, the joint manager of acting, "by the Management and method of matters at the . . . Duke's Theatre, the profits arising out of and by the same had in a reasonable measure Answered the Expectations of the persons concerned therein."[93]

NOTES FOR CHAPTER V

1 (197). Page 17 (ed. J. Knight, 1708). This story has been repeated by almost every recent historian of the stage.

2 (197). *Studies in Philology*, 1921, p. 331.

3 (197). Whitelocke, *Memorials*, 1732, p. 699.

4 (197). *Middlesex County Records* (ed. J. C. Jeaffreson), iii, 282.

5 (198). *Ibid.*, pp. 279, 280.

6 (198). Parton, *Some Account of the Hospital and Parish of St. Giles in the Fields*, p. 236.

7 (198). Adams, *Dramatic Records of Sir Henry Herbert*, p. 81.

8 (198). *Ibid.*, p. 121.

9 (199). See Appendix, p. 400.

10 (200). State Papers, Dom., Charles II, viii, 1.

11 (200). Ibid., x, 108.

12 (200). Printed in Malone's *Prolegomena*, 1813, pp. 301–303.

13 (201). *Cal. State Papers, Dom., 1660–1661*, p. 196. Regarded as genuine by Nicoll, *Restoration Drama*, p. 273.

14 (202). State Papers, Dom., Charles II, x, 169.

15 (202). Adams, *Dramatic Records*, pp. 85, 86.

16 (202). C. P. Plea Roll 2751, Mem. 317. Halliwell-Phillipps printed a mutilated copy of this contract, signed only by Burt (Adams, pp. 84, 85), which lacks the clause granting the £4 a week.

17 (203). Adams, pp. 113–115, 121. Nicoll, *Restoration Drama*, p. 276n.

18 (203). C. P. Plea Roll 2751, Mem. 317.

19 (204). Adams, p. 93.

20 (204). *Ibid.*, p. 95.

21 (204). L. C. 5/137, 332. Public Record Office. Lowe, *Thomas Betterton*, p. 68. Cf. Nicoll, p. 274.

22 (204). Mr. Nicoll (pp. 273, 274) is at some pains in attempting to show that Lowe was wrong in his conclusion for an amalgamated company. It will appear from what follows, however, that Lowe was right.

23 (205). C. P. Plea Roll 2753, Mem. 1190.

24 (205). Adams, p. 93.

25 (206). *Ibid.*, pp. 93, 94. Lowe is mistaken in concluding that "on October 13, 1660, the actors were under the control neither of Killigrew nor Davenant."

26 (207). No. 100.

27 (208). Following Malone, historians have been accustomed to think that there was an interval of ten days here, and that they did not begin to play until 15 Nov. This "15" is, however, a scribal error for "5," and is found in the copy of Herbert's declaration of 6 May, 1662 (Adams, pp. 108–110). The court record of the suit gives 5 Nov., the correct date. C. P. Plea Roll 2767, Mich., 1662, Mem. 512.

28 (208). *Hist. MSS Comm., Rep. V*, App., p. 200. That same afternoon they had given *The Unfortunate Lovers* at Gibbons's. Cf. *Ibid.* and Adams, p. 116.

29 (208). "THE / PROLOGUE / TO HIS / MAJESTY / At the first PLAY presented at the Cock-pit in / WHITEHALL; / Being part of that Noble Entertainment which Their MAIESTIES received *Novemb.* 19. from his Grace the Duke of ALBEMARLE. LONDON, *Printed for* G. Bedell *and* T. Collins, *at the* Middle-Temple Gate *in* Fleet-street. *1660.*" [MS. Nov. 23.] B.M., 669 f.26/30.

30 (210). State Papers, Ireland, Charles II, ccciv, 171.

31 (210). State Papers, Ireland, cccxlv, 50.

32 (210). Signet Office Docquet Books.

33 (211). C. P. Plea Roll 2746, Mem. 318.

34 (211). Ibid. 2753, Mem. 1190.

35 (211). Ibid. 2765, Mem. 2216.

36 (212). Malone, *Variorum*, iii, 263.   Adams, pp. 119, 120.

37 (212). C. P. Plea Roll 2767, Mem. 512.   Cf. Adams, p. 108.

38 (212). *Middlesex Sessions Books*, iii, 322.

39 (213). State Papers, Dom., Charles II, lviii, 15.

40 (213). Nicoll, p. 283.

41 (213). *Ibid.*, p. 298.

42 (214). *Ibid.*, pp. 277, 278.

43 (214). *Ibid.*, p. 278.   L. C. 5/138, p. 91.

44 (215). *Hist. MSS Comm., Rep. III*, App., p. 215a.

45 (215). J. L. Van Gundy has no reference to it in his dissertation.

46 (215). Nicoll, p. 356.

47 (216). See above, pp. 5, 26.

48 (216). Nicoll, pp. 278, 279.

49 (217). By a slip, Professor Nicoll (p. 285) gives the date of Davenant's patent as 15 Jan., 1662, instead of 1663, thus erroneously making it precede Killigrew's.   Lowe (*Betterton*, p. 76) has the correct date.

50 (217). *Cal. State Papers, Dom., 1661–1662*, p. 460.

51 (217). Signet Office Docquet Books, xxi, 170.

52 (217). Ibid.

53 (217). Given in full by Fitzgerald (i, 73) under the misleading date 1662, which should be 1662/3.

54 (219). POEM, / TO THE / KING'S / MOST / Sacred Majesty. / BY / Sr WILLIAM D'AVENANT. / *LONDON,* / Printed for *Henry Herringman,* at the *Anchor* in the Lower / Walk of the *New Exchange.* 1663.

55 (220). Nicoll, p. 339.

56 (220). No. 37.

57 (220). B. M., Additional Charters, 9296.

58 (220). Nos. 31, 99.

59 (220). No. 96.

60 (220). No. 97.

61 (220). No. 98.

62 (221). B. M., Additional Charters, 26,514.

63 (221). No. 97.

64 (221). No. 36.   See Appendix, p. 373.

65 (222). No. 64.

66 (223). No. 36. See Appendix, p. 368.

67 (223). Pages 6, 7 (London, 1668). Cf. Lowe, *Betterton*, pp. 106, 107.

68 (224). Bodleian, Wood 429, f. 27. Cf. the copy printed by Mr. G. Thorn-Drury in *A Little Ark* (1921), p. 35.

69 (226). *Wills from Doctors' Commons* (Camden Society), p. 160.

70 (227). *Betterton*, p. 108.

71 (227). No. 30.

72 (228). P. R. O., C24 1144/11, *Pro* Killigrew *c.* Davenant.

73 (229). No. 38.

74 (229). See Adams, *Shakespearean Playhouses*, p. 371, for a plan of the property.

75 (229). Marsh, *Records of the Worshipful Company of Carpenters* (1913), i, 35, 75.

76 (229). No. 96.

77 (229). The "self-seeking" of Betterton, mentioned by Mr. Nicoll (*Restoration Drama*, pp. 289, 335), is thus seen to be merely his taking part as sharer in the above-mentioned agreement.

78 (230). No. 97.

79 (231). No. 64.

80 (232). *Betterton*, p. 112.

81 (232). *Shakespere to Sheridan*, p. 213. Thaler here mistakenly says that Sir William Davenant built the Dorset Garden Theatre.

82 (232). *Restoration Drama*, p. 289.

83 (232). Fitzgerald, i, 141.

84 (232). No. 36. See Appendix, p. 369.

85 (232). No. 37.

86 (233). See the accompanying plate.

87 (233). No. 61.

88 (234). B. M., Add. MS. 35,177, pp. 79 ff.

89 (235). Lowe, *Cibber*, i, 233, 234 and n. Cf. Genest, ii, 98, 99.

90 (235). Lowe, *Betterton*, p. 29.

91 (236). *Cal. State Papers, Dom., 1678*, p. 371. Cf. *Ibid., 1677–1678*, p. 616.

92 (236). No. 32.

93 (238). No. 61.

CHAPTER VI

THE KING'S COMPANY, 1660–1682

BESIDES the Duke's, the other monopoly company, as we have seen, was Killigrew's (the King's) company, made up of an older and more experienced set of actors, among whom were numbered Mohun, Hart, Burt, Lacy, Wintershall, and others. Although at first they outshone the Duke's company of younger players in spite of Betterton's rising star, they were destined to be quite eclipsed before twenty years had passed. Advancing age and (more disastrous still) dissension, greed, and bad management combined to bring about their downfall.

A good share of the blame must go to Tom Killigrew, the patentee. Though, like Davenant, Tom was a dramatist and courtier, we shall find that, unlike the knight, he had little notion of sound methods of playhouse rule. He could boast to Pepys of the great physical improvements of the Restoration stage over its predecessor; but when we read of the disintegration of his company because of mismanagement, the boast rings hollow.

To go back to 1660 — by virtue of his joint grant of monopoly with Davenant of 21 August, Killigrew took over the original Mohun company (part of which had been formed into the united company under the joint monopoly, in October) and brought it from the Red Bull to Gibbons's Tennis Court on 8 November, 1660. At this time the company included Michael Mohun, Charles Hart, Nicholas Burt, John Lacy, Edward and Robert Shatterell, William Wintershall, William Cartwright, Walter Clun, Richard Baxter, and Thomas Loveday. And although Killigrew's theatre in Gibbons's was of the old Elizabethan style, — unadorned with scenery, — he embellished his troupe with the addition of six women actors, Mrs. Corey, Mrs. Eastland, Mrs. Hughes, Mrs.

Knepp, Mrs. Anne Marshall, Mrs. Uphill, and Mrs. Weaver. These actresses (contrary to the system first employed by Davenant, by which he received extra shares of the profits to support the actresses) must have been on the basis of hirelings, whose wages were to be paid out of the gross receipts. We have no record of a sharing agreement between Killigrew and his company until after they had secured ground for building their future Theatre Royal.[1]

The ground was obtained on 20 December, 1661. By an indenture of that date between (1) William, Earl of Bedford, and (2) Sir Robert Howard, Thomas Killigrew, and the eight actors, Hart, Burt, Lacy, Mohun, Robert Shatterell, Clun, Cartwright, and Wintershall, and (3) William Hewett and Robert Clayton,[2] the earl leased a plot of ground to Hewett and Clayton for forty-one years, in trust for the others. This plot was the "Riding Yard" between Drury Lane and Bridges Street, late in the possession of one Richard Rider, a carpenter, and measured 112 feet in length and between 58 and 59 feet in width. The condition of the lease was that before Christmas, 1662, Howard, Killigrew, and the actors should spend £1500 in building a theatre on the ground, and that they should pay an annual ground rent of £50.

On 28 January, 1661/2, Hewett and Clayton (the trustees) made over their property in the plot of ground — the interest in which was thereby divided into 36 parts — to the building sharers in the following proportions: Sir Robert Howard, nine, Killigrew, nine, Lacy, four, and two each to Mohun, Hart, Burt, Shatterell, Clun, Cartwright, and Wintershall.[3] On the same day the acting company, composed of thirteen members (the eight actors just mentioned as building sharers and five others — Theophilus Bird, Richard Baxter, Edward Kynaston, Nicholas Blagden, and Thomas Loveday), entered into articles with Howard and Killigrew and the actor-builders, by which the former promised to act in the projected theatre and no other, as soon as it could be finished, and to pay the building sharers the sum of £3 10s. for every acting day. It is important to keep the shares in the building (the 36 parts of the

daily "rent" of £3 10s.) clearly distinguished from acting
shares in the company. The former were based on the amounts
of money invested in the building, while the latter were allotted according to the value of an actor to the company.

The first agreement which I can discover concerning the acting shares took place two weeks before these agreements last
mentioned, that is, on 10 January, 1661/2.[4] I regret to say
that I cannot find all the details, but it is at least clear[5] that
the actors' shares were hereby divided into 12¾ shares, of
which Killigrew was to have two.[6] The three leading actors,
Mohun, Hart, and Lacy, each had a share and a quarter.
Five other actors, — Wintershall, Cartwright, Burt, Clun, and
Bird, — held one share apiece; that is, they were "whole"
sharers.[7] This brings the total of allotted shares to 10¾, leaving
two to be accounted for. These were probably reserved for
poets and others (since we know that Dryden later owned a
share and a quarter), and one Robert Lewright also had some
proportion. Clun, a whole sharer, died in 1664. Shortly afterwards Kynaston was appointed to a whole share, probably
that vacated by Clun. Another sharer, Bird, also died not
long before 1664; and when Killigrew, by virtue of his authority as patentee, attempted to appropriate the "dead"
share to himself, a dispute arose which throws interesting
light on the organization of the King's company.

From an undated report to the King by the Lord Chamberlain and two other officers,[8] concerning this dispute, it appears that Killigrew had delegated the actual direction of the
company to the leading actors, Mohun, Hart, and Lacy, and
that these three actor-managers had paid themselves for their
additional trouble by "taking in" one of the acting shares, and
dividing three quarters of it among themselves. This proceeding increased their shares to one and one half apiece. The
actors who had formerly enjoyed this share were thereupon
turned into hirelings, whose annual wages of £100 each had
now to be paid out of the general receipts. Such an arrangement, which held for about a year, naturally displeased the
rest of the company. They protested to Killigrew, and he

withdrew the delegated power from the three actors, giving the three quarters of a share back to the company. But since Bird, one of the sharing actors, had just died, Killigrew claimed his share. This again outraged the company, and they complained to the King. The Lord Chamberlain's opinion supported Killigrew's action, on the ground of the sweeping powers as master of the company granted to him by his patent. Despite this judgment, however, which supported him in his seizure of the "dead" share, it is probable that the feeling of the company was too strong to allow him to retain it. He was constrained to relinquish his hold, and confine himself to his two original shares.[9]

Two things are clear from this dispute: that Killigrew failed for a time to direct the company himself, and that the dissensions had begun which were ultimately to wreck the concern.

What the approximate annual value of one of the 12¾ acting shares was, is uncertain. The familiar petition of the managers of the Theatre Royal, made about 1678,[10] asserts that Dryden "received for his share and a quarter, three or four hundred pounds, *communibus annis*." Let us take a mean of £350, which on this showing makes the income on one share come to £280, and the total annual profit on 12¾ shares, to £3570. On looking back at the total income of the 20 shares in the Duke's Theatre (which was at least equally prosperous) and finding it to be £1800, or at most £2000, we may conclude that the foregoing estimate of the profits of the King's company is considerably inflated.

Killigrew's separate patent, as we have said before, was issued to him on 25 April, 1662, while the first construction work had been begun on the Bridges Street Theatre, and his company at Gibbons's Tennis Court was rivalling Sir William's at Lisle's. We turn with relief, after trudging through the legal and financial records, to an interesting letter in rime doggerel, which, I think, has been unknown to stage historians. It was written by a man-about-town to apprise his friend in the country of the plays current in London prior to the summer of 1662, and runs as follows:[11]

To omitt the antient salutation
Of after my hartie Comendation
With hopeing that you are in good health
As I am at writeing hereof my selfe
5 Since you command me to send you downe
The newes of all the Playes in Towne
Knowe they a Monopoly of them have made
And Courtiers have engross't the Trade
Nor shall we ever have good they suppose
10 Till every one medle with the trade that he knowes
First then to speake of his Majestys Theatre
Where one would imagine Playes should be better
Love att the first sight did lead the dance
But att second sight it had the mischance
15 To be so dash't out of Countenance as
It never after durst shew itts face
All though its bashfullnesse as tis thought
Be far from being the Authors ffault
For the surprizall it was a good proofe
20 By its getting them mony it took well enough
Without which Divell take the Play
Be it never so good the Actors say
But they may thanke God with all their hart
That Lacy plaid Brankadoros part
25 For Cornelia they all doe say
There was abundance of witt in the play
Indeed t' had soe much t' was the worse for 't
For t' was to witty for the vulgar sort
And they who 'd have poetts their Benefactors
30 Say witt without mony's naught for the Actors
O' th' contrary Salendina for witt
Most say did come far short of it
And though I confesse there was some fault there
Yett this I 'll say in defense of the Author
35 A good Plott though ill writt lookes more like a Play
Then all your fine lines when the plott is away
    To come to the other Theatre now
Where the Knight with his Scenes doth keep much adoe
For the Siege of Rhodes all say
40 It is an everlasting Play
Though they wonder now Roxalana is gon
What shift it makes to hold out so long
For when the second part tooke, but for Bully
The ffirst did not satisfie soe fully

45   The Cutter of Coleman street had more fame
      Before the Author chang'd its name
      And shewd himselfe an Englishman right
      By mending of things to spoyle them quite
      And hee's more to blame because he can tell
50   (No better) to make new strings soe well
      Then came the Kn*igh*t agen *wi*th his Lawe
      Ag*ains*t Lovers the worst that ever you sawe
      In dressing of w*hi*ch he playnely did shew it
      Hee was a far better Cooke then a Poet
55   And only he the Art of it had
      Of two good Playes to make one bad
      And these are all the new playes wee have had
      Indifferent good or indifferent bad
      When they'l be worse, or when they'l be better
      Is more for a Prophesie then for a Letter.

Metre could hardly be worse; but the dramatic criticism is fresh and apt. In the first place, the new Davenant–Killigrew monopoly is none too well liked by the town: a free stage would produce better plays. At Gibbons's Tennis Court — "His Majesty's Theatre" — the first new play was Tom Killigrew's *Princess: or, Love at first Sight*. Pepys saw this play on 29 November, 1661, "the first time that it hath been acted since before the troubles."[12] The piece had little luck, lasting but two days. Its bashfulness in thus retiring from public view, our rimester observes, is hardly a fault to be attributed to its author, whose effrontery was notorious.

Mentioned next is *The Surprisal*, by Sir Robert Howard, who, as we have just seen, was the capitalist who laid out a quarter of the sum for building the new theatre. His play was acted 23 April, 1662.[13] We are told that it took, thanks largely to the acting of Lacy in the part of Brancadoro, "A rich Senator's Son." As for Sir William Berkeley's *Cornelia*, played for the first time on 1 June, 1662, we learn that it was full of fine things, over the heads of the common crowd, and brought little revenue.[14] Killigrew also accepted a play by his elder brother, Sir William Killigrew, entitled *Selindra*.[15] Acted on 3 March, 1661/2, it met a doubtful fate, says our critic, although he allows it a good plot.

At Lisle's, where the bustling Sir William was putting on "show" as well as drama, this playgoer finds that *The Siege of Rhodes* is enjoying an unheard-of vogue, even after the withdrawal of Elizabeth Davenport from the rôle of Roxalana.[16] And the Second Part of this operatic hit is even more attractive than the First. Cowley's changing the name of his *Guardian* to *Cutter of Coleman Street* (put on in December, 1661) is here deprecated, especially as the dramatist's originality is highly thought of. Finally, Davenant's harebrained effort at combining *Measure for Measure* and *Much Ado about Nothing* into one play called *The Law against Lovers* (performed 18 February, 1661/2) meets with the contempt it deserves.

While the patentees had been trying their luck with these plays, Sir Henry Herbert had harassed them, as we have seen in the preceding chapter, with repeated lawsuits. In this summer of 1662, while Davenant and his company still combined to repel the determined attacks of the Master of the Revels, Tom Killigrew came to terms with the enemy, on 4 June. Malone [17] has printed their treaty, by which Killigrew agreed not only to pay Herbert all the licensing fees in arrear since 11 August, 1660, and the expenses of Herbert's lawsuits, but also to give him a gratification of £50. He did more: he pledged himself to help reëstablish the ancient powers of the Office of the Revels, even to the extent of opposing Davenant and the Duke's company. In return, Herbert promised to stand by Killigrew, and restored to him the articles of 11 August, 1660, whereby (as has been shown above) Mohun and his fellows had bound themselves to Herbert. This separate peace between Killigrew and Herbert, which left Davenant on the firing line, indicates that friendship between the rival patentees was none too strong in 1662.

To emphasize that rivalry, Killigrew's players were now preparing to move into their new playhouse, built between Bridges Street and Drury Lane. Both patentees must have felt cramped in their small tennis-court theatres, the scenes of their early Restoration successes and failures. But though Davenant was destined never to see the gorgeous playhouse to be built in 1671 by his company, in the winter of 1662/3 Killigrew pushed on his building, that he might the sooner have a large house with scenery to emulate the embellishments of Davenant's operas, for which the knight had contrived to make space at Lisle's Tennis Court.

The proposed cost of this Bridges Street Theatre Royal was, as we already know, £1500. I have found, however, that before it was complete the cost had mounted to £2400; [18] and though this increase (60 per cent) is considerable, it is nothing to the additional burden of 200 per cent which the builders of the Dorset Garden Theatre had to shoulder in 1671.

Killigrew's new theatre was opened on 7 May, 1663. Six months later, on 23 November, I find [19] that Walter Clun, who, it will be recalled, owned two of the 36 building shares, sold them for £430 to Thomas Johnson, a barber-surgeon. A share, therefore, on which £66 13s. 4d. (that is, one thirty-sixth of £2400) had been laid out, now brought £215 in the open market. Such a price shows a prosperous state of affairs in 1663, and squares with Pepys's remark that the actors were grown "proud and rich." Some of them, I find, while the Bridges Street theatre was building, had enough extra funds to build three dwelling-houses close adjoining the theatre:

Bartholomew Baker, Michael Mohun, Robert Shotterel, Walter Clunne, William Wintershall, and William Cartwright, 10 June 1663 leased to Margaret Nephway widow . . . for £24 [rent per annum] all the newbuilt messuage, being the middle house of 3 houses lately built by the parties of the 1st part, in St. Martin's in the Fields, on the south East side of a way or passage leading from a street or lane called Drury Lane alias ffortescue Lane to the Theater Royall for 21 years.[20]

Theatrical prosperity received a heavy blow, however, just two years after, in 1665. Plague closed the doors of the London theatres for a year and a half. On 5 June, 1665, the Lord Chamberlain ordered complete cessation of acting until further notice.[21] When the house had been dark for half a year, and the plague showed no signs of abating, Killigrew and his actors, having concluded that the stage had been designed too narrow for scenic convenience, seized this opportunity to alter it; for on 19 March, 1665/6, Pepys found the carpenters in, widening it, and the place all dirt. Improvements of this nature, however necessary, were an added burden to a theatre over which hung the blight of the pestilence. By October, 1666, the two companies were eagerly seeking permission to open their houses, and, having agreed to give the proceeds of one day in every week to the poor, they gained the right to act. Unfortunately for them, the Archbishop of Canterbury complained to the King, and performances were again stopped on the first of November.[22] Four weeks later, on offering still larger gifts for charity, they were granted definitive permission to play. As Henry Muddiman writes on 29 November, 1666: "The Players have upon great proffers of disposing a large share to charitable uses prevailed to have liberty to act at Both Houses, which they begin this day." [23]

Two years and a half after this reopening, Dryden's tragedy, *Tyrannic Love: or, The Royal Martyr*, was acted at the Theatre Royal. In connection with the production of this play — in which figures the God-defying Emperor Maximin — I have found an instructive Chancery suit.[24] Therein Killigrew, Hart, and Mohun lodge their complaint against Isaac Fuller, a scene painter, showing that the King's comedians, being appointed to act

. . . a new play or Tragedy called the Royal Martyr or St. Katherine about the latter end of April, 1669, and there being a necessity of making a new Scene of an Elysium to be presented in the said Tragedy . . . and one Isaac Fuller . . . being a Painter and one who sometimes did apply himself for painting of Scenes,

Hart and Mohun, according to their version of the story, treated with him on 14 April, 1669. The terms of their agreement ran as follows. Fuller was to paint the said scene

. . . of such largeness as should fit the stage of the said house or Theater Royal and . . . paint the same so well as other Scenes belonging to the said Theater were usually painted by other Painters and as was fitting for the same to be painted for the best advantage of the said Tragedy.

He was to finish the work within the fortnight next following. The complainants now make a great talk of the eagerness of the King and the nobility to see the play, and allege that they had warned Fuller to get his work done promptly, since the Easter and Trinity terms at the law courts, when most people were in town, were then coming on. Fuller, nevertheless, did not finish it until the end of June; on account of which delay the managers (so they say) "received very great blame from his said Majesty, and by reason of his distaste thereat he did much forbear his coming to the said Theater," and the nobility stayed away too. Moreover, they say that the scene was painted "very meanly and inconsiderably," and that because of this the acted play was "disparaged and lost its reputation and not half the company resorted to see the acting thereof which would have come in case the said Scene had been painted according to the said Agreement." They assert that they are damaged by Fuller's breach of the agreement to the extent of £500. They were in hope that Fuller would make them some recompense for their loss, the more so since they had paid him £40 on account. But he did not, and has lately brought action at law against Hart and Mohun, and has recovered £335 10*s.* for painting the scene.

To this complaint Fuller replies that it is true that

about the latter end of April or the beginning of May in the year . . . 1669, One Mr Dryden (a Poet as this Defendant hath heard that Sometimes makes Plays for the Company of Comedians or Actors in the Bill mentioned) and one Mr Wright (a Joiner belonging to the said Company) by the order . . . of the said Company . . . did come unto this Defendant then lying sick at his own house and did propose unto him the painting of the said Scene of an Elysium . . . and to encourage this Defendant to undertake the painting thereof the said Dryden and Wright or one of them told this Defendant he should be well Satisfied for the same. . . . And . . . about four or five days after, this Defendant having recovered his health went to the said Company at their said house and there met with all or most of them together, particularly with the Complainants Hart and Mohun; and then and there treated with them about the painting the said Scene; and then (and not about the 14th of April . . .)

it was agreed that he should paint it to fit the stage. Fuller denies that he ever agreed to finish it within a fortnight — a thing which, he avers, would have been impossible for him or any other to accomplish. No time was fixed, but Hart and

Mohun promised him satisfaction and "did also expressly Say that he should not Stay a minute for his money after his work was done." Fuller insists that he painted quickly and well, completing the work "within the space of Six weeks or thereabouts, beginning to paint the same about the 12th day of May . . . and perfecting the Same about the 23d of June." He avers that he has reason

. . . to believe that no painter in England could have finished the same and have done the work So well . . . in So Short a Space, for that at the trial at Law hereafter mentioned . . . One Mr Streeter [25] an eminent Painter (being produced by the now plaintiffs themselves as a witness on their behalf) did acknowledge that this Defendant had a quicker hand at painting than any other, And if he Performed the Said Work in Six weeks time it was very fair, And did also acknowledge that the Said work was excellently well done. And this Defendant saith that he was so far from neglecting or delaying the said work that for three weeks . . . he did not put off his Clothes but lay upon a pallet-bed in the Room and rose up to work as Soon as he could See.

In addition, Fuller does not believe that the company received any blame from the King, for the reason that Killigrew "some few days after the finishing thereof gave this Defendant thanks for the Same And told him that he . . . had very well pleased his Majesty and the whole house." What is more, he refuses to believe that because of the delayed production "the said Play when Acted was disparaged or lost any reputation," since at the trial some of the complainants' own witnesses,

. . . some of them being their own Servants, [testified] that the said Scene was very well painted and gave great content to the Spectators that came to see the said Play Acted, And that the . . . Company acted the Same about 14 days together, and received all that while about 100[li] per diem, Whereas at other plays they are not wont usually to receive above 40 or 50[li] per diem And that their said House all the said 14 days was very full, the Pit Boxes and other Places thereof being thronged with Spectators.

After trying in vain to collect his pay for the work done, Fuller says he brought suit in the Court of Exchequer against Hart and Mohun. At the trial, held in Guildhall in Easter term, 1670, the jury found for Fuller and valued the work at £335 10s. Forty pounds had been paid, and Fuller adds that he has obtained an execution on Hart and Mohun for the remaining £295 10s. He says that he was loth to go to law, and was

. . . also deterred by their or Some of their great words and threats; One of them, by name Mr Wintersell, plainly telling this Defendant that they could spend more at Law than [he] could And that they would keep him out of his money till he should be glad to take what they would please to give him.

It seems clear that Fuller had the right on his side, and that the company's behavior toward him was both unworthy and contemptible. By pleading their privilege as His Majesty's Servants, they had prevented him from suing them at law until, on petitioning, he at length got permission from the Lord Chamberlain to sue. I do not find that Killigrew, Hart, and Mohun proceeded any further in this Chancery suit.

The labor of jogging through such a long-winded answer in Chancery is well rewarded if we can picture Glorious John calling on the sick artist to paint him an Elysium; if we can learn that such a scene when finished was appraised at £335 10s. (well over $10,000 in modern values), and that its elaborate perfecting occupied a facile artist six long weeks, during three of which he never took off his clothes, but snatched a brief sleep in the studio; and if, finally, we can be told that *Tyrannic Love*, put on at the end of June, 1669, was played for fourteen days to packed houses, averaging what to-day would be $3000 to $4000 a night.[26]

Before the Theatre Royal had been standing for nine years, it was destroyed by fire, on Thursday evening, 25 January, 1671/2. The fire was a disastrous one: beginning under the stairs at the back of the playhouse, it burned down half the building and all the stock of scenery and costumes. From there it spread, urged on by a southwesterly wind, to the adjoining houses toward Drury Lane. Profiting by their experience in the great fire of 1666, the fire-fighters blew up the houses in the path of the flames with gunpowder, and so stopped the conflagration, after a loss of fifty or sixty houses, valued in all at £20,000. An actor named Bell was killed in one of the explosions.[27]

One thing only lightened the gloom of the players after this misfortune: they were able to find a temporary theatre in Lisle's Tennis Court, vacated eleven weeks earlier by the Duke's company, which had gone over to the new house in Dorset Garden. At Lincoln's Inn Fields the unlucky King's company, on 26 February, 1671/2, began to play after a fashion, with stock pieces and borrowed costumes, while they set about raising funds for a new theatre on the site of the old. Appealing to the King, they asked not only for the arrears owing to them for court performances, but also for a subsidy, on the ground that the new theatre would cost them "neere Two Thousand pounds more than when it was first built." I can find no record that Charles gave them a gift of money, but it is certain that a letter or "brief" was sent out in 1673 to the parish churches of England, and thereupon a collection was made to assist the rebuilding.[28] Coming so close on the hostility of the religious under the Commonwealth, this aid from the Church is surprising. Was it servility to Charles, or a kindly Restoration interest in the theatre, which loosened the parishioners' purse strings?

As we have seen, the cost of the first Theatre Royal had been £2400. The "rent" or daily income to the building investors had been £3 10s. (half as much as the £7 "rent" at the Dorset Garden). On 17 December, 1673, the sharers in the company (Killigrew, Dryden, Robert Lewright, Hart, Mohun, Burt, Lacy, Shatterell, Cartwright, Wintershall, and Kynaston) entered into articles with the building investors (Edmund Ashton, Esq., Thomas Sheppey, John Wolfe, John Tombes, Joseph Nickens, and Thomas Johnson). Killigrew and the company thereby agreed to act exclusively in the theatre which was being rebuilt, and to pay the building investors at the rate of £3 10s., if the cost were £2400, and proportionally more for any additional cost.[29] What the exact price of the new Theatre Royal was, has not been known, although Genest (i, 160) learned that it was said to be "near £4000," and Mr. Lawrence found another statement that the playhouse cost "neere Two Thousand pounds more than when it was first built."[30] Since he regarded the original cost of the first Theatre Royal as £1500, this estimate would mean near £3500. But as we now know that the cost of the first theatre was £2400, the estimate should be read near £4400. The actual sum can be found by the proportion between the rent of the first theatre and that of the second. We now learn [31] that the ultimate rent of the rebuilt theatre was £5 14s.; and the result of the proportion, "£3 10s.:£2400 = £5 14s.:x," gives £3908 11s. 5d. as the price of the second Theatre Royal in Drury Lane.

Besides the theatre building, scenery and costumes had also to be replaced; and the company resolved to erect a scene-house in Vinegar Yard adjoining the rear of the theatre. This scene-house was to be the property of the company, and distinct from the theatre, which was owned by the building investors. The funds required for scene-house, scenery, and costumes were raised by contributions from the members of the company in proportion to their shares.[32] Articles of agreement were signed 20 March, 1673/4, by which the terms were settled. Hart, Mohun, and Lacy, each of whom had one share and a quarter, contributed £200 apiece. The single sharers, Wintershall, Cartwright, Burt, Kynaston, and Shatterell, put in £160 each. Since the shares numbered 12¾ in all, and £160 was the charge on one share, the whole sum raised must have been £2040.[33]

The understanding with the sharing actors concerning their contributions to the stock was as follows:

1. If the sharer should die within three years (and had acted until his death), his heirs should be paid £1 13s. 4d. out of the acting profits each acting day until his contribution had been repaid.

2. If within three years after date a sharer should give three months' notice of his decision to retire from acting, at the end of such three months he should be paid £1 13s. 4d. for every acting day until his contribution had been repaid, even if he should meanwhile be judged by the majority of the company incapable of continuing to act.

At six performances a week, the daily payment of £1 13s. 4d. comes to £10 a week; so that a whole sharer at this rate would be repaid his investment of £160 in sixteen acting weeks, or half a season, after leaving the company. This agreement should be kept in mind, as we shall return to it shortly.

We have seen that the dimensions of the first Theatre Royal on this site were 112 feet in length by 58 or 59 feet in width. With the addition of the scene-room on the rear, the width of the new theatre was the same, but the length was increased to 140 feet.[34] The size of the scene-room built by the acting company is therefore seen to be 58 by 28 feet. I find that the scene-room was provided with a cellar — perhaps for the storing of "machines." For the plot on which it stood in Vinegar Yard, the company paid £30 annual ground rent, entirely separate from the £50 a year paid to the Earl of Bedford as rent for the theatre plot.

At this point it is necessary to attack a subject of which little has been known, and that little misunderstood: the transactions concerning Killigrew's patent and his acting and building shares.

First I shall mention the document given by Malone,[35] which bears on Tom Killigrew's two shares in the company. Dated 31 December, 1666, it recites that on 4 July, 1662, Killigrew granted £4 a week, to be paid out of the profit of his two shares, to his son and heir, Henry, during his life. Shortly after, Henry made this stipend of £4 over to Thomas Porter, Esq., for life. The latter in turn bargained to sell it for £600 to Sir John Sayer and Katherine, his wife. To accomplish this end, Porter deeded it back to the Killigrews, who thereupon assigned it to the Sayers. These took it as trustees for the benefit of their eldest son, George Sayer, for his life. If they outlived him, they were to enjoy it for themselves.

The foregoing is, however, a small matter when compared to the main question, which affects Killigrew's patent and his shares in the theatre building. As early as 1 May, 1663 (a week before the opening of the Theatre Royal in Bridges Street), Killigrew made over his nine shares (out of the 36 into which the building shares had been divided) to the aforesaid Sir John Sayer.[36] That these shares were to be held by Sayer in trust for Killigrew is suggested by the next document, dated

27 June, 1670,[37] by which Killigrew sets up a trust in Dame Katherine Sayer (Sir John's widow) and one Thomas Elliott, Esq. Killigrew hereby grants his patent and all his interest in the Theatre Royal to Elliott and Dame Katherine Sayer (with exception of the aforesaid annuity of £4 a week), in trust for himself during life. After his death the Sayers are to have the £4 a week during Henry Killigrew's life, but on Henry's death it is to go to James, Henry's heir. The rest of the theatrical estate is to be divided into five parts, of which two are to be held in trust for Charlotta, Killigrew's wife, during her life. The three remaining after Tom's death, with the two others available after her death, are to be held in trust for all their children in equal proportions; except that Charles Killigrew, the eldest, is to have a double share and, after coming of age, is to be governor of the theatre.

Now, although it is clear that Tom Killigrew's nine building shares were thus in the hands of his trustees, nevertheless, on 21 June, 1673, he calmly made them over as security to Sir Lawrence Debusty, for a loan of £950.[38] Eight years later Thomas Sheppey, the actor, testified that Debusty (about the time he lent the sum aforesaid to Killigrew) told him that Dame Katherine Sayer

... had acquainted him that she had a good title to Mr. Thomas Killigrew's Interest in the said Playhouse long before he had assigned the same to the said Sir Lawrence Debusty; but she had promised that she would not trouble or hinder him [Sir Lawrence] from receiving the rents and profits arising out of the said Theatre or Playhouse until he should be fully satisfied and paid the moneys and Interest which he had lent to the said Thomas Killigrew.

On 22 July, 1673, just a month after the assignment to Debusty, Killigrew borrowed again, this time £1600, of one Richard Kent, Esq., through an agent named James Magnes; and for security assigned his theatrical patent and authority to Magnes for ninety-nine years, reserving an equity of redemption.

These two hypothecations, which, it is clear, involve nothing but Tom Killigrew's property (his patent, his nine building shares, and part of the income of his two acting shares), have been for some reason taken by Fitzgerald (i, 138) to imply a mortgage "of the ground" on the part of the company, for the purpose of raising building funds. In this error he is followed by Nicoll (p. 289). True, Killigrew may have used this expedient to raise his part of the money, but no other shareholders were involved.

Debusty received profits of the building shares until there remained only £500 of his debt still due. The £1600 owing to Kent through Magnes (little affected by the small profit arising from the remnant of the two acting shares), accumulated interest, however, until at the beginning of 1676 it amounted to £1850. On 22 March, 1675/6, Kent paid the £500 which Killigrew still owed to Debusty, thus increasing Killigrew's debt to himself to £2350. In return, Killigrew now made over to Kent (through the latter's trustees, Charles Tucker and Thomas Smith) his patent, his building shares, and his acting shares — all his interest in the Theatre Royal — for the remainder of the ninety-nine years. Kent was to try to repay himself out of the theatre profits. That he was badly disappointed in this expectation will appear from what follows later.

Not only, therefore, had Killigrew resigned most of the manager's function to Hart and Mohun, but in 1673 he had also pawned, not merely his building shares, but his patent and interest in the acting profits as well, in return for ready money. Small wonder that with such improvidence on his part the prosperity of the venture rapidly disappeared!

Let us return now to the agreement of 20 March, 1673/4, noted above, for refunding the stock contributions of the sharing actors by daily payments of £1 13s. 4d. We learn from the testimony of Charles Killigrew given in January, 1676/7,[39] that, shortly after the sealing of this agreement, profits

. . . did fall much short of expectation and did daily decrease; and the said Actors did get very little profit by their Acting: insomuch that the said Wm. Wintershall, Charles Hart, Edwd. Kynaston, and Wm. Cartwright did each of them at several times in the year 1675 give notice in writing to your Orator's Father [Tom Killigrew] that they were minded to give over and desist from acting, and did each of them demand to be allowed the several sums of money according to the above mentioned Articles.

On this account the company "was like to break up and be dissolved for want of their principal Actors."

Killigrew was alarmed at the prospect of losing outright the profitable building shares which he had mortgaged, and the more so when the dissatisfied chief actors ceased to play, thereby stopping the whole company. Displeased at the closing of the house, on 14 February, 1675/6, the King ordered the company to resume performances.[40] Unrest still ruled, however, and in April Killigrew told his son Charles that he wanted to retain Hart, Wintershall, Kynaston, and Cartwright, who were threatening to "give over Acting, by which he said that he feared the House would be Destroyed." He proposed that Charles should act as mediator: persuade them to stay on, and, on cancelling their former articles, to enter into new ones "which might be more moderate and more practicable considering the abatement of profits." Killigrew was, nevertheless, aware that this desired consummation could not be achieved without labor and expense. To get Charles to undertake the task, he promised to make over to him the patent and "all his right, Claim, and Power in and to the Governing, Ordering, and regulating of the said Theatre, and all profits, privileges, and powers relating thereunto." At length Charles agreed; and by dint of much persuasion of the actors, and especially by giving Hart £100 and Kynaston £60, he not only got Hart, Wintershall, Kynaston, and Cartwright to continue, but also prevailed on them and Mohun, Lacy, Burt, and Shatterell to cancel all their former articles,[41] and to seal a new agreement dated 1 May, 1676. The terms of this I find detailed in a suit of 1696 between Kynaston and William Clayton, Wintershall's heir.[42]

The contracting parties in this agreement are Killigrew, Lewright, Mohun, Hart, Burt, Lacy, Kynaston, Wintershall, Cartwright, and Shatterell. Dryden, we notice, is omitted from the list of sharers. As before, three months' notice in writing is to be given of intention to retire from acting; and it is here provided that "such Notice should not be given but in playing weeks, and that such weeks wherein the said Company should not Act or play should not be accounted any part of the said three months." Whereas by the former articles each whole sharer was to be paid at the rate of £1 13s. 4d. each acting day until his contribution of £160 should be repaid, it is now stipulated that each whole sharer, after the three months' notice, should have five shillings each acting day for life, and at his death his executors should be paid £100. The holders of a share and a quarter (of whom Kynaston was now one) were to receive 6s. 3d. every acting day for life, and their executors similarly £100.

Wintershall's executor, Clayton, here gives his view of Charles Killigrew's activities in bringing about the new agreement:

> Charles Killigrew . . . so contrived that matter that, unknown to the rest of the Company, he proposed to advance a hundred pound to the said Mr. Hart and sixty pound to [Kynaston] . . . (he finding them to be most unwilling to lessen the said allowance of two hundred pounds) in Case they would persuade and procure the rest of the Company to agree for a hundred pound only. [They] did at length persuade the rest of the Company . . . telling them that two hundred pounds was a great deal too much, and that they feared it could not be paid . . . and that they as for their parts would willingly consent thereto; and thereupon the whole Company agreed to do the like being altogether Ignorant of the underhand dealings of [Kynaston] and the said Mr. Hart, and of the rewards they were to have for the said service.

If, as Clayton says, the sums paid by Charles Killigrew to Hart and Kynaston were in the nature of clandestine bribes, there was sharp practice, and the characters of all three are considerably lowered in our eyes.

Dissension did not cease even with the sealing of these last articles. Once they were signed, Tom Killigrew failed to carry out his promise to make over his authority and shares to Charles. So disrupting was the quarrel between father and son that on 9 September, 1676, the Lord Chamberlain appointed four actors — Hart, Mohun, Kynaston, and Cartwright — to be a committee of control. Later, Hart was made sole manager. On 23 January, 1676/7, Charles Killigrew complained in Chancery in order to force his father to give him the promised government of the theatre. Elliott and Dame Katherine Sayer were included as defendants in the suit,[43] because, as trustees of Killigrew's property, they had a power in its disposal. Before the case came to trial, the elder Killigrew and his trustees acceded to Charles's demands, and the hearing was merely a form. On 22 February, 1676/7, it was decreed by the Court that Killigrew should perform his agreement and "transfer all his power and authority in the government of the said Playhouse to the Complainant," and that Elliott and Dame Katherine should join in the conveyance.[44]

Three weeks before this date, which marks old Tom's surrender of his theatrical rights, he had resigned to Charles his power as Master of the Revels, which he had exercised since Sir Henry Herbert's death in 1673.[45] Charles had been granted the reversion of the office in 1668.

Although Charles now wielded authority over the King's company, the profits were still being paid to Kent, his father's creditor. It was not long, as we shall see, before Killigrew took steps to alter this unsatisfactory state of affairs.

The players were so dissatisfied with the new rule under the son of their former master that by the summer of 1677 they were petitioning for autonomy. King Charles granted their wish for self-government, with reservations, provided that they would continue to act.[46]

On 28 September following, Killigrew tried a new plan, which seems to indicate friction in the company. He gathered several of the building sharers together until he had a group representing a majority of the 36 shares, as follows: Charles Killigrew (that is, with the consent of Kent, to whom they were mortgaged), 9; Captain Thomas Morley (formerly Sir Robert Howard's), 4½; Thomas Sheppey (ditto), 1½; Joseph Nickens (ditto), 1; John Tombes (from Michael Mohun), 2; William Cartwright, 2—in all, 20 shares. This group then entered into an agreement with the younger actors, Philip Griffin, Cardell Goodman, Martin Powell, Carey Perin, Thomas Disney, Marmaduke Watson, and Sarah Cooke, virtually forming a new company. The latter agreed not to act elsewhere than in the Theatre Royal, and to pay the "rent" of £5 14s. every acting day.[47] We may infer that a new sharing agreement had also been made about this time, and that Henry Killigrew, Charles's half-brother, had interested himself in the company; for I find that in 1678 Henry Killigrew, Charles Killigrew, Thomas Morley, Philip Griffin, Cardell Goodman, Thomas Clarke, and Robert Shatterell were "Master Partners or sharers." [48]

Of the vicissitudes of the dejected King's company in 1678 and 1679 we learn much that is new through a suit in Chancery brought by James Gray in 1682.[49] After relating that he was employed as treasurer by the "Master Partners" aforesaid in 1678, Gray tells us that "soon after, several discords and dissensions arising between the said [Henry and Charles and other partners] the said Playhouse was shut up and no Plays were acted . . . therein for some Considerable time after." For this reason Gray joined with Cardell Goodman and Thomas Clarke, and went to Edinburgh, where he was "employed as Master or Principal of the Company of his Majesty's Comedians or Actors there, which was a place of Considerable Advantage." In 1679, not long after he and the other actors had settled themselves in Scotland, the Killigrews, Morley, and certain other sharers, pretending that all discords were reconciled, and that "they then had the regulating and governing" of the Theatre Royal, importuned Gray to come back and bring the two actors with him, offering to pay their travelling expenses. Gray, Goodman, and Clarke accordingly arrived in London in February, 1679/80. Gray charges that the sharers not only neglected to pay the promised travelling expenses, but also delayed his appointment as treasurer until the middle of 1681. Further, he accuses Charles Killigrew and Shatterell of secretly mortgaging the stock of the theatre to George Sayer, Thomas Sheppey, and Thomas Morley, for £300. Charles Killigrew and Morley, in a joint answer to Gray's complaint, deny that they asked him back or offered to defray his expenses. As for the alleged mortgage of the stock, they admit "that there being a great Debt due and owing by the Old Company of Players to several Tradesmen for Wares Delivered," Charles Killigrew and Shatterell, "being as they were advised the only persons Interested and who had power so to do," sold the costumes and scenes and other materials to Sayer, Sheppey, and Morley for £300. Henry Killigrew and Philip Griffin make a separate answer to Gray,[50] in which they show their hostility to Charles Killigrew and Shatterell, and agree substantially with Gray's statement of the case, and say that "no plays or Interludes could well be shown or Represented in the said Playhouse for want of the said Players or Actors. Wherefore it was Agreed between the said Partners and Sharers of the said Playhouse or the major part of them that Letters should be written unto the said" Gray to persuade him to come to London. They say that Gray should be paid by Charles Killigrew, who has the profits in his hands; that they have none of them, "but are much wronged and Injured by the secret and private Dealings of the said Charles Killigrew and Thomas Morley and other Partners," since Charles Killigrew and Shatterell, without their consent, mortgaged the "Scenes, habits, Stock of Plays, and other materials." Obtaining no satisfaction from his suit in Chancery, Gray appealed to the King; and the case came before the Lord Chamberlain on 8 February, 1683/4, when it was settled in Gray's favor.[51]

Not to get ahead of the story, we must go back to the spring of 1680. Here we find the King's players applying to the Vice-Chancellor for permission to play in Oxford during the Act, the great academic celebration which was to take place in July. On 15 May the Lord Chamberlain, at the King's order, wrote to the Vice-Chancellor, recommending that His Majesty's players be accepted.[52] The very next day, the Duke of Ormonde wrote to the Bishop of Oxford, informing him that he had recommended his own players to the Vice-Chancellor, and implying that he was not anxious that they should be received, provided no other company was allowed to play.[53] The unfortunate Vice-Chancellor was thus caught between two mutually exclusive requests — one from a king and the other from a duke — for the same thing. On 30 May he wrote to Sir Leoline Jenkins as follows:

These two inclosed letters I lately received the one in behalfe of his Ma^tys players, the other of those who belong to his Grace the Duke of Ormond. Since which time I am informed that the Earle of Ossory [that is, Ormonde's son] hath been with my L^d. Chamberlain who was pleased to signify unto him that he would not oppose any thing my L^d. of Ormond desired, nor would any further interpose in this affair. I am not at all versed in the modes of the Court, yet I am very unwilling to shew any disrespect. I am very desirous to know what is my L^d. Arlington's sence in the matter and what will be expected from me.[54]

Apprised of the attempts of the Ormonde company to gain permission, the King's players appealed again to the King, who ordered the Lord Chamberlain (Arlington) to require the Vice-Chancellor to receive his actors to the exclusion of all others.[55] On 22 June, the Bishop of Oxford told Ormonde as his opinion that "if the Vice-Chancellor be forced to receive them [that is, the King's players], he will so shorten them in time as may discourage them from coming on such terms." [56] Despite the threatened discouragement, the King's players in July set up their stage in an Oxford tennis court.

At the end of the same month I find that the company, no doubt having returned to London, signed and sealed an acting agreement as follows: [57]

On 30 July, 1680, Griffin, Shatterell, Clarke, Goodman, Powell, Watson, Sheppey, and Charles Killigrew, as acting sharers, covenanted and agreed with Charles Killigrew (as master of the theatre), that Cartwright, Shatterell, Kynaston, Griffin, Clarke, Goodman, Powell, Watson, and Sheppey, respectively,

. . . should and would at all times thereafter during their respective Lives, Every one of them with their best care and Skill, Act and Represent all such persons and parts in the King's Majesty's Theatre Royal or elsewhere as should be Allotted and Appointed for him by the said . . . Charles Killigrew or his Assigns, and should likewise during the Time aforesaid Observe, perform, pay, fulfill, and keep all such Orders, Articles, Payments, Forfeitures, and Rules as were or should be made by the said Charles Killigrew or his Assigns for regulating and Governing the said Theatre Royal; And the said . . . Charles Killigrew and the said [company also agreed that if any of them] should at any time thereafter be Disabled from Acting by Sickness or other infirmity or incapacity (the same to be Examined and Allowed to be so by the said Charles Killigrew his heirs or Assigns under his or their hands), That then . . . there should be paid and allowed unto such person during his respective life so much money as should amount unto one Moiety of one share according to the profits and proportions of a whole share for the Time being had and received out of the profits of acting as aforesaid. And lastly it was thereby Agreed and Declared by and between all the said parties to the said presents That all former and other Articles, Agreements and Covenants whatsoever made by or between all the said parties or any of them touching or concerning any stipends or Salaries for acting or playing in the said Theatre Royal should from thenceforth be, and were thereby Declared to be, void and of no Effect: Except such Covenants and Agreements as had been at any time theretofore made for payment of the Rent due and to be due for the said Theatre Royal, and Except also all Covenants and Agreements for not acting in any other place save only in the said Theatre Royal; But that the said last mentioned Covenants and Agreements should stand and Remain in full Force.

It is to be noted that the names of Hart, Mohun, Burt, and Wintershall are absent from this agreement. Wintershall had died in July, 1679, and Burt had retired. Hart and Mohun, both well advanced in years and afflicted with disease, seldom acted after 1679. As the prologue to Crowne's *Ambitious Statesman* tells us, in 1679:

> The Time's Neglect, and Maladies have thrown
> The two great Pillars of our Playhouse down.[58]

Continuing the subject of the new acting agreement, I find Griffin in 1682 asserting that it was also agreed in 1680 by Killigrew that his half-brother, Henry Killigrew, with Griffin, Sheppey, Goodman, Clarke, Powell, and Watson, were to be "received as Adventurers Sharers or Participants," and that the whole profits should be divided into $6\frac{3}{4}$ shares, thus:

Charles Killigrew	1
Henry Killigrew	1
Philip Griffin	1
Cardell Goodman	1
Thomas Clarke	1
Martin Powell	$\frac{3}{4}$
Thomas Sheppey	$\frac{1}{2}$
Marmaduke Watson	$\frac{1}{2}$
Total	$6\frac{3}{4}$

On the other hand, Killigrew and his allies against Griffin in 1682 deny that by the agreement of 30 July, 1680, the acting profits were divided into 6¾ shares. They are careful, however, not to deny that such division was made by another agreement; and we have the word of the treasurer, James Gray, that such division was agreed on.[59] Gray gives a list of sharers coinciding with that furnished by Griffin, with the omission of Henry Killigrew. This omission is, however, explained by the fact that in this suit all the sharers except Henry Killigrew were defendants.

We may surmise that in the autumn of 1680, after making these two agreements just mentioned, Charles Killigrew formed a coterie consisting of himself, Captain Thomas Morley, Thomas Sheppey, and William Cartwright, representing roughly half the building shares, and left the other sharers out of his councils. At all events, by February, 1680/1, Kent (who, it will be recalled, held the nine Killigrew shares and other theatrical property as a mortgage), together with Burt, Lacy, William Clayton (Wintershall's executor), and one Anthony Stevenson (who had Johnson's — originally Clun's — two shares), complained in Chancery against Killigrew and his friends.[60] They allege that they are being kept out of their profits, and that Killigrew and his allies "pretend that their title is paramount to your Orators'." The various actors in the company are made defendants. Their answers are illuminating, showing that the regular "rent" of £5 14s. was paid each acting day until the beginning of February, 1680/1, when they found that the profits were not enough to cover the outlay, and therefore ceased acting. On this discovery, Sheppey approached some of the owners of the building shares and proposed an abatement of their demand, on days when the receipt was extraordinarily small. Accordingly, Morley, Sheppey, Nickens, and Tombes agreed with the actors to accept half-rent (57 shillings) on days when the total receipt was less than £10. Hereupon they began acting again, at the said half-rent; but after six days of it, the audiences were so small that they stopped acting entirely. One of the treasurers, William Mur-

ray, gives the miserable sums taken on three of the worst days:
"11 May, 1681, £3 14s. 6d.; 30 May, 1681, £3 2s.; 18 June,
1681, £3 13s."

On sixteen other days the receipts were not sufficient to meet
the necessary expenses. James Gray deposes to the effect that
the company "did heretofore sometimes desist from acting of
plays" when the takings were too small;

> ... and that they have for the same reason dismissed the Audience and re-
> turned their respective moneys And . . . all the young Players and Ser-
> vants in the said house, both men and women, did consent . . . to accept
> of half wages on such days as the moneys . . . would not answer the full
> Wages; . . . All the said Actors that did . . . agree to the said Abate-
> ment did proceed again to represent and act plays . . . as formerly; and
> for that the money then received was not sufficient for many days to defray
> the charge of half wages, they did again desist from acting.

Cartwright, on 1 June, says that he does not know how
many acting days there have been since the beginning of February, as he "hath been sick and kept his house for almost the
whole six months last past, and hath not been amongst the
said Players in the said house above four or five times, as he
believes, in all that time."

The more important question at issue, however, was not the
theatre's miserable condition, but the title to the Killigrew
theatrical property made over to Kent's trustees. Charles
Killigrew, on 28 June, meets this question by maintaining
that the property, long before it was made over to Kent's
trustees, had been assigned to Sir John Sayer and Dame
Katherine Sayer. The case dragged on for two years, involv-
ing a suit at law on the issue whether the deed of 27 June, 1670
(by which Tom Killigrew set up the trust in Elliott and Dame
Katherine Sayer), was fraudulent or not. Finally, on 14 December, 1682, the Court decreed that the Killigrews should be
"for ever debarred and foreclosed of all Equity of Redemption" of the property made over to Kent's trustees, and that
the latter should hold and enjoy it.[61] In due course we shall see
what the practical result of this decree was. Not to anticipate
matters, however, we shall turn now to the question of the

dissolution of the King's company, which preceded the union of the two patents in 1682.

Besides internal dissension and bad management, fruitful of a lamentable falling off in the size of audiences, the members of the Theatre Royal were taxed with another vice, equally pernicious. I refer to the appropriation by individuals of common property — in this case, the stock of costumes. We have seen that Henry Killigrew accused his half-brother, Charles, of exceeding his powers in mortgaging the company's stock. And although Charles maintained that he was within his rights, on 30 October, 1679, the King, on hearing of his doings, forbade him to dispose of "the said Clothes and other properties." [62]

We may notice, by way of contrast, another accusation of pilfering costumes before this time, levelled by Kynaston some years later at Henry Killigrew, and at the memory of the departed William Wintershall, as follows:

William Wintershall, living in a house which Joined to the said Playhouse and had a door into the same, did . . . (while he was an Actor there) by contrivance and agreement with Henry Killigrew let the said Henry Killigrew through the said Door into the said Playhouse; who thereupon by and with the aid and assistance of the said William Wintershall possessed himself of all the said Clothes, apparel, and books; the doing whereof very much contributed to and forwarded the dissolution of the said Company . . . the said Company being . . . greatly indebted, and the said Henry Killigrew then seizing the said Clothes, apparel, and books . . . the same put the said Company into such great disorder and confusion that his . . . Majesty King Charles the Second . . . soon after, in the year of our Lord 1680, did by Express Command dissolve the said Company, and ordered them to unite with the other Company . . . in Dorset Garden.[63]

Henry Killigrew denied this accusation *quoad* himself, and Wintershall's executor, Clayton, said he knew of no such order from King Charles dissolving the Theatre Royal company. Meeting Kynaston with a counter accusation, Clayton recited the terms of the agreement between the owners and managers of the Duke's Theatre in Dorset Garden — Charles Davenant, Thomas Betterton, and William Smith — and Hart and Kynaston. This agreement, a copy of which was given by Gildon in his *Life of Betterton*, is dated 14 October, 1681.[64] Its terms follow:

1. The managers are to pay Hart and Kynaston each 5s. for every regular acting day at the Duke's Theatre, so long as they do not act for the King's company, or assist them.

2. If Kynaston can get free to act at the Duke's Theatre, his 5s. is to cease.

3. Hart and Kynaston promise to make over to the managers their rights in the stock of the Theatre Royal, and likewise their claim to 6s. 3d. a day from the Theatre Royal.

4. Hart and Kynaston promise to promote an agreement between the two companies; Kynaston promises to try to get free to act at the Duke's, but is not obliged to play until he can have 10s. a day, whereupon his 5s. a day is to cease.

5. Hart and Kynaston promise to go to law, if necessary, to have these articles performed.

With all our new light on the dubious doings of the King's company, this agreement does not seem by comparison to us now as very high-handed or unfair; nor is it so puzzling as it was to Lowe, when he wrote on the subject in 1891.[65] Kynaston, as he himself tells us,[66] gave notice, in or about 1677, of his intention to retire, ceased acting three months after, and for some time received his payment, every acting day, of 6s. 3d. Hart, being ill, gave up acting a year or two later. We have seen that in the new division of the acting shares on 30 July, 1680, neither Kynaston nor Hart was included. Inasmuch as the takings of the house were barely sufficient to pay the rent, it is most probable that the company failed to pay the pensions of these retired actor-sharers. Moreover, when Killigrew and Shatterell presumed to mortgage the stock, into which Hart and Kynaston had each put £200 (equivalent to some $6000 or $8000 to-day), one can see that the old actors' hopes of a healthy Theatre Royal were small, and that their provocation for seeking a change in the organization and some security for their interests was great. Whether the action of the Dorset Garden managers, in making this agreement with them, was outrageously unfair or not, depends a good deal on the state of mind of the Theatre Royal company at the close of 1681. It is true that Clayton asserts that the agreement was unknown to the rest of the company, and was entered into "the better to bring them to a Compliance with the said Duke's Company and to unite them." But he does not say that this agreement was the disruptive power which broke the company. On the contrary, as we shall presently see, the immediate cause most frequently given in these new documents for the dissolution was lack of money and the misappropriation of costumes from the Theatre Royal stock. Behind both of these troubles lay the original cause — bad management.

In April, 1682, the Theatre Royal closed its doors, and shortly afterwards negotiations were set on foot for the union. The unimportant question as to who took the first step is a matter of doubt. Griffin avers that Killigrew acted on his own initiative; Killigrew says that the Dorset Garden owners came to him with a proposal; and the latter declare that Killigrew applied to them. The following interesting statement is from William Smith, joint manager of acting with Betterton at the Dorset Garden Theatre:

[The Theatre Royal company,] being much in Debt for Habits, Scenes, and Utensils . . . and several of the persons of whom the said Company did Consist being dead and others of them refusing or leaving off to act therein, And many differences arising amongst them, And [Charles Killigrew] being Sensible as this Defendant Believes That it would be Impossible or extremely difficult for him to compose the said Differences, and by Such acting of the same Company or Such of them as were or might be prevailed with to act . . . to raise sufficient clear Moneys to pay the Debts owing upon the Account of the same Playhouse, and to buy Clothes and other things necessary for his said Company to act there again; And the said [Killigrew] (as this Defendant believes) being in great despondency of making any advantage Suitable to the charge of their future acting . . . and Observing (as this Defendant believes) that by the Management and method of matters at the said Theatre called the Duke's Theatre the profits arising out of and by the same had in a reasonable measure Answered the Expectations of the persons concerned therein, He . . . applied himself not only to the said Charles Davenant but likewise to Thomas Betterton Gent. . . . and to this Defendant,

and proposed a union of the patents.[67]

Whichever party actually made the first move, it is clear that Killigrew acted on his own responsibility, and did not carry the other shareholders of the Theatre Royal with him until later.

On 4 May, 1682, [68] Charles Killigrew entered into an indenture with Davenant, Betterton, and Smith, which may be summarized as follows:

1. The two patents are to be united.

2. All plays are to be acted by the Dorset Garden company under the joint direction of Killigrew and Davenant.

3. Killigrew undertakes
   (*a*) to dissolve the Theatre Royal company within six days;
   (*b*) to deliver the stock of playbooks and possession of the Theatre Royal (with the exception of the scenes and scene-room) to Davenant.

4. Davenant agrees
   (*a*) to pay Killigrew £3 for each day any play shall be acted at either house;
   (*b*) in case Killigrew should not be able to deliver possession of the Theatre Royal after dissolving the company, to pay him 20*s*. 6*d*. a day for one whole year, the payment to change to £3 each acting day when possession shall be given;
   (*c*) to divide all acting profits into 20 shares, of which Killigrew is to have three: that is, 1½ for dissolving the company, and paying its debt of £500, and 1½ for uniting his patent to Davenant's.

That by the terms of this agreement Killigrew was usurping power and property which did not belong to him is clear, when we recall that at most he had a claim to only one fourth of the building shares and to one of the 6¾ acting shares. For example, he hereby agreed to deliver up the whole stock of plays, of which, in equity, he owned less than 15 per cent.

A fortnight after this agreement, and when Killigrew had dissolved the company, Griffin brought suit against him in Chancery on this very issue of usurpation of power.[69] Killigrew, he maintains, was only a part sharer; and he, Griffin, and the other actor-sharers had contributed each his part to buy the stock — in all, some £1000. From a certain Mr. Jacob Holton the four chief sharers, Griffin, Killigrew, Goodman, and Clarke, had borrowed £100, which sum "was laid out in buying

Roman habits or shapes for some Plays," and ought to have been paid by the company at large. Goods were also bought, by the sharers, of "one Robert Baden, a Copper lace man, of one Thomas Biggs, a Coalmonger, of one Francis Stamper, a Silver lace Man, and of one Richard Chase, a Feather man." Killigrew, nevertheless, has paid all these debts himself, and together with Sheppey and others has seized the common stock of costumes and will dispose of the same to repay himself. Griffin insists that the goods and playbooks seized in this manner are worth a great deal more than the debts Killigrew has paid.

Killigrew meets this charge by asserting that he has paid no one but Holton, and by denying that he has seized the stock. As a counter-charge, he brings in Andrew Perryman, the wardrobe keeper, to testify that Griffin himself carried off costumes from the theatre.

Several months later, depositions were taken in this suit [70] which cast considerable light. William Murray, the treasurer, shows that, while Kent was at law with Killigrew over the mortgaged theatrical property, the company took money out of Kent's share of the "rent" to the extent of £150 or £200. Daniel Golding, Killigrew's appointee as housekeeper of the theatre, says that the company owes £400 to the several tradesmen named above, and gives as the cause of dissolution

... for that [Griffin] and other actors carried away divers of the Clothes and other habits belonging to the said Theatre which were to be used in representing plays . . . And [Griffin] was many times requested or desired to bring back the said Clothes and Habits . . . but . . . refused to do the same; whereupon . . . Mr. Killigrew, Mr. Clarke, and Mr. Goodman did send this deponent with a Letter to [him, desiring him] to bring those Clothes and Habits he had taken away, in to the Wardrobe for that the Company could not go on Acting without them; And the said [Griffin] told this deponent that he would not bring back the said Clothes or Habits, and that the same were as safe in his hands as in the Wardrobe or Mr. Killigrew's hands, or to such effect; And upon [Griffin's] refusal . . . this deponent had Orders and did lock up the doors to keep the said Company of Actors from Acting till the Clothes or Habits were returned. And this deponent saith that there were suits and differences between . . . Killigrew and Richard Kent Esqr. and his Trustees touching the Title of the said Theatre And a verdict passed against . . . Killigrew's Title; but the said suits and differences were not any occasion of breaking up and dissolving the said Company (as this deponent doth verily believe) for that this deponent heard the said . . . Mr. Killigrew tell the said Company that although there were differences between Mr. Kent and him, yet he would have them keep on their Acting and that he would take care they should not be damnified by the said suits.

Andrew Perryman, the wardrobe keeper, corroborates Golding's story, and adds that Griffin, since July, 1680,

. . . hath at several times taken and carried away several of the Clothes, Habits, and other materials belonging to and bought for the use of his Majesty's Theatre Royal, as particularly: one French Habit, A laced Coat and Breeches, A Night Gown; besides Hats, shoes, stockings, periwigs, and Trimming, being all of the value of above three score pounds.

Whatever the result of this quarrel between Griffin and Killigrew may have been, it is clear that the latter was not seriously disturbed by it. After his agreement of 4 May, 1682, to unite his patent with Davenant's, he energetically set about persuading the other building sharers in the Theatre Royal to join him in a lease of the theatre for twenty years to Davenant, Betterton, and Smith. A draft agreement for a lease was prepared in June, 1682; and, although the proposed rent of £3 per diem was little more than half the former £5 14s., the following building sharers signed: Charles Killigrew (9 shares), Thomas Morley (4½), Charles Hart (2), Thomas Sheppey (1½), William Cartwright (2), Nicholas Strawbridge (2). These represent 21 shares, or more than half the shares in the property. The £3 "rent" was to begin on the first acting day after 24 August, 1682, and the Dorset Garden managers agreed to pay the annual £50 ground rent to the Earl of Bedford, beginning on Michaelmas Day. On the advice of counsel, however, this paper draft agreement was cancelled in November, and a new one made — a draft lease of the Theatre Royal to Charles Davenant for nineteen years, beginning 9 November, 1682.

Before we let the King's company be swallowed alive by the Duke's players, we must pause long enough to examine an interesting suit brought on by the dissolution of Killigrew's band of actors. This suit [71] reveals a purchase of scenario material for a play — the earliest transaction of its kind that I know. The dramatist, Elkanah Settle, and Elizabeth Leigh, the actress,[72] are the parties to this suit, which was brought on 21 April, 1687. Settle, "of St. Andrew's, Holborn, gent.," alleges that in 1681 he agreed with Elizabeth Leigh, spinster, to

> ... write or compose a certain Interlude or Stage Play upon A certain Subject or Theme given ... by the said Elizabeth Leigh; which said Stage play your said Orator did engage and promise to write, invent, compose, and finish, in the Space of Eight months . . . and also within the Said time to tender into the hands of the actors or Comedians of his then Majesty's Theatre Royal to be forthwith by them acted or represented upon the Stage in the said Theatre Royal at their first & speediest opportunity.

In consideration of receiving the "Theme or Subject" from her, Settle says he agreed to pay her £20 "whenever the Said Stage play should be acted" at the Theatre Royal, and for security gave her a bond of £40 penalty, conditioned on the payment of the £20 within ten months. The poet insists, however, that it was fully agreed that the £20 should become payable only when the play was acted. He admits that he promised also that, if the profits from acting, "together with the printing, publishing, and dedication," should amount to more than £40, he would pay Mrs. Leigh half of the overplus.

Proceeding, he avers that he finished the play on that subject within the time agreed on, but that then "it so happened that his then Majesty's Actors in the said Theatre Royal did not act plays in the said Theatre." Settle, nevertheless, delivered his play to some of the actors, asking them to act it, when they should resume performances, at their earliest convenience. The company did meet again; but, after less than ten days of acting,

> ... through Variances & Differences arising between themselves did forever after dissolve & Separate, and from thence never Acted Plays again: by this means Your Orator was wholly uncapable of having the said Stage Play Acted according to his Agreement & Covenant, nor has the said Play been ever Acted by them or any other Comedians in any Theatre whatsoever.

Notwithstanding these circumstances beyond Settle's control, Mrs. Leigh has had him arrested several times on the bond, and has now obtained a judgment against him in the King's Bench. He prays for an injunction to quash her proceedings.

In answer to Settle's complaint the actress says that, after she had

... designed the Subject and story of a Tragedy or Stage Play and having composed and reduced part of the Story into writing, and the Complainant having notice thereof and pretending himself skillful in poetry and in the composing and finishing Stage Plays,

they talked it over, with the result that on 13 October, 1681, she gave Settle "the Theme, Subject, and design of the said Play with what she had written thereof." He thereupon entered into a bond to her of £40, conditioned for the payment of £20 on or before 1 June, 1682 ("towards the design and subject of the said Stage Play)." Mrs. Leigh insists that this £20 was to be paid whether the play were acted or not. Further, she says that on the same thirteenth of October Settle entered into a second bond (this time of £100 penalty) with a condition reported as follows:

... Whereas ... Elkanah Settle was at that present time composing and writing a certain Stage Play or Tragedy in which one of the principal Characters or persons in the stage play was to be a woman that gives and contracts her soul to the Devil to be made a beauty, and afterwards seduces a certain Prince in the said Play from the affection & bed of his Princess and causes the said Prince to murder the said Princess, Then in Consideration That the design, subject, and story on which the said Tragedy or Stage Play was to be written was made & given by the said . . . Elizabeth Leigh to the said Complainant, If the said Complainant should at any time before the tenth day of April next ensuing the date of the said obligation have composed, written, & perfectly finished the said Stage Play to the best of his Capacity and made fit to be represented either at the then Theatre Royal or the Duke's Theatre, and should likewise within the same tenth day of April have delivered or caused to be delivered the said Stage Play into the hands of the Comedians or Actors of the then Theatre Royal or the Duke's Theatre to be forthwith acted upon the stage, and if the said . . . Elkanah Settle should moreover pay or cause to be paid to the said Defendant a full moiety or half of all manner of profits that should arise to him from the said Play either by representation, Printing, or dedication, or any other ways whatsoever, Then the obligation was to be void, or else to remain in full force.

After reciting this bond at length, Mrs. Leigh proceeds to declare her belief that Settle neither wrote the play within the time agreed nor ever delivered it to the actors. She says that the Theatre Royal was playing at the stated time, and never refused to act Settle's play. She has taken action to recover her debt of £20 and costs; and since the poet has not performed the conditions of the £100 bond, she hopes she may be at liberty to prosecute him on that also.

Since she admits that the play has never been acted and consequently has brought the unfortunate Settle no profit, Mrs. Leigh, in demanding both her bonds, seems very much the female Shylock. Although I cannot find the upshot of the dispute in Chancery, no doubt the litigants came to a compromise; for we are told that, as late as 1716, Settle was writing drolls for Mrs. Mynn (Elizabeth Leigh's mother), who had booths at Bartholomew and Southwark Fairs. It has been said, too, that Settle had an "annual salary from Mrs. Mynn and her daughter, Mrs. Leigh, for writing Drolls." [73]

More interesting for our purposes than the outcome of the suit, however, is this record of a sale of a dramatic plot for a sum which should equal half of all the proceeds of the production. One wonders whether such a practice was common. As for the identity of the piece in question, Mrs. Leigh's *aperçu* of the plot reveals it as *The Ambitious Slave, or A Generous Revenge*, a weak tragedy by Settle, in blank verse. Being at length acted and damned in 1694, it was published in the same year, and Settle's epistle dedicatory speaks of "the severity of this poor Plays Fortune." Even Mrs. Barry's acting in the rôle of Celestina, the "Beautiful Scythian of unknown Birth" who causes all the trouble, could not save it.

Discovery of this Chancery suit alters the Settle chronology somewhat, throwing the date of composition of *The Ambitious Slave* back a dozen years,—from 1694 to 1681/2,—and giving point to the remark in the epilogue that here was an "*Out-of-Fashion*" drama. The play was simply a shelf-worn commodity left over from the palmier days of heroic blank-verse tragedy in the early sixteen-eighties. One can no longer regard it, as Mr. Nicoll does, as a late example of the heroic style.[74]

Returning from this excursus, we are brought to the close, after a troubled two-and-twenty years, of the independent life of the King's company. The date for the beginning of the nineteen-year lease of the house to Davenant and his allies (9 November 1682) is just a week before the date given by the old prompter, Downes, for the opening of the united company at the Theatre Royal. It must be remembered, of course, that, although the King's company had been dissolved in April, the Duke's had been playing regularly at Dorset Garden until the move to the theatre in Drury Lane in November. From this time on for twelve years London was to have but one company of players.

NOTES FOR CHAPTER VI

1 (243). Following a grossly erroneous entry in Fitzgerald (i, 27 n.), Professor Nicoll (*Restoration Drama*, p. 271 and note) states that Killigrew's first agreement with his players took place in 1660 and is contained in certain articles printed by Fitzgerald. It is obvious, however, that these articles have nothing to do either with 1660 or with profits of acting. They are drawn between Sir Robert Howard, Killigrew, and certain of the actors, and concern the building of the theatre. The real date of these articles is 28 Jan., 1661/2, as we shall see below. See B. M., Add. MS. 20,726.

2 (243). In the copy of this indenture printed by Fitzgerald (i, 81, 82) from a document in the British Museum, Theophilus Bird is included among the lessees. This is a mistake, as I find from another copy of the lease in No. 46. Bird was a member of the company at this time, but did not take part as a "builder."

3 (243). Nicoll's list of these shares (p. 282) follows Fitzgerald's (p. 82 n.), which in turn follows a defective document in the British Museum (Add. MS. 20,726). All three leave out Burt's name; and the sum of the shares they give is 34 instead of 36, which makes the omission evident.

4 (244). No. 44.

5 (244). Malone, *Var.*, iii, 170 ff. And cf. the indenture of 31 Dec., 1666, between Thomas and Henry Killigrew, Thomas Porter, Thomas Elliott, and Dame Katherine Sayer. This is included in "Killigrew's Abstract of Title to the Playhouse" (B. M., Add. MS. 20,726).

6 (244). Not two and three quarters, which is the amount quoted by Bellchambers and repeated in Lowe, *Cibber*, i, 197 n.

7 (244). No. 44.

8 (244). Printed by Chalmers in his *Apology*, 1797, p. 529.

9 (245). Cf. the indenture of 31 Dec., 1666, mentioned above, and Nicoll, p. 291 n.

10 (245). Cf. Malone, *Var.*, iii, 170 ff.; Lowe, *Cibber*, i, 197 n.; Nicoll, p. 294 n.

11 (245). B. M., Add. MS. 34,217, fol. 31*b*. Another copy is given in part in *Hist. MSS Comm., Rep. X*, App., pt. 4, p. 21.

12 (247). Nicoll (p. 366) has overlooked this performance.

13 (247). Adams, *Dramatic Records*, p. 118.

14 (247). *Ibid.*

15 (247). *Ibid.* Nicoll, pp. 129, 366.

16 (248). Pepys, on 18 Feb., 1661/2, mentions that this actress had retired.

17 (248). *Var.*, iii, 269.

18 (249). No. 51.

19 (249). Ibid.

20 (249). C10 82/82. Norris *v.* Baker *et al.*

21 (249). L. C. 5/138, p. 417. Nicoll, p. 286 n.

22 (250). State Papers Dom., Charles II, clxxvii, 6.

23 (250). Ibid., clxxix, 136.

24 (250). No. 27. See Appendix, pp. 348 ff.

25 (252). Robert Streeter was "His Majesty's Sergeant Painter," and in 1671 and 1672 painted scenes for the Court Theatre in Whitehall. Cf. *Cal. Treasury Books, 1669–1672*, pp. 1158, 1330.

26 (253). It is interesting to compare with the foregoing the scene-painting agreement of 1699/1700, printed by Mr. Nicoll (p. 344), between Robert Robinson and the Theatre Royal company. Robinson thereby agrees to paint the scenes for an opera by Settle (probably *The Virgin Prophetesse*) within seven weeks from the date of the agreement.

27 (253). See *Reliquiæ Baxterianæ* (1696), iii, 89, 90. *Hist. MSS Comm., Rep. II*, App., p. 22a.

28 (254). *Notes and Queries*, Eighth Ser., x, 7. Wheatley, *London Past and Present*, i, 525.

29 (254). No. 52. Fitzgerald, in printing this document (from B. M., Add. MS. 20,726), gives "Lewens" for Lewright and "Wickens" for Nickens. Nicoll (p. 290) mistakenly says that the £2400 was a loan, to be repaid by the daily £3 10s. On the contrary, the £3 10s. was a rent, to be paid by the company, or users of the theatre, to the building investors, or owners of it, for every acting day. It must be kept in mind that the building investors named above (Ashton, Sheppey, etc.) were not the only owners of the building. Killigrew owned nine building shares, a full quarter of the total, and most of the actors each owned two.

30 (254). *The Athenæum*, 18 April, 1903.

31 (255). No. 51.

32 (255). No. 44.

33 (255). Not £1600, as Fitzgerald says (i, 139). Burt's part of these articles was printed in *The Shakespeare Society's Papers*, iii, 147 and copied thence by Fitzgerald. Not realizing that these articles with Burt were merely part of a larger agreement, Fitzgerald regarded the £160 as a special loan from Burt to the company. In this he is followed by Nicoll (p. 289), who also misdates the articles by a year.

34 (256). No. 80.

35 (256). *Var.*, iii, 172. Cf. B. M., Add. MS. 20,726.

36 (256). Chancery Reports, vol. 209, Kent *v.* Killigrew.

37 (257). B. M., Add. MS. 20,726.

38 (257). No. 47.

39 (258). No. 44.

40 (259). L. C. 7/1, p. 5. Nicoll, p. 292.

41 (259). Dated 10 Jan., 1661/2, 10 June, 1670, 12 Nov., 1672, and 20 March, 1673/4.

42 (259). No. 77.

43 (261). No. 44.

44 (261). Chancery Decree Roll 1164.

45 (261). *Gazette*, 1–5 Feb., 1676/7. Cf. L. C. 7/1, and Nicoll, p. 293 n.

46 (261). L. C. 5/142, p. 98. Nicoll, p. 293.

47 (262). No. 46.

48 (262). No. 42.

49 (262). Ibid.

50 (263). No. 43.

51 (263). L. C. 7/1. Nicoll, p. 297. Mr. Nicoll furnishes us with the outcome of the case, but mistakenly refers the Edinburgh journey to a
period after the union in 1682. As has been shown, the players were
in Scotland in 1679, and returned to London in Feb., 1679/80.

52 (263). L. C. 5/143, p. 506. Cf. Thaler, *Shakspere to Sheridan*, p. 293.

53 (263). *Hist. MSS Comm., Ormond Papers*, v, 320. Cf. Lawrence, *The
Elizabethan Playhouse* (Second Ser.), p. 197.

54 (264). J. P. Collier's Manuscript History of the Restoration Stage,
p. 230 (Harvard College Theatre Collection).

55 (264). L. C. 7/1, p. 9. Thaler, *loc. cit.*

56 (264). *Hist. MSS Comm., Ormond Papers*, v, 338. Cf. Lawrence,
loc. cit.

57 (264). No. 41.

58 (265). Cf. Lowe, *Betterton*, p. 125.

59 (266). C24 1058.53. 1681, 12 Oct.

60 (266). No. 46.

61 (267). Chancery Decrees and Orders, B1682, 14 Dec.

62 (268). Nicoll, pp. 293, 294.

63 (268). No. 77.

64 (269). Cf. Fitzgerald, i, 148.

65 (269). *Thomas Betterton*, pp. 126, 127.

66 (269). No. 77.

67 (270). No. 61.

68 (271). Not 14 May, as the date is incorrectly printed by Fitzgerald, i,
154, and Nicoll, p. 296.

69 (271). No. 41.

70 (272). C24 1070/63, *Ex parte* Killigrew *ads.* Griffin.

71 (274). No. 54.

72 (274). There were two actresses by the name of Leigh, besides a Mrs.
Mary Lee. The famous Mrs. Leigh, wife of Anthony Leigh, whom
Cibber applauded for her "droll way of dressing the pretty Foibles of
superannuated Beauties," cannot, however, be identical with the
Elizabeth Leigh of our Chancery suit, for the latter is described in
1681 as "spinster." A petition discovered by Mr. Nicoll (pp. 330,
340) clinches the matter by showing that the Mrs. *Ellen* Leigh who
signed was Anthony Leigh's widow. Lowe is wrong in concluding
(*Cibber*, i, 163 n, and *Betterton*, p. 144) that Leigh's wife was named
Elizabeth.

73 (276). Cf. Dodsley, *Theatrical Records*, p. 69; Cibber, *Lives of the
Poets*, iii, 353; *Biographica Dramatica*, vol. i, pt. II, p. 640; and F. C.
Brown, *Elkanah Settle*, p. 35.

74 (277). *Restoration Drama*, p. 140.

CHAPTER VII

THE UNITED COMPANY, 1682–1694

BETTERTON, now at the height of his powers, became as natural a leader of the united company as he had been of the Duke's players. Henry Harris, his chief rival at Dorset Garden, had just retired from acting. Among the veteran leaders of the King's company, Mohun was infirm, and seldom acted after the union; and as for Hart, Downes tells us that this great actor "being the Heart of the Company under Mr. *Killigrew's* Patent never *Acted* more, by reason of his Malady; being Afflicted with the Stone and Gravel, of which he Dy'd some time after." According to an elegy noted in Luttrell's *Diary*, "that Worthy and Famous Actor, Mr. Charles Hart . . . departed this Life Thursday August the 18th. 1683." [1] Wintershall and Lacy had died before the union, and Shatterell was dead before 1684. Burt had retired. Of the elder actors only Cartwright, Sheppey, and Kynaston remained as active members of the company for varying periods after 1682. From the younger group, Clarke, Perin, Disney, and Watson disappeared from view, while Griffin, Powell, and Sarah Cooke were taken into the united ranks.

As we learned in the preceding chapter, a decree in Chancery was passed on 14 December, 1682, making Kent's title to the Killigrew patent and shares absolute. On 19 March following, old Tom Killigrew died. Charles II contributed £50 toward the funeral expenses of his Jester, the quondam Master of his Players and of the Revels.[2] Two months later Tom's heir, Henry Killigrew, brought a suit against his half-brother, Charles, and Richard Kent,[3] from the record of which we take the following details.

Henry complains that he has been obliged to pay some of his father's debts out of his own estate, and accuses Kent of having "craftily and subtly" possessed himself of Tom's theatri-

cal interest; and alleges, further, that about the time of his
father's death there was a private agreement by which Kent
made over all his interest to Charles.

In answer, Kent quotes the decree which confirmed his title,
and then relates a subsequent agreement between himself and
Charles by which, "in consideration of £500 and a greater
sum to be thereafter paid," he absolutely sold to Charles all
his right and interest in the property. Unfortunately, I cannot
discover the total price Charles Killigrew was to pay. It is,
however, no wonder that Kent was ready to sell, when one
considers the negligible profit he had made from the Theatre
Royal property. From March, 1675/6, to July, 1682, his takings amounted in all to £563 5s. 10d. Even when we allow
for "rent" held back from him and put to other uses in 1681
and 1682, this sum shows that the King's company, in the last
seven years of its life, made pitifully small returns. His building shares alone, if the company had acted and paid for a nor-
mal 200 days a year, would have brought him more than
£1800.

Thus it is clear that with the union and the resulting good
management, even taking into account the reduction of the
"rent" from £5 14s. to £3 a day, a more prosperous era for the
Theatre Royal sharers was ushered in. I find that in June,
1683, the 36 building shares were held as follows:

Charles Killigrew	9
Thomas Morley	4.5
Thomas Sheppey	3.3
Nicholas Strawbridge	1.2
Joseph Nickens	1
Henry Tichburne	2
Charles Hart	2
Nicholas Burt	1
Richard Burt	1
William Cartwright	2
William Clayton	4
John Tombes	1
Margaret Lacy	4
Total	36 [4]

Under the new régime, the actors were more heavily taxed than before, since the managers had undertaken the continued support of two theatre buildings with but one company of actors. The building investors of the Dorset Garden theatre would never have consented to a plan which stopped their daily "rent" of £7; therefore the combined "rent" of £7 for Dorset Garden and £3 for the Drury Lane theatre had to be paid first out of the receipts of every acting day at either house. Although it seems to us a plan thoroughly disadvantageous, especially since the Dorset Garden house was but little used after the union, we shall see that a respectable profit was made on this arrangement for at least ten years.

The union, I find, had a disturbing effect on a perquisite formerly enjoyed at the Duke's Theatre by Dame Mary Davenant. In a certain answer in Chancery [5] her son, Charles Davenant, says that ever since the building of the Dorset Garden theatre his mother had enjoyed

. . . the sole liberty of selling and vending of fruit, Lemons, oranges, and Sweetmeats within the said Theatre . . . And being by reason of the said Union much prejudiced in and likely to lose the benefit she formerly enjoyed of, from, and by such persons that did use to sell fruit and Sweetmeats in the said Duke's Theatre at such times when plays were more constantly acted there than they were likely to be, both the said Companies being so united, That when any plays were acted at the said King's Theatre there was none like to be acted at the said Duke's Theatre,

Dame Mary, some time after the union, applied to Killigrew, Betterton, Smith, and Davenant, "who then were the owners of all or the principal and greatest shares of the profits arising by, from, and under both the said Letters patents," for some compensation. Accordingly, the four owners, "in Consideration and in lieu and recompense of such loss and also in Consideration of fifty pounds or fifty Guineas" paid by Davenant to Killigrew, executed a deed, 1 November, 1683, between themselves and Dame Mary, whereby it was agreed that from 9 November, 1683, for eighteen years, they should pay her five shillings "on every day any play or Interlude should be acted or shown at the said Theatre Royal and not at the said

Duke's Theatre." This sum was to be paid out of the gross receipts, and there was a proviso that Betterton and Smith should be bound by the agreement only so long as they continued as actors with the company. On acting days at the Theatre Royal, then, Dame Mary enjoyed this income in lieu of her fruit money until 30 May, 1687, when she sold it to Richard Middlemore and Andrew Card.[6] There was also a license granted for selling fruit at the Theatre Royal, concerning which we shall have more to say later.

The death of the merry monarch, Charles, in 1685 was a sad blow to a theatre which could ill afford to lose its chief patron. To make matters worse, his loss was accompanied by a ruinous expenditure on the scenes and machines devised by Betterton for Dryden's opera, *Albion and Albanius*. Unluckily, this magnificent production, written to celebrate Charles and James, opened on the day of Monmouth's landing, when England was in an uproar. More than half the outlay was lost, leaving the company in debt.

During the next few years the fortunes of the theatre were chiefly affected by the dealings of the Davenants. It will be recalled that Sir William Davenant at his death left 3.3 of his original 10 shares, and that another 1.2 reverted to his estate on the death of Ashburnham, making a property of 4.5 shares which came to Charles Davenant at his majority. On 8 October, 1678, Charles deeded one half-share to his mother. A certain courtier, Sir Thomas Skipwith (who assumes importance later), made his appearance in the theatrical arena by buying this half-share of Dame Mary Davenant on 31 March, 1682.[7]

Alexander Davenant supplanted his step-brother, Thomas Cross, as treasurer of the Duke's company on 30 November, 1675, and continued in that office until his marriage, which occurred in May, 1683, not long after the union. He married well, receiving £3000 with the hand of Allett, the daughter of one Henry Brome.[8] Able now to set up for himself, he bought a wood-wharf next to the theatre in Dorset Garden, and became a wood and coal merchant.[9] Later he also acquired a brewing establishment on Saffron Hill, London. On his resignation as treasurer another brother, Ralph Davenant, was appointed in his room.

Alexander's activity in these business ventures gave him an appearance of prosperity, by means of which he seems to have been able to deceive even his brother Charles as to his financial ability. No one knew that he had lost heavily in several unsuccessful speculations. Keeping the secret of his losses close, Alexander resolved to try his hand at making money from the playhouse. In May, 1687, he proposed to buy out Charles's interest in the theatrical concern for £2400, and Charles, not too provident in his own affairs, and an occasional heavy plunger himself, agreed to the bargain. Alexander had, however, conducted secret negotiations with the aforesaid Sir Thomas Skipwith and a certain lawyer named Christopher Rich. Thus it came about that when, on 30 August, 1687, Alexander paid down the £2400, only £400 of it was his own money, the remaining £2000 belonging to Skipwith.[10] This fact appears in a deed by which Alexander Davenant declared that five sixths of the profits were for the use of Skipwith, and only one sixth for himself.[11]

Charles Davenant professes ignorance of this arrangement, and says that he thought that Alexander was buying the property with his own money. The parcels so sold by Charles — his trustees, Thomas Betterton and one Edmond Bolsworth [12] being included in the deed — may be listed as follows:

1. All his acting or adventurers' shares (4 shares — $\frac{2}{10}$, or $\frac{4}{20}$);
2. His interest in apparel, scenes, clothes, and furniture;
3. His right to the Davenant patent;
4. The nineteen-year lease of the Theatre Royal, beginning 9 November, 1682;
5. All plays mentioned in the schedule annexed to the indenture of union (4 May, 1682).[13]

Charles reserved, however, "a Liberty of sending twelve Tickets a week for Persons to be admitted to see Plays in either of the said Theatres." [14]

Less than two weeks after the purchase, on 12 September, 1687, Skipwith made over his five sixths to Alexander for a period of seven years. Alexander was to farm the shares for his own advantage, and pay Skipwith £312 a year rent, in weekly payments of £6. Skipwith reserved the right to two box tickets, four pit tickets, or six middle-gallery tickets every week, and Alexander was to have the privilege of purchasing the five sixths from Skipwith at their cost price. By March, 1689/90, Alexander had sold his one sixth for £400 to Christopher Rich, who allowed him to farm it on similar terms, for £1 4s. a week. Rich was allowed the same number of free tickets as Skipwith.

In 1688, almost immediately after taking over the property, Alexander Davenant assumed control, and exercised his power with a high hand. Deposing Smith and Betterton, the veteran managers of acting, he appointed in their place his brother Thomas Davenant, a young man of twenty-four. And whereas they had each been receiving twenty shillings a week for their extra pains, Thomas now received their combined salary of forty shillings. Heretofore the managers of acting under the Davenant patent had been a distinguished group of dramatists and fine actors. Sir William himself had acted as manager until his death in 1668. From that time Betterton and Harris jointly directed the artistic policy of the theatre until 1677, when Harris withdrew, to be replaced by Smith. The latter, through no fault of his own, was forced off the stage in 1685 by a cabal of Mohawks; and although he continued in the management until the autumn of 1688, he may well have been ready to withdraw after Alexander's advent. We learn, too, that young Thomas Davenant was counselled by Betterton in his handling of affairs, though Betterton received no compensation for this service.

The company which young Davenant managed in the spring of 1688, before James was driven from the throne, consisted of the following persons: Betterton, Smith (nominally), Underhill, Nokes, Sandford, Pavy, and John Downes (all of the early Duke's company), and Sheppey, Kynaston, Griffin, and Martin Powell (the elder actors from the King's company before the union), together with Joseph Williams, Anthony

Leigh, Thomas Jevon, John Verbruggen, John Bowman, Francis Baker, George Bright, William Mountfort, John Freeman, George Powell, Henry Boutell, John Barr, Thomas Simpson, and Aaron Darby. As actresses there were Elizabeth Barry, Margaret Osborne, Francis Maria Knight, Katherine Davies, Anne Bracegirdle, and Sarah Cooke.[15] The actress last mentioned died in this very spring of 1688. This and other details are found in a letter written by Lord Granville, 5 May, 1688:

> We have had a new play called The Fall of Darius (written by Crowne) by which the poet, though he could get no fame, yet had a most extraordinary third day by reason of the King's presence at it; the first day of its acting Mrs. Bower [Bowen ?] was taken so violently ill in the midst of her part that she was forced to be carried off, and instead of dying in jest was in danger of doing it in earnest. Mrs. Cook is dead and Mrs. Boute[ll] is again come upon the stage, where she appears with great applause.[16]

In our preoccupation with the Davenants we must not lose sight of Killigrew. At the union, it will be recalled, he was to have not only joint control (as owner of the Killigrew patent), but also his $\frac{3}{36}$ of the Theatre Royal "rent" of £3 daily — fifteen shillings — and $\frac{3}{20}$ of all the acting profits.

Concerning this $\frac{3}{20}$ there arose a disagreement which was settled only by a long suit in Chancery.[17] Briefly, Alexander Davenant testified that Killigrew came to him (as treasurer) after the union and told him that by the agreement he was to have "three shares equal to three shares in twenty of the said clear profits, and did then and there contrive . . . the method and manner of charging his three shares in the Book of accounts." Actually, Killigrew received, not $\frac{3}{20}$, but $\frac{3}{23}$ of the profits. And that this adjustment was not a dishonest trick of Alexander's is shown by the testimony of Betterton and Smith, who insist that the understanding of all concerned was that Killigrew's shares were to be calculated on this basis, that is, $\frac{3}{23}$. After receiving his shares on this computation for three years, however, Killigrew began to complain that he had been wronged, and demanded of Charles Davenant payment of his arrears. Charles referred the matter to George (later

Baron) Bradbury, the theatre's counsel, who decided, upon reading the articles as written, that Killigrew should receive ³⁄₂₀ and not ³⁄₂₃. Ralph Davenant, having come in as treasurer in 1684, was therefore ordered to pay Killigrew his arrears of £159 4s. Payment continued at the rate of ³⁄₂₀ until Alexander got control of the Davenant patent and shares, in 1687. Then, on the ground that "other sharers complained of the wrong," he ordered Ralph to reduce Killigrew's payment to the former scale, ³⁄₂₃. This action urged Killigrew to seek redress in the courts. He complained not only on the foregoing grounds, but also, among other things, because Alexander had put in Thomas Davenant as manager without his consent.

On 7 December, 1691, the court decreed [18] that Killigrew should have his ³⁄₂₀, and directed Sir Robert Legard, a master in Chancery, to take an account of profits in the theatres since the union. Legard's report, made 27 July, 1693,[19] contains the following statement:

I have looked into the Books of Account relating to the Theatres, And do find that the profits . . . from the 4th day of May 1682 to the 3d of August last [that is, 1692] inclusive amount to the sum of £103,988 5s. 7d. And I find that the Constant and Incident Charges for and by Reason of Acting of Plays for the same time amount to the sum of £85,393 19s. 0d. Which being deducted out of the said sum of £103,988 5s. 7d. There remains Clear Profits the sum of £18,594 6s. 7d. Which being divided into 20 Equal parts, Three parts thereof do belong to the plaintiff, and do amount to the sum of £2,789 2s. 11¼d. And I do find that there hath been paid to the plaintiff and his order several sums amounting in the whole to the sum of £2,790 6s. 0d. (The Particulars of all which Receipts, Charges, and Payments to the plaintiff are set forth in Two Paper Books Each containing Three Schedules which I have signed with my hand and delivered one to each of the said Parties) Which sum of £2,789 2s. 11¼d. being deducted out of the said sum of £2,790 6s. 0d., there remains due to the defendants which they have paid to the plaintiff beyond his said three shares . . . the sum of £1 3s. ¾d. Which sum I appoint the Plaintiff to pay to the Defendants according to the said order . . . And as to the Defendants' demand of Allowance at the rate of £30 per annum to be charged upon the plaintiff for Ticket Money, I take it to be a consequence of what shall be the opinion of this Court touching the State of the Government . . . and of the Rights of the Patentees and their Assigns. And if this Court shall be of opinion that the plaintiff hath no other Rights or powers than according to his shares of three in Twenty then I find that the Tickets which the plaintiff hath given gratis for seeing of Plays do when valued in money exceed that proportion after the rate of £30 per annum at Least; which being reckoned from the Time of the Union of the Patents to the year 1692 comes to 10 years and makes in all £300.

From this report it appears that Killigrew was ill-advised to sue for arrears, for it was proved that he had been overpaid. I cannot find the court's decision on the matter of the £300 ticket money, which the other sharers made as a counter-charge against Killigrew. Legard's report is chiefly valuable for its statement of the receipts, expenditures, and profits of the united company during the ten years from 1682 to 1692. Receipts averaged about £10,400 a year, or roughly £50 a day (allowing 200 acting days to a year), of which £9 6s. (to-day equivalent to between $280 and $370) was clear profit. When the profits were divided into 23 shares, each sharer received about £2 9s. a week; but when Killigrew obtained his ³⁄₂₀ first, before any division, he received £2 16s. 4d. for each of his three shares, and the rest of the sharers, redividing the remaining ¹⁷⁄₂₀ again into 20 shares, were reduced to £2 7s. 10d. for each share.

While this report was being prepared, Killigrew, on 17 March, 1691/2, complained in a petition to the court that Alexander Davenant

. . . who takes upon him the sole government of the Playhouses is . . . endeavoring to make a lease to some person . . . in Trust for himself for some long term of years of . . . the after money (that is money given by persons who come in after the first and second Acts) and that for some small and inconsiderable Fine; whenas the same is of more than 3 times the value of such Fine, and the same like to prove of very mischievous Consequence in creating differences touching the receipt of the said profits.

Killigrew therefore prayed that Davenant might be enjoined from leasing such after-money.

Evidently this custom of coming in after the second act of a three-act play, and after the third act of a five-act play, at a reduced rate, was a common proceeding among those who could not afford the whole price of a ticket. Ned Ward, in his *London Spy* (1700), describes certain ladies in the park, who "began to flow as fast into the Walks, as Whores into the Eighteen-Penny Gallery, at the third Act." In an affidavit, Alexander Davenant claims the honor of having discovered that money could be made for the theatres in this fashion, asserting "that he was the first person that found out the said profit of after Money, which hath turned to good Account." [20]

Argument for and against the proposed lease of the after-money was heard by the court on 13 May, 1692. Davenant's counsel insisted that such a lease should be made for a term of seventeen years, to raise £1000 "to pay the debts of the Theatres and to leave a fund of £200 to buy goods for the future with ready money." Convinced of the desirability of this plan, the court ordered the lease to be made accordingly, under Sir Robert Legard's direction. [21]

Not only does the foregoing suit show that the theatre was not prospering, — being £800 in debt in February, 1691/2, — but several depositions of Williams, Mountfort, and Bowman [22] evince the discontent of the actors. It appears that they made a request to Killigrew and Thomas Davenant, as managers, for a redress of grievances "relating to the management of the moneys." Audiences were slim in 1691 and 1692, and the managers began the apparently logical but really ruinous policy of reducing the salaries of the actors. "And," says Colley Cibber, who had joined the company in 1690, "what seem'd to make this Resolution more necessary at this time was the Loss of *Nokes*, *Monfort*, and *Leigh*, who all dy'd about the same Year." [23] While quite accurate in the case of Mountfort and Leigh, who died in December, 1692, Cibber's memory played him a trick over Nokes's death, which did not occur until four years later. From a Chancery suit [24] I find that he died in September, 1696, leaving a personal estate of more than £1500. A number of *The Protestant Mercury* adds the following particulars:

September 9. Last night dyed Mr. *Noaks*, the famous Comedian, some miles out of Town, and 't is said, has left a considerable Estate, tho' he has not frequented the Play-house constantly for some years. [25]

In 1692 Mountfort and Leigh were among the leaders of the company, and their loss was a serious blow.

Another useful denizen of the Theatre Royal had also died the year before — the chief orange-woman, universally called Orange Moll. This personage not only quenched the thirst of the playgoer with oranges at sixpence apiece, but dispensed playhouse news and gossip to her patrons, among whom had been numbered Sir William Penn and Samuel Pepys.[26] Doubtless her most lucrative occupation was the carrying of messages about the theatre; but on one occasion, at least, her capable tongue got the better of her. There was an unfortunate altercation with Beck Marshall, a leading actress of the company, and Moll no doubt uttered some plain and stinging truths in public, for the Lord Chamberlain ordered her arrest for "abusing Mrs. Rebecca Marshall."[27] We may, however, offset this indiscretion of hers by pointing out that she once heroically brought a gentleman who had choked on some of her fruit back to life by pushing the obstruction down his throat.[28] She used to keep her stock of fruit under some stairs at the back of the playhouse; and, as we have seen, it was there that the disastrous fire began which destroyed the Theatre Royal on Thursday evening, 25 January, 1671/2.[29]

Orange Moll's legal name was Mrs. Mary Meggs. She was a widow, and lived in the parish of St. Paul's, Covent Garden. Concerning her and her relations with the theatre I have uncovered a deal of information in the records of the Chancery.

We first hear of her just after the completion of the Theatre Royal in Bridges Street, and three months before its opening. On 10 February, 1662/3, the builders and owners of the theatre (Sir Robert Howard, Tom Killigrew, Burt, Mohun, Hart, and the rest) granted to her, on payment of £100,

. . . full, free, & sole liberty, license, power, & authority to vend, utter, & sell oranges, Lemons, fruit, sweetmeats, & all manner of fruiterers & Confectioners wares & commodities in all that new built messuage or house made & intended to be used as a public Theater or Stage . . . excepting unto the use, benefit, & advantage of the uppermost Galleries in the said Theater . . . [with] full & free access & liberty of ingress, egress, & regress for her . . . and assigns, not exceeding three persons in one day to appear in number (That is to say, two persons to be in the pit, & one in & about the boxes & lower rooms) into the said Pit, boxes, & lower Rooms at all & every seasonable time & times . . .[30]

The license was to run for thirty-nine years, and Mrs. Meggs was to pay 6s. 8d. every acting day. How she used her privileges is the subject of a suit in Chancery brought by the owners of the theatre in 1684,[31] who assert that, after they had entrusted the counterpart of the aforesaid agreement to a scrivener, Mrs. Meggs very cunningly got it away from him, and hid it. And knowing that the owners, deprived of their documentary evidence, could not sue at law, she made her payments to them very few and small. To their demand for payment of arrears she replies that, although she kept no account (her method being to pay daily), she is positive that she owes only for three days or so. She insists that she paid in full up to 21 June, 1680; and that

when after that time the Players began to act, The said Mr. Killigrew and Sheppey took this Defendant out of the said Playhouse by force and violence whilst she was selling her Fruit and sweetmeats and withheld her out by the Space of Six weeks at the least.

For some unexplained reason she was thereafter allowed gratis to sell until the union, when the Duke's company

. . . put in a person of their own to sell Fruit and sweetmeats and kept the Defendant out until about the beginning of October [1683] . . . Since which time this Defendant hath constantly paid her said rent.

She submits it as her opinion that she should not be required to pay rent either while she was kept out, or while she was permitted gratis to sell in the playhouse.

Whatever the result of the 1684 suit may have been, Orange Moll's later payments were unsatisfactory to the owners, for in 1690 we find them complaining again. She now admitted that something was really due, but that after 10 February, 1689/90, she had been wrongfully excluded from selling fruit, contrary to the terms of her license.

Before this second suit was heard, we learn that Orange Moll died, on 21 January, 1690/1, having by her will of 24 April, 1682, made the actor, Captain Philip Griffin, her executor. To him she left her fruit-selling lease, which, it was alleged, had gone up in value to £150 or £200. A picture of Griffin, found among her effects, was claimed by its original. She also left to her brother, a mariner, a good property of three houses, one of which was let to a minister at £50 a year.

So passed Orange Moll, who, as we have seen, had other claims to fame besides that of having employed the young and as yet unknown Nell Gwyn to help her sell oranges and lemons in the King's playhouse.

Not only was the theatre weakened by the loss of valuable actors and priceless orange-wenches, but Alexander Davenant had used his ill-got credit to carry through a long series of swindling operations. We shall not get involved in the devious strands of his dishonesty. Enough to say that two of his favorite tricks were to sell the same property twice, and to borrow up to the limit on property which did not belong to him. Managing, however, to avoid arrest even at the last minute, he fled (23 October, 1693) to the Canary Islands. Disclosure of his knavery was naturally followed by a shower of complaints in Chancery from his victims.

Skipwith and Rich, who had allowed Alexander to farm their shares, complained that he was a year behind with his payments to them.[32] At the beginning of December, 1693, Rich and Skipwith, as they themselves testify, "discovered to the said Charles Killigrew, Mr. Betterton, and others concerned the said Conveyance and assignment so made by the said Alexander Davenant"; and Rich thereupon "entered on the said Theatres and concerned himself in the Government of the Company . . . in Conjunction with the said Charles Killigrew and others." This is Rich's modest way of saying that by one means or another he arrogated the whole power to himself. Within the next few years he earned the name of being "as sly a Tyrant as ever was at the Head of a Theatre." Rich also informs us that his friend Skipwith's real proportion of the £2400 purchase money was not £2000, but £1500; and that his (Rich's) was not £400, but £900.

Whether that be true or not, it is undeniable that the company went rapidly from bad to worse as soon as this crafty lawyer took control. Not content with further salary reductions, he began to divide the actors against themselves by giving Betterton's chief parts to George Powell. Alarmed at this stroke, Betterton adroitly gathered a large group of the best actors about him, who, as Cibber tells us, "enter'd with him into a sort of Association to stand or fall together." [33]

The cunning Rich fancied that as patentee he could ride the storm, and continued his ill-treatment of the best actors. At the end of a year the latter could endure it no longer, and in December, 1694, Betterton laid a long paper of grievances before the Lord Chamberlain, signed by himself, Underhill, Kynaston, Bowen, Bowman, Williams, Doggett, Bright, Sandford, Mrs. Barry, Mrs. Bracegirdle, Mrs. Verbruggen, Mrs. Bowman, Mrs. Betterton, and Mrs. Ellen[or] Leigh.[34] A categoric answer submitted by Rich and Skipwith gave no satisfaction to the complainants, and a hearing before Sir Robert Howard failed to compose their differences.

When, on 22 December, the company ceased acting because of the grave illness of Queen Mary, the unexpected leisure gave Betterton and his fellow actors an opportunity to consolidate their position and to enlist the sympathy of influential courtiers in their favor. After several abortive attempts on the part of the patentees and the Lord Chamberlain to effect a settlement, the players began definitely to work toward independence. By this time Sir Robert Howard and the Lord Chamberlain, Lord Dorset, had both been won to their side, and the latter recommended the King to grant them permission to set up a separate company. By March, 1694/5, Betterton was so confident of victory that he and his band hired the old Lisle's Tennis Court, — where he had begun as actor under Sir William Davenant more than thirty years before, — and moved rapidly to reconvert it into a playhouse. A subscription raised by "several persons of quality" aided them in their undertaking. Rich protested in vain. Betterton, Mrs. Barry, and Mrs. Bracegirdle appealed to Caesar; and after hearing their story in private audience, King William granted them a separate license. Issued through the Lord Chamberlain's office on 25 March, 1695, to Betterton, Mrs. Barry, Mrs. Bracegirdle, Bowman, Williams, Underhill, Doggett, Bowen, Mrs. Verbruggen, Mrs. Leigh, and Bright, this license destroyed the one-company monopoly which had existed since 1682.[35]

NOTES FOR CHAPTER VII

1 (281). Luttrell, i, 62. I owe this note to the kindness of Professor Rollins. Cf. the copy of the elegy, printed by Mr. G. Thorn-Drury, in *A Little Ark* (1921), p. 47. 18 Aug., 1683, was, however, not Thursday, but Saturday.

2 (281). *Secret Services, Charles II and James II* (Camden Society), p. 70.

3 (281). Nos. 48–50.

4 (282). No. 87.

5 (283). No. 84.

6 (284). No. 104.

7 (284). No. 98.

8 (284). Chancery Decree Roll 2034, Davenant *v.* Powell.

9 (284). C6 316, Powle *v.* Davenant.

10 (285). Chancery Decrees and Orders, Entry Book A1708, p. 130*b*.

11 (285). Indenture 30 Aug., 1687, between Charles Davenant, Thomas Betterton, William Smith (1) and Alexander Davenant (2). Recites lease of Theatre Royal 7 June, 1683, to Charles Davenant, and witnesses that for 10*s.* Charles has sold to Alexander all the shares in the Theatre Royal for the rest of the term of nineteen years. Alexander promises to pay the rent regularly.

> [*Signed*] "CHARLES DAVENANT THO: BETTERTON"

[*Endorsed*] "I Alexander Davenant do assigne & sett over unto Christopher Rich gent The Indenture of Lease of the Theatre and p'misses within menconed with the appurtenances To Hold to him the said Christopher Rich his Executors . . . [for the rest of the 19 years] In Trust nevertheless for the use & Benefitt of Thomas Skipwith of Lincolns Inne ffeilds in County of Midd Esqr & the said Chr. Rich But subject to certain Articles of Agreemt bearing date" 12 Sept. 1687 between Alexander and Skipwith, and an endorsement thereon 18 March 1689/90. Hand and seal this 24 March 1690/1

> [*Signed*]
> "ALEXAND^R D'AVENANT"
>   [B. M., Add. Ch. 9298.]

Articles 12 Sept., 1687, between Skipwith and Alexander Davenant. Recite that Charles Davenant, 30 May, 1687, agreed to convey before 30 Aug. to Alexander the patent, his interest in the Dorset Garden theatre, and his ⁷⁄₁₀ of the profits of acting forever, for £2300. Recite deed of 10 Aug., by which Alexander declared that the said agreement was made by him as to £2000 of the purchase money in trust for Sir Thomas Skipwith, and as to the other £300, for himself. It was agreed that since Alexander had "driven on and sollicited" the bargain with Charles Davenant, that he should proceed therein; that when Charles's trustees should execute the conveyances, Skipwith should pay his £2000 and Alexander his £300, and the writings relating to the title should be delivered into the custody of Skipwith or Rich. Also declared that assignment of lease of Theatre Royal in Bridges Street and the agreement with Hart and Kynaston were included in the purchase. Further agreed that Alexander might reckon charges and fees for conveyances and his consideration at £100, which added to £300 makes his share of purchase £400, and the whole sum to be paid, £2400. Agreed that profits should be divided into six parts, five for Skipwith, and one for Alexander. Alexander was to do nothing without the consent of Skipwith.

Now agreed that when the premises are fully conveyed Skipwith will lease his five parts to Alexander for seven years from 10 September, instant, at a yearly rent of £312, to be paid £6 weekly. Skipwith reserves two box tickets every week, or four pit, or six middle-gallery tickets, and he is to have free access to the account books. Alexander is to have the privilege (on six months' notice) of buying Skipwith's shares for £2000, provided that he has regularly paid the £6 a week rent.

[*Signed*] "THO SKIPWITH"

[*Endorsed*] Recites that Alexander, 17 March, 1689/90, sold his sixth part to Christopher Rich for £400. Hereby agreed that Alexander shall hold and manage the sixth part for the rest of the seven years (to expire 10 Sept., 1694) at a weekly rent to Rich of £1 4*s*., with a privilege of redemption for £350. Dated 18 March, 1689/90.

[*Signed*] "ALEX. D'AVENANT"

[B. M., Add. Ch. 9299.]

The completed agreement is set out at large under date of 26 March, 1691, in B. M., Add. Ch. 9302.

12 (285). Bolsworth, as trustee for Davenant's wife, disapproved of the sale, and declined to put his name to the document, thus causing Charles considerable embarrassment.

13 (285). No. 83.

14 (285). No. 98.

15 (287). Nicoll, p. 298.

16 (287). *Hist. MSS Comm., Rep. V*, App., p. 197.

17 (287). No. 61.

18 (288). Chancery Decrees and Orders, Entry Book A1691, pp. 371–373.

19 (288). Chancery Reports, vol. 246 (1693).

20 (290). Chancery Register of Affidavits, vol. 31. E1692, No. 460.

21 (290). Chancery Decrees and Orders, Entry Book A1691, p. 775.

22 (290). C24 1144/11.

23 (290). Lowe, *Cibber*, i, 188.

24 (290). C5 290/63, Huxley *v.* Nokes.

25 (290). 7–9 Sept., 1696. This passage was pointed out to me by Professor Rollins.

26 (291). Pepys, 29 Aug., 1666; 22 and 26 Aug., 1667.

27 (291). Nicoll, p. 285 n.

28 (291). Pepys, 2 Nov., 1667.

29 (291). See above, p. 253.
30 (292). No. 58.
31 (292). No. 56.
32 (293). No. 96.
33 (294). Lowe, *Cibber*, i, 189.
34 (294). L. C. 7/3.   Printed by Nicoll, pp. 330 ff.
35 (295). L. C. 7/1.   Cf. Nicoll, p. 301

CHAPTER VIII

RIVAL COMPANIES, 1695–1705

KING WILLIAM'S grant of independence to the seceding players galvanized Rich and his fellow patentees into
action. If they hoped to continue their company, they must
not only try to buy back some of the rebels, but also secure the
adherence of the remnant of their staff by large increases in
pay. At the outset the Betterton company made the mistake
of refusing to admit Mrs. Verbruggen (formerly Mrs. Mountfort) and Williams as sharers; whereupon these excellent players went back to Drury Lane. A week before the Lord Chamberlain forbade any actors to leave either company for the
other (16 April, 1695), Rich managed to get back Verbruggen,
but it is not certain that he was able to keep him permanently
from Betterton's camp. In similar fashion, Doggett seems to
have shifted masters more than once during the next few years,
in spite of the Chamberlain's prohibition.

Betterton got off to a flying start on Monday, 29 April, 1695,
with Congreve's new play, *Love for Love*, which proved a
phenomenal success. Everything indeed seemed to favor the
rebels, except the inconveniency and smallness of their house;
for they had a large part of the nobility on their side, and their
actors were far better and more experienced.

Over against them, Rich presented a sorry front, in spite of
his hold on the two good theatres. We find him (some five
years later) testifying[1] to the financial strain to which he
and his allies were subjected during this crisis. After Queen
Mary's death, and throughout the suspension of acting, which
lasted until 30 March, 1695,[2] Rich says that

subsistance money was allowed not only to several actors and others who
did not desert . . . But also to several persons who were hired and entertained to act, sing, or dance under the said Letters patents to fill up the
Company; And moneys were expended in and about Rehearsals of plays

and preparations for acting, and with intent to hinder the said deserting actors and others from setting up or acting for themselves in Opposition and prejudice to the said Letters patents and the Interest under the same.

Killigrew, Skipwith, and Rich, as owners of the patents, even contemplated giving up altogether,

it being debated between them . . . whether to carry on acting or to desist by reason of the said chief actors and others deserting as aforesaid . . . it was thought that if acting were not carried on under the authority of the said Letters patents that the whole concern might be lost; And therefore it was resolved . . . to carry on acting with all possible vigor, and for that purpose to hire and entertain Actors and others, and to Endeavor to procure the Return of all (or so many as could be) of such as had deserted, and to use such means as should be advised for the Recalling or annulling of the said License granted . . . by the Earl of Dorset.

All these proceedings told heavily on their pocketbooks. We have it from Cibber that the salaries of the chief actors who stood by Rich were doubled. An additional expense was incurred when Skipwith and Rich appointed Captain Griffin as manager of their tail-end of a company — a post which he held until his journey to Ireland in August, 1699.

In the ten years which elapsed from 1695 to 1704, Rich paid no dividends to the adventurers, and none of the "rent" due to the building investors of the Dorset Garden theatre. That he fraudulently kept profits for himself during this time is not proved, but may be strongly suspected. At all events, the shareholders were thoroughly dissatisfied. At this point it may be interesting to insert selections from a complaint in Chancery which reveal the attitude of mind of some of the minor adventurers. At Queen Mary's death the twenty shares (into which the seventeen which remained after Killigrew's three had been taken out were redivided) were claimed, ten by the sharing actors, and ten as listed on the opposite page.

Bridget, the widow of Richard Bayly, married Sir Edward Smith. In 1704 this Sir Edward and two other small shareholders brought suit [3] against Skipwith, Rich, Davenant, and others on the ground that "they shuffle, conceal, and refuse to discover" the profits of acting. These complainants make ex-

Skipwith	1.75
Rich	1.75
Sir John Brownlow	2.
John Metcalfe	.5
Ann Syderfin	.5
Mrs. Gooding and Ann Syderfin	.5
Bridget Bayly	.5
Thomas Goodall	.75
Ashburnham Froude	.333
Ashburnham Toll	.333
Ann Shadwell and Mr. Pierce	.25
Benjamin Godwin	.5
Paul Cross	.25
Thomas Davenant	.084
Total	10.⁴

traordinary and novel charges, which include an assertion that Betterton's group,

. . . who had been bred up and taught at the Charge of the said Patentees and Adventurers . . . by the Instigation, Contrivance, and promotion of the said Doctor Davenant, mutined and pretended to be dissatisfied, and . . . withdrew themselves from further Acting under the said Patents.

The patentees (the complaint continues) falsely pretend that, because of the separation and the expenses arising therefrom, not only has there been no profit, but the theatrical enterprise has accumulated a debt of £10,000; whereas

in truth such division of the said Betterton and his Accomplices . . . was set on foot by . . . Sir Thomas Skipwith, Christopher Rich, and Doctor Davenant and their Accomplices on purpose to give a pretence to the stopping of the payment to your Orators of their respective shares . . . of the profits; which is the rather probable in regard when the said New Playhouse in Lincoln's Inn fields hath been destitute of Actors or needed such persons as were fit to act parts therein, occasion hath been given of Disgust to some of the principal Actors from time to time at the said Playhouses in Dorset Garden and Drury Lane, to the end they might with the better color retire from thence and go over to the New Playhouse . . . (when in truth they could not have done so without their permission), in order to keep up and support the said Playhouse which must long ere now have declined and totally sunk if it had not had and received secret supplies and support from such . . . as have the management of the said Theatres in Dorset Garden and Drury Lane . . . And the same is further manifest for that by Agreement between the said Managers under the . . . patents and the Managers of the said New Playhouse . . . plays were and are often times in Lent times, the Long Vacation, and at several other times when the Town is thin of Company . . . acted by turns in Succession by each Society so that their showing plays might and may not interfere to their mutual prejudice: one Society or Company being to Show under the said Patents one day, and for that time no acting was and is to be at the said New Playhouse; and on the Subsequent day there was and is to be acting at the said New Playhouse, and for that time . . . no acting at either of the said Playhouses in Dorset Garden and Drury Lane; which manner of Dealing between the two Societies plainly demonstrates there is a Very good Correspondence kept up between their respective Managers, and that such Division and Animosities as seemed to be between them were not real but only colorable, and done on purpose and with design to blind the matter and give the said Managers of the said Theatres in Dorset Garden and Drury Lane an Opportunity and a fair pretence to defeat and defraud your Orators of their said respective shares and Interests.

Further charges follow, such as one to the effect that the patentees collected money from the adventurers to pay for an effort to obtain the revocation of Betterton's license, which effort was never made or intended to be made; and another, that in the nine years from 1696 to 1704 the patentees had given the actors on an average sixty benefit plays every year, "to prevent their desertion and mutining."

While it certainly may be true that Rich defrauded the adventurers to some extent, it is quite impossible to believe in any such elaborate system of deceit as Sir Edward's complaint pictures. How he hoped to persuade the court to believe it is a mystery.

To return to the facts of the matter, it is clear that Betterton's company would have been wiser to mix enough of the Drury Lane tyranny with their new freedom to guarantee to themselves a stable government. Carelessness and dissension within their ranks proved their undoing. Betterton did all he could to maintain order; but in spite of his best efforts the players grew more and more slack.

The dignity of the stage had been seriously impaired by the division into two theatres, one managed by a fop and a lawyer (neither of whom knew anything of theatrical art), the other almost in a state of disintegration. The contemporary drama was susceptible of censure in more than one regard; and when the Reverend Jeremy Collier, in his famous *Short View of the Immorality and Profaneness of the English Stage*, smote it hip and thigh, the theatres as well as the playwrights staggered under the blow.

This was in 1698. In the year following, a vigorous word-picture appeared in *The Country Gentleman's Vade Mecum*,[5] which gives a more impartial and perspicuous view of the temple of the decadent drama. I can do no better than to quote:

The *Stage*, I must needs own, was originally (till so many immoral Practices and Irregularities broke in upon it) of admirable use and Design. . . . If you will come there now, you must take it as Men do their Wives, For Better, for Worse; 't is already in a state of Declension, and for my part, I am not so much a Friend to the *Mob*, or the *Phanaticks* either, to give my Vote for its utter Extirpation. To go on then, if it be a New Play, the House is commonly very full, especially if the Author be a new One too; upon such occasions, every body that has any Inclination for the *Playhouse*, is willing to gratify his Itch with a Novelty.

Tho' indeed I must confess, when I look into the Plays that were writ formerly, and compare them with the generality that have been writ here a late, in my poor Judgment, the *Plots* and *Characters*, and (what's more strange) the *Stile* too, is grown so profoundly dull and flat that a Man must have a very good Appetite, that can digest such intolerable trash, without a Surfeit. Well, let it be what it will, provided it be stampt with a New Name, and a strange title, it certainly raises the *Mob*, calls together the *Whores* and *Bawds*, the *Squires*, *Beaus*, *Cits*, *Bullies*, &c. that come all crowding in shoals to hear what this wondrous New Man can say, or do, to please 'em. The third Day, if by the help of a good *Prologue* and *Epilogue*, good *Acting*, good *Dancing*, and *Singing*, good *Scenes*, and the like, the Sickly half-got Brat can be kept alive so long, is commonly the grand Day; then you may observe the general Humours of the *House*. In one part of it you'll see the *Judges*, and the *Wits*, with abundance of Hangers-on, and *Interlopers*, censuring and mistaking the *Scene*, if there be any, for the *Non-sence;* 't is ten to one if there be any Part above the rest, but some of these pretending *Coxcombs* unluckily pitch upon that, for their Subject to laugh at: the Reason of this is very plain, perhaps they may know a little of the *Merry Andrew* Parts, the dull *Jokes* and *Drolls*, which at best are but the Rubbidge and Lumber of the *Play;* but for the Flights and *Extasies*, and the shining Parts of it, those are utterly out of their Element; and so consequently they are forc'd to damn and censure 'em in course, because they don't understand 'em; the poor Poet must be confounded and maul'd, and, what's worse, if there be e're a *Phanatick* that sets up for a

Judge, if there's but a few accidental Expressions, that don't exactly square with his Opinion, and Inclination, the whole *Play*, upon the score of one single Character or Paragraph, must be esteem'd a *Satyr* against the Government, and have an *Embargo* laid upon it and the poor Author be doom'd as an Enemy to the Publick, to be taken into Custody, and whipt, &c. This, within the compass of my own Knowledge, has been the Fate of some of 'em; and indeed I have known One of the best *Tragedies* that ever was writ, stopt upon such a Peque. In another part of the House sit the *Poet's* Friends, which are resolv'd to carry him off, right or wrong; 't is no matter to them, whether the *Play* be well or ill done, they're engag'd either for Friendship, Interest, or else by a Natural Spirit of Contradiction, to oppose the other Faction; and those you'll observe stradling upon the Seats, hollowing, clapping, and flouncing, and making such an impertinent Clatter and Noise, and using so many insolent and indecent Actions, that I advise you as a Friend, to keep as far from 'em as you can. But, what's worse still, perhaps, in the very nick of all, comes in a drunken Lord, with a Party of *Low Country* Warriours; or, what's more common, a Country *Squire*, that has lately taken up the Noble Profession of Scowring and Revelling; and to shew their Parts and their Courage, raise a Quarrel, and put the whole House into a Hurly-burly; then you'll see fine Work, indeed; the *Whores* tumbling over the Seats, and the poor *Squires* and *Beaus* tumbling after 'em in a horrible fright, and disorder; the whole *Pit's* in Arms in a Minute, and every Man's Sword drawn, to defend himself; so that if the Uproar be not instantly supprest, 't is great odds but there's some body murder'd. These Insurrections, I confess, don't often happen, and 't is well they do not; for if they shou'd, they might ev'n play by themselves: for, who but a mad Man would run the risque of being stab'd, or trode to Death, to gratify himself with an empty, insignificant Curiosity? And, indeed, most of our *Novel Farces* have little else, but barely that to recommend 'em.

While we are on the subject of armed violence and the theatre, it is possible to draw up quite a little list — disregarding casual affrays between enraged playgoers — of fatal accidents in which players figured. On the night of 2 August, 1664, Clun, while passing Tottenham Court on his way home, was set upon by highwaymen, "robbed, and most inhumanly murdered." Ralph Davenant met a similar fate on 18 May, 1698; we read that "about 12 last night Mr. D'avent, treasurer of the play house, was murthered by 3 soldiers, as he was goeing into his own lodgings in Grayes Inn Lane, who designed to have robbed the house." [6]

More brutal still was the notorious and dastardly murder of

Mountfort by Captain Hill, with the help of Lord Mohun, on 9 December, 1692, thus reported by Luttrell:

Last night lord Mohun, captain Hill of collonel Earles regiment, and others, pursued Mountfort the actor from the playhouse to his lodgings in Norfolk Street, where one kist him while Hill run him thro' the belly: they ran away, but his lordship was this morning seized and committed to prison. Mountfort died of his wounds this afternoon. The quarrell was about Bracegirdle the actresse, whom they would have trepan'd away, but Mountfort prevented it, wherefore they murthered him thus.[7]

Colley Cibber deplored the loss in 1696 of Hildebrand Horden, a promising young player, "who was kill'd at the bar of the Rose-Tavern, in a frivolous, rash, accidental quarrel."

Murders and brawls were not alone in taking toll; players and managers were not above duelling in cold blood. Under the date of 19 March, 1691/2, we read: "A duell was yesterday fought between captain Hoard of the Provo, and Williams the player; the former was killed." [8] And again, on 31 January following: "A duell was yesterday fought between Mr. Chamberlain and Mr. Killigrew of the play house." [9] Tragedy was acted to the life on 6 September, 1693, when

one Mr. Pavey, father and son belonging to the playhouse, being together at Temple tavern in Fleetstreet, the father reprimanding the son for some extravagancies, but he not being able to bear the same, threw himselfe on his sword, and fell down dead.[10]

The freedom of certain of the actors with their swords aroused the indignation of the Lords on 5 May, 1698:

The lord Monmouth moved the house against the impudence of the actors at the playhouses, upon Powells wounding a gentleman; and the lords with the white staves are to desire his majestie that none of the players wear swords.

A year later the players were still armed, and ready if need be for a pitched battle, for on

Saturday night [June 17] one Brown, a baylif, with 13 more, beset the playhouse, in order to arrest Capt. Hodgson [one of the company]; but the players comeing out in a body, beat and wounded them, and in the scuffle Captain Hodgson's man was cowardly run through the back by a baylif, and immediately dyed, having nothing but a stick in his hand.[11]

And even if unarmed, some of the theatrical employees were dangerous in a quarrel. It is reported that on the evening of 24 January, 1704/5, "captain Walsh quarelling with Mrs. Hudson, who keeps the boxes in the play house, she pulled out his sword and killed him." [12]

On this exploit of Mrs. Hudson, the stabbing *ouvreuse*, we may well leave this dark side of playhouse life and return to our acrimonious and energetic Chancery suits. By 1700 Rich, by his tyrannical methods and his failure to pay the "rent," had thoroughly alienated Killigrew, the owner of the other patent, as well as many of the building investors. Killigrew and a body of the latter joined forces to oust Rich and regain control of the Theatre Royal building,[13] on the expiration of the nineteen-year lease of the theatre to Charles Davenant, which, it will be remembered, Alexander Davenant had sold to Skipwith and Rich. This lease expired 9 November, 1701; but, secure in his "nine points of the law," Rich refused to budge. Killigrew and his allies thereupon resorted to Betterton, who was naturally anxious to move from the Lincoln's Inn Fields tennis court, if he could obtain a better house. He offered the building investors £5 a day (instead of the £3 which Rich was supposed to pay, but which was actually far in arrears). On 11 June, 1702, a lease was drawn up [14] to Betterton and John Watson, for five years, at £5 a day, with an agreement to grant a further term of eight years, if Betterton and Watson should wish it. Unfortunately, Rich and Skipwith were able to checkmate Killigrew and his friends by persuading some of the building investors not to sign. And of course Betterton was wise enough not to execute his part of the instrument until he had the signatures of all the owners of the theatre. Killigrew and his allies immediately attacked Skipwith and Rich in Chancery,[15] but the attempt failed. In his separate answer to the bill of complaint, Skipwith declared that he had had nothing to do with the management of the theatres since 1694, having left it all to Rich.

Lady Penelope Morley, who, on the death of her husband (Captain) Sir Thomas Morley in July, 1693, had inherited his shares in the "rent" of the Theatre Royal, brought suit in 1701 against the patentees for her arrears. In their answer [16] Rich and Skipwith insist that since Betterton's secession the profits have not been sufficient to pay the expenses of the house; that arrears of "rent" are owing to Killigrew and others, and that she has received proportionally as much as anyone. What is more, since she has demanded arrears of "rent" for the vacation days on which the young actors acted for their own benefit, they think it only reasonable to charge her for "her and her friends seeing performances, as in the Schedule annexed," which sums (according to Mr. Baggs, the treasurer) amount to more than her arrears.

The annexed schedule of performances at Drury Lane attended by Lady Morley and her friends is a valuable document. It gives the dates of 108 performances between 6 November, 1696, and 9 June, 1701, among which are several that materially alter accepted ideas, or make certainty where before was doubt. For example, Lady Morley saw Vanbrugh's *Relapse* (hitherto supposed to have had its *première* in December) on 25 November, 1696. In connection with this date should be read the following letter written by Robert Jennens on Thursday, 19 November:

There has been for four or five days together at the play house in Lincolns Inn Fields acted a new farce translated out of the French by Mr. Monteux called the Shame [Sham] Doctor or the Anatomist, with a great concert of music, representing the loves of Venus and Mars, well enough done and pleases the town extremely. The other house has no company at all, and unless a new play comes out on Saturday revives their reputation, they must break.[17]

The Anatomist; or the Sham Doctor (heretofore assigned to March, 1697) [18] was a translation, not by Motteux, but by Ravenscroft, Motteux being responsible only for the musical part of the entertainment. To offset this success at Betterton's theatre, *The Relapse* was no doubt the play which arrived in the nick of time.

I may add two further selections from the list of performances. Vanbrugh's *Country House* (a translation from Dancourt's *Maison de Campagne*), whose production was heretofore assigned to 1703, was seen by Lady Morley five years earlier, on 18 January, 1697/8. The date of production of D'Urfey's opera, *Cinthia and Endimion*, usually given as September, 1697, is thrown back six months, to 5 April. But the student will find things of this kind for himself in the schedule, which I reproduce in the Appendix.

We now turn from the subject of plays performed to that of the number of acting days at the patentees' theatres. Rich and Skipwith were always reluctant to produce their books of account; but in a further answer to Sir Edward Smith's bill,[19] they were obliged by the court to show the following instructive list of acting days between 25 March, 1695, and 1 August, 1704:

25 Mar. 1695 to	7 Jul.	1695	. . . .	84
9 Oct. " "	13 "	1696	. . . .	214
11 " 1696 "	7 "	1697	. . . .	200
6 " 1697 "	19 May	1698	. . . .	161
18 May 1698 "	10 Jul.	1698	. . . .	41
9 Oct. " "	9 "	1699	. . . .	209
9 " 1699 "	26 "	1700	. . . .	218
13 " 1700 "	27 "	1701	. . . .	207
9 " 1701 "	18 "	1702	. . . .	151
10 " 1702 "	24 "	1703	. . . .	185
23 Jul. 1703 "	1 Aug.	1704	. . . .	175

And the days on which the "young people" acted were listed as follows:

6 Jul. to 10 Oct.	1695	. . . .	68
12 " " 12 "	1696	. . . .	57
7 " " 7 "	1697	. . . .	58
10 " " 10 "	1698	. . . .	24
9 " " 10 "	1699	. . . .	27
26 " " 12 "	1700	. . . .	15
26 " " 10 "	1701	. . . .	28
17 " " 11 "	1702	. . . .	29

These acting days, says Rich, were "most frequently" at Drury Lane. Sir Edward Smith estimates that, from 1695 to 1704, plays were given at Dorset Garden only fifty times. On this calculation, then, between March, 1695, and August, 1704, there were 50 performances at Dorset Garden and some

1800 at Drury Lane, exclusive of vacation acting. The average regular season was 196 days. Before 1702 the average was well over 200, but a sharp falling off appears in 1702, 1703, and 1704.

Theatrical art, taste, and business in London had all become lamentably poor in these years — so much so that when Betterton, in the summer of 1703, took his company to Oxford University for the Act, he could utter the following lines from his heart:

> Our *London* Muses . . .
> Glad to retire from that degen'rate Town:
> Where spurious Criticks in false Judgment sit,
> Debauch'd with Farce, and negligent of Wit.
> Our Indignation equally they raise
> Whether they frown or smile upon our Plays,
> And damn us with the Scandal of their Praise.
>
> . . . .
>
> Then rise, *Athenians!* in the just defence
> Of Poetry opprest, and long neglected Sense;
> The Reputation of our Art advance,
> Suppress the Exorbitance of Song and Dance
> And in one pow'rful Party conquer *France* . . .[20]

Advancing age and infirmity had made it increasingly hard for Betterton to carry on, from a smaller theatre, the contest with the younger company at Drury Lane. When, therefore, at the end of 1704 Captain John Vanbrugh offered to build a new theatre for the company in the Haymarket, Betterton willingly agreed to transfer to the dramatist his license as manager. The latter, with the aid of a subscription among the nobility, erected the new theatre, and opened it on 9 April, 1705.

We may regard this point as a fitting close to a study of the Restoration stage, since the managements of Vanbrugh and Swiney open a new chapter, and belong rather to the era of Colley Cibber.[21] Further vicissitudes of Rich likewise carry us into the age of Queen Anne, and are not proper to a study of the Restoration. Not, however, to leave the old villain, who made life miserable for so many actors, without a good word, I may finish with a sketch of the later history of the fruit-selling privilege, in connection with which he appears after the death of Orange Moll.

On 21 August, 1695,[22] the owners of the Drury Lane theatre granted another license to one Thomas Phillips, and gave him and his assigns access to the playhouse "(not exceeding six persons in one day) four persons to be in & about the Pit & Boxes & two other persons in the two Upper Galleries." His right was to run for seven years, at a rent of £4 a week (13*s*. 4*d*. every acting day). Phillips tells us that it was his wife who carried on the business in his name, he being by trade a bricklayer. She found the audiences so thin, however, that she could not get enough to pay the rent, and so was often in arrears. To add to their distress, Phillips says that he

. . . is informed by his said wife and Servants that . . . Christopher Rich who had, or took upon himself the Chief management of the said house . . . would not suffer this Defendant's wife or Servants or any of the Six persons in number to be in and about the Pit, Boxes, and Galleries according to the agreement when the Play began to be acted, but only during the time of the playing of the music, and not at all when Operas were acted Except in the Eighteen penny Gallery for several Years together, but caused them to be thrust out of the house by force, which was A very great Damage and loss.

After the opening of the Haymarket, and the desertion to it of some of his actors, Rich sent for Phillips,

. . . and told him that there would be nothing but Operas acted twice a week only which would be worth nothing to the Defendant, and bid this Defendant go and tell . . . Mr. Killigrew that the Lessors or Builders owed him money on account of the Fruit; and he [Rich] would put in persons on his own account to sell fruit and sweetmeats in the said Theatre Royal, and that this Defendant should not continue any longer in that business.

Phillips took the message to Killigrew, who told him to "send a Servant or two and endeavour the selling fruit and sweetmeats there" — which the latter did, in 1706; yet "Rich would not suffer any of them to be in the said Theatre, but thrust them out."

Rich has been roundly and rightly execrated for his many crafty tyrannies, but I think the least of his crimes was forbidding the orange-wenches to cry their wares during the opera!

THE DUKE'S THEATRE IN PORTUGAL STREET, LINCOLN'S INN FIELDS, 1813

(From Wilkinson's *Londina Illustrata*, vol. ii.)

NOTES TO CHAPTER VIII

1 (299). No. 83.

2 (299). I take this date from Rich. Cibber gives the date for their re-opening as "Easter Monday in April following," which cannot be right, as Easter in 1695 fell on 24 March. Monday, a week after Easter, was 1 April, which I presume to be the correct date.

3 (300). No. 97.

4 (301). No. 98.

5 (303). For 1699, pp. 45–49. This passage was pointed out to me by Dr. Arthur Sprague.

6 (304). Luttrell, *Diary*, iv, 382.

7 (305). *Ibid.*, ii, 637.

8 (305). *Ibid.*, ii, 394.

9 (305). *Ibid.*, iii, 25.

10 (305). *Ibid.*, iii, 179.

11 (305). *Ibid.*, iv, 529.

12 (306). *Ibid.*, v, 512. These valuable passages from Luttrell were kindly communicated to me by Professor Rollins.

13 (306). In 1695 they had secured from the Earl of Bedford a further lease of the ground, to run from Christmas, 1702, for fourteen years, at the old rent of £50 a year.

14 (306). No. 88.

15 (306). No. 87.

16 (307). No. 81.

17 (307). *Hist. MSS Comm., Rep. XII*, App., pt. ii, p. 367.

18 (307). Nicoll, pp. 244, 370.

19 (308). No. 98.

20 (309). *Oxford and Cambridge Miscellany*, edited by Elijah Fenton. This reference was kindly given to me by Dr. Arthur Sprague.

21 (309). I cannot, however, deny a place in the Appendix to several new documents bearing on a well-known and amusing episode related by Cibber. It will be recalled that Cibber tells his reader how Skipwith, being tired of his theatrical patent, which brought him no profits and many lawsuits, gave it away to his friend, Colonel Henry Brett. The latter, however, turned it to such good account through his sagacious management that profits soon made their appearance. Upon this, Skipwith changed his mind and complained in Chancery for restitution of his former property. Having discovered the original bill of complaint and Brett's answers (Nos. 110 and 111), I reproduce them, without comment, in the Appendix, pp. 386 ff.

22 (310). No. 107.

APPENDIX

APPENDIX

CHANCERY BILLS AND ANSWERS

New Documents from the Public Record Office used for History
of Stage, 1640–1710

1.	C3 390/47	1623,	25 Oct., *bill* 6 Nov., *answer*	Th. Woodford *v.* Aaron Holland *Share in Red Bull*
2.	C2 ChI M78/29	1636/7,	20 Mar., *b.*	Sir Matt. Mennes *v.* Ch. Gibbons John Poole *Lease of premises on which stood* *Gibbons's Tennis Court*
3.	C2 ChI M26/35	1647, 1647/8,	14 Dec., *b.* 1 Feb., *a.*	Sir Matt. Mennes, *et al. v.* John, Earl of Clare Ch. Gibbons, *et al.*
4.	C2 ChI G21/51	1647/8,	18 Feb., *a.*	Sir Matt. Mennes *v.* Ch. Gibbons
5.	C5 434/21	1655,	June, *b.* 3 July, *a.*	Theoph. Bird *v.* Th. Morrison *Bond of Blackfriars Players*
6.	C10 32/31	1654,	24 Oct., *b.* 1 Oct., *a.* [*i. e.,* Nov.]	And. deCaine *v.* Wm. Wintershall and wife Margaret *Bond with Gunnell (Prince's* *Servants) at Fortune*
7.	C2 ChI P6/6	1651/2,	16 Feb., *a.*	Wm. Phillipps *v.* Eliz. Beeston *Bond into which Chr. Beeston en-* *tered as security*
8.	C2 ChI H44/66	1647,	9 July, *b.* [1]9 July, *a.*	Th. Hussey *v.* Robt. Rolleston, *et al.* *Cockpit in Drury Lane*
9.	C2 ChI H28/26	1647,	4 Nov., *a.* 8 Nov., *a.*	Th. Hussey *v.* Robt. Rolleston Sir Lewis Kirke Dame Eliz. Kirke
10.	C2 108/34	1650,	1 May, *b.*	Th. Hussey *v.* Sir Lewis Kirke
11.	C7 181/44	1650,	23 Oct., *plea*	Th. Hussey *v.* Dame Eliz. Kirke
12.	C2 160/113	1651,	2 June, *b.*	Wm. Beeston *v.* Robt. Rolleston Sir Lewis Kirke Dame Eliz. Kirke David Leader *Lease of Cockpit in Drury Lane*
13.	C10 35/29	1651,	10 June, *a.*	Wm. Beeston *v.* Dame Eliz. Kirke
14.	C5 18/37	1654,	? *b.* 25 May, *a.*	Th. Hussey *v.* Robt. Rolleston, *et al.* *Rent of Cockpit in Drury Lane*

15.	C5 21/89	1655,	8 May, *b.* — Robt. Rolleston *v.* Sir Lewis Kirke
			3 Nov., *a.* — Dame Eliz. Kirke
			24 Nov., *a.* — James Kirke
			Th. Hussey
			Cockpit in Drury Lane
16.	C10 25/33	1655/6,	16 Feb., *a.* — Robt. Rolleston *v.* Sir Lewis Kirke
			Dame Eliz. Kirke
17.	C10 128/27	1672,	7 June, *b.* — Wm. Beeston *v.* Mary Rolleston
			3 Oct., *a.* — *Debt for Cockpit in Drury Lane*
		?	? *b.*
		?	? *a.*
18.	C10 129/9	?	? *plea* — Wm. Beeston *v.* Mary Rolleston
19.	C10 124/13	1672/3,	3 Feb., *a.* — Wm. Beeston *v.* Mary Rolleston
20.	C10 53/7	1658,	25 June, *b.* — Wm. Beeston *v.* Rich. Earl of Dorset
			19 Aug., *a.* — Henry Wheeler
			2 Nov., *a.* — *Salisbury Court Playhouse*
21.	C10 80/15	1666,	8 May, *b.* — Wm. Beeston *v.* Thomas Silver
			22 May, *a.* — Edward Fisher
			Salisbury Court Playhouse
22.	C7 237/86	1661/2,	1 Feb., *b.* — Horatio Moore *v.* Thomas Lisle
			Wm. Witherings
			John Howell
			Anne Moore
			Lisle's Tennis Court
23.	C7 455/70	1662,	2 April, *a.* — John Harris ⎱ *v.* Thomas Lisle
			Rich. Harris ⎰ Anne Lisle
			Horatio Moore
			Anne Moore
			Lisle's Tennis Court
24.	C10 99/21	1661,	15 July, *a.* — George Blake ⎱ *v.* Sir Wm. Davenant
			Jere. Copping ⎰ William Cutler
			Thomas Harper
			John Wilcox
			Charterhouse enterprise
25.	C7 100/68	1663,	13 Nov., *b.* — Wm. Davenant *v.* John Carew
			20 Nov., *a.* — Wm. Walker
			25 Nov., *a.* — Wm. Witherings
			28 Nov., *a.* — *Lisle's Tennis Court*
26.	C10 237/65	1689,	15 Nov., *b.* — Anne Lisle, *vid.* ⎱ *v.* Horatio Moore
		1689/90,	27 Jan., *a.* — Rich. Reeve ⎰ Anne Moore
			Anne Reeve
			Thomas Reeve
			Lisle's Tennis Court
27.	C7 486/74	1670,	6 June, *b.* — Th. Killigrew ⎱ *v.* Isaac Fuller
			16 June, *a.* — Ch. Hart ⎰
			Mich. Moone
			Agreement for painting scenes

28.	C8 335/129	1671/2, 13 Mar., *b.*	Th. Duckworth *v.* John Perin *Building Nursery in Bunhill*
29.	C10 126/6	1675, ? *b.* 1675/6, 20 Jan., *a.*	Wm. Beeston *v.* Rich. Francis *Periwig for Bartholomew Fair*
30.	C8 299/134	1676/7, 8 Mar., *b.* 1677, 24 April, *a.*	Paul Crosse *v.* Dame Mary Davenant Ch. Davenant Alex. Davenant Rich. Brawne *Share in Dorset Garden Theatre* *Schedule of profits 1674-77 annexed*
31.	C10 184/2	1677, 7 May, *b.* ? May, *a.* ? July, *a.*	Edm. Brawne *v.* Th. and Paul Crosse Wm. Mercer *Share in Dorset Garden Theatre*
32.	C10 188/2	1677, 24 May, *a.*	Edm. Brawne *v.* Dame Mary Davenant Ch. Davenant Alex. Davenant Rich. Brawne *Share in Dorset Garden Theatre* *Schedule of profits 1674-77*
33.	C8 215/50	1677, 17 July, *b.* 1 Aug., *a.*	Paul Crosse *v.* Edm. Brawne Th. Crosse Wm. Mercer *Share in Dorset Garden Theatre*
34.	C5 431/11	1679, 30 June, *b.*	John Roffey. *v.* Wm. Mercer *Bond on share in Dorset Garden Theatre*
35.	C8 294/90	1680, 25 May, *b.* 9 June, *a.* 12 June, *a.*	Wm. Mercer *v.* Dame Mary Davenant Ch. Davenant Alex. Davenant Rich. Brawne Paul Crosse *Share in Dorset Garden Theatre*
36.	C6 250/28	1684, 13 Nov., *b.* 1684/5, 14 Feb., *a.*	Dame Mary Davenant *v.* Th. Crosse Paul Crosse Ph. Cademan *Family and Dorset Garden affairs*
37.	C7 575/62	1680/1, 26 Jan., *b.* 1681, 4 May, *a.*	John Roffey *v.* Th. Betterton *Share in building Dorset Garden Theatre*
38.	C7 581/135	1682, 28 Nov., *b.*	John Roffey *v.* Th. Betterton Mary Betterton Rich. Bayly *Share in building Dorset Garden Theatre*
39.	C6 243/103	1682/3, 20 Jan., *a.*	John Roffey *v.* Th. Betterton Mary Betterton
40.	C6 243/82	1682/3, 24 Jan., *a.*	John Roffey *v.* Rich. Bayly

41.	C7 133/82	1682,	22 May, *b.*	Phil. Griffin *v.* Ch. Killigrew
			1 June, *a.*	Th. Shepey
			2 June, *a.*	And. Perryman
			10 June, *a.*	Daniel Golding
			26 June, *a.*	Jacob Holton
				Robt. Baden
				Th. Clarke
				Marmaduke Watson

Share in Theatre Royal

42.	C8 262/26	1682,	23 Nov., *b.*	James Grey *v.* Henry Killigrew
			30 Nov., *a.*	Charles Killigrew
				Th. Morley
				Ph. Griffin
				Cardell Goodman
				Th. Clarke
				Robt. Shotterel

Stock of Theatre Royal

| 43. | C8 300/168 | 1682, | 8 Dec., *a.* | James Grey *v.* Hy. Killigrew |
| | | | | Ph. Griffin |

Stock of Theatre Royal

44.	C6 221/48	1676/7,	23 Jan., *b.*	Ch. Killigrew *v.* Th. Killigrew
			2 Feb., *a.*	Dame Kath. Sayer
			20 Feb., *a.*	Thomas Elliott

Government of Theatre Royal

| 45. | Decree Roll 1164 | 1676/7, | 22 Feb., *dec.* | Ch. Killigrew |

| 46. | C7 194/57 | 1680/1,
1681, | 23 Feb., *b.*
1 June, *a.*
8 Nov., *a.*
15 Nov., *a.*
18 April, *a.* | Rich. Kent
Ch. Tuckyr
Th. Smith
Ch. Hart
Nich. Burt
John Lacy
Ant. Stevenson
Wm. Clayton | *v.* Ch. Killigrew
Th. Morley
Th. Shepey
Wm. Cartwright
Ph. Griffin
Carey Perin
Th. Disney
Marmaduke Watson
Martin Powell
Cardell Goodman
Sarah Cook
Daniel Golding |

Rent of Theatre Royal

| 47. | C7 331/29 | 1681, | 30 June, *a.*
28 June, *a.*
30 June, *a.* | Ch. Tucker
Th. Smith
Rich. Kent | *v.* Ch. Killigrew
Th. Killigrew
Hy. Killigrew
Th. Shepey |

Rent of Theatre Royal

48.	C7 194/51	1683,	4 May, *b.*	Hy. Killigrew *v.* Rich. Kent
				Ch. Killigrew
				Dame Kath. Sayer

Ownership of Theatre Royal

49. C7 194/47   1683,   24 May, *b.*   Hy. Killigrew *v.* Rich. Kent
   7 July, *a.*   *Interest in patent and Theatre Royal*

50. C7 198/29   1683,   7 Nov., *a.*   Hy. Killigrew *v.* Rich. Kent
   Interest in patent and Theatre Royal

51. C7 317/57   1683,   14 May, *b.*   Nich. Strawbridge *v.* Ch. Killigrew
   4 June, *a.*   Th. Morley
   9 June, *a.*   Ch. Hart
   13 June, *a.*   Th. Shepey
   Wm. Clayton
   Ch. Davenant
   Th. Betterton
   Wm. Smith
   Rent of Theatre Royal

52. C7 298/35   1684,   30 Sept. } *a.*   Nich. Strawbridge *v.* Ch. Killigrew
   7 Oct., }   Th. Morley
   Ch. Hart
   Th. Shepey
   Wm. Clayton
   Ch. Davenant
   Th. Betterton
   Wm. Smith

53. C6 297   1686,   27 Nov., *b.*   Th. Sheppey *v.* Sackvile Beeston
   18 Dec., *a.*   *Will of Alice Beeston*

54. C7 302/12   1686 [7?], 21 April, *b.*   Elkanah Settle *v.* Eliz. Leigh
   1687,   29   *a.*   *Bond for giving idea for play*

55. C7 596/55   1689/90, 15 Feb., *b.*   Eliza Goodwyn *v.* Alex. Davenant
   ? Mar., *a.*   *Share in theatre*

56. C6 246/74   1683/4, 16 Feb., *b.*   Ch. Killigrew } *v.* Mary Meggs
   1684,   12 April, *a.*   Th. Morley   Nich. Burt
   15 April, *a.*   Hy. Tichburne   Mich. Mohun
   Th. Shepey   Nich. Strawbridge
   Jos. Nickens   Henry Hale
   Th. Napier
   Rich. Burt
   Wm. Cartwright
   Wm. Clayton
   John Tombs
   Marg. Lacy, *vid.* }
   Rent for fruit license in Theatre Royal

57. C6 249/44   1684,   24 April, *a.*   Ch. Killigrew *v.* Henry Hales
   Rent for fruit license in Theatre Royal

58. C7 161/32   1690,   3 Nov., *b.*   Sir R. Howard } *v.* Mary Meggs
   Nich. Burt   { Mich. Mohun
   Th. Napper } Admrs { John Lacy
   Wm. Clayton } of { Rt. Shatterall
   { Walter Clunne
   Rent for fruit license

59. C10 284/34	1692,	16 June, *b.*	Sir Robt. Howard } *v.* Ph. Griffin
		11 Nov., *a.*	*et al.* } Th. Thomas
	1692/3,	23 Jan., *a.*	

Rent for fruit license

60. C10 291/37	1696/7,	1 Feb., *a.*	Sr. Robt. Howard } *v.* Th. Thomas
			et al. }
	(further answer)		*Rent for fruit license*
61. C6 316	1690/1,	23 Jan., *b.*	Ch. Killigrew *v.* Ch. Davenant
	1691,	30 April, *a.*	Th. Betterton
		5 May, *a.*	Wm. Smith
		7 May, *a.*	Dame Mary Davenant
		19 June, *a.*	Th. Davenant
			Alex. Davenant
			Ralph Davenant

Government of theatre, and shares

62. C8 348/95	1691,	7 Nov., *b.*	Alex. Davenant *v.* Dame Eliz. Harvey, *vid.*
			Sir Th. Harvey

Share in theatre

63. C8 560/39	1691,	16 Nov., *a.*	Alex. Davenant *v.* Dame Eliz. Harvey

Share in theatre (sched. of balance due)

64. C8 542/88	1693,	9 May, *b.*	Hen. Harris *v.* Alex. Davenant
			Ralph Davenant
			George Bradbury
			Rich. Bayly
			Robt. Garter
			Th. Betterton
			Wm. Smith
			James Noke
			Cave Underhill
			Th. Crosse
			Sir Th. Hervey
			Eliz. Hervey

Share of rent of theatre

65. C8 542/86	1693,	24 July, *a.*	Hen. Harris *v.* Alex. Davenant

Share of rent of theatre

66. C8 443/43	1693,	12 Oct., *a.*	Hen. Harris *v.* Ralph Davenant

Share of rent of theatre

67. C5 280/38	1693/4,	26 Jan., *b.*	Benj. Godwin *v.* Alex. Davenant
		1 Feb., *a.*	Rich. Cowper
	1694,	16 May, *a.*	Robt. Cowper
			Anne Patterson

Recovery of loan

68. C10 287/24	1694,	6 Nov., *b.*	Rich. Cowper *v.* Benj. Godwin
		19 Nov. *a.*	Eliz. Godwin
			Alex. Davenant
			Ch. Davenant

Recovery of loan

69.	C10 513/37	1694,	16 Nov., *b.*

Ch. Davenant *v.* Benj. Godwin
Gregory King
Catherine Loggan
Eliz. Wooding
Rich. Wooding
Joan Wooding
Alex. Davenant
Recovery of loan

70.	C6 401/50	1695,	23 Oct., *a.*

Ch. Davenant *v.* Benj. Godwin
Gregory King
Recovery of loan

71.	Decree Roll 1372	1695,	1 July, *dec.*

Benj. Godwin *v.* Alex. Davenant
Rich. Cowper
Robt. Cowper
John Cowper
Anne Patterson
Recovery of loan

72.	C9 143/13	1694,	16 Aug., *b.*
		1694/5,	? *b.*
		1694,	12 Nov., *a.*
		1694/5,	16 Feb., *a.*
		n.d.	*a.*

Roman Russell *v.* Sir Jno. Sherrard
Rich. Middlemore
Robt. Moor
Ralph Davenant
Christopher Rich
Rent of theatre

73.	C9 143/17	1694,	9 Nov., *a.*

Roman Russell *v.* Rich. Middlemore
Rent of theatre

74.	C9 163/79	1696(4),	? *b.*
		1695,	16 Dec., *a.*
		1696,	20 June, *a.*

Roman Russell *v.* Sir Jno. Sherrard
Rich. Middlemore
Robt. Moore
Alex. Davenant
Ralph Davenant
Rent of theatre

75.	C9 163/89	1697,	12 June, *a.*

Roman Russell *v.* Rich. Middlemore
Rent of theatre

76.	C9 455/116	1695/6,	24 Feb., *b.*

Jos. Williams *v.* Sr. Th. Skipwith
Ralph Davenant
Articles as actor

77.	C6 438/34	1696,	31 Oct., *b.*
			15 Dec., *a.*

Ed. Kynaston *v.* Wm. Clayton
Ch. Killigrew
Articles as actor

78.	C8 573/34	1697,	8 June, *a.*

Ed. Kynaston *v.* Ch. Killigrew
Articles as actor

79.	C8 459/35	1699,	10 July, *b.*
			11 Oct., *a.*

Edw. Rich *v.* Sir Edw. Smith
Dame Bridget Smith
Sir Th. Skipworth
[*read* Skipwith]

79. C8 459/35   1699,   11 Oct., *a*   Edw. Rich *v.* John Baggs
                                                   [*read* Zach.]
                                        Christopher Rich
                                  Share in Davenant patent

80. C10 360/16   1700,   21 June, *b.*   Eliz. Clayton ⎱ *v.* Sir Th. Skipwith
                                   Th. Clayton ⎰   Chris. Rich
                                            Th. Betterton
                                  Rent of theatre

81. C10 364/8   1701,   10 May, *b.*   Penelope Morley *v.* Ch. Davenant
                    26 July, *a.*   Sir Th. Skipwith
                                            Chris. Rich
                                            Th. Betterton
                                  Share in rent of theatre
                           (Schedule of performances at Theatre
                     Royal, 6 Nov., 1696, to 9 June, 1701)

82. C6 438/55   1700,   24 April, *b.*   Ch. Killigrew *v.* Sir Th. Skipwith
                    12 July, *a.*   Chris. Rich
                                            Ch. Davenant
                                            Marg. Lacey
                                            Th. Betterton
                                  Rent of theatre

83. C10 297/57   n.d.   *a.*   Ch. Killigrew *v.* Sir Th. Skipwith
                                                Chris. Rich
                                  Rent of theatre

84. C10 260/6   1701/2,   18 Mar., *a.*   Ch. Killigrew *v.* Ch. Davenant
                                  Rent of theatre

85. C9 316/91   1702,   13 April, *a.*   Ch. Killigrew *v.* Sir Th. Skipwith
                                                Chris. Rich
                                  Rent of theatre

86. C9 317/6   1702,   14 April, *a.*   Ch. Killigrew *v.* Sir Th. Skipwith
                                  Rent of theatre

87. C10 261/51   1702,   30 June, *b.*   Ch. Killigrew   ⎫ *v.* Ch. Davenant
                    1702/3,   ? Feb., *a.*   Pen. Morley   Sir Th. Skipwith
                               3 Feb., *a.*   Marg. Lacy   Chris. Rich
                               4 Feb., *a.*   Th. Clayton   Grace Shepey
                                           Th. Napier   ⎬ John Sherman
                                           Hen. Mordant   Th. Musters
                                           Fran. Stanhope Barbara Bradley
                                           Th. Kinaston   Rich. Symes
                                           Grace Davies   ⎭ James Stone
                                                          Owen Swinney
                                                          Th. Betterton
                                                          John Watson
                                  Rent of theatre

88.	C10 299/33	1702, 1704, 1704,	30 June, *b.* 1 April, *a.* 21 July, *a.*	Ch. Killigrew ⎱ Pen. Morley Th. Cleyton Th. Napier Th. Kinaston John Sherman ⎰	*v.* Sir Th. Skipwith Chris. Rich Grace Shepey Barbara Bradbury Rich. Symmes Anne Davies James Stone Marg. Lacey Henry Mordant Fran. Stanhope Paul Burrard Ralph Young Th. Betterton John Watson

Rent of theatre

89.	C9 317/3	1704,	18 Dec., *a.* 16 Dec.. *a.* ? *a.*	Ch. Killigrew ⎱ *et al.* ⎰	*v.* Sir Th. Skipwith Chris. Rich Henry Mordant Fran. Stanhope

Rent of theatre

90.	C10 300/25	1703,	1 June, *a.* 4 Nov., *a.*	Ch. Killgrew *v.* Th. Skipwith Chris. Rich Th. Betterton

(Cf. nos. 83–86)

91.	C10 301/16	1704,	9 May, *b.* 10 May, *a.*	Ch. Killigrew *v.* Th. Skipwith Chris. Rich

(Cf. nos. 83–86)

92.	C10 390/17	1710,	10 Nov., *b.* 4 Dec., *a.*	Ch. Killigrew *v.* Sir George Skipwith

Estate of Sir Th. Skipwith

93.	C9 294/57	1711, 1711/12,	27 Mar., *b.* 5 Feb., *a.*	Sir Geo. Skipwith ⎱ Chris. Rich ⎰	*v.* Ch. Killigrew

Share in theatre

94.	C6 523/204	1702,	2 July, *b.*	Ch. Davenant *v.* Roger Pitkin

Bond

95.	C9 171/39	1703,	8 Oct., *a.*	John Leche *v.* Sir Th. Skipwith

Debt

96.	C5 284/40	n.d. 1702, 1704,	*d.* 17 July, *a.* 12 April, *a.* 8 June, *a.*	Sir Ch. O'Hara ⎱ Hen. Harris Roman Russell *et al.* ⎰	*v.* Sir Th. Skipwith Chris. Rich Zach. Baggs Ashburnham Frowde Hy. and Mary Bradbury Barbara Bradbury John Metcalfe Wm. [?] Millman

Rent of theatre

97.	C8 599/74	1704, ?	30 May, b. a.	Sir Edw. Smith Wm. Shiers Th. Savery Robt. Gower } v. Lord John Harvey Sir Th. Skipwith Dame Alice Brownlow Dame Mary Davenant Ch. Davenant Ch. Killigrew Chris. Rich John Metcalfe Zach. Baggs Ashburnham Froud Ashburnham Toll Ann Siderfin *vid.* Ann Shadwell *vid.* Th. and Mary Betterton Cave Underhill Eliz. Barry Anne Bracegirdle Geo. Powell Robt. Wilks John Vanbruggen Phil. Griffin Th. Doggett John Bowman and wife George Bright Edw. Kynaston

Profits in theatre

98.	C8 599/77	1704, 1705,	19 Dec., a. 23 May, a. 15 Sept., a. 20 Sept., a.	Sir Edw. Smith v. Lord John Harvey *et al.* *et al.*

Profits in theatre

99.	C8 604/6	1705,	27 June, a.	Sir Edw. Smith v. Lord John Harvey *et al.* *et al.*
100.	C5 337/72	1705,	10 Nov., a.	Sir Edw. Smith v. Th. Betterton and wife *et al.* Cave Underhill Eliz. Barry Ann Bracegirdle John Verbruggen John and Eliz. Bowman Geo. Bright

Profits in theatre

101.	C8 604/5	1705,	17 Dec., a. 17 Dec., a.	Sir Edw. Smith v. Robt. Wilks *et al.* Geo. Powell

01. C8 604/5   1705,   29 Dec., *a.*   Sir Edw. Smith *v.* Phil. Griffin
                    1705/6,   16 Feb., *a.*   Zach. Baggs
                                                 Th. Dogget
                                                 Sir Th. Skipwith
                                   Profits in theatre

02. C8 619/34   1706,   24 April, *a.*   Sir Edw. Smith *v.* Zach. Baggs
                                                  et al.
                                   Profits in theatre

03. C8 620/35   1708,   21 Dec., *a.*   Sir Edw. Smith *v.* Zach. Baggs
                                                  et al.
                                   Profits in theatre

04. C8 595/71   1704,   13 Nov., *b.*   Rich. Middlemore ⎫ *v.* Ch. Killigrew
                      1704/5,   2 Mar., *a.*   Andrew Card   ⎭   Ch. Davenant
                               5 Mar., *a.*   Sir Th. Skipwith
                               12 Mar., *a.*   Chris. Rich
                                                          Zach. Baggs
                                                          Th. Betterton
                                                          Wm. Smith
                                     Rent of theatre

05. C7 642/44   1707,   3 July, *b.*   Richard Steele *v.* Chris. Rich
                                           19 Nov., *a.*   *Profits of* "The Tender Husband"

06. C9 464/126   1707,   8 Nov., *b.*   Robt. Wilks *v.* Chris. Rich
                                           Stay of process at law on articles

07. C10 383/15   1707/8,   5 Mar., *b.*   Ch. Killigrew   *v.* Th. Phillipps
                      1708,   29 Apil, *a.*   Geo. Morley   James Stone
                      1708,   30 April, *a.* ★   Th. Cleyton   Nich. Straw-
                            ★Out of place.   Marg. Lacey, *vid.*   bridge
                                                          Grace Shepey, *sp.*
                                                          Robt. Moreton
                                                          Susan. Waring, *vid.* ⎬
                                                          Chris. Rich
                                                          Rich. Symes
                                                          Sir John Mordant
                                                          Th. Napier
                                                          John Chaworth
                                                          Th. Kinaston
                                     Fruit-selling lease

08. C10 518/23   1710/11,   26 Jan., *b.*   Ch. Killigrew ⎫ *v.* Mich. Webster
                                              Geo. Morley ⎪   Jno. and Eliz. Lawrence
                                              Th. Clayton ⎬   Jno. and Kath. Brock
                                              Marg. Lacey, ⎪   Nich. Strawbridge
                                                 vid., et al. ⎭   Eliz. Stone
                                                          Andrew Card
                                                          John Rookesby
                                     Fruit-selling lease

| 109. | C7 229/34 | 1708, | 5 July, *b.* | Lawrence Morein *v.* Wm. Pinkethman |
| | | | | Mary Morein —— Dimock |

Contract to act at Bartholomew Fair

| 110. | C8 481/66 | 1708/9, | 1 Feb., *b.* | Sir Th. Skipwith *v.* Col. Hy. Brett |
| | | | 17 *a.* | *Assignment of patent* |

| 111. | C10 545/39 | 1709, | 29 July, *a.* | Sir Th. Skipwith *v.* Col. Hy. Brett |
| | | | | *Assignment of patent* |

| 112. | C10 537/22 | 1709, | 29 June, *b.* | Colley Cibber *v.* Chris. Rich |
| | | | | *Stay of process on articles* |

| 113. | C10 528/33 | 1709, | 31 July, *b.* | Benj. Johnson *v.* Chris. Rich |
| | | | | *Stay of process on articles* |

| 114. | C6 555/27 | 1710, | 22 May, *b.* | Owen Swiney *v.* Nicolini Grimaldi |
| | | | | *Performance of articles* |

115.	C8 621/30	1710/11,	10 Feb., *a.*	Robt. Wilkes ⎫ *v.* Owen Swinney
			24 *a.*	Th. Dogget ⎬ John Hall
				Colley Cibber ⎭

Breach of articles

116.	C8 493/77	1711,	15 May, *a.*	Robt. Wilkes ⎫ *v.* Owen Swinney
				Th. Dogget ⎬ John Hall
				Colley Cibber ⎭

Breach of articles

117.	C7 668/31	1710/11,	12 Jan., *b.*	Owen Swiny *v.* Robt. Wilks
			17 Feb., *b.*	Th. Doggett
		1711,	17 April, *a.*	Colley Cibber
			3 July, *a.*	John Vanbrugh
				Fran. Champelon

per vid.

Accounts of Haymarket Theatre

118.	C7 299/10	1710/11,	20 Feb., *a.*	Owen Swiny *v.* Robt. Wilkes
				Th. Doggett
				Colley Cibber

Accounts of Haymarket Theatre

| 119. | C8 378/17 | 1711, | 19 June, *b.* | Owen Swinny *v.* Lucret. Champelon |
| | | | | John Smith |

Accounts of Haymarket Theatre

No. 1. WOODFORD *v.* HOLLAND

C3 390/47

WOODFORD'S BILL

25 Octob: 1623   Tothill

To the Right honourable and right reverend ffather in God John Lord Bishop of Lincolne Lord Keeper of the Great Seale of England

Humbly complayning sheweth vnto you^r Honor you^r dayly Orator Thomas Woodford of London Merchant   That Whereas one Aaron Holland of the parish of St James at Clerkenwell in the county of Midd*lesex* yeoman by vertue of a Lease or of some other good & lawfull assurance [was possessed for the terme of] divers years yet to come of & in one Messuage or Tenem*en*^{t} now commonly called or knowne by the name or signe of the Red Bull at the vpp*er* end of St John street w*i*th the Gardens Courts Cellars Wayes & lib*er*ties therevnto belonging or app*er*teyning sometymes in the tenure of one John Waintworth or his assignes [scituate lyinge and beinge] in the parish of St James at Clerkenwell aforesaid did lately erect & set vp in & vpon part of the premisses diu*er*s & sundry buildings & galleries to serue & to be vsed for a Playhouse or a place to play & present Comedies Tragedies & other matters of that qualitie And the sayd Aaron Holland being of the premisses [soe possessed, and] hauing made & erected such buildings & galleries therein as aforesaid he the said Aaron Holland did by his deed Indented for the consideracon therein expressed graunt vnto one Thomas Swynnerton one of the then Players & Servants to the late Queene Anne deceased for diu*er*s yeres [then vnexpired the] eighteenth penny & iust eighteenth part of all such sum*m*e & sum*m*es of money and other com*m*odities & benefits whatsoeu*er* that at any tyme or tymes thereafter during the said yeares should be collected gotten or receiued of all & eu*er*y p*er*son & p*er*sons whatsoeu*er* that should or did come into or sit stand or be placed or [take place in anie] the gallery or galleries or other places in or belonging to the said Playhouse dayly or at th'end of eu*er*y weeke   To wh*i*^{ch} Eighteenth part there was then & still is incident & belonging by the vsuall Custome a Gatherers place whereby in respect of certen orders made by & betweene the sayd Company [of Players and the Parteners and] Sharers or owners of the said house for th'avoyding of all differences & controu*er*sies concerning their dayly charge of Gatherers there did arise & grow due vnto the said Eighteenth part Three

pence profit a day amounting to Eighteene pence a weeke to be
payd dayly or at th'end of every weeke [to the said] Swynnerton
or to such Gatherer as he should nominate or appoint during to the
tyme of theyr playing By vertue of whi^ch Graunt the said Thomas
Swynnerton receiued & enioyed aswell the said profits of the said
Eighteene pence a weeke as also the said Eighteenth penny & iust
[eighteenth part of all] such summe & summes of money and other
benefit & profits & commodities whatsoeuer to be collected gotten
or receiued for diuers yeares togither wi^th the good liking of the
sayd Aaron Holland and the rest of his partners players of the sayd
Play house according to theyr Custome wi^thout any Denyall [or
interruption And thereafter] the sayd Thomas Swynnerton being
of the same so possessed did for the Consideracon of ffiftie pounds
of good & lawfull money of England before hand payd by Phillip
Stone of London gent bargayne & sell vnto the said Phillip Stone
all the said premisses wi^th th'appurtenances [in as full a manner &]
to all intents & purposes as he the said Thomas Swynnerton had
could or might enioy the same or any part thereof Wherevpon it was
concluded & agreed by & betweene the said Phillip Stone & the
said Thomas Swynnerton for th'avoyding of all former incum-
brances that the sayd Thomas [Swynnerton should] procure the
said Aaron Holland to seale & deliuer a new Lease or Graunt of the
premisses vnto the said Phillip Stone for the Terme of yeares then
to come & vnexpired of & in the said Indenture made by the sayd
Aaron Holland vnto the sayd Thomas Swynnerton as afore said
[And the said Aaron] Holland being therevnto required did seale
& deliuer to the said Phillip Stone accordingly a new Indenture or
Deed Indented bearing date the Thirtieth [*sic*] day of ffebruary
Anno Domini 1608 and in the Sixt yeare of the Kings Majesties
reigne that now is The said Indenture or Graunt [formerly made
by the said] Aaron Holland vnto the sayd Thomas Swynnerton
being then surrendered & cancelled at the sealing & deliuery
thereof) The sayd Aaron Holland thereby covenanting & graunting for him his executors administrators & assignes to & wi^th the
said Phillip Stone his executors & assignes [that he the said Aaron]
Holland his executors administrators & assignes should & would
from tyme to tyme from thenceforth during the Terme of Twenty
& fyue yeares & three quarters of a yeare to be accompted from the
ffeast of the Birth of our Lord God then last past before the Date
of [the said Indenture] well & truly pay & deliuer or cause to be
deliuered vnto the said Phillip Stone his executors or assignes at
the sayd Play house the Eighteenth penny & iust Eighteenth part
of all such summe & summes of money and other commodities
profits & benefits what soeuer that at [all times within] the said

Terme of Twentie & fiue yeares & three quart*er*s of a yeare should
be collected had made gotten or receiued of all & eu*er*y or any p*er*-
son or p*er*sons whatsoeu*er* that should or did come into and sit
stand or be placed or take place in any the Gallerie or Galleries or
[other places in or belonginge] to the sayd Play house or vpon the
Stage of the said Play house or in or vpon any p*ar*t or p*ar*cell of the
said Play house weekly or at th'end of eu*er*y week The said Phillip
Stone or his assignes demaunding the same of the said Aaron Holland his executors [& assignes at the] Great Gate leading into the
sayd Play house called the Red bull the Actors & Players p*ar*ts &
duties and all other ordinary charges & duties arising to be paid out
of the same And the whole p*r*ofit of the selling of bread beere ale &
fruit being first deducted [And that by the said] Indenture made to
the sayd Phillip Stone there is an Agreeme*n*t made that he the sayd
Phillip Stone his executors or assignes should in further consideracon of the p*r*emisses eu*er*y yeare yearly during the continuance of the said Terme of Twenty & fyue years [& three quarters
of a yeare therein] specified well & truly pay or cause to be payd
vnto the said Aaron Holland his executors administra*t*ors or assignes at the Great gate aforesaid leading into the said Play house
called the Red bull the sum*m*e of ffiftie shillings of lawfull money
of England At [the four principal feasts of the] yeare that is to say
At th'annunciacon of our Lady the Natiuity of St John Baptist
St Michaell th'archangell and the Birth of our Lord God or W*i*thin
ffowreteene dayes next after eu*er*y the sayd ffeasts & dayes by euen
porcons w*i*th a Provisoe [within the same Indenture] conteyned
That yf the said Phillip Stone his executors administra*t*ors or assignes should not pay or cause to be payd vnto the sayd Aaron
Holland his executors administrators or assignes the sayd annuall
or yearly Rent of ffifty shillings at the dayes [therein limited &
appointed] for payme*n*t of the same, but should make default of the
payme*n*t thereof or any p*ar*t thereof contrary to the forme aforesayd That then the benefit & Com*m*oditie to him the sayd Phillip
Stone his executors administra*t*ors or assignes in & by the sayd
menconed [Indenture] or Covenaunt to be to him & them paid &
deliu*er*ed togither w*i*th the said Indenture should cease determine
& be vtterly void to all intents & purposes whatsoeu*er* as though
the same had been neu*er* made As by the said Indenture it may &
doth at large appeare [And that by the said] Indenture made by
the said Aaron Holland to the said Phillip Stone the sayd Phillip
was lawfully possessed of the p*r*emisses thereby graunted as aforesayd and did receiue & enioy the same w*i*th all p*r*ofits & commodities therevnto incident or belonging [in as full] ample & beneficiall
manner & forme as the sayd Thomas Swynnerton had before that

tyme enioyed the same wthout any denyall or interrupcon of the
sayd Aaron Holland or of any other person or persons whatsoeuer
The state Right title interest [term of years and demand] whi^{ch} the
said Phillip Stone had from the said Aaron Holland of in & to the
said Indenture & the premisses thereby graunted the said Phillip
Stone by good & lawfull Conveyance in writing Dated the Seauen-
teenth day of June In the Tenth year [of the Kings Majesties
reigne of England] for the consideracon therein expressed Did bargayne sell & assigne vnto you^r Orator & his assignes to receiue &
pay as Attorney for him & to you^r Suppliants vse all & euery
summe & summes of money as were to be receiued or paid out of or
for the profit of the [premisses at the tyme] & tymes afore limitted
for the Receipt & paymen^t thereof during the residue of the said
yeares to come And you^r said Orator hauing shortly after occasion
to trauell beyond the Seas about his affaires of Merchandize &
other busynes of import did [will and appoint] one Anthony Payne
(who had beene formerly a Servant to you^r Orator) to receiue &
pay such summes of monyes as should from tyme to tyme grow
due and especially the sayd ffiftie shillings to the sayd Aaron Holland at the dayes & tymes limitted [in the said Indenture] of Covenaunts according to the true meaning thereof and the said Aaron
Holland did permit & suffer the said Anthony Payne to receiue all
the sayd proffits & commodities of the said premisses according to
all true meaning for the space of allmost a quarter of [a year without any] disturbance or gaynsaying But so it is right honourable
That in the absence of you^r Orator beyond the seas the sayd Anthony Payne often resorted to the said Aaron Holland intreating
the said Holland to demaund of him the sayd Anthony Payne the
[twelve shillings and sixpence] payable quarterly when it should be
& grow due, whi^{ch} the sayd Anthony Payne assured the said Aaron
Holland should be ready at all tymes vpon demaund To whome
the sayd Aaron Holland answered & said that the said Anthony
Payne need not trouble [himself touching the payment] thereof,
for that the sayd Aaron Holland his loue was such towards you^r
Orator that he would do anything for you^r Orators content & good,
but would do nothing to hinder you^r Orator by taking any advantage agaynst you^r Orators payments vnto him [of the sums of
moneys aforesaid] To whi^{ch} said Relacon & Answere of the sayd
Holland the sayd Anthony Payne giuing certen confidence & beleiue
did omit & neglect by mistaking of a day of paymen^t to pay vnto
the said Aaron Holland Twelue shillings & six pence [which was
due to] him at the ffeast of the Birth of our Lord god In the yeare
of our Lord God One thowsand six hundred & twelue or wthin
ffowreteene dayes after according to the very day & tyme in the

sayd Indenture limitted but tendered [the said twelue shillings & six pence] vpon the sixteenth day to the said A*a*ron Holland after the sayd ffeast of the Birth of our Lord god 1612 as aforesayd But the sayd Aaron Holland then refused to accept thereof and willed the sayd Anthony Payne to keepe the said Quarters Rent vntill the return [of your Orator from beyond] the seas saying that he would talke & conferr w*i*th you*r* Orator concerning the same & other matters at his returne And therevpon the said Anthony Payne did keepe in his hands the sayd Twelue shillings & six pence without any further tender [of the same Whereas the] speeches & practice so vsed by the said Aaron Holland to the sayd Anthony Payne (as now appeareth) tended onely to defraud you*r* said Orator of his interest benefit & p*r*ofit of in & to the p*r*emisses And afterwards you*r* sayd Orator [having returned from] beyond the seas, he repayred vnto the sayd Aaron Holland and vpon Con-ference had w*i*th the said Aaron Holland did desire him to accompt w*i*th you*r* said Orator for & concerning all & eu*er*y p*a*rt of the said p*r*ofits & benefits of the sayd Eighteenth [part arising to your said] Orator in the tyme of his absence out of England amounting some-tymes to Twenty shillings a weeke sometymes more & sometymes lesse for the space then of Three yeares and to yeild pay & deliu*er* the same to you*r* said Orator and also to [account for seven pounds and eighteen] shillings then due to you*r* Orator for the said p*r*ofits of the Eighteene pence a weeke vsually receiued for the said Gath-erers place as aforesaid The w*hi*ch Accompt the said Holland then refused to make taking strickt advantage of the [clause of reserva-tion concerning the] p*r*emisses in the said Indenture of Coven*a*nts for that the said Twelue shillings & six pence was not payd at the very day (but offered to be payd Two dayes after) when it was due Wherevpon you*r* Orator (as his learned Counsell informed him [being without all remedy by] the strickt course of the Com*m*on Law of this Land and by their aduise for his releife did exhibit his Bill into his Ma*jestie*s Court of Requests agaynst the sayd Aaron Holland about some Tenn yeares sithence who appearing thervnto the first day [of — in the eleventh] yeare of his Ma*jestie*s reigne of England answered you*r* Orators said Bill there, and being moved & pricked in his conscience therein did in his then Answere vpon his oath therevnto playnly confesse that he verily beleeued that the state right title Terme [of years interest and] demaund of the said Phillip Stone of in & to the same Indenture of Coven*a*nts made by him the sayd Aaron Holland to the said Phillip Stone was bar-gayned sold & assigned vnto you*r* sayd Orator and that you*r* sayd Orator was possessed of the sayd Eight[eenth part so purchased] by him & his assignes [did] enioy the same about one Quarter of a yeare Without the denyall or interrupcon of the sayd Aaron Holland the then defendant And also did therein proffer & offer vpon his oath voluntary that yf the sayd then Complaynant [would make even] & pay such summes of money as were iustly due vnto the said Aaron Holland by the said Phillip Stone or any from whome he claymed He the sayd Aaron Holland would be contented to make a new Lease vnto you^r Orator the then Complainan^t in his owne [name with the like covenants] articles condicons & agreements as were conteined & specified in the same Indenture formerly made vnto the said Phillip Stone Wherevpon shortly after that is to say the Thirteenth day of June in the same Eleuenth yeare of his Majesties sayd Reigne [of England upon opening of] the same Matter before his Majesties Counsel of the said Court of Requests in presence of the Counsell learned on both sides and vpon consideracon had of the then Defendants Answere and other Circumstances of the Cause And for that the sayd Aaron [Holland had] not made apparent to the said Court what monyes were iustly due vnto him there being in truth none at all from the then Complaynant It was therefore ordered by his Majesties said Counsell of the sayd Court of Requests That you^r Orator [the then Complaynant should] from thenceforth haue & receiue the profits & benefits of all the premisses in as large & ample manner and in such manner & forme as the said Phillip Stone before him or any other person for or in the behalfe of the said Complaynant or of the said [Phillip Stone ever before] that tyme had & enioyed the same without the Let denyall disturbance or contradiccon of him the said Defendant or any other person or persons clayming in by from or vnder him vntill such tyme as other & further order should be in that Court [taken and made (which hath not] hitherto beene) to the contrary And it was also then further ordered That the sayd Complaynant should & might draw a new Indenture or Deed Indented to th'effect of the former with such Covenants & prouisoes as in the said former Indenture [granted to the said] Phillip Stone was conteyned whi^{ch} the said Aaron Holland the then defendant should forthwith vpon request in that behalfe to be made seale & deliuer and execute the same to all intents & purposes as the said former Indenture was made [and executed notwithstanding] any pretended forfeiture thereof And for the other demaunds aswell of the Complaynant as Defendant the said parties were left at libertie to proceed according to the ordinary Course of that Court And it was lastly then thereby ordered [that an Injunction] vnder his Majesties priuy seale vpon payne of Three Hundred pounds should be directed to the said defendant and all & euery other person & persons clayming in by from or vnder him to whome in that cause it should app*e*rteyne for the due [performance of the same order] as thereby may appeare Wherevpon p*r*esently after you*r* Orator did according to the said Order cause a new payre of Indentures to be drawne & engrossed betweene the said Aaron Holland and you*r* said Orator like & agreeable [to the former which were so] had & made betweene the sayd A*a*ron and the said Phillip Stone as is aforesayd and did offer & tender the same to the said Aaron Holland to be sealed & deliu*e*red according to the same order w*hi*ch was then also shewed vnto him w*i*th [a writ or Injunction under your] Ma-*jestie*s priuy seale de execuci*one* ordinis therein for the p*e*rformance thereof W*hi*ch he the said Aaron Holland then seemed willing to do accordingly But for asmuch as at that tyme he p*r*etended he was vtterly vnlearned & [illiterate not being able to read; and then] knew not whether the same were agreeable to the former Indentures and to the said Order He therefore requested you*r* said Orator to forbeare a litle tyme & to giue him so much libertie onely as his Counsell might p*e*rvse the same [and see whether those new In-dentures] did agree w*i*th the form*e*r Indentures of the said Phillip Stone and w*i*th the said before recited Order because he could not read them nor compare them togither, promising then also that as soone as his said Counsell might p*e*rvse the same [he would seal and] deliu*e*r th'one p*a*rt thereof as his Act & Deed vnto you*r* sayd Orator yf they were so agreeable to the form*e*r Indentures w*hi*ch he had sealed to the said Phillip Stone, p*r*ouided that you*r* said Orator should seale & deliu*e*r th'other p*a*rt thereof as his act & deed [unto the sayd] Aaron Holland, W*hi*ch you*r* Orator agreed vnto and de-liu*e*red the sayd new Indentures so ingrossed vnto the sayd Aaron Holland for that purpose to be p*e*rvsed by his said Counsell But the said Aaron Holland intending no such matter did rather Con-spire & confederate [with his] said Counsell how to finde a meanes to avoyd & ou*e*rthrow or p*r*event the sayd Order and thereby to auoyd the sealing & deliu*e*ring of the said Indenture by him the said Aaron Holland to th'end you*r* Orator should be w*i*thout Remedy either in law or equitie w*hi*ch [was also] accomplished, Wherevpon the sayd Aaron Holland and his said Counsell con-cluded that his said Counsell should moue in his Ma*jestie*s Court of the Kings Bench for a Prohibicon in the said Cause and to obteyne the same vnder hand against you*r* Orator, [which was done] ac-cordingly, W*hi*ch Prohibicon was graunted in respect that the sayd Indenture made by the said Aaron Holland vnto the said Phillip Stone was not any Lease at all but onely an Indenture of Cove-n*a*nts, W*hi*ch you*r* said Orator before that tyme [did not under-stand,] but now of late p*e*rceiuing that the Counsell of his Ma*jestie*s Court of R'equests and you*r* Orator had beene so much deluded &

abused therein by the said Holland and his Counsells indirect proceedings you^r Orator did resort to his owne Counsell learned in the
Law [to be therein advised] what he should do, who did then perswade him to exhibite a new Bill in his Majesties said Court of Requests for the same matter in the name of the sayd Phillip Stone
against the said Aaron Holland hauing authority vnder the [hand
and seal of the said Phillip] Stone so to do, whi^{ch} you^r said Orator
so also did   And the sayd Aaron Holland being warned by the Messenger of the said Court to appeare & to answere the same new Bill
preferred in the said Stones name he the said Aaron Holland procured [one Marie Phillips for ten shillings] to bring the said Phillip
Stone vnto him the said Holland to be dealt withall touching the
premisses, whi^{ch} she then shortly after did accordingly   And at the
said Phillip Stones coming to the said Aaron Holland he the said
Phillip Stone by the faire speeches of [the said Holland] and for
some Gratuitie to him giuen or promised to be giuen was drawne
to combine himself with the said Holland and to plott how they
might defraud & deceiue you^r Orator   And for th'effecting of such
their fraudulent purpose the said Phillip Stone [was persuaded
and drawn] by the said Aaron Holland to seale a generall Release
to the said Holland aswell of the same Suite commenced agaynst
him the sayd Holland in the name of the said Stone as of all Covenants accons & demaunds Whatsoeuer betweene [the said Holland
and the said] Stone, By whi^{ch} Release the said new Bill and the
sayd Order and the true intent & meaning thereof were avoyded
whi^{ch} new Bill the sayd Aaron Holland could not answere nor
avoyd but by pleading therevnto (as he did) the Release so procured & [gotten from] the said Phillip Stone so vnduely so vncon-
scionably and by fraud & deceipt as aforesaid to th'abuse of the
said honourable Court and to the great preiudice & hurt of you^r
said Orator contrary to all right equitie & good conscience   In tender consideracon whereof [and for] that the said Aaron Holland
hath most vnconscionable drawne the sayd Phillip Stone against
his owne Act & Deed to release vnto him the sayd Aaron Holland
as aforesayd that whi^{ch} in all equitye doth duely & truly belong
vnto you^r Orator and agaynst the [act and deed of] said Aaron
Holland as he hath confessed vpon his oath as aforesaid and hath
betweene him the sayd Aaron and the said Phillip Stone combined
togither to defraud you^r Orator of his right & interest whi^{ch} he
hath in the sayd Indenture of Covenaunts [And] you^r Orator being
thus by their fraudulent Combinacon locked vp from the recouering
of his said Right & interest in & to the said premisses both by the
strickt course of the Common Law and in equitie as aforesaid   And
being thus frustrated of all hope or [reliefe as] in this case except in

this honourable Court Wherefore and to th'end & purpose that
the full & whole truth concerning the said Matters & premisses
may appeare by the Answeres of the said Aaron Holland and the
said Phillip Stone [and that they may show the reasons] & consideracons why the said Phillip Stone did release vnto the sayd
Aaron Holland his sayd Covenants contrary to the sayd Stones
Graunt vnto your said Orator made vnder his hand & seale, and
that the whole truth vnto [   ] & premisses may appeare by the Answeres of the said Aaron Holland & Phillip Stone
vpon their oathes, which your said Orator hopeth that they will
therein confesse and desireth may be so done accordingly And to
th'end also that your sayd Orator [may be] releiued therein, for
that the sayd Aaron Holland by theis vniust shifts & fraudulent
devises and invencons hath vniustly deteyned allthis said right
title & interest claymed by your said Orator as aforesayd now for
the space of Tenn yeares or thereabouts [to your Orators] great im-
pouerishment And to th'end that the said Aaron Holland may be
compelled to make good & performe his owne offer as aforesaid
made voluntary vpon his oath vnto your Orators sayd first Bill
exhibited in his Majesties Court of Requests and to [be compelled]
as also to giue a iust & true Accompt of all such profits & commodities as haue been euer sithence vniustly & wrongfully deteyned
by the said Aaron Holland & his assignes or Confederates due &
arising from the said Eighteenth part of the said profits of the sayd
Play house [and the three]pence a day incident & belonging vnto
the said Gatherers place And to th'end that he the said Aaron
Holland according to equitie & good conscience may giue your
said Orator present satisfaccon for the same in respect the said
profits haue been so vniustly and wrongfully by the said Aaron
Holland deteyned May it there fore please your Honor to graunt
vnto your said Orator his Majesties most gratious writt of Subpena
to be directed vnto the said Aaron Holland & Phillip Stone thereby
commanding them & either of them at a certen day and vnder a
certen paine therein to be limitted personally to be & appeare before your good Lordship in his Majesties high Court of Chancery
then & there to answere the premisses vpon their Corporall oathes
And further to stand to & abide such further order & decree
[therein as] to your good Lordship shall seem to stand with right
equitie & good conscience And your Orator shall dayly pray for
your Lordships long life & happy estate/

HOLLAND'S ANSWER

Jurat 6° die Novembris 1623
      Saunders

    The severall Aunswere of Aaron Holland one of the defendants to the Bill of Complaint of Thomas Woodford Complaynant./

The said defendant both nowe and at all tymes hereafter savinge and reservinge vnto himselfe all excepcons to the incertentie and insufficiencie of the said Bill of Complaint, ffor aunswere to such points thereof as concerne him this defendant, And for manifestacon and playne declaracon of the truth of so much of the matters and things therein conteyned as concerne him this defendan^t He this defendant saith That true it is That he this defendant was lawfully possessed for the terme of divers yeres yet to come of and in the said messuage or tenement nowe comonlie called or knowne by the name or signe of the Redd Bull at the vpper end of St Johns streete w^{ith} the courts gardens Cellars wayes and libertyes therevnto belonginge or app*er*teyninge scituate lyinge and beinge in the p*a*rishe of St James at Clerkenwell in the Countie of Midd*lesex*, And that this defendant to his greate charge and expences did erect & sett vpp in and vpon parte of the said p*re*misses divers buildinges and Galleryes for a Play howse to present & playe Comedyes, Tragedyes and other matters of that qualletie in such sorte as in the said bill of Complaint is sett forth and alleadged, And this defendant further saith That true it is, that he beinge of the said premisses soe possessed, And havinge erected and made such buildinges and galleryes as aforesaid Did by deed Indented as in the said Bill is alleadged graunte vnto Thomas Swynnerton in the said Bill named beinge then one of the Players and servaunte to the late Queene Anne for divers yeres then vnexpired the eightenth penny or iust eightenth parte of all such sum*m*e and sum*m*es of money and comodities that should be collected of everie p*er*son that should come and take place stande or sitt in anie the said galleries or roomes belonginge to the said Playhowse (exceptinge and deductinge as in the said Indenture is excepted and deducted) As in the said Bill of Complaint is also sett forth. To w*hi*^{ch} deed for more certentie hereof this defendant referreth himselfe, But this defendant vtterlie denyeth, That there is or ever was (to his this defendan̄tes knowledge) incident or belonginge to the said eightenth parte by anie vsuall Custome a Gatherers place in respect of anie orders made betwene the said Company of Players and the Parteners and Sharers of the said playhowse in such sorte as in the said bill of Complaint is vntruly surmised, Neither doth this de-

fendant knowe of anie such three pence a daie proffitt arysinge to
the said Thomas Swynnerton or to such gatherers as he did appointe duringe the tyme of their playinge by reason of anie such
Gatherers place as incident or belonginge to the said eightenth
parte as in the said Bill is alleadged, But saith if the said Swynnerton did receave anie such three pence a daie, he did not receave the
same as incident to the said eightenth parte, but rather in respect
of some speciall wordes conteyned in his said graunte whi^{ch} are not
menconed or conteyned in the graunte afterwards made to the
said Phillipp Stone as will hereafter appeare, Or if there were noe
such speciall wordes in the said graunte as this defendant re-
membreth not certenlie after soe longe tyme and the deed beinge
nowe cancelled, Then he saith he *p*ermitted him the said Swynnerton to take the same oute of his love and favor towards him; in
respect of the hard penny worth the said Swynnerton then afirmed
he had thereof, And this defendant further saith, That he thincketh
it to be true that the said Swynnerton (by vertue of the said deed
made to him from this defendant) beinge possessed of the said
eightenth parte as aforesaid some agreament was betwene the
said Thomas Swynnerton and the said Phillipp Stone in the said
Bill named for the buying of the said eightenth parte of him the
said Thomas Swynnerton But this defendant denyeth to his
knowledge that the said Phillipp Stone did paye ffiftie Poundes
before hand to the said Thomas Swynnerton for the said eightenth
parte or for anie bargayne for the same in such sorte as in the said
bill of Complaint is surmised, Neither doth this defendant thincke
it to be true that the said Phillipp Stone did paie anie such sum*m*e
for the same In respect this Defendant vpon the makinge of the
first graunte thereof to him the said Thomas Swynnerton had and
receaved onlie the sum*m*e of five and twentie Poundes or there-
aboutes, and that by divers and severall small payments vide*l*ic*et*
some thereof by five Poundes quartelie and other some thereof by
ffiftie shillinges and fortie shillinges and such like small sum*m*es
severallie at manie paymentes the said Swynnerton then sayinge
that it was not worth so much. And this defendant further saith
and confesseth that true it is as he thincketh That he this defendant vpon the request and intreatie of the said Thomas Swynnerton and Phillip Stone, and vpon the surrendringe vpp of the
said former deed Did by a Newe Indenture bearinge date the said
Thirtieth [Thirtinth?] daie of ffebruary A*n*no d*o*mini 1608 and in
the sixte yere of his Ma*jes*ties raigne covenante and graunte to
paie and deliver to the said Phillipp Stone his executors and assignes the said eightenth penny or iust eightenth parte of all such
sum*m*e and sum*m*es comodities and benefittes duringe the said

terme of twentie and five yeres and three quarters of a yere (except
as before is excepted) That should be collected or receaved of anie
person that should come to take place sitt or stande in the said
roomes or galleryes or vpon the stage in the said Playhowse weeke-
lie or at the end of everie weeke in such sorte as in the said Bill of
Complaint is sett forth and alleadged, And this defendant saith
That true it is That in the same Indenture made to the said Phillipp Stone as aforesaid, there is a Covenante or reservacon whereby
the said Phillipp Stone his executors or assignes should yerelie
well and trulie paie or cause to be paide to this defendant his executors administrators or assignes at the greate gate of the said Playhowse the summe of ffiftie shillinges of lawfull money of England
at such feasts & dayes and in such sorte manner and forme as in
the said bill of Complainte is sett forth, And that in the same Indenture there is likewise a Provisoe conteyned, That if defaulte of
payment thereof were made contrarie to the forme afore in the
same Indenture expressed and lymitted, That then the said benefitt to the said Phillipp Stone by the said Indenture graunted togeather with the same Indenture should cease determyn and bee
vtterlie voide to all intentes and purposes, As in and by the same
Indenture wherevnto this defendant for more certentie referreth
himselfe more at large appeareth, In w*hi*^{ch} said Indenture soe made
to the said Phillipp Stone there is noe mention made of a Gatherers place by anie custome incident or belonginge to the said
eightenth penny or eightenth parte graunted to the said Phillipp
Stone as aforesaid Neither was there anie such thinge by the same
Indenture graunted, Nor was it the intent or meaninge of this defendant to graunte anie such Gatherers place to him the said Phillipp Stone, And this defendant saith That if such a Gatherers place
by such custome were incident or belonging to the said eightenth
penny or eightenth parte as indeed there is none but by the said
Complaynantes presumpcion It is verie likelie and probable that
the said Phillipp Stone at the tyme of the makinge of the said Indenture to him by this defendant would have speciallie menconed
the same in the said Indenture, All w*hi*^{ch} notw*i*thstandinge he the
said Phillipp Stone and the said Complaynant have and did for a
longe tyme vpon pretence of such a Gatherers place to be incident
and belonginge to the said eightenth parte or eightenth penny as
aforesaid receave and take divers summes of money for and in respect of three pence a daie by them pretended to be due and ap-
perteyning to the said gatherers place daily to be paide oute of the
proffites arysinge of the said playhowse over and besides the said
eightenth parte or eightenth penny covenanted by this defendant
to be paide to the said Phillipp Stone as aforesaid, To w*hi*^{ch} said

Gatherers place and the said three pence a daye thereto belonginge
as by the said Complainant is pretended he the said Phillipp Stone
nor the said Complaynant nor either of them hath or ever had any
iust or lawfull right title or interest. But have and did intrude
themselves thereinto, and wrongfully receave the same to the
greate losse and preiudice of him this defendant to whome the same
of right did and doth truly belonge and apperteine, And he this
defendant saith. That he this defendant therevpon demaunded
restitution of the said Phillipp Stone of the said summes soe by
him wrongfullie receaved which the said Phillipp Stone refusinge
this defendant then saide he would bringe his accon at the common
Lawe against him the said Stone for the same as vnder the favor of
this honorable court this defendant thincketh it was lawfull for
him to doe, vpon which occation he the said Stone ymagyninge
this defendant would have molested him for the said summes soe
by him wrongfully receaved, and perceavinge that he should not
nor could not any longer quietlie receave the said proffitts in respect he had noe iust nor lawfull title right or clayme therevnto did
therevpon as this defendant thincketh and conceaveth to be ridd
of further trouble for some good consideracon bargayne sell or assigne over the said eightenth parte or eightenth penny to the said
Complaynant to be by him receaved and taken duringe the residue
of the said yeres then to come But by what conveyaunce or what
manner of assurance this defendant saith he knoweth not nor was
made privy therevnto, And this defendant further saith And
denyeth that (to the knowledge of him this defendant) the said
Anthony Payne in the Bill of Complaynt named to be substitute
to the Complaynant for the receavinge of the said eightenth parte
or eightenth penny and to paie the said fiftie shillinges yerelie to
this defendant as in the Bill is alleadged did before the daie lymitted for the payment of the said fiftie shillinges yerely resorte to
this defendant in the absence of the said Complaynant concerninge the same payment, Or that this defendant did therevpon saie
That he should not need to trouble himselfe touchinge the payment thereof, for that he this defendant would doe nothinge to
hinder the Complaynant by takinge advauntage against the said
Complaynantes paymentes as in the said Bill of Complaint is vntruly surmised, ffor this defendant saith that he never had any
meddlinge or dealinge with the said Complaynant concerninge the
said eightenth parte or eightenth penny or other the premisses Nor
ever accompted him as his tenante therevnto but onlie the said
Phillip Stone to whome this defendant had geven his covenante as
aforesaid for the payment thereof duringe the terme menconed in
his said deed vpon the said clause or provisoe in the same deed also

conteyned that if the said yerelie rent of fiftie shillinges were be-
hinde at the dayes lymitted therein for payment thereof, Then the
same deed and all the benefitt thereof to come to the said Phillipp
Stone should cease & be voide Accordinge to whi^{ch} clause of reservacon this defendant at the feaste of the Birth of ou^r lord god in
the yere of ou^r lord god one thowsand sixe hundred & twelve and
wi^{th}in fourtene dayes after expectinge payment of the quarters
rent of the said yerelie summe of fiftie shillinges then due from the
said Phillipp Stone, and noe payment thereof beinge then or wi^{th}in
the said fourtene dayes after made or tendred by the said Phillipp
Stone or by anie in his behalfe accordinge to the said clause of
reservacon the said deed and the Covenante on the parte of this
defendant therein conteyned concerninge the payment of the said
eightenth parte or eightenth penny to the said Phillipp Stone did
cease and become absolutelie voide frustrate & of none effect to all
intents and purposes, And although the said complaynant sup-
poseth in his said bill of complainte that the said Anthonie Payne
his substitute did shortlie after the said fourtene dayes next after
the said feaste daye of the birth of ou^r lord god 1612 in the said
Complaynants absence tender the said quarters rent to this defendant, This defendant saith That the same was tendered to be
paide to this defendant in the name of the said Phillip Stone, whi^{ch}
this defendant then refused to accept of, And this defendant saith
vnder favor of this honorable court That he then had and yet hath
good reason to take and holde the forfeicture of the said eightenth
parte or eightenth penny soe forfeicted as aforesaid, for that the
said summes of money intruded vpon & wrongfullie receaved by
the said Phillipp Stone in respect of the benefitt & proffitt of the
said Gatherers place (whi^{ch} of right did belonge to this defend$a$nt)
was farr more worth then the said eightenth parte or eightenth
penny of the proffits and summes aforesaid, and this defend$a$nt
could not but wi^{th} much suite trouble & expences remedie or helpe
himselfe therein, And therefore this defend$a$nt (the premisses duelie
considered hopeth this honorable Court will thincke it reasonable
that he this defend$a$nt for his releife and satisfaccon therein did
take the said forfeicture in manner & forme aforesaid, And although this defendant did vpon the reasons aforesaid take the said
forfeicture, yet at the tyme of the foresaid tender, this defendant
did offer that if the said Phillipp Stone or the said Complaynant
would have made even and have paide the said defend$a$nt all &
everie such summes as were by him the said Phillipp Stone and the
said Complaynant wrongfullie receaved as aforesaid and whi^{ch}
truly belonged to him this defend$a$nt, That then he this defend-
ant would have made good the said graunte of the said eightenth

parte or eightenth penny to him the said Complaynant for & duringe the residue of the said Terme then to come; wh^{ch} the said
Complaynant refused to accept of. But therevpon shortlie after
the said nowe Complaynant exhibited his bill of Complaint into
the honorable court of requests about the tyme in the said bill of
complainte now exhibited into this honorable court menconed,
To wh^{ch} Bill this defendant confesseth That he thincketh in his
aunswere therevnto he did not denye the said assignement of the
said Covenants concerninge the said eightenth parte or eightenth
penny from the said Phillipp Stone to him the said Complaynant,
And that this defendant thincketh it to be true, That he this defendant for avoydinge of tedious suites and costes & expences
therevpon did in his said aunswere in the said court of requests
offer That if the said Phillipp Stone or such as claymed vnder him
would satisfie this defendant all such summes of money as were
then iustlie due to this defendant by the said Stone or by any
clayminge vnder him for the said summes soe wrongfully receaved
That then this defendant would make a newe covenante of the said
eightenth parte or eightenth penny to the said complaynant in his
owne name wth the like convenantes and agreementes as were in
the said Indenture made to the said Phillipp Stone: To wh^{ch}
Aunswere this defendant for more certentie referreth himselfe, But
this Defendant denieth That anie mencon was therein or by him
therein confessed to be agreed or assented vnto for the graunting
of any such Gatherers place or of anie such threepence a daie, or
that the said gatherers place was incident and belonginge to the
said eightenth parte or eightenth penny As by the same Aunswere
more at large appeareth And this defendant further saith that duringe the dependencie of the said suite in the said court of requests
the said nowe Complaynant and defendant vpon some conference
had betwene them concerninge the premisses did referr them
selves to stande to the arbitrament of Clement Goldsmith of Greys
Inne in the Countie of Middlesex Esqr and Anthonie Dyott of the
Middle Temple london Esqr arbitrators equallie & indifferentlie
chosen by the said parties for the fynalle determyninge & endinge
of the said controversies then dependinge betwene them, and did
then assure & promise each to other to stande to the same awarde
& arbitrament, wh^{ch} the said Arbitrators vndertakinge to make
& sett downe their awarde accordinglie, They did amongst other
things awarde (as this defendant hopeth to prove to this honorable
court That the summe of twenty marks should bee paide to this
defendant for the said summes soe wrongfullie receaved by the
said Stone and the said Complaynant for the said threepence a
daye or gatherers place and soe by them wrongfullie deteyned from

this defend*a*nt and for this defend*a*nts greate charges expended in
suites concerninge the same, But the said Complaynant well p*er*-
ceavinge there was noe bond nor other consideracon geven each to
other betwene this defend*a*nt and the said complaynant whereby
the said Complaynant was bound or compellable in lawe to stande
& obey the same awarde and therefore might easilie avoyde the
same and refuse to p*er*forme the same awarde w*ith*out any daunger
as this def*endan*t is informed did accordinglie vtterlie refuse to
stande to or p*er*forme the same awarde, & therevpon did, whilest
this defend*a*nt was busyed & ymployed aboute the said awarde or
arbitram*en*t not thinckinge of any further suite or proceedinges in
the said co*u*rt of requests, and before this defend*a*nt could be sufficientlie provided to w*ith*stande the same or to give his councell
direccons & informacons concerninge the said busynes Did ob-
teine an order in the said co*u*rt against this defend*a*nt, By force
whereof the said Complaynant againe entered into and had &
enioyed the said eightenth p*a*rte or eightenth penny of the proffits
aforesaid and by color thereof intruded and tooke likewise the
proffits of the said Gatherers place or three pence a daye as incy-
dent to the said eightenth p*a*rte for some tyme vntill this defend-
*a*nt vpon good reasons therefore shewed by his councell obteyned
a writt of prohibition oute of the co*u*rt of Kinges bench at west-
m*inste*r as hereafter is more at large shewed And this defend*a*nt
confesseth that the said Complaynant did tender an Indenture to
him this defend*a*nt to be sealed w*hi*ch he the said Complaynant
tould this defend*a*nt was drawne vpp accordinge to the said former
deed Indented made to the said Stone of the said eightenth parte
or eightenth penny w*hi*ch this defend*a*nt did not denye to seale,
but desired respitt of tyme to be advised therevpon by his councell
whether the same were drawne vpp accordinge to the said former
deed and the true meaninge of the said order, At or aboute w*hi*ch
tyme or shortlie after there beinge some treatise or conference betwene the said Complayn*a*nt and this defend*a*nt of a newe refer-
rence to be had of all the said differences to Raph Wormelaighton
of Greys Inne Esqr, the said Indenture soe tendred was not afterwards much vrged vpon this defend*a*nt to be sealed and therefore
this defend*a*nt hopinge all the said differences would have been
ended vpon the said arbitram*en*t did therevpon forbeare to seale
the same Indenture soe tendred And this defend*a*nt further saith
That he beinge still desirous of an Arbitram*en*t and peaceable end
concerninge the p*re*misses for the avoydinge of multeplicitie of
suites and the greate charges & expences in lawe vpon a second
treatie of agream*en*t had betwene the said Complayn*a*nt and this
defend*a*nt, They both referred themselves to the arbitrament of

the said Raph Wormlaighton Arbitrator [jointlie?] chosen betwene them to end & determyn all matters & differences betwene them And became bound by severall obligacons each to other in the penall sum*me* of twenty poundes of lawfull money of England to stande to the Arbitrament Awarde & fynal end of the said Raph Wormelaighton, To be geven vpp at or before the Ninth daie of october then next followinge, As by the said obligacon bearinge date the fiftenth daye of September in the eleaventh yere of his Ma*je*sties raigne more at large appeareth, And therevpon the said Raph Wormleighton takinge vpon him the makinge of the said awarde and hearinge the allegations and proofes of both p*ar*ties, And beinge willinge to sett them at vnitie did arbitrate that this defend*ant* vpon the said Complayn*ant*s request should make a newe graunte to the said Complaynant of the said eightenth p*ar*te of the sum*me*s & proffites to be gathered in the said Playhowse (the Players p*ar*tes and other dueties beinge first deducted) Secondlie that this defendant should enioye the Gatherers place Thirdly that this defendant should be absolutelie discharged against the Complaynant for the meane proffites of the said eightenth p*ar*te by him receaved since the said forfeicture. And fourthlie that the said Complaynant should paie to this defendant forty shillinges in discharge of arrerage of rent due to this defendant And that the said suite in the said Court of requests and all other suites betwene them should cease and determyn. As by the said Awarde vnder the hand & seale of the said Raph Wormelaighton bearinge date the the [*sic*] Nynth daie of october in the said eleaventh yere of his Ma*je*sties raigne ready to be shewed to this honorable co*ur*t more at large appeareth. After w*hi*ᶜʰ said awarde and arbitram*en*ᵗ soe made this defend*ant* thinckinge that the said Complaynant would not refuse but stande to & obey the same as he this defend*ant* was then willinge to obey and p*er*forme the same of his p*ar*te did accordinglie divers tymes require him the said Complaynant to p*er*forme the said awarde of his p*ar*te But he the said Complaynant beinge a contentious p*er*son and beinge more desirous of suites and controuersies then of peace & vnity did refuse to obey or p*er*forme the contentes of the said awarde, And notw*i*ᵗʰ-standinge the said Complaynant had enioyed & receaved the said eightenth p*ar*te or eightenth penny of the proffites aforesaid by force of the said order made in the said Court of requestes And therevpon wrongfullie intruded vpon the said gatherers place and receaved the proffits thereof w*hi*ᶜʰ of right belonged to this defend*ant*, yet the said Complaynant deteyned & refused to make payment of the quarters rent of the said yerelie rent of fiftie shillinges payeable to this defendant for the rent of the p*re*misses at

the feaste of St Michaell tharchaungell next followinge after the
said order made wherevpon this defendant havinge noe other present remedy for his said wronges was inforced to make meanes for
the said prohibition And by his Councell moved in the said Court
of Kings bench where the full and whole matter beinge plainly and
truly sett forth and opened to the said court It pleased the said
court vpon the iust reasons there shewed to graunte the said writt
of prohibition to this defendant for the avoydinge of the said order
and proceedinges in the court of requests concerninge the premisses
As by the said writt of prohibition ready to be shewed to this
honorable Court more at large appeareth. After which tyme the
said defendant although the said prohibition was had & obteyned
vpon good matters and reasons grounded as well vpon lawe as
equitie he the said Complaynant havinge a desire and delight to
variety of suites and controuersies did afterwards as this defendant
is informed make divers motions in the said Court of kings bench
for the makinge voide and adnihillatinge of the said prohibition.
And thereby putt this defendant to greate and vnnecessarie expences in answere of the said seuerall mocions And at last perceavinge he could not prevayle therein he the said Complaynant
thinckinge himselfe as this defendant conceaveth) to be an excellent Tragedyan and purposinge to vexe and vndoe this defendant
(beinge an aged man) with suites and controversyes exhibited another Bill of Complainte in the said said [*sic*] Court of requests in the
name of the said Phillipp Stone against this defendant conteyninge
in effect as this defendant hath heard and beleeveth the selfe same
matters before in his said former Bill Complayned of in the said
court of Requestes. And therevpon this defendant beinge served
with his Majesties writt of privy seale oute of the said Court of
Requests to appeare and aunswere the said Bill exhibited in the
name of the said Phillipp Stone, he this defendant meetinge with
the said Phillipp Stone and vpon conference had betwene him and
this defendant he the said Phillipp Stone well perceavinge howe
he had formerly wronged this defendant in intrudinge vpon and
takinge the proffits of the said Gatherers place as aforesaid. And
likewise perceavinge howe this defendant was molested & wronged
withoute anie iust cause, he the said Stone then saide this defendant should be noe further troubled therein Neither should his
name be vsed as an instrument to vexe and trouble this defendant.
And therevpon he the said Phillipp Stone vpon the request of him
this defendant did seale and deliver vnto him this defendant a
generall release of all Accons claymes and demaundes whatsoever
from the begynninge of the world vntill the tyme of the date of the
same release As by the said generall release bearinge date the

sixtenth daie of Maye in the twelveth yere of his Ma*jes*ties raigne
ready to be shewed to this honorable court appeareth. And this
defend*an*t confesseth he pleaded the said Release to the said Complaynants said second Bill in the Co*u*rt of Requestes. W*hi*ᶜʰ this
defend*an*t hopeth vpon all the matters and reasons aforesaid this
honorable court will thincke it was lawfull for him to doe, W*hi*ᶜʰ
Release this defendant saith he did not obteyne in respect he this
defendant knewe not howe otherwise to aunswere the said Complaynants second bill in the said Court of requestes but by plead-
inge the said release As in the said Bill of complainte in this court
is vntruly surmised But because this defendant beinge wearied
oute w*i*ᵗʰ costes and expences in suites was growne vnable to
mainteine defence a'gainst such tedious suits w*i*ᵗʰ such a *per*verse
and contentious adversarie, and therefore by this meanes was
desirous to putt a peryodd to these controversies, And this defendant denyeth that he gave or promised to give to the said
Phillipp Stone any gratuity for & vpon the makinge of the said release as aforesaid, Nor that the same was made for and vpon any
other causes & reasons then are before alleadged, And this defend*an*t likewise saith That if he the said Complaynant receaved
any pr*e*iudice vpon or by reason of the said release, Then the said
Complayn*an*t as this defendant hath heard therevpon had or
might have had or maie have his remedy by Accon at the co*mm*en
Lawe or otherwise against the said Phillipp Stone vpon his the
said Stones covenantes betwene him & the said Complaynant vpon
the assigninge of the said eightenth p*ar*te as aforesaid. But the
said Complaynant not restinge but still *per*severinge in the vex-
inge & molestinge of this defendant caused an Accon of the case to
be brought in the Co*u*rt of Kings bench in the name of the said
Stone against this defend*an*t vpon a supposed Assumpsit to be
made by this defendant to the said Stone at the tyme of the makinge of the said release to discharge him the said Stone of a Bond
of one hundred Poundes wherein the said Stone stood bound to the
said Complaynant w*hi*ᶜʰ Accon cominge to a Tryall by nisi prius
before the lord Cheife Justice of the Kings bench the said Complaynant was therein overthrowne and this defendant found to
have made noe such promise for and in consideracon of the said
release, But that the same release was freelie made from the said
Stone to this defend*an*t vpon the causes and reasons before herein
sett forth and alleadged, By reason of all w*hi*ᶜʰ said tedious suites
and vexacons prosecuted by the said Complaynant against this
defendant he this defendant for the defence and mainteyninge of
his right hath bene putt to greate charges and expences and therevpon compelled to borrowe many sum*m*es of money and for satis-

faccon thereof hath bene enforced not only to sell his whole benefitt
and proffit in the said Playhowse, but also all his interest and
terme of yeres in the said Messuage called the Redd Bull and in
divers tenementes therevnto neere adioyninge for the sum*m*e of
one hundred Poundes reservinge a small An*n*uytie for the maintenance of him and his wife for the terme of their severall lives
whereby it maie plainlie appeare that the whole benefitt of the
said Playhowse togeather w*i*ᵗʰ the messuage & divers other tenementes beinge solde by this defendant for such a small consideracon That the said eightenth penn'y or eightenth parte of the benefitt and proffitt aforesaid, for w*hi*ᶜʰ the said Complaynant hath
soe wrongfullie molested and sued this defendant and putt him to
such vniust costes and expences as aforesaid can be by all proba-
billity but of small worth or consequence, And this defendant
likewise hopeth that it will apparantlie appeare to this honorable
court the passages and Circumstances aforesaid beinge duelie
weighed and considered that the said Complaynant (after this
defendant hath nowe bene for the space of these eight yeres in
quyett) hath noe iust cause to complayne in this honorable Court,
But that the said Bill of Complaint nowe exhibited into this court
is meerlie framed of purpose to scandalize and vexe this defendant
vpon some hope to wrest or gayne a sum*m*e of money vpon some
composicon from this defend*a*nt, and not vpon anie iust or lawfull
ground The consideracon whereof this defendant leaveth to the
censure of this honorable Co*u*rt, W*i*ᵗʰoute that that this defendant
to his knowledge or remembrance did saie to the said Anthony Payne
that he need not trouble himselfe touchinge the payment of of
[*sic*] the said yerely rent, or that this defendant would doe nothinge
by takinge any advauntage of the same paymentes Or that this
defend*a*nt by anie such speeches or practise intended to defraude
the said Complaynant of his interest as in the said bill of Complainte is vntruly surmised, Nor otherwise then is before herein
expressed and declared, And w*i*ᵗʰoute that that any such sum*m*e
of Seaven Poundes & eightene shillinges was due to the Complaynant for the proffitt of the Gatherers place As in the said Bill
is also vntruly surmised, And w*i*ᵗʰoute that that to this defend-
*a*nts knowledge the said writt of prohibition was vnduly obteyned
Or that the said Co*u*rt of Requestes by any indirect proceedinges
of this defendant or his Councell have bene deluded and abused in
such sorte as in the said bill of Complainte is vntruly surmised nor
otherwise then is before herein expressed. And w*i*ᵗʰoute that that
this defend*a*nt by anie fayre speeches or gratuityes to the said
Stone given or to be given by this defendant he the said Stone was
drawne to Conioyne himselfe w*i*ᵗʰ this Defendant to defraude the

Complaynant, and therevpon to seale the said release to this defendant in such sorte as in the said Bill of Complaynt is also vntruly surmised, nor otherwise then is before declared. And w*ith*oute that that this defendant and the the [*sic*] said Stone Combyned togeather to defraude the Complaynant of his right in the said Indenture of covenantes and *p*remisses, Or that this defendant by any vniust shiftes or fraudulent devises hath or doth deteyne the said Complaynantes right or title in such sorte as in the said Bill of Complainte is vntruly surmised otherwise then is before herein alleadged. And w*ith*oute that that anie other matter or thinge in the said bill of Complaynt conteyned materiall or effectuall in the Lawe to be aunswered vnto by this defendant, and herein before not sufficientlie aunswered vnto confessed avoyded traversed or denyed is true. All w*hich* matters and things this defendant is ready to averr and prove as this honorable court shall awarde, And humbly prayeth to be from hence dismissed w*ith* his reasonable costes & damages in this behalfe wrongfully susteyned./

Edward Campion

The Court's Decree

(Chancery Decrees and Orders Entry Book B1623, p. 948a.)

Thomas Woodford pl }
Aaron Hollande dft }

3 Maij [1624]
The p*laintiff* is adiudged to paye to the d*efendan*t xlvi*s* viii*d* Costs for want of a Replica*t*ion and the matter of the p*laintiff's* bill is from henceforth cleerlie and absolutelie dismissed out of the courte according to the generell order of the courte in thet behelff m*a*de

NO. 27. THOMAS KILLIGREW, CHARLES HART, AND MICHAEL MOHUN *v.* ISAAC FULLER

C 7 486/74

BILL OF KILLIGREW *et al.*

"1670, 6 June

To the Right Honble Sr Orlando Bridgman knt & Bart Lord Keeper of the Great Seale of England."

Th. Killigrew, Esq., Groom of the Bedchamber, Ch. Hart, and Michael Mohun of the parish of Covent Garden. Killigrew being "Mr of the Company of his said now Mats Comedians or Actors at his said Mats house called the Theater Royall" and "being intended according to his Mats appointmt in that behalfe that the said Company of Comedians or Actors should Act a new play or Tragedy called the Royall Martir or St Katherine about the latter end of Aprill one thousand six hundred sixty nine and there being a necessity of making a new Scæne of an Elysium to be p'sented in the said Tragedy or play of St Katherine and one Isaack ffuller of the pish of St Gyles in the ffeilds . . . gent, being a Painter & one who sometimes did apply himselfe for painting of Scænes" Hart and Mohun, for Thomas Killigrew, treated and agreed with Fuller "touching the painting of the said Scæne of Elysium" 14 April, 1669; Fuller should paint the said scene "of such largenes as should fitt the stage of the said house or Theater Royall and that he should paint the same so well as other Scænes belonging to the said Theater were vsually painted by other Painters and as was fitting for the same to be painted for the best advantage of the said Tragedy" and should perfect it within a fortnight next following. And Hart and Mohun for Killigrew then told Fuller that they "who were to have considerable shares in the benefitt and profitt to be gotten by the said play or Tragedy and your Orator Thomas Killigrew were exceedingly concerned to have the said Scæne finished by the time agreed on for that the said play was appointed by the said Kings Maty to be Acted psently after the said time wherein by the said agreemt the said scæne was to be finished and alsoe for that notice was given to yor Orators that a very great number of psons of Honor & of the greatest quality attending on his sd Mats pson & his Royall consort the Queenes Matie in & about the Cort were very vrgent to see the Acting of the said Tragedy or play and for that at the time of the said agreemt the pts in & about London were very full of nobillity & Gentry & psons of quality who daily called on yor Orators & pressed them to see the Acting of the

same and also for that Easter & Trinity termes were then coming
on wch were times for great resort of Gentry & psons of quality to
the pts in & about the Cittys of London & Westmr & very many at
that time more then ordinary for that it was in pliamt time also)
so that great numbers did resort to the said house or Royall Theater to see Comedyes or playes Acted these sumer terme times being
vsually the greatest times of pfitt to yor Orators throughout the
whole yeare." Therefore Hart and Mohun gave Fuller "great caution and warning" not to fail to finish the scene in time, but he did
not finish it till the latter end of June; for which reason "yor Orators received very great blame from his said Maty & by reason of
his distast thereat he did much forbeare his coming to the said
Theater or house to see other playes or Comedyes presented or
Acted & did alsoe occasion the Nobility & Gentry & psons of quality
attending vpon his Matys & his Royall consorts persons & Cort
to forbeare very much their coming therevnto for the said purposes."

They allege that the scene when finished "was painted very
meanly & inconsiderably & not at all answearable to what became
such a play or to the curiousity wherewith the said Isaack ffuller
agreed to paint the same by reason whereof the said play when it
was Acted was dispaged & lost its reputacon & not halfe the company resorted to see the acting thereof which wold have come in
case the said Scæne had been painted according to the said Agreemt
the painting & finishing of the said Scæne not being worth ffifty
pounds whereas if the same had byn painted according to the said
Agreement the painting & finishing thereof wold have byn worth
as much more."

They say that they are damaged to the extent of £500 by Fuller's
breach of the agreement. They hoped that Fuller would make them
some recompense for their loss, the more so as they had paid him
£40 on account. But he did not, and has lately brought action at
law against Hart and Mohun, and has recovered £335 10s. for
painting the scene.

Fuller's Answer

1670, 16 June

Answer of Isaac ffuller to Bill of Complaint of Killigrew,
Hart, and Mohun.

. . . Hee Saith hee knoweth nothing of any appointment of his
Matie for the Acting of the Play or Tragedy in the Bill menconed
Save only that the plte Thomas Killigrew a few dayes before this
Defendant had made and Perfected the Scheane of an Elizyum in

the Bill menconed as an Argument or motive to perswade this defendant to hasten the finishing thereof Did tell this Defte that his Matie was desirous to See the Said Tragedy acted within a day or two after or to that effecte Wherevpon this Defte did Sitt vpp all night to finish the Said Scheane Butt this defendant Saith true it is that about the latter end of Aprill or the beginning of May in the yeare of our Lord 1669 One Mr Dryden (a Poett as this Defendant hath heard that Sometimes makes Playes for the Company of Comedians or Actors in the Bill menconed) and one Mr Wright (a Joyner belonging to the Said Company) by the order or direccon as this Defendant believes of the said Company or Some of them did come unto this Defendant then lying Sicke att his owne house and did propose vnto him the painting of the said Scheane of an Elizyum for the said Company in their house called the Theatre Royall in the Bill menconed and to encourage this Defendant to vndertake the painting thereof the said Dryden and Wright or one of them told this Defte hee should bee well Satisfyed for the same or vsed Severall expressions to that effecte And this Defte saith that about foure or five dayes after this Defte haveing recovered his health went to the said Company att their said house and there mett with all or most of them togeather particularly with the Complaynants Hart and Moone and then and there treated with them about the painting the said Scheane and then (and not about the 14th of Aprill 1669 as in the Bill is Suggested) it was att length agreed by and betweene this Defte and the said Company or Some of them on the behalfe of the rest of them to this or the like effecte that this defte should paynte the said Scheane of an Elizyum so as should fitt the Stage of the said house or Theatre Royall and so as was fitting for the same to be paynted Butt this Defte doth not remember that it was expressely Agreed that hee should paynte the same as well as other Scheanes belonging to the said Theatre were vsually paynted by other Paynters as the Bill suggests Howbeit this Defte saith hee believeth and hopeth if need bee to prove that the Same was paynted as well as any other Scheane belonging to the said Theatre was or had been paynted by any other Paynter whatsoeuer And this Defte doth positively deny that it was then or att any other time agreed betweene this Defte and the said Company or any of them that this Defte should or would paynte or perfect the said Scheane within a ffortnight as the Bill very vnreasonably suggests (the same beeing in truth impossible for this defte or any other as this Defte believeth to doe within that time) And denyeth that any other certaine time was agreed for the finishing thereof And this Defte saith that by the said Agreement the said Company or some of them were to pay vnto this Defte what hee should deserve for painting the said Sceane And to encourage this Defte to vndertake the painting thereof they or Some of them particularly the said Hart and Moone did not onlie promise that this Defte should have Satisfaccon for doeinge the said worke but did also expressly Say that hee should not Stay a minute for his moneye after his worke was done And this Defte saith that there was noe other Agreement betweene this Defte and the Said Company or any of them or any other on their behalfe but Such or to Such effecte as herein before is Sett forth And denyeth that att the time of the said Agreemt the Compltes or any of them did acquainte this Defte that they were exceedingly concerned to have the said Sceane finished by the time in the Bill pretended to be Agreed on for any of the reasons in the Bill for that purpose alleadged or for any other reason whatsoever And denyeth that att the time of the said Agreemt the pltes Hart and Moone or either of them or any other of the said Company did give any Caution or Warneing to this Defte that hee should not fayle to painte and finish the said Scheane by the said time ptended to bee agreed on Butt this Defte believeth that while the said worke was goeing on they or some of them might call vpon him to dispatch the same with what expedicon hee could, and might vse Some Such Argumts as in the Bill are alleadged to quicken him therein And this Defte Saith hee did make what haste therein hee could and believeth hee finished the Same in as little time as any other painter could have done the same and believeth that the said pltes or some of them might mind him to painte the said Scheane well and for the best advantage of the Said Play And this Defte believeth for the reasons herein after expressed that hee did and hath painted the Same very well and that the said Company of Actors have had very greate Advantage thereby And this Defte denyeth that hee did willfully neglect or delay the painting and Pfecting of the sd Scheane ffor hee saith hee painted the Same within the Space of Six weekes or thereabouts beginning to painte the Same about the 12th day of May in the sd yeare of our Lord 1669 and Pfecting the Same about the 23th of June then next following And hath reason to believe that noe painter in England could have finished the same and have done the worke Soe well as this Defte did it in Soe Short a Space ffor that att the tryall att Law hereafter menconed had touching the pmisses wherein the now pltes Hart and Moone were Deftes and this Defte was plte One Mr Streeter an eminent Paynter beeing pduced by the now pltes themselves as a wittnesse on their behalfe did acknowledge that this Defte had a quicker hand att painting then any other And if hee Pformed the Said Worke in Six weekes time it was very fayre And did also acknowledge that the Said worke was excellently well done And this Defte saith that hee was so farre from neglecting or delaying the said worke that for three weekes of the said Six weekes hee did not putt off his Cloathes but lay vpon a pallatt-bed in the Roome and rose vpp to worke as Soone as hee could See and for the rest of the Said Six weekes hee made what haste hee could and entred vpon no other worke till the said worke was finished And if in the meane time the two Termes of Easter and Trinity that yeare were past as is Suggested in the Bill this Defte conceiveth it not materiall to him for that hee beganne the Said worke within Three or foure dayes after the Said Agreemt which three or foure dayes was time little enough to provide materialls and Servants for the entring vpon Such a worke and finished the Same within Six weekes after as aforesd And if the pltes would have had the said worke Pfected against the said two Termes they should have Employed this Defte about it Sooner good pte of Easter Terme that yeare beeing in truth Spent before the Said Agreemt for doing thereof Nor is it materiall to this Defte as hee humbly conceiveth that the Compltes or any of them did importune and presse this Defte to finish the Said Scheane with all expedicon or acquainte him with the greate losse and damage that they had or should Sustaine by reason of the not finishing thereof Sooner this Defte denying that by any Agreemt with them he was to finish the Same against any certaine time And denying that hee did willfully neglect or delay the finishing thereof as aforesd ffor which reason also this Defte humbly conceiveth it no way materiall to him if the Plts did receive any blame from his Matie or that by reason of his Distaste thereof his Matie did forbeare the comeing to the sd Theatre to See other Playes psented and acted Or if the Nobillity and Gentry or any others did forbeare comeing therevnto or if for any other cause they received any losse or Damage by reason the sd Scheane was not finished Sooner Howbeit this Defte saith hee doth not believe that they did receive any blame from his Matie for that the sd worke was not done sooner as is ptended by their Bill and hee doth the rather So believe for that the Complte Thomas Killigrew Some few dayes after the finishing thereof gave this Defte thankes for the Same And told him that hee this Defte had very well pleased his Matie and the whole house And then also told this Defte that hee the sd Thomas Killigrew would see him this Defte payd for the doeing thereof And this defte doth vtterly deny that the sd Scheane was painted very meanely or inconsiderably and not att all Answerable to what became Such a play or to the curiosity wherewth this Defte Agreed to paynt the same as in the Bill is very falsely and vnworthily Suggested Nor doth this Defte believe that by reason

thereof the sd Play when Acted was disparaged or lost any reputacon or that not halfe the Company resorted to see the Acting
thereof which would have come in Case the sd Scheane had been
well painted ffor this Defte Saith it appeared att the sd tryall as
well by the testimony of Wittnesses pduced by this Defte as also
by wittnesses pduced by the pltes themselves Some of them beeing
their owne Servts that the sd Scheane was very well paynted and
gave greate content to the Spectators that came to see the sd Play
Acted And that the pltes and their said Company acted the Same
about 14 dayes together and received all that while about 100^{li} p
diem Whereas att other playes they are not wont vsually to receive
above 40 or 50^{li} p diem And that their sd House all the said 14
dayes was very full the Pitt Boxes and other Places thereof beeing
thronged with Spectators And for that also this Defte hath been
informed and hopeth if need bee to prove by diverse Psons of
Quallity whoe in the sd 14 dayes time did See the sd Play Acted
and the sd Sceane therein psented that the sd Scheane did give a
generall content to the Spectators thereof ffor which reasons also
this Defte taketh the sd Allegacon touching ye meane pformance
of the sd worke and the Disparagmt the sd Play received thereby to
bee not only false but alse a very greate and vniust Scandall to this
Defte in his pfession which hee humbly hopeth will in due time bee
considered by this Honoble Court And as for the Suggestion in the
Bill that the painting & finishing of the sd Scheane was not worth
50^{li} And that if the same had been done according to the sd
Agreemt the Same would have been worth as much more this
Defte taketh the Same to bee a very vaine and idle Suggestion after
that by a verdict vpon full Evidence att the sd Tryall the sd worke
hath been found to bee worth 335^{li} 10^s And in truth this Defte was
in disburse well nigh 100^{li} in pviding materialls and paying Servts
for and about the same And this Defte denyeth that the pltes or
any of them did resort vnto this Defte and acquaint him that they
were dampnifyed 500^{li} or any other sume by his this Deftes breach
of the sd Agreemt and pposed to him to make them satisfaccon for
the Same Howbeit it may bee true that when this defte did resort
vnto them or Some of them or to some of the said Company to bee
payd for his sd worke to delay and putt off this Defte they might
ptend Some Such Damage as by their now Bill the Pltes Suggest.
But this Defte doth absolutely deny that hee ever was willing or
did expresse himselfe to bee willing to make them any recompence
or Satisfaccon in any pporcon whatsoever for such their ptended
damages Nor doth this Defte believe that they were att all dampnifyed, but on the contrary hee verily believeth that they received
greate benefitt and Advantage by the Pformance of the sd worke in

Such good and workeman-like manner as this Defte pformed the
Same And if they did receive any losse or damage this Defte doth
vtterly deny that they received the Same by any breach of Agreemt
on his Pte this Defte haveing made no breach of Agreemt att all as
herein before is declared And this Defte confesseth that while the
sd worke was carrying on the sd pltes Some or one of them did pay
or cause the sume of 40^{li} to bee payd to this Defte towards his
Satisfaccon for painting and finishing the sd Scheane which this
Defte did acknowledge att the sd Tryall And the same was considered by the Jury whoe were Summoned to try the sd Cause And
this Defte also confesseth it to bee true that after hee had often in
vaine resorted vnto the Compltes or Some of them or of the sd
Company to bee payd for his sd worke They Still delaying and
putting him off from time to time and offering him very inconsiderable Satisfaccon for his great paynes taken therein Hee this Defte
did bring or cause to bee brought an Accon att Law in his Maties
Court of Exchequer against the sd Pltes Charles Hart and Michaell
Moone vpon a quantum meruit as this Defte is informed by his
Attourneye in the Sd Cause the sd Accon was call'd And it is true
that vpon full Evidence given on both Sides att the Tryall of the
sd cause in Yield hall London about the end of Easter Terme last
this Defte did obtaine a Verdict for 295^{li} 10^s The sd Jury who were
to try the sd Cause valueing the Said worke at 335^{li} 10^s but diduct-
ing the sd 40^{li} this Defte did acknowledge hee had received as
aforesd And that Judgmt is therevpon entred as this Defte is likewise informed by his sd Attourneye in the sd Court of Exchequer
for the sd Sume of 295^{li} 10^s and Costs of Suite Vpon which Judgmt
this Defte is likewise informed as aforesd that Execucon is Since
taken out and Executed vpon the sd Hart and Moone or one of
them And that therevpon they or one of them have payd or
caused the sd moneyes recovered against them by the sd Judgmt
to be payd into the hands of the Sheriffe to whome the sd Execucon
was directed and this defte expecteth that the sd Sheriffe will very
Suddenly pay the Same over vnto him this Defte As this Defte
humbly conceiveth vnder the favour of this Honoble Court hee is
and ought to doe And this Defte Saith that before hee brought his
Said Accon hee did desire the pltes or Some of them or of the sd
Company to referre the matters in difference betweene them to
any indifferent Psons this defte beeing very vnwilling to contend
with them att Law which would distract and hinder him in his
worke & businesse by which hee supports himselfe and family And
beeing in truth also deterred by their or Some of their great words
and threats One of them by name Mr Wintersell playnly telling
this Defte that they could Spend more att Law then this defte

could And that they would keepe him out of his moneye till he should bee glad to take what they would please to give him And this defte further Saith that before hee could bring his sd Action att Law the sd Company of Actors did putt him this Defte to great trouble charge and expence of time to gett liberty to bring his sd Action against them they insisting vpon their priviledge as his Maties Servts and refuseing to appeare gratis therevnto Butt att length the Earle of Manchester beeing fully Satisfyed as this Defendt believeth of the greate Justice and honesty of his Cause did give this Defte liberty to bring his sd Action against them And did Order the sd Hart and Moone to appeare therevnto on the behalfe of the sd Company And this Defte Saith that att the Said Tryall att Law the most materiall allegacons in the pltes now Bill pticularly the allegacon touching the time by the Bill ptended to bee Agreed on for the doeing of the sd Worke and touching the goodnesse thereof were insisted on by the now pltes Hart and Moone and were endeavoured to bee proved but no such Agreemt as to time Appeareing to the said Court and Jury and it appeareing that the sd Worke was very well done One of the now pltes owne Wittnesses then affirmeing that the Same was excellently well done this Defte did obteyne Such verdict as aforesd And this defte positively Saith that hee would not doe the like worke againe for the Same moneye as is given him by the said Verdict for the painting and finishing the said Scheane And that in the Same time hee was about the said worke hee could have gotten more else where iff hee had not been Employed therein And this Defte doth vtterly deny that hee ever agreed to make the pltes or any of them any manner of recompence or Satisfaccon for any their ptended Damnificacons or for any other Damnificacons whatsoever as by their Bill is very falsely Suggested Without that [etc.]

No. 36. DAVENANT *v.* CROSSE

C6 250/28

Mary Davenant's Bill

13° die Novembr
1684

Garth

> To the right honoble Francis Lord Guilford Lord Keeper of the great seale of England.

Humbly Complayning sheweth vnto your Lordship your oratrix Dame Mary Davenant of London Widdow and Relict of Sr William Davenant late of London aforesaid Knt deceased That in the year of our Lord 1653 the said Sr. William Davenant (your Oratrixes late husband) having then Living but one Child (which was a Daughter) by Mary his first wife And having after her decease intermarryed with Dame Anne Cademan widow (of Sr Thomas Cademan Knt deceased, And formerly of one Crosse) who had then four sonns living namely Thomas Crosse Paul Crosse John Crosse And Phillip Cademan als Crosse And the said Sr William Davenant haveing A kind intention to be helpfull and Assistant to them And to doe some what for them out of his small estate towards their maintenance in Case they should live to attaine their respective ages of two and twenty years And the said Sr. William Davenant should not by yt time or in some reasonable time procure or provide for them the said Thomas Crosse Paul Crosse John Crosse and Phillip Cademan als Crosse respectively some office or Imployment for their respective subsistance, He the said Sr William Davenant gave order to the said Thomas Crosse or some person by his privity or procurement to prepare or to gett drawn A Bond from him the said Sr William Davenant to the said Thomas Crosse to be Conditioned to pay to him the said Thomas Crosse and his said Brothers Paul John and Phillip 100ˡⁱ A peice att their respective ages of two And twenty years in Case Hee the said Sr William Davenant should not before that time have procured or provided for them respectively some office or Imployment whereby they might respectively gett A Competent livelyhood, And to pay to such of them as should not be soe provided for by such office or Imployment 100ˡⁱ A peice att their respective ages aforesaid or to this or some such Effect, But soe it is may it please your Lordship that the said Thomas Crosse or some person by his appointment or privity designing to surprise ye said Sr William Davenant brought to him A Bond of 800ˡⁱ penalty dated on or about the seventh day

of February in the aforesaid year of our Lord 1653 Conditioned as
followeth or to that effect that is to say that if the said Sr William
Davenant his heires Execors Admrs or Assignes should pay or
Cause to be paid to the said Thomas Crosse his Execrs Admrs or
Assignes 400^{li} of Lawfull money of England by or upon the seventh
day of February then next ensuing att A certaine place of payment
in the Condition of the said Bond exprest that is to say 100^{li} for
the use of the said Thomas Crosse and 100^{li} for the use of the said
Paul Crosse and his Assignes 100^{li} for the use of the said John
Crosse And 100^{li} in full of the said 400 for the sole use of the said
Phillip (yongest brother of the said Thomas Crosse) and his
assignes, or of as many of the said Brothers as should be living on
the said seventh day of February next after the date of the said
Bond to be Equaly shared amongst them and allso if the said Sr
William Davenant his heirs Execrs Admrs or Assignes should att
his and their Cost and Charges maintaine and keep the said Thomas
Crosse and the said Paul Crosse John and Phillip his brothers with
dyet lodging washing linnen and woolen and all other necessaries
till the said Sr William Davenant his heirs Execrs Admrs or Assignes have truely paid the sume of 400^{li} as above exprest then the
said Obligation should be voyd, which Bond being drawn the said
Sr William Davenant not suspecting that the Condition thereof
was otherwise then he had given his said instructions for it to be
made, And the said Sr William Davenant and Thomas Crosse
both declareing and the said Thomas Crosse then promiseing and
agreeing to and with the said Sr William Davenant that in Case
the said Sr William should (before the respective ages aforesaid of
the said Thomas Crosse and his said brothers) procure or provide
for them respectively any office or Imployment whereby they might
respectively subsist or have A Competent livelyhood and pay vnto
every such of them as should not be so provided for by such office
or Imployment 100^{li} A peice att their respective ages of two and
twenty years then the said Bond should be cancelled, or to this or
the like effect, Wherevpon the said Sr William Davenant putting
great Confidence in And having A good Beleife of the honesty and
integrity of the said Thomas Crosse (to whome onely he had communicated these matters) did voluntarily and without any manner of Consideration therefore paid or given him, Execute the said
Bond Conditioned as the same is above exprest as by the said Bond
and Condition thereof when produced (whereunto your oratrix for
more certainty thereof referreth) may appeare, And your oratrix
further sheweth unto your Lordship that the said Sr William
Davenant having sealed and delivered the said Bond of 800^{li}
penalty upon such declaration promise and agreement aforesaid

The said Sr William Davenant did from and after the sealing and delivery thereof not onely untill the seventh day of February 1654 on which by the words of the Condicon of the said Bond (though obteyned by Surprise as aforesaid) the said 400^li was made payable, but afterwards at their respective requests of the said Thomas Crosse and his said brothers for severall years or for some long time at his own Charges find and provide for them respectively dyet lodging Apparell and washing and all other necessaries (as well before as after he had intermarryed with your oratrix) The said Thomas Crosse and his said Brothers having in truth no estate or calling whereby to subsist or gaine A livelyhood nor other freind to maintaine help or preferre them save onely the said Sr William, who from time to time supplyed all their wants Att his great Cost and Charges, And the said Sr William Davenant did put the said Thomas Crosse into the office of Receiver of the proffits of the operas and Representacons which he Caused to be performed and shewed in publique untill his now majestyes happy Restauracon, soon after which his said majesty having by his letters patent vnder the great seale of England Impowered and given Licence to the said Sr William Davenant and his heires to erect or Cause to be erected A Theatre and therein to Cause to be acted and shewed in publique certaine playes he the said Sr William Davenant did putt the said Thomas Crosse into the office of Receiver of the proffits therof and of paying thereout all Charges of and concerning ye premisses and of paying to the respective persons who by Agreement with the said Sr William Davenant had shares in the cleare and neat proffits thereof, their respective shares of the same proffits In which office or Imployment the said Thomas Crosse Continued untill about ye middle of the year of our Lord 1673 [read 1675] And duely rec'd or reteyned for such his Imployment 30^s per weeke or thereabouts out of the proffits of the said Playes and allso of the said operas and Representacons aforesaid (A great parte of which proffits belonged to the said Sr William Davenant) dureing the respective times of such respective Imployments but it being discovered that the said Thomas Crosse had imbecelled misimployed or detayned great sums of money of the sayd sharers which were due to them respectively of the proffits of the said playes as allso severall summs amounting together to 1500^li and upwards of the moneys paid and deposited in his hands towards the Charge of building the Theatre or playhouse now in Dorsett garden in London aforesaid commonly called the Dukes Theatre as allso moneyes of y^r oratrixes in his hands deposited, your oratrix who from and after the death of the said Sr William Davenant (which was in or about Aprill in the yeare of our Lord 1668) during the infancy of her sonne Charles Davenant (Eldest sonn and heir of the said Sr William Davenant) had the Government and ordering of the said Theatre and of the Company that acted there for and in behalfe of the said Charles Davenant did afterwards forbear to Imploy the said Thomas Crosse any longer in such his Imployment nor in [   ]aine being forced to abscond himselfe for fear of being sued by the said sharers for a great parte of their respective monyes by him recd and with him deposited and misimployed or deteyned as aforesaid, Howbeit your oratrix doth affirme that the said Thomas Crosse in the lifetime of the said Sr William Davenant and after the said Sr William had by surprise and by the said promise Agreement and declaration of the said Thomas Crosse & his Continuance aforesaid been wrought upon to execute ye sd bond, having in his custody severall of the goods of ye sd Sr Williams to ye value of one hundred pounds at ye least & ye sd Sr William then understanding how he was intangled by such contrivance above menconed and not knowing how to gett the said goods out of his hands without suit and trouble it was agreed between them that the said Thomas Crosse should acknowledg the said goods to be in full satisfaction of his proporcon of the benefitt of the said bond: and the said Sr William Davenant did then pay to the said Thomas Crosse 11^{li}: 15^s: 4^d in full for the maintenance of his said three brothers, which said summe of 11^{li}: 15^s: 4^d: (the said Sr William Davenant having thentofore paid severall summs of money and provided other things for or towards their maintenance aforesaid was then to be in full satisfacon of & for their maintenance by intent of the Condition of the said Bond to be provided ye receipt of which said 11^{li}: 15^s: 4^d: And goods aforesd by Indorsm^t on the said Bond (to which Idorsmt your Oratrix doth referre) if produced would appeare, And your oratrix further sheweth that the said Sr William Davenant did allso putt ye said Phillip into the Imploym^t of an actor in the said playes in which Imploym^t he continued for many years and gayned considerably thereby untill by some misfortune he became incapable of performing the same, after which neverthelesse he had for severall years and still hath allowed and Continued to him out of the said proffits of the said playes (as having been an Actor as aforesaid) thirty shills per weeke And the said Phillip well knowing the truth of the premisses and how the said Sr William Davenant had been surprised as aforesaid did after the death of the said Sr William Davenant by deed or deeds in writeing under his hand and seale bearing date in or about the 26th day of May in the year of our Lord 1684 Release unto your oratrix and vnto the said Charles Davenant all right Interest Claime benefitt demand and pretence of or to the said bond or any money or other thing to him thereby or by the Condition thereof made payable or to performed, or to that or the like effect, And your oratrix further sheweth unto your Lordship that the said John Crosse in or about the year of our lord 1668 dyed intestate and without any disposition made of any of his goods or personall estate nor hath any person taken out letters of Administration of any his estate whereby to make title to any money to him due or payable And your oratrix further sheweth that the said Thomas Crosse & his sd Brothers respectively did promise acknowledge declare or say y^t w^t money the sd Sr William Davenant had lent or disbursced or should lend or disburse to or for y^{e}m respectively & w^t dyet clothes or nessicaryes he had provided or should provide for y^{em} respectively should be satisfied alowed or deducted or was to be satisfyed allowed or deducted by or out of ye sd 100^{li} a peice to them respectively payable by ye Condicon of ye sd Bond & yt they never intended ye same should be put in suit or to some such effect And your oratrix further saith that the said Charges of dyet lodging Apparell washing & necessaries found & provided for the said Thomas Crosse and his said Brothers respectively after the time limited for paymt of the said 400^{li} as aforesaid, even if the sd bond had beene duely obteyned by the said Thomas Crosse, and without any surprise or Contrivance as aforesd, ought in all Equity and good Conscience to have bin allowed satisfied or deducted out of the said respective summes of 100^{li} A peice to them respectively made payable by the Condition therof, if such 100^{li} had not been otherwise satisfied And if such provisions after such time of paymt amounted to more then was vnsatisfyed of their sd respective 100^{li} A peice y^{en} such overplus to have been payd or satisfyd to the said Sr William Davenant his Executors or Administrators, and your oratrix further sheweth unto your Lordship that besides such provisions made for the said Thomas Crosse and his said Brothers by maintaining them and providing Imployments for the said Thomas and Phillip as aforesaid the said Sr William Davenant did after the executeing of the said Bond pay and disburse to and for the said Thomas Crosse and his said Brothers respectively severall summes of money which summes by them were respectively acknowledged to bee payd by the said Sr William Davenant & had the sd Condicon duely obteyned, ought to have bin in for or towards satisfaction of wt was not otherwise satisfied of the said 100^{li} A peice And your oratrix further sheweth that since the death of the said Sr William Davenant she hath discovered And finds he dyed much in debt and left very Little personall estate that could be recd or gotten in to satisfy the same, Howbeit whatsoever the sd personall estate was your oratrix hath good title therevnto for that the said

Sr William Davenant dyed intestate and after his decease Administration was duely comited thereof vnto John Allway gent who Afterwards by deed sold and assigned to your oratrix the same, And your oratrix hath in the Charges of the sd Sr Williams funerall and by paymt of money due by the said Sr William Davenant at his death, expended more then the value of what she hath yet recd or could receive of his said personall estate; neverthelesse soe it is may it please your Lordshipp that the said Thomas Crosse Paul Crosse and Phillip Cademan als Crosse Combineing and Confederating together and with other persons unknown to your oratrix (whose names when discovered she humbly prayes may be incerted in and they made partyes to this Bill with apt words to Charge them) to defeat and defraud your Oratrix of the sd personall estate to her sold and assigned as aforesaid The said Thomas Crosse by such Combinacon hath sued your oratrix at the Common law upon the said Bond (being entred into above thirty years agoe) and prosecutes the same suit ag^t your oratrix with great violence And the said Confederates give out in speches that he shall recover agt her the whole penalty of the said Bond allthough the said Confederates or any of them or the said John Crosse (and soe your oratrix doth expressly Charge) did never till of late demand aske or require of her any money whatsoever upon Account or by reason of the said Bond which your oratrix doth expresly affirme is satisfyed and it cannot otherwise be reasonably presumed to be, being of soe ancient a date And the said Sr William Davenant for severall years last past before his decease had A plentifull Revenue and the said Thomas Crosse and his said brothers were frequently and allmost every day with him and in his Company yet in all that time never demanded any money of him for or upon the same nor had they any reason soe to doe for ye reasons aforesaid and your oratrix doth affirme that the said Sr William Davenant some years or Considerable time before his decease had been at above 1000^{li} Charge for and upon Account of the said Thomas Crosse and his said brothers to feed, clothe, educate and maintayne y^{em} yet the said Confederates now unconsionably seeke to ruine your oratrix by compelling her (if they could) to satisfy their most unjust demands allthough your oratrix doth affirme that the said Confederates or any of them allthough the said Sr William dyed about Aprill 1668 never demanded of your oratrix soe much as one farthing upon the said Bond or ever menconed the same to her untill abt two years agoe the said Thomas Crosse (being putt out of his said Imploymt for the reasons aforesaid) by the aforesaid Combinacon Theartned to sue your oratrix thereupon and the said confederates now pretend that the said Sr William Davenant never found or provided for them any dyet lodging Apparell or washing nor ever paid any money to or for them or any of them nor procured or provided for them or any of them any office or Imployment or that there was any such promise trust or agreemt made by the said Thomas Crosse unto the said Sr William Davenant as aforesaid or any such declaracon made by them or either of them as herein above is set forth And that the said John Crosse did in his life time duely assigne his proporcon of the benefitt of the said bond to the said Thomas Crosse Paul Crosse and said Phillip some or one of them thereby to make to them a pretence of title thereunto; all which actings and dealings of the said Confederates are Contrary to all equity and good Conscience wherefore and forasmuch as your oratrixes wittnesses who could and would have proved the said deed of sale & Assignm^t from the said John Alway to yr oratrix and the said Release from the said Phillip and could make proofe of other the premisses are dead or beyond the seas or in places remote and unknowne to your oratrix soe that she cannot have the benefitt of their testimoney nor make her defence at the Common Law to the said suit, & for as much as your oratrix hath no means to discover or to be releived in the premisses save in a Court of Equity and the same are properly discoverable and releivable in this honoble Court, And for as much as the said Confederates do well know the truth of all and singular the premisses, To the intent therefore that the said Thomas Crosse Paul Crosse and Phillip Cademan als Crosse may upon their Corporall oathes set forth and discover the truth thereof and perticulary whether any summs of money and other and what Consideracon was given or paid unto the said Sr William Davenant for or that he should enter into the said Bond and whether he did not for a long time and for how many years and for w^t and how long time or times after the date thereof at his proper Costs and Charges find or provide for the said Confederates or any and which of them for ye sd John Crosse dyet lodging Aparell and washing or any and which of these provisions or other necessaryes and whether the said Confederates & ye sd John Crosse & for whom such respective provisions were made & monyes lent pd or disbursed as aforesd or any & wch of them did not promise or declare, or say to the said Sr William Davenant or to some other person & to whome that they would respectively or some of them & whiche of them pay or satisfy allow or deduct for the same or for any such and what provision or maintenance and for what times respectively, By or out of the sayd Respective summes of one hundred pounds to them respectively made payable by the condicon of the said bond or by or out of any and wch of them And whether any Administracon be committed to the said Confederates or any and which of them or to whome of the goods of the said John Crosse and when & where, and if soe, by whome was the same granted and whether there be not such Indorsmt as aforesaid or any and what Indorsmt on the said Bond, And may sett forth all the perticuler words of the Indorsmt there upon, and that the said Phillip Cademan als Crosse may set forth whether he did not by deed under his hand and seale Release unto your oratrix All demands by vertue of the said Bond or execute some Release to her to that or some such or what effect; And that the said Thomas Crosse and Phillip Cademan als Crosse respectively may sett forth whether the said Sr William Davenant did not provide or procure for them respectively such respective offices or Imploymts aforesaid or what offices or Imploymts did he provide or procure for them or either and which of them and of what yearly value were they respectively and what and how long and for what times respectively did they respectively Enjoy the same; and that the said Confederates may respectively sett forth what moneys the said Sr William Davenant or any by his order or appointmt did after the date of the said Bond pay vnto or for or upon Accot of them the said Confederates & the sd John Crosse respectively or for their respective Apparell lodging dyet necessary Phisick washing or other necessaries, and how much and when and at what time or times, and to whome, and whether such respective moneys so paid to for or upon accot of them respectively were not promised or declared & by & to whome to be allowed for or towards satisfacon of the said respective summs of 100^{li} to them respectively made payable by the Condicon of the said bond And that the said Confederates may true Answer make to all and singular the premisses as if particulary interrogated thereunto And that your oratrix may be releeved in the premisses according to Equity May it therefore please your lordship to grant vnto your oratrix his majestyes gracious writt or writts of Subpena to be directed to the said Thomas Crosse Paul Crosse and Phillip Cademan als Crosse thereby comanding them and every of them at a certaine day and vnder A certaine paine therein to be limitted personally to be and appeare before your lordship in his majestyes high Court of Chancery, then and there to Answer the premisses and further to stand to and abide such order and decree therein as to your Lordships Grave Judgement shall seeme agreeable to Equity, And your oratrix shall ever pray &c./

Ri : Bayly

Answers of Thomas and Paul Crosse

Ambo Iurat
14° die Febry
1684 [*i. e.* 1685]

The joint and severall Answers of Thomas Crosse and Paul Crosse gent Two of the Defts. to the Bill of Complt. of Dame Mary Davenant Widow the Relict and Executrix of Sir William Davenant deceased Complt.

The said Defts. saving to themselves now and at all times hereafter all and all manner of benefit and advantage of exceptions to the manifold imperfections incertainties and insufficiencies in the sayd Complainants Bill [contained] for answer unto so much thereof as matterially concerneth these Defendts. or either of them to make answer unto.

These Defts. severally say that before the yeare of our Lord 1653 the sayd Sir William being Prisoner in the Tower of London as the Deft. Paul Crosse knows and the other Deft. Thomas believes and in danger of losing his life as was then reported and as they doe verily believe and being then in great want of money as these Defts. believe and as the Deft. Paul has heard him declare when the other Deft. Thomas was beyond the seas and these Defts. mother being then the widdow of one Sir Thomas Cademan in the Bill named and of a considerable fortune did supply the wants of him the said Sir William Davenant with the greatest part of the summe of Eight Hundred pounds as the Deft. Thomas Crosse believes for that he received part of it immediately after his returne home from beyond sea with the other Deft. Paul his brother for the sayd Sir William and delivered it to him by her appointment and the Deft. Paul is well assured thereof for that (to the best of his remembrance) he was at the receipt of the whole Eight hundred pounds which was lodged by this Defts. mother in the hands of [   ] Richardson an Apothecary in Warwick Lane and all or most drawne from him to supply the wants, as this Deft. Paul conceives, of the sayd Sir William Davenant as aforesaid, which sayd summe or the greatest part thereof the Deft. Paul Crosse says was left by the sayd Sir Thomas Cademan at his death to his sayd Lady these Defts. mother for her and their support the sayd Deft. Paul then living with the sayd Sir Thomas Cademan during the time of his whole sicknes and till the time of his death who heard him expresse the same injoyning her to see it equally devided amongst her and her Fower Sons and the reason as this Deft. Paul conceives that induced him so to doe was for that the sayd Sir Thomas Cademan as

this Deft. hath heard losing his whole Estate in a Vessel sunk at Sea
going over for Holland with the Queen Mother and having nothing
left as the Deft. Paul has heard the sayd Sir Thomas Cademan declare but the clothes on his back these Defts. Mother did then supply him with a considerable summe of money before she intermar-
ried with the sayd Sir Thomas which money the Deft. Paul believes
and hath heard his Mother declare was part of the Estate which
Thomas Crosse the father of these Defts. left her at his death for
her and her Childrens maintenance and the Deft. Paul further says
that his sayd Mother was possest of severall other considerable
summes of money and Jewels to a considerable value Vizt. a Dia-
mond Ring valued by a Goldsmith at Two hundred broad pieces in
gold a paire of Pendants vallewed likewise at One hundred and
Sixty pounds a Necklace of Pearle valued at Sixty pounds with
many other things of value, as Rings, Bracelets &c which in all
might amount (as this Deft. believes) to the vallue of Six hundred
pounds or thereabouts the greatest part of all which as this Deft.
believes were disposed to supply the wants of the sayd Sir William
Davenant before and after his intermarriage with their Mother the
then Lady Cademan which was in the yeare of our Lord God 1652
at the time of which marriage the sayd Sir William made large
promises of his care for these Defendts. and their brothers without making any certaine provision for these Defts. and their sayd
Brothers maintenance being at the time of these Defts. Mothers
intermarriage with the sayd Sir William Davenant which was
about the month of October in the yeare of our Lord 1652 as aforesayd of the Ages hereafter mentioned that is to say this Deft.
Thomas Crosse was then about the Age of Twenty Two yeares and
the Deft. Paul Crosse was then about the Age of Sixteen yeares
and these Defts. brother John Crosse was then about the Age of
Eleven yeares and these Defts. brother Phillip Cademan was then
about the Age of Nine yeares. That shortly after these Defts.
Mothers intermarriage with the sayd Sir William Davenant notwithstanding the considerable supplys their sayd Mother had
brought him in marriage yet he the sayd Sir William Davenant was
carelesse of these Defts. and their Brothers maintenance it being
as he pretended soe low with him that after discharging such necessary debts as he had contracted that he was scarce able to provide
for himself yet these Defts. Mother was in hopes as these Defts.
believe that the sayd Sir William would be in a better condition in
some reasonable time but finding him then not able to give any
other security for her Childrens maintenance and for the paying of
them One hundred pounds a piece than only his owne Bond these
Defts. Mother as these Defts. believe was perswaded to accept of a

Bond of Eight hundred pounds penalty not only for the payment of One hundred pounds a piece unto these Defts. and their sayd brothers but also to finde and provide sufficient maintenance for these Defts. and their sayd brothers untill they should receive their sayd One hundred pounds a piece and to that purpose the sayd Sir William Davenant did as these Defts. believe give order to some person unknowne unto either of these Defts. for the drawing up of the Bond in the Bill mentioned which was given to the Deft. Thomas Crosse to write out faire and then he did afterwards signe seale and deliver the same to this Deft. Thomas Crosse to the uses intents and purposes mentioned in the Condition of the sayd Bond as in the Bill is mentioned which Bond was sealed and delivered in the presence of Sir Sackvile Crowe and Paul Hagget Esquire and these Defts. deny that the sayd Sir William Davenant did to the knowledg of either of these Defts. give order to either of these Defts. or any other person for the Drawing up of the sayd Bond he entered into unto the sayd Thomas Crosse to be in any other manner than is expressed in the sayd Bond and Condition by which sayd Bond the sayd Sir William Davenant did become bound unto the sayd Thomas Crosse in the penall Summe of Eight hundred pounds bearing date the Seaventh day of February in the yeare of our Lord 1653 with a Condition thereunto Vizt. The Condition of this Obligation is such that if the above bound William Davenant Knight, his Heires Executors Administrators and Assignes or any or either of them doe well and truly pay or cause to be payd unto the above named Thomas Crosse his Executors Administrators or Assignes the full summe of Fower hundred pounds sterling of lawfull money of England by or upon the Seaventh day of February next ensueing the date above written which shall be in the Yeare of our Lord God One Thousand Six hundred Fifty and Fower at or [in] the now dwelling place of him the sayd Thomas Crosse in Tutle Street to and for the uses hereafter mentioned that is to say One hundred pounds of lawfull money of England to and for the sole proper use and uses of Thomas Crosse his Executors Administrators or Assignes, One hundred pounds of like lawfull money of England to and for the sole proper use and uses of Paul Crosse brother of the sayd above named Thomas Crosse and his Assignes One hundred pounds of like English money to and for the sole proper use and uses of John Crosse another brother of the sayd above named Thomas Crosse and his Assignes and One hundred pounds more of current English money in full of the sayd summe of Fower hundred pounds to and for the sole proper use and uses of Phillip Crosse the youngest brother of him the above named Thomas Crosse or his Assignes or to the sole proper use and uses of as many of the sayd brothers as shall be living on the sayd Seaventh day of February whereon the sayd summe of Fower hundred pounds ought to be payd as aforesayd to be equally shared amongst them and also if the sayd above bound Sir William Davenant his Heires Executors and Assignes or any or either of them doe and shall at his and their or some of their owne proper costs and charges maintaine and keep the sayd above named Thomas Crosse and the sayd Paul Crosse, John Crosse and Phillip Crosse his brothers and every of them with meat drink lodging washing linnen and woollen and all other necessarys whatsoever till he the sayd above bound William Davenant Knight his Heires Executors Administrators or Assignes have truly payd the sayd Summe of Fower hundred pounds as above expressed, then this Obligation to be voyd or else to stand in full force and vertue. As by the sayd Bond and Condition unto which for more certainty these Defts. referre themselves, ready to be produced, more fully and at large may appeare. And this Deft. Thomas Crosse for himself Sayth that before the sayd Sir William Davenant marryed his this Defts. Thomas Crosse Mother Sir William Davenant finding this Deft. capable to be serviceably to him did desire this Deft. to goe with him in the nature of a Secretary or Gentleman to wayte upon him to Mary Land in the West Indies of which place the sayd Sir William Davenant had, as this Deft. believes, a Commission to be Governour from his late Majesty and this Deft. going with him they were both taken Prisoners at Sea by the then Parliaments forces in the late rebellious times where this Deft. Thomas lost a considerable venture his sayd Mother then sending him out in very good Equipage and thereupon Sir William Davenant was put Prisoner in the Tower of London at which time this Deft. Thomas Crosse left the sayd Sir William D'avenant and went to Barbadoes upon his owne account to the late Lord Willoughby of Parham then Governour there and served him as Secretary and after this Deft. Thomas Crosse his returne into England the sayd Sir William Davenant having newly marryed this Defts. Mother did desire this Deft. not to leave him promising him large rewards when he should be able and although this Deft. was profferd good Employment under the Duke of Ormond (and other persons of Quality) having before served the Earle of Ossory in France as his Gentleman, yet this Deft. by the importunity and faire promises of great rewards by the sayd Sir William Davenant did continue to serve him for the most part during his life in such Employment as the sayd Sir William Davenant found this Deft. capable to serve him which was in constant hard writing and goeing of his Errands and that during this Defts. service with the sayd Sir William he did not allow him any wages or

Salary at all besides ordinary Clothes lodging and diet for which last he was often put to shift untill after his Majesties happy restauration when the said Sir William as he believes having gotten his late Majesties Letters Pattents under the Great Seale of England whereby he was impowered and had licence to erect or cause to be erected a Theatre for the acting and shewing in publique certaine Plays as in the sayd Bill is set forth and true it is the sayd Sir William Davenant did afterwards as in the sayd Bill is alleadged put this Deft. Thomas Crosse into the Office of one of the Receivers of the profits of the sayd Plays and of paying thereout all charges of and concerning the premises and of paying to the respective persons who by Covenants and agreement with the sayd Sir William Davenant had shares in the cleere and neat profits thereof their respective shares of the same profits in which office or Employment this Deft. Thomas Crosse continued untill about the time in the sayd Bill mentioned and during that Employment he did receive for such weeks only as they acted after the rate of Twenty Five Shillings p*er* week and some time after his decease was by the sayd Company advanced to Thirty shillings in consideration as he conceives of his great paines and care and no more and not only from the sayd Sir William and the sayd Company of Actors but also by and from the respective persons sharers interest in the sayd Plays. And whereas the Complt. by her sayd Bill doth charge him to have imbeaziled misemployed or detained great summes of money of the sharers which were due to them respectively of the profits of the sayd Plays as also severall summes amounting together to Fifteene hundred pounds and upwards of the moneys payd and deposited in this Defts. hands towards the charge of building the Theatre or Playhouse now in Dorset Garden in London called the Dukes Theatre as also of the Complts. money deposited in this Defts. hands: To which Charge this Deft. sayth that he did demeane himself in the sayd Employment as one of the Receivers or Treasurers faythfully and justly during the sayd Sir William Davenants life time and since his death, since which time this Deft. had more businesse heaped upon him than was reasonable for one man to undergoe, yet this Deft. did performe the same to the best of his ability honestly and faythfully by delivering out Tickets to his fellow Treasurers who had an equall power with this Deft. both in Receipts of money payment of charges and making up the Charge of the Theatre and then to receive the Tickets in againe from all the Dorekeepers together with such Tickets as this Deft. had delivered out during the whole time of his Receipts with the Dorekeepers of the Pitt, Galleries and Boxkeepers moneys, as also making up the whole Receipts and expences of the day comparing the number of Tickets with the money brought in wherein the Company had alwaies a check upon this Deft. and they might and did almost dayly view and examine this Deft. Accompts which one or other of them did or might have done when they pleased And also this Deft. had the sole trouble of paying the whole charge of the House weekly that is to say the Salaries of all hireling Players both men and Woemen, Musick Masters, Dancing Masters, Scene men, Barbers, Wardrobe keepers, Dorekeepers and Soldiers, besides Bills of all kinds, as for Scenes, Habits, Properties, Candles, Oile and other things, and in making and paying, if called for, all the Dividends of the Sharers, deviding each man his particular share according to his proportion, and often in the crowd of this Defts. [business] and all this done by this Deft. without having any Receipts from any of the Company, or any of the Hirelings or any others belonging to the Company for any one Summe payd them by this Deft. And also this Deft. had the paying the sharers of the Ten Shares (being the Assignees of the sayd Sir William Davenant) who came or sent for their moneys when they pleased having free accesse by themselves servants or Agents to the Books of Accompts of all the Receipts and disbursements of the foregoing week with the severall Dividends, this Deft. being ever ready when required to Sattisfy them in every particular and to deliver them their shares at every weeks end which he conceives by the Setlement he was to doe and to stand no further charged then from week to week And if this Deft. kept it longer it was their fault and not this Defts. for this Deft. never denyed them when they came for it, till the Accompts fell short. And although one Mr. Bayly was nominated Treasurer and Expenditor to the building of the new Theatre (who is a sharer in the Ten Shares) by the sharers putting in a Stock of Three Thousand pounds into his hands, yet most part of the trouble was imposed upon this Deft. in defraying the remaining charge being about Six Thousand pounds more, for this Deft. receiv'd all or most of the Bills for work done and payd them and delivered them over to Mr. Bayly or his wife he being appointed Expenditor, and this Deft. constantly carryed his loose Bills Receipts of money and other papers to Mr. Bayly's house where he or his wife did peruse them she being concerned in point of interest, and by that meanes and by too much busines imposed upon this Deft. some of the Receipts were lost or misplaced as this Deft. believes, so that this Deft. having had his Books of Accompts taken from him by their or some of their appointment could not perfectly state it in so short time as it was desired he should make it out nor does he conceive himself lyable by the sayd Setlement to accompt farther than a Week, but he does believe the

Plt. the Lady Davenant having many Children unprovided for having fitted her son Alexander for his the Defts. Employment as Treasurer the sayd Alexander (imediately upon his remove) was put into his sayd office as Treasurer where he remained till he marryed. yet this Deft. doth positively affirme that he hath neither mispent nor misemployed one penny of the publique money of the Theatre nor any Sharers or any other concerned in those Receipts otherwise than to their owne uses and when this Deft. found the Accompts fall short this Deft. did lay out much of his owne money to their uses in hopes thereby to purchase this Defts. quiet and in doing of the same this Deft. was forced to borrow money of severall persons for which he still stands indebted and at last to sell his shares in the Building and proffits of acting at an under rate to his this Defts. ruine. And if this Defts. Papers and Books of Accompts had not been taken away so soone from this Deft. so that he might have had longer time to have examined those that he had payd monies to their Receipts for the same being mislayd or lost this Deft. doubted not but to have made it appeare that there was little or nothing due from this Deft. for before and after this Defts. Books and Papers were taken from him this Deft. found upon examination and confession of severall persons that he payd money unto whose Receipts were mislayd or lost and therefore not as he believes charged upon the sayd Accompt he gave in although no ways obliged to accompt as he conceives by the first setlement for more than a week yet this Deft. made it appeare he payd to the Plummer the summe of One hundred and seaventy pounds to the Carpenter the summe of Forty pounds, to the Bricklayer the summe of Twenty pounds for which money the Receipts were either lost or mislayd, besides he believes severall others took advantage by this Defts. Books and Papers being taken from him for the Master Builder did owne unto the sayd Deft. before he knew his Accompts came into question being asked what was owing to him the sayd Master for the Building, answered that there was only Thirteene hundred pounds due in Arreare upon his Accompt yet afterwards hearing that his Accompts were called into question, and that this Defts. Papers and Receipts were lost he chargeth to be owing unto him Seaventeen hundred pounds, being Fower hundred pounds more than was formerly demanded. Now if those summes which this Deft. hath discovered were allowed him upon his Accompt with Ninety Nine pounds Fowerteen shillings and Three pence that this Deft. hath payd in his owne wrong upon review of this Defts. Accompts, and his fellow Receivers who for some time payd weekly part of the Charge of the House to ease this Deft. it would appeare there were nothing at all due to the Plt.

nor any of the Sharers, but that the Deft. Thomas Crosse rather
lost by the Trust they imposed upon him in leaving their money in
his hands longer than a week which was more than the first Setlement required as aforesayd and as afore to his utter undoing. And
this Deft. Thomas Crosse denyes that he ever received of the sayd
Sir William Davenant before or after the sealing of the sayd Bond
any mony, dyet, lodging, apparrel, washing or other necessaries, or
any goods or other thing whatsoever for or in respect of the aforesayd bond but what this Deft. ever received or had from the sayd
Sir William Davenant this Deft. very dearly merited it for the
service he had done and performed to and for the sayd Sir William
and not in any manner of sattisfaction of the aforesayd bond or
condition thereof for though this Deft. Thomas Crosse did at the
desire of the sayd Sir William Davenant write on the backside of
the sayd Bond that he had received One hundred pounds in goods
and moveables prized to the rate of the sayd summe which this
Deft. alleadged he took in full sattisfaction of this Defts. right and
proportion in the sayd Bond and that he did likewise write on the
sayd Bond that he had received over and above the sayd One
hundred pounds, Eleven pounds fifteen shillings and fower pence
out of the value of the sayd goods for the maintenance of this
Defts. three younger brothers in part of payment of what is mentioned in the sayd Bond and to which this Deft. did set only his
hand thereto, yet the same was done only for prevention and to
secure the seizure of the sayd Sir William Davenants goods from
his Creditors as he conceives upon some Judgment or Judgments
against the sayd Sir William Davenant and to no advantage to this
Deft. the sayd Sir William taking the house in Tutle Street where
the Goods were in the name of this Deft. for the purpose aforesayd
and not otherwise for that after this Deft. had made that acknowl-
edgment on the backside of the sayd Bond at the request of the
sayd Sir William Davenant who told this Deft. it should be no
prejudice to this Deft. in regard this Deft. never had any part of
the sayd goods except the Picture of this Defts. Mother which
the Complt. gave to this Deft. since the sayd Sir Williams death
and that most part of the sayd goods the sayd Sir William upon
his removall from his house in Tutle Street to Rutland house in
Charter house Yard did sell and had the money for the same to his
owne use and that this Deft. had no part thereof and that such of
the sayd goods as were not sold by the sayd Sir William Davenant
the Complt. as this Deft. Thomas believes had all or most part of
the same for that this Deft. did lately see a Tin Cabinet in the
custody of Doctor Charles Davenant which was valued at three
pounds in the Inventory of the goods pretended to be made over

to the Deft. Thomas in sattisfaction of his proportion in the Bond aforesayd And this Deft. further denies that he ever made any agreement with the sayd Sir William Davenant for the sayd goods or that he received Eleven pounds Fifeteen shillings and Fower pence or any part thereof in such manner as the sayd Bill chargeth or in any other manner whatsoever but this Deft. confesseth he made such Endorsement upon the sayd Bond at the desire and request of the sayd Sir William Davenant and for the reasons aforesaid and not otherwise, being then prevailed with to doe the same upon some assurance as this Deft. believes that the sayd Endorsment would not prejudice the sayd Bond (in regard the same was not under this Defts. Seale) at Common Law nor in Equity unlesse some proof could be made that this Deft. had the sayd Goods which Endorsement is as followeth Memorandum that I Thomas Crosse have received One hundred pound in Goods and moveables priz'd to the rate of the sayd summe which I take in full sattisfaction of my right and proportion in this Bond and likewise over and above the sayd Hundred pound I have received Eleven pounds Fifteene shillings and Fower pence out of the value of the sayd Goods for the maintenance of my Three younger brothers in part of that payment which is mentioned in this Bond I say received by me One hundred Eleaven pounds fifteene shillings and Fower pence. And this Deft. further sayth that as to his brother Phillip Cademans share of the sayd Bond he believes the sayd Phillip Cademan hath given unto the Complt. a Release of his interest and share in the sayd Bond so that this Deft. is willing to abate the Complt. the Same if he may so doe legally. And the sayd deceased John Crosse did in his life time by writing under his hand and seale ready to be produced give one half of his interest in the sayd Bond to this Deft. Thomas Crosse so that this Deft. is advised that he hath good right to one half of his the sayd John Crosse his interest and share of the sayd Bond without taking any Letters of Administration of his Estate. And this Deft. Thomas Crosse further sayth that neither he nor any of his brothers, except the sayd Phillip Cademan, to the knowledg of this Deft. did ever promise, acknowledg, declare or say that what money the sayd Sir William Davenant had lent or disbursed or should disburse to and for this Deft. or his brothers respectively or that what diet, clothes or necessarys he the sayd Sir William had provided for them respectively should be sattisfy'd allowed or deducted or was to be sattisfyed allowed or deducted by or out of the said Bond or that the sayd Bond should never be put in suite as in the sayd Bill is untruely alleadged And this Deft. Thomas Crosse denyes that the sayd Bond was gott, had or obtained by surprize or that this Deft. ever had any moneys,

Cloathes dyet or any other necessaries or imployment for or in
respect of the sayd Bond but what this Deft. had he did dearely
deserve for his service, paines and imployment as aforesayd having
never received one penny of sallary or wages for his sayd service as
aforesayd; and what this Deft. had acknowledged on the back of
the sayd Bond was done for the reason above sayd and not otherwise
And this Deft. believes that what his Two Brothers Paul and John
had from the sayd Sir William Davenant was in no part of sattisfaction of the moneys due to them on the sayd Bond, or that the Dyet
clothes or other necessaries that the sayd Sir William Davenant had
so slenderly provided for them was suitable either to their Mothers
quality or portion she brought him with whom the sayd Sir William
had a great fortune (considering his then condition) And this Deft.
conceives the sayd Sir William ought to have provided better for
them besides the sayd hundred pounds a peece considering the fortune he had with this Defts. sayd Mother the sayd Sir William being
at the time of their intermarriage in a very low condition. And this
Deft. further saith that he believes that the sayd Sir William Davenant dyed in debt besides the aforesayd Bond, yet he believes that
the sayd Sir William left at his death a good personal Estate for
that he believes that the sayd Sir William Davenant at the time of
his death left a personal Estate consisting in ready money housel
stuffe, plate, Jewels, Pictures and other things to a very considerable value besides Three fifthes of Five shares and a half of the
profits in the sayd Plays with a like share of the Scenes and Habits
which are now worth to be sold Eight hundred pounds a share
which Three fifths amounts unto near Three Thousand pounds
which the Complt. hath possessed as this Deft. is informed and
does believe as Executrix in her owne wrong for that this Deft. is
advised that the Administration graunted unto John Alway was
fraudulent by the Statute in the 43 yeare of the Reigne of the late
Queen Elizabeth, And in regard the sayd Complt. hath kept the
sayd shares unsold: this Deft. is advised that the sayd Complt.
shall be answerable for the profits she hath since received for the
sayd shares which, as this deft. believes, amount unto about
Seaven Thousand pounds. And this Deft. denyes the combination
in the Bill charged but confesseth that he hath sued the sayd
Complt. upon the aforesayd Bond entered into above Thirty yeares
since as this Deft. hopes is lawfull for him so to doe and the reason
why this Deft. did not put the sayd Bond in Suite sooner was for
that the sayd Sir William Davenant was but in a low condition
untill his late Majesties happy restauration which was in the yeare
1660 and since that unto the time of his death which was in the
yeare 1668 This Deft. and his sayd Brother Paul Crosse did by

themselves and severall others sollicite the sayd Sir William to pay the sayd money due on the sayd Bond who promised to Sir William Bolton late Lord Major of the City of London and others in the behalf of these Defts. that in regard he had not present moneys that he the sayd Sir William Davenant would setle some part of the shares upon them of the profits of Acting in lieu of the sayd bond and thereupon these Defts. were prevailed with to for-beare sueing him the sayd Sir William during his life; and after his death one John Alway took out Letters of Administration of the sayd Sir William Davenants personal Estate who was a man of no residence as these Defts. could heare of so that these Defts. knew not where to finde him to put the sayd Bond in suite against him, but afterwards these Defts. were informed that the sayd Adminis-tration graunted to Alway was fraudulent and that what personall Estate that these Defts. could prove came to the hands of the sayd Complt. would be lyable to make good the sayd Bond but all things were so secretly transacted between the sayd Alway and the sayd Complt. and her son Doctor Charles Davenant that these Defts. till about the yeares 1677 or 1678 could not discover what personall Estate of the sayd Sir William Davenant came to the hands of the sayd Complt. Yet the sayd Defts. doe verily be-lieve and hope to prove that demand was made for them to the sayd Complt. of sattisfaction of the condition of the sayd Bond after the death of the sayd Sir William Davenant Notwithstand-ing these Defts. till of late could not be sattisfyed that the shares of the cleere profits of the Plays which the sayd Sir William left at his death were Assets the sayd Complt. and her sonne Doctor Davenant till of late afirming that the sayd profits were only In-heritance and not Assets: and besides the sayd Deft. Paul Crosse sayth the sayd Deft. Thomas Crosse having an Employment under the sayd Complt. and the Actors this Deft. Paul Crosse could not prevaile with him to sue the sayd Bond. And this Deft. Thomas doth confesse he may have given out in speeches that if he doe re-cover he shall recover the whole penalty of the Bond, for the in-terest of the sayd Fower hundred pounds in the sayd Condition mentioned comes to more than the penalty of the sayd bond. And this Deft. denies that the sayd Sir William Davenant to the time of his death had been at any charge to feed, clothe, educate and maintaine him this Deft. in any greater manner than as his servant or better than this Defts. service did deserve having never received one penny of wages from him. And this Deft. Thomas Crosse doth confesse that he hath given out in speeches that his brother John Crosse had in his life time assigned one moyety of all his in-terest in the sayd Bond unto him by writing under his hand and

Seale and is advised that he hath good right and Title to the same
without taking any Letters of Administration of his sayd Brothers
Estate and therefore no Administration of the sayd John Crosse
his Estate is taken out as this Defendant believes And this Deft.
Thomas Crosse further sayth that the consideration, as he believes,
why the sayd Sir William Davenant entered into the aforesayd
Bond was because the sayd Sir William had all this Defts. mothers
Estate upon his marriage with her and she had not made any provision for this Deft. and his sayd brothers. And the Deft. Paul
Crosse further sayth that he never received one penny nor ever
had any other sattisfaction on discount of the sayd Bond nor lived
above Two yeares under the care of the sayd Sir William Davenant
since the sealing of the sayd Bond, during the major part of which
Two yeares the sayd Deft. Paul Crosse often wanted both meate,
drink and clothes and does verily believe he should have been absolutely starved had not some friends of the Deft. Pauls often relieved him, yet notwithstanding the Deft. Paul spent most of the
sayd time (when required) in gooing and coming in the busines of
the sayd Sir William Davenant and often in writing for him and
doeing what else he commanded who would seldome or never suffer him to want imployment. Three yeares more, to the best of
this Deft. Pauls remembrance, he spent in one Tracy Pauncefote
Esqr. his service as his Clerk, and about one yeare more he spent
as a Souldier in Flanders under his Majesty that now is, and for
above Twenty Five yeares last past he the sayd Deft. Paul has lived
upon his owne Estate and industry without receiving the least sattisfaction upon the sayd Bond upon any account whatsoever.
And both of these Defts. the sayd Thomas and Paul Crosse say
that during their sayd brother John his time of Tuition under the
sayd Sir William Davenant, he the sayd Sir William Davenant
seldome took care to give him necessaries suitable to the portion
the sayd Sir William had with their said Mother wanting all manner of necessaries as one that had no manner of Parents left to look
after him, and often neer famished with hunger till he gott into the
service of Major Generall Jephson as his Page which was long before the yeare 1660 and after till the time of his sicknes lived as
these Defts. have heard from him and doe verily believe without
relief from the sayd Sir William or any sattisfaction upon the sayd
Bond being, by the Deft. Paul Crosse, put into the Earle of Ox-
fords Troop at the first raising thereof and there often relieved by
both these Defts. Thomas and Paul Crosse untill the time of their
sayd brother John his sicknes in which they maintained him to
their cost of above Twenty pounds and after his death buried him
likewise at their owne charge; and both the sayd Defts. deny all

manner of Combination to defraude or defeate the sayd Complt. And the Deft Paul Crosse further sayth that John Crosse his brother did on the Sixth day of November One Thousand Six hundred Sixty Three under his hand and seale assigne the sayd Paul Crosse fifty pounds of his share of Sir William Davenants debt. And this Deft. Thomas Crosse denyes that he does owe or is any way indebted to the Complt. upon any accompt whatsoever any summe or summes of money upon any receipts or actings in relation to the sayd Playhouse as Treasurer or otherwise but sayth the House is indebted to him a considerable summe of money, and he is now Debtor to severall persons for monys taken up for supply of the occations of the Playhouse. Without that that any other matter or thing in the Complts. sayd Bill of complaint contained matteriall or effectuall in the Law to be answered unto and not herein and hereby well and Sufficiently answered or denyed is true. All which matters and things these Defts. are and will be ready to averre, justify, maintaine and prove as this Honorable Court shall award And therefore humbly prays to be hence dismist with their reasonable Costs in this behalf wrongfully susteyned.

Will : Killingworth

No. 81. MORLEY *v.* DAVENANT

C10 364/8

The Schedule or Account Referred to in the Answere whereunto this is annext

			li	s	d
Anno Dni 1696					
Novemb^r 6th:	The Lady Morley and two in the Box at Oroonoko			12	
" 25th	Lady Morley in the Box at the Relapse			4	
Decemb^r 29th	" " and ffower in the Box at Loves last Shift		1		
January 2^d	" " " three " " " " Timon of Athens			16	
" 22th	" " " two " " " Esop			12	
March 9th	" " " one att the Prophetesse			10	
" 13th	" " " two " " Indian Queen			15	
1697 27th	" " " two in the Box at the Libertine			12	
Aprill 5th	" " " Three " " " " Cynthia and Endimion			16	
" 8th	" " " two " " " " Psyche			15	
" 23th	" " " one " " " " Oroonoko			8	
May 8th	" " " one " " " " Plott and noe Plott			8	
" 24th	" " " two " " " " Esopp			12	
" 25th	" " one in the Pitt att the Tempest			3	
" 26th	" " and ffour in the Box att Don Seabastian		1		
" 27th	" " one in the Pitt at Lancashire Witches			2	6
" 31th	" " and one in the Box att Sham Lawyer			8	
June 5th	" " " three " " " " Indian Queen		1		
" 12th	" " " " " " " " Oroonoko			16	
" 18th	" " " two " " " " Marryage Allamode			12	
Novr 19th	" " " " " " " Scornefull Lady			12	
" 26th	" " " one " " " " Timon			8	
Decr 4th	" " " " " " " prophetesse			10	
" 9th	" " " " " " " Esop			8	
January 5th	" " two in the Pitt at the Relapse			5	
" 18th	" " and one in the Box att Country House			8	
ffeb^{ry} 7th	" " " two " " " " King Arthur			15	
" 25th	" " " one " " " " "			10	
March 19th	" " " " / " " " " "			10	
anno 1698					
Novr 19th	" " " two " " " " Allexander			12	
" 26th	" " " " " " " " Oedipus			12	
" 28th	" " " " " " " " Little Theife			12	
Jan^{ry} 28th	" " " one " " " " Bonduca			8	
ffeb^{ry} 2^d	" " " " " " " " Spanish Wives			8	
" 3^d	" " " two " " " " King Lear			12	
" 7th	" " " one " " " " the Island princesse			10	
anno 1699					
March 25th	" " " two " " " " " " "			15	
June 29th	" " " two " " " " the Joviall Crew			12	
October 24th	" " " one " " " " the Comittee			8	
" 28th	" " in the Box at the Traytor			4	

[anno 1699]										li	s	d
Nov^r	11th	"	"	and two		in the Box at Caius Marius					12	
"	21th	"	"	"	"	" "	" "	the Orphan			12	
"	28th	"	"	"	"	" "	" "	Constant Couple			12	
Dec^r	14th	"	"	"	three	" "	" "	Marryage hater			16	
"	16th	"	"	in the Box at Earle of Essex							4	
ffebr	3^d	"	"	and two		in the Box at Venice preserved					12	
"	10th	"	"	"	one	" "	" "	ye Relapse			8	
"	13th	"	"	"	two	" "	" "	Constant Couple			12	
"	19th	"	"	"	one	" "	" "	the Grove an Opera			10	

anno 1700

										li	s	d
May	2^d	"	"	"	three	" "	" "	the ffox			16	
June	15th	"	"	"	two	" "	" "	Constant Couple			12	
"	18th	"	"	"	three	" "	" "	the Pilgrim			16	
Octob^r	19th	"	"	in the Box at			"	"			4	
"	26th	"	"	and two		in the Box at Constant Couple					12	
"	29th	"	"	"	one	" "	" "	London Cuckolds			8	
Nov^r	19th	"	"	one		in the Box at the Pilgrim					4	
"	21th	"	"	"		" "	" "	the prophetesse			4	
"	23th	"	"	and two		in the Box at Love at a losse					12	
"	27th	"	"	one		in the Box at the plaine dealer					4	
"	29th	"	"	"		" "	" "	Marryage allamode			4	
Dec^r	4th	"	"	and three		in the Box at the prophetesse				1		
"	5th	"	"	in the Box at ye Island princesse							4	
"	6th	"	"	one		in the Box at Rule a Wife &c:					4	
"	9th	"	"	"		" "	" "	Love makes a Man			4	
"	12th	Idem									4	
"	13th	Idem									4	
"	14th	Idem									4	
"	18th	Lady Morley and two				in the Box at Love makes a Man &c					12	
"	21th	"	"	one		in the Box at the Silent Woman					4	
"	27th	"	"	"		" "	" "	the ffox			4	
"	28th	"	"	"		" "	" "	Marryage Hater			4	
Jan^{ry}	1st	"	"	in the Box at the Tempest							4	
"	2^d	"	"	and three		in the Box at Island Princesse				1		
"	7th	"	"	one		in the Box at all for love					4	
"	9th	"	"	"		" "	" "	the Relapse			4	
"	11th	"	"	"		" "	" "	the Indian Queen			5	
"	15th	"	"	"		" "	" "	Love Makes a Man			4	
"	17th	"	"	"		" "	" "	Timon			4	
"	18th	"	"	"		" "	" "	venice preserved			4	
"	23th	"	"	"		" "	" "	plaine Dealer			4	
"	25th	"	"	one		in the Box at Constant Couple					4	
"	29th	"	"	"		" "	" "	King Arthur			5	
ffebr	1st	"	"	and one		in the Box at King Arthur					10	
"	4th	"	"	one		in the Box at the Unhappy pennitent					4	
"	7th	"	"	"		in the Box at the Tempest					4	
"	20th	"	"	and two		in the Box at Allexander					12	

								li	s	d

[anno 1700]

							li	s	d
ffebr	22ᵗʰ	"	"	in the Box at Alexander			4	
March	1ˢᵗ	"	"	and two	in the Box at the Humours of the Age		12	
"	4ᵗʰ	"	"	one	in the Box at the Tempest		4	
"	13ᵗʰ	"	"	"	" " " " the Humors of yᵉ Age		4	
"	15ᵗʰ	"	"	"	" " " " Like to Like or a Match well made		4	
"	18ᵗʰ	"	"	"	" " " " the ffox		4	
"	24ᵗʰ	"	"	"	" " " " Rule a Wife &c		4	

Anno 1701

							li	s	d
	25ᵗʰ	"	"	"	" " " " Old Batchelor	4	
"	27ᵗʰ	"	"	"	" " " " the Alchimist	4	
Apr:	1ˢᵗ	"	"	in the Box at Alchimist		4	
"	5ᵗʰ	"	"	" " " " the Rivall Queene		4	
"	8ᵗʰ	"	"	" " " " King Arthur		5	
"	12ᵗʰ	"	"	" " " " Carius Marius		4	
May	2ᵈ	"	"	" " " " Sʳ Harry Wildair		4	
"	3ᵈ	"	"	and two	in the Box at " " "	12	
"	19ᵗʰ	"	"	" " " " " " the Virgin prophetesse	15	
"	20ᵗʰ	"	"	one	in the Box the same	5	
"	28ᵗʰ	"	"	one	in the Box at Sʳ Harry Wildair	4	
"	30ᵗʰ	"	"	"	" " " " Loves last Shift	4	
"	31ᵗʰ	"	"	"	" " " " the Bath &c:	4	
June	5ᵗʰ	"	"	"	" " " " the Silent Woman	4	
"	9ᵗʰ	"	"	"	" " " " the Bath &c:	4	

Totall   45 11 6

John Hoskyns

No. 105. STEELE *v.* RICH

C7 642/44

1707, 3 July

 Bill of Richard Steele, showing that "Yr. Orator haveing writt severall Comedyes & Playes at the request of & for Christopher Rich Esqr. for the use of the Theater or Playhouse in or near Bridges Street in Covent Garden . . . Christopher Rich to induce yr. Orator to write further for him on or about . . . December" 1702 advanced Steele £72 "upon this Agreement then . . . made between them That yr. Orator should bring to him . . . the next Comedy yr. Orator should be the Author of and out of the Profitts when the same should come to be acted that belonged to yr. Orator as the Author according to the Usage and Custome in such Cases he the said Christopher Rich was to deduct & pay himself for the said [£72] & Interest thereof and in the meane time for the said . . . Rich's Security yr Oratr. was prvailed with to give . . . his bond of [£144] condiconed for ye paymt of the said [£72] and alsoe a Warrant of Attorny to Enter up Judgement of the sd bond"

 "Sometime in Aprill [1704] Your Oratr. being the Author of the Comedy called the Tender Husband he did bring to & deliver into the hands of the said Christopher Rich the said Comedy being the next Comedy yr. Oratr. was Author of and it being then in an ill season of the Year and Yr. Orator being therefore unwilling to have it then acted [Rich] promised to & agreed with yr. Oratr. that it should not be to yr. Orators losse or Detriment but that yr. Oratr. should have assigned to him the profitts of Two Nights made by Acting of the said Play the next following Winter in Lieu of his Two dayes Profitts according to the Usage & Custome in such Case And [Rich] did cause the said Comedy or Play to be Acted on the said Theatre in or about the Month of April [1704] aforesd And Severall dayes in the Autumne or Winter following which proved very successefull and [Rich] made & received great pfitt thereby and by the Agreement aforesd and according to usage & Custome in the like Cases your Oratr. was to have the whole pfitts of the first third day it was acted in Autumne or Winter aforesd without any deduccon of Charges of Acting and alsoe of the second third day or sixth day it was acted on as aforesd deducting only the charges of Acting Which pfitts of the said two dayes came to the hands of [Rich] and was more then sufficient to pay & satisfye the said [£72] & interest Whereupon yr Oratr expected as he had reason that [Rich] would have delivered up to yr. Orator the said bond and acknowledged satisfaccon on the Record of the Judgmt. which [Rich] had caused to be Entred upon Record against yr. Oratr. and would have pay'd yr. Oratr. what was over & above the said [£72] . . . But [Rich] minding to oppresse yr. Oratr. and extort great sumes of Mony from him refuses to allowe yr. Oratr. the pfitts of the said two dayes Acting in Autumne or Winter following according to his Agreemt or any dayes pfitts or any other pfitt whatsoever in Consideracon of the said Comedy or Play but threatens to Sue yr. Oratr. on the sd Judgment"

Asks injunction to stay proceedings at law, and that Rich may come to an account.

ANSWER OF CHRISTOPHER RICH

1707, 19 Nov.

Says "the Complaynant in or about [October 1701] brought a Comedy or play to this Defendt. which he the Complaynant alleadged he had written and stiled the ffunerall for which he the Complaynant came to an Agreement with this Defendt. in writing on or about the Ninth day of October Anno Dni 1701 and thereby for the Consideracons therein menconed sold the same to this Deft to be acted by the Actors under this Defts Government assoone as they could conveniently, which Comedy was soone after acted in pursueance of the said Agreemt and the said Complaynant was paid and satisfyed in full according to the Conditions and the tenor and true Intent of the said Agreemt. and to the Content and Satisfaccon of him the Complt as he acknowledged and Declared and this Deft is informed and beleiveth that he the Complt gave a Receipt to Mr Zachary Baggs the then and now Treasurer of the said Company for his the Complaynts. profitts arising by acting of the said Comedy by vertue of the Agreement aforesaid

And this Defendt. further sayth that the Complaynt. in or about [January 1702/3] informeing this Defendt. that he had neare finished another Comedy which he intended to call the Election of Goatham He proposed to sell the same to this Deft and accordingly in or by a certaine writing or Agreement bearing date on or about the [7 January 1702/3] Signed by the Complaynant in Consideracon of one shilling to him the Complt then paid by this Deft and for the Consideracon therein and herein after menconed he the said Complaynant did sell or is therein or thereby menconed to sell unto this Defendt. his heires and assignes A Certaine Comedy which he the Complaynt. was then writing called the Election of Goatham and which he was to deliver to this

Defendt. on or about the [20 February] then next in order to be acted by the Company of Actors under this Defendts. Governmt. assoone as they could conveniently

In Consideracon whereof the said Complaynt. was to have all the Receipts of the third day on which the said play should be acted Hee the Complt paying out of the same all the Charges of the house both Constant and Incident But if the Receipts of the ffourth day should double the Charges thereof then the Charges of the third should be returned to him and he thereby obliged himselfe to make good the Charges of the second day out of the profitts of the third day in case the Charges of the Second day should not arise to Soe much

Item if the Receipts on the ffourth day of acting the said play should amount to fforty pounds or upwards the said Company was to act it the ffifth day And if the ffifth dayes Receipt should be fforty pounds Then they were to act it the Sixth day for the Benefitt of the Complaynt. Hee paying out of the same the Charges of that day

But if at any time there should appeare Reason to doubt whether the play would bring Charges or not Then the Company should not be obliged to act it the next day unlesse he the Complaynt. would oblige himselfe to make good the full charges

And lastly the Complaynant was not to print the said play untill a Month should be expired from the ffirst day it should be acted and three of the printed Bookes in Marble paper Covers and Gilt Edges were to be delivered into the Office for the use of the Patentees assoone as the same should bee printed"

Rich is ready to produce this agreement in court.

"And this Deft sayth that there being a ffreindship contracted between him the Complt and this Deft and the Complt expressing greate kindnesse to this Deft and telling him of his the Complts want of Money and of his being likely to be arrested for moneys oweing by him prevayled with this Deft to advance lend and pay to him" £72 & Steele by bond 7 Jan 1702/3 became bound to Rich in £144 conditioned for payment of £72 with interest on 8 March 1702/3 & also executed warrant of attorney as above & Steele, "as an Additionall Security for the better payment of the said Debt did by a writing [7 January 1702/3] assigne and sett over or is therein menconed to assigne and sett over unto this Deft all the Money and profitts which was or were to come to him the Complt for his Play intended to be called the Eleccon of Goatham by the Agreemt. therein before written Upon this Condition That if the said Debt should not be paid unto this Deft before the acting of the said play That then this Deft . . . might retaine and apply

Such profitts for or towards paymt of the said Debt of [£72 with damages] But if such profitts should amount to more moneys then should be due to this Deft or his assignes att the time of acting such play then the Overplus of the moneys and profitts arising due to the Complaynant on his play by the agreemt. aforesaid was to goe to the use of the Complt . . . as by an Agreement" under Steele's hand of that date appears.

"And this Deft sayth that the Complt did not pay or cause to be paid unto this Deft the said Debt of" £72 on 8 Mar. following, and has never paid any part of it and "did not deliver to this Deft the said Comedy sold as aforesaid to this Deft . . . on" 20 February following nor has he "ever since that time delivered to this Deft any Comedy called the Election of Goatham altho this Deft very often requested him . . . for the same

But this Deft Confesseth that the Complt about the latter End of March Anno Dno 1705 brought a Comedy to this Deft which he stiled or called the Tender Husband or the Accomplished ffooles & desired and urged this Deft and his cheife Actors that the same might be acted by them with all Speed which he the Complt said was in leiw and in stead of the said play which he intended to have called the Election of Goatham and the same was the next and onely play or Comedy which the Complt has brought sold and delivered to this Deft since the" loan aforesaid.

"Beleiveth that his . . . Company of Actors did according to his the Complts desire gett up the said Comedy called the Tender Husband with all the speed they could and acted the same the first time on" 23 April 1705; second time next day, and third time on Wednesday 25 April "for the Benefitt of the Complt the Author according to the same Conditions in the said ffirst and second Agreements mencaned and acted the same the fourth time" the next day Thurs. 26 April, on which day the receipts being but £26 11s, or £13 9s short of the agreed £40, Rich was not obliged to cause it to be acted on the sixth day or any more for the benefit of the Author, "save as hereinafter is mencaned"

"the said Mr Baggs the Treasurer computing each dayes charge of acting the said play called the Tender Husband to amount to [£38 15s 10d] and the Receipts of the third day being [£61 6s] out of which the said [£38 15s 10d] being deducted there then rested [£22 10s 2d] but the Receipts of the second day of acting the same play amounting to but [£26 14s] being deficient [£12 1s 10d] to make up the charges of that day which [£12 1s 10d] being deducted out of the said [£22 10s] the Residue of Neate and cleere profitts to come to the Complt pursueant to the Agreement aforesaid amounted to [£10 8s 2d] with which this Deft beleives the Complt was acquainted and that he was well contented and satisfyed with the account given to him the Complt of the Receipts and Charges of and for the sayd play called the Tender Husband for the ffower ffirst dayes of acting thereof And this Deft sayth that the profitt accrewing due to the Complaynant being soe small the Complaynant applyed himselfe to this Deft and alsoe to the principall Actors under this Defts Governmt. That he the Complt would waive his profitt by the said play being [£10 8s 2d] as aforesaid and permitt the same to goe to the use of the Company provided they would act the said play the then next Winter one day for his the sd Complts: Benefitt instead of the third day aforesaid he paying or allowing out of the Receipts on Such day in Winter the Constant and incident charge thereof and alsoe what money the Receipts on the said second day of acting the said play wanted to make up the full charge for that day being [£12 1s 10d] as aforesd which this Deft as well as most of the Cheife Actors Consented to or to such Effect And thereupon the said Treasurer made the full Receipts on the third day of acting the said play called the Tender Husband to be charged for the use of the Company without chargeing any part thereof paid to the Complaynant in regard the Complaynant refused to receive the profitts due to him for that day But chose to have a day in Winter in Leiw thereof as aforesaid And this Deft Sayth That in pursueance of such Request made by the Complt to this Deft and the Cheife actors as aforesaid a day was appoynted in the Winter following according as the Complaynant desired and Bills were sett up the day before it was to have been acted and it was ordered by this deft to be given out that Night and Bills putt up for the same to be acted the next day for the Authors Benefitt; But a little before it was to have been given out the Complt forbidd the same to be given out on the Stage or putt into the Bills for his Benefitt Saying that he did not thinke there would be such an Audience att it, as would please him or used words to some such or the like Effect But however the same play was acted on the then next day and the whole Receipts that day being Thursday" 25 Nov 1705 amounted to £64 3s 6d "which was about two pounds seaventeen shillings more then the Receipts came to on the said third day that the same play was acted as aforesaid which two pounds seaventeen shillings and Six pence this Deft and the said Principle Actors were willing should be paid to the said Complt as well as the sume of Ten pounds Eight shilling and two pence before menconed And this Deft sayth that as to the [£10 8s 2d] which was due to the Complt out of the Receipts of the said third day according to the agreement before menconed this Deft never received the same or any part thereof nor the said

[£2 17s 6d] But both the said sumes remaine in the said Treasurers hands for the use of the Complt . . . And this Deft gave order to the said Mr Baggs the Treasurer to pay the same to the Complayn-ant amounting together to [£13 5s 8d] and that Mr Baggs hath sev-erall times offered to pay the same to the Complt and is still ready to doe the same But that he the Complt hath neglected or refused to receive the same as the said Trear has informed this Deft And this Deft Denyeth that the said play called the Tender Husband was acted att any time in the yeare [1704] either in the Sumer or Winter as in the Complts Bill is suggested But the first time the same was acted was on [23 April 1705] And sayth that he . . . did never agree to stay for the said Debt untill the Complt should bring the said play called the Eleccon of Goatham or any other play to this Deft"

Is informed that The Tender Husband "hath been severall times acted in the last yeare by the Company of Actors in the playhouse in the Hay Markett without this Defts consent or direccon & in Opposition to this Defts Interest which this Deft had Reason to beleive was so done by the Incouragemt. or att least the Conni-veance of the Complt"

Nos. 110, 111. SKIPWITH *v.* BRETT

C8 481/66

[1708/9, 1 Feb.]

To the Right Honble William Lord Cowper Baron of Wing-
ham Lord High Chancellor of Great Britain

Humbly Complaining sheweth unto your Lordship your Orator
Sr Thomas Skipwith of Twickenham in ye county of Middlesex
Baron^t That your Orator being well Entituled to and Legally in-
terrested in Three ffifth Parts ye Whole into five parts being divided) or some part Share or proporcon of ye Benefitt and Advantage of Certaine Letters Patents for ye Theatre or playhouse granted
by his Late Majestie King Charles ye Second to Sr William Davenant deacesed under ye great Seale of England dated ye ffifteenth
day of January in ye fourteenth year of his Reigne and all Rooms
to ye said Playhouse belonging Scenes and Apparell and power to
Act playes and all other Priviledges and Appurtenances therewith
or Otherwise granted and also to and in some part or Proporcon of
ye Acting profits in ye playhouse or Theatre in Drury Lane in y^e
County of Middlesex which cost your Orator on ye first purchase
thereof two thousand and five hundred pounds or some other very
Considerable summe of money. Henry Brett of Sandiwell in y^e
County of Gloucester Esqr knowing such your Orators Interest
and Concern in ye said Letters Patents Theatre and Playhouse did
somtime in ye year of our Lord One thousand seven hundred and
Seven Earnesly press and sollicit your Orator to come to his ye said
Henry Brett's house at Sandiwell aforesaid in ye said County of
Gloucester and to make some stay there, ye said Henry Brett making att ye same time great Protestations of ye Friendship and Kindness he had for your Orator and professing a Gratefull Sence of y^e
Civility's Kindness and Unusual Friendship your Orator had for
a Long time past shewed to him And your Orator by ye Importunity of ye said Henry Brett was prevaled upon to promise to
make him ye said Henry Brett a Visitt att Sandiwell aforesaid And
your Orator did Accordingly in or about ye Month of August which
was in ye said Year One thousand seven hundred and Seven or
sometime in ye said Year go to ye said Henry Brett's house at
Sandiwell aforesaid where your Orator was Entertained with a
great deal of seeming Civility by him ye said Henry Brett. And
your Orator farther sheweth that While your Orator was att Sandiwell aforesaid ye said Henry Brett was frequently talking to and
discoursing with your Orator about your Orators Interest Share or
Concern in ye said Letters Patents or Theatre or Playhouse telling

your Orator of ye ill Management of ye same and that ye same was much Abused and your Orator much wronged and imposed upon and that if ye same was Carefully Look'd after and put upon a better foot then itt had been for some time Last past thatt itt might be of great Advantage to your Orator and your Orator might gain a Considerable profitt thereby and that he ye said Henry Brett wonder'd your Orator would suffer himslfe to be so much injured or so much Neglect ye same or ye said Henry Brett discoursed with your Orator to that or ye like Effect And your Orator further sheweth that ye said Henry Brett while your Orator was att Sandiwell aforesaid and was in all outward Appearance very much Caressed by ye said Henry Brett he ye said Henry Brett told your Orator that your Orator had shewed him ye said Henry Brett so many Kindnesses and been so generous a friend to him even when He ye said Henry Brett was under ye greatest Streights Necessity's and dificulty's as to his fortune in ye world and that he to shew his Gratitude to your Orators Great and many Friendshipps to him should be Glad of any Opportunity to returñ your Orators Kindnesses and that he beleived that if your Orator would intrust him ye said Henry Brett with ye Management of your Orators Interest in ye said Playhouse that he would restore itt to a flourishing Condition and make ye same turn very much to ye profitt and Benefitt of your Orator and his family which was att psent ye only thing he could think of to returne ye great Kindnesses received by him but y^t itt would be Necessary or proper that your Orator should by some deed or Writeing Assign or make over to him ye said Henry Brett all your Orators Interest Right and Title to ye P^rmisses and ye said Henry Brett often discoursed with and proposed to your Orator to that or ye Like Effect And your Orator further sheweth that your Orator giving Creditt to such fair Speeches and pretensions of ye said Henry Brett and Considering ye many Obligations ye said Henry Brett had to him and not being able to beleive that after ye many signal services done to ye said Henry Brett by your Orator he could be capable of deceiving or injuring your Orator. Your Orator was in ye Month of September or October in ye said year One thousand seven hundred and seven or some time in ye said Year One thousand seven hundred and seven prevailed upon to make and Execute some Deed or Writing whereby your Orator did without any Consideration whatsoever paid unto your Orator Assign over to ye said Henry Brett All your Orators Right Title and Interest in and to ye said Letters Patents and playhouse in which Deed or Writing thô your Orator told ye said Henry Brett that itt ought to be declared that itt was only a Trust for your Orator his Heires Executors and Administrators yet v^e said Henry

Brett prevailed upon your Orator not to insist upon any such Declaration of Trust and told your Orator that itt would not be in ye Power of him ye said Henry Brett so well or Effectually to serve your Orator if in ye said deed or Writing itt should Appear that ye same was only in Trust for your Orator but y^t your Orator might safely rely upon ye Fidelity and Integrity of him ye said Henry Brett and that itt should be Considered only as a Trust for your Orator thô ye same was not y^n Declared in Writing in ye said deed and that he ye said Henry Brett would afterwards make a Declaration in Writing that ye said Deed of Assignmt. or Writing Executed as aforesaid by your Orator was only in trust for your Orator his Heirs Executors and Administrators when your Orator should think fitt to require ye same or ye said Henry Brett said or promissed to your Orator to that or ye Like Effect And your Orator further sheweth that your Orator was prevailed on to Execute ye said Deed of Assignm^t or Writing att ye house of ye said Henry Brett att Sandiwell aforesaid and ye said Deed or Writing was drawn by a Freind of ye said Henry Brett and ye same was never read over to your Orator before ye same was Executed and your Orator had no Councell or any Person to Advise wth about ye same nor had your Orator any Draught of ye same to peruse and Consider upon before ye same was Engrossed but ye same was prepared and brought ready Ingrossed to your Orator to Execute and your Orator did Unadvisedly execute ye same without taking any Copy or Counterpart of ye same ye said Henry Brett who took upon himself to direct ye preparing ye said Deeds designedly and on purpose Neglecting to Order any Copy or Counterpart of ye same for your Orator and told your Orator y^t itt was not Necessary or proper for your Orator to have any Copy or Counterpart thereof, because ye said Deed or Writing was designed onely to Colour his Intentions of serving your Orator and to make some persons whom itt was Necessary to Make Use of in Carrying on such his Intentions beleive that your Orator had no Interest in ye said Letters Patents and Playhouse, or ye said Henry Brett told your Orator to that or ye Like Effect And your Orator hoped and Expected that ye said Henry Brett would either have made some Declaration in Writing of ye said Trust or have cancelled ye said Deed of Assignm^t or Writing. But Now so itt is May itt please your Lordship that ye said Henry Brett Combining and Confederating with divers persons to your Orator as yet Unknown (whose Names when discovered your Orator pray's may be made party's hereunto with Apt words to Charge them as Defendants) how to defeat and Defraud your Orator of ye benefitt and Advantage of ye said Letters Patents and Playhouse and Shares in ye Profits of Acting doth somtimes pretend and insist that ye said Deed of Assignm^t or Writing made as aforesaid by your Orator to ye said Henry Brett was an Absolute Gift of yor Orator to him ye said Henry Brett and that he ye said Henry Brett never made any promise or said any thing of Declaring that ye said Deed of Assignm^t or Writing was only in Trust for your Orator or that he said any thing of reassigning ye same to your Orator when He your Orator should desire ye same or when he ye said Henry Brett should by his managem^t have put ye said playhouse into a better and more flourishing Condition. And att other times ye said Henry Brett pretends that he bought your Orators Interest in ye said Letters Patents and Playhouse for a valuable Consideration and paid your Orator a Considerable sum*m* of Money for ye same and pretend's that there is in ye said Deed of Assignm^t or Writing some sum*m* of Money Expressed as ye said Consideration thereof whereas your Orator Expressly Chargeth that no Money whatsoever was ever paid to your Orator by ye said Henry Brett or any other person for his Use as ye Consideration of ye said deed of Assignm^t or Writing nor was ye same made upon any other Consideration or with any other Intention or on any other Motive then as aforesaid and if any sum*m* of money be menconed in ye said Deed of Assignm^t or Writing to have been paid unto your Orator by ye said Henry Brett as ye Consideration thereof ye same was fraudulently and unfairly put into ye said Deed or Writing And att other times ye said Henry Brett pretendeth that no particular time having been agreed upon for ye reassignm^t of ye said *p*remisses to your Orator itt remaines in ye Discretion and Power of him ye said Henry Brett to reassign ye same when he shall think itt proper so to Do and sometimes he pretendeth that he doth purpose and design to keep ye same for ye Benefitt of your Orators family but y^t your Orator shal not have any Advantage thereby or power over ye same dureing yor Orators Life) and att other times he pretendeth that some of ye Actors in ye said Playhouse having been very Instrumentall in Assisting him in Bringing ye said Playhouse into a fflourishing and thriving Condition y^t he will Dispose of some Interest or Proporcon in ye Benefitt of ye said Letters Patents to some or one of ye Actors in ye said Playhouse And Your Orator further Sheweth that thô Your Orator hath From time to time by himself or some other person Importuned or desired ye said Henry Brett to make some Declaration in Writing whereby itt may Appear that he is onely a Trustee for your Orator and ye said Henry Brett hath sometimes promised so to do Yet now he refuseth and declineth to Execute any such Declaration and your Orator hath sent to him a Writing to such Purpose but he refused to Execute ye same And ye said Henry Brett

hath wrote severall Letters to your Orator since yᵉ Executing yᵉ
said Deed of Assignmᵗ or Writing which Manifest by his yᵉ said
Henry Brett's own Confession that itt was not your Orators Intention to alienate absolutely yᵉ said pʳmisses but only to Assign
yᵉ same to yᵉ said Henry Brett upon yᵉ Trust and for yᵉ Reason or
upon yᵉ Motives aforesaid some of which Letters your Orator hath
Left with his Clerk in Court to yᵉ intent that yᵉ said Henry Brett
may view and Inspect yᵉ same and which yoʳ Orator pray's yᵉ said
Henry Brett may veiw and Inspect and may in his Answer to this
your Orators Bill sett forth Whether yᵉ same are not all of his yᵉ
said Henry Bretts owne hand-Writing and Whether yᵉ same were
not wrote and sent by him yᵉ said Henry Brett to yoʳ Orator yet
he yᵉ said Henry Brett sometimes Deny's that ever he wrote such
Letters to your Orator and that yᵉ same do not relate to yᵉ said
Deed of Assignmᵗ or Writeing made as aforesaid by your Orator or
any Way Concern yᵉ same And your Orator further sheweth yᵗ yᵉ
said Henry Brett hath since yᵉ said Deed of Assignmᵗ or Writing
received very Considerable summs of Money or some Money raised
by yᵉ playhouse in Drury Lane in yᵉ County of Middˣ which was
sett up under Colour or by Authority of yᵉ said Letters Patents
and acting play's therein or some other Way by Vertue or under
Colour of yᵉ said Deed of Assignmᵗ or Writing and Converted yᵉ
same to his Own Use or hath taken upon him to Dispose of yᵉ same
or some part of yᵉ same and refuseth to Account unto yoʳ Orator
for yᵉ same, and yett yᵉ said Henry Brett suffereth your Orator to
be sued troubled or Molested for yᵉ Rent or some part of yᵉ Rent
or other Charges of yᵉ sᵈ Playhouse and yᵉ said Henry Brett
knoweth hath heard or doth beleive that your Orator hath been
sued or troubled or threatned to be sued or troubled for such Rent
or Charges or for some money upon Accᵗ of yᵉ said Playhouse and
that a Considerable summ of Money is now Demanded or Claimed
from your Orator upon Accᵗ of Rent or Arrears of Rent or in some
other Manner for yᵉ said Playhouse which yᵉ said Henry Brett refuseth to Discharge or Pay All which Actings and pʳtensions of yᵉ
said Henry Brett and his Confederates are Contrary to Equity and
good Conscience and tend to yᵉ Manifest Wrong and Injury of
your Orator IN TENDER Consideration whereof and forasmuch
as your Orator is remediless in yᵉ Premisses by yᵉ Strict Rules of yᵉ
Common Law of this Kingdom and is proper to be releived in a
Court of Equity before your Lordship where your Orator may com-
pell a Discovery of yᵉ Trust of yᵉ Pʳmisses upon yᵉ Oath of yᵉ said
Henry Brett and his Confederates and where Matters of Fraud
and Trust are properly Cognisable and yᵉ Execucons of Trust are
proper to be enforced which is yᵉ more necessary because your Ora-

tors Witnesses who could prove a great part of your Orators Case
to be as herein before is sett forth are either Dead or in parts remote and beyond yᵉ seas or in places unknown to your Orator so
that your Orator cannot have yᵉ benefitt of there Testimony To the
End therefore that yᵉ said Henry Brett and his Confederates (when
Discovered) may full true perfect and Direct Answer make to all
and singular yᵉ Matters Charges Allegacons and things herein before sett forth as he or they do know have heard and do beleive as
fully as if yᵉ same were herein again particularly and Distinctly
repeated and he and they particularly interrogated thereunto and
particularly that yᵉ said Henry Brett may sett forth Whether your
Orator did not Execute to him such deed or Writing of Assignmᵗ
and yᵉ Date and Contents of such Deed or Writing and between
whom yᵉ same was made and when and where yᵉ same was Executed and upon what Motives or for what reason or upon what
Considerations your Orator Executed such Deed of Writing by
whom by name yᵉ same was prepared and who gave Orders or
Directions for preparing such Deed or Writing and who by Name
Engrossed yᵉ same and may produce and Leave such Deed with
his Clerk in Court to be Copied by your Orator and may Discover
whether itt was not intended to be in Trust only for your Orator
and Whether he hath not refused and doth still refuse to make or
give any Declaration in Writing to your Orator that yᵉ same was
only Designed to be in Trust for your Orator his heirs Executors
and Administrators and for what Reason he did and doth so refuse
and may either Execute to your Orator a Declaration in Writing
of such Trust or may Shew Cause (if he can) why yᵉ sᵈ deed of Assignmᵗ or Writing should not be delivered up to your Orator to be
Cancelled and that yᵉ said Henry Brett may sett forth a particular
Accᵗ of all ye sumes of money or all the money he or any other by
his Order or by his permission or with his privity Knowledge or
Consent hath received out of yᵉ money arising by yᵉ said playhouse or Under Colour of yᵉ said Letters Patents and how yᵉ same
hath been Disposed of or how yᵉ Money arising by yᵉ sᵈ Playhouse
or by acting plays under Colour or by Authority of yᵉ said Letters
Patents hath been Disposed of since he Concerned himself in the
Managemt of yᵉ said playhouse and since yᵉ said Deed of Assignmᵗ or Writing And that yᵉ said Henry Brett may Accᵗ with
your Orator for all yᵉ Money which hath been raised by Acting
plays in yᵉ said playhouse or Otherwise under Colour Or by Authority of yᵉ said Letters Patents According to yᵉ share and proporcon your Orator Ought to have therein or which he yᵉ said
Henry Brett claimes therein or pretends Title unto by vertue or
under Colour of yᵉ said deed of Assignmᵗ or writing And that your

Orator may have such further and other Releife in yᵉ premisses as
yᵉ Nature of his Case shall require and shall be Agreeable to Justice
and Equity May itt please your Lordship to grant unto your Orator her Majesties Most gracious Writt or Writts of Subpœna to be
Directed to him yᵉ said Henry Brett (and yᵉ other Confederates
when discouered) Thereby Commanding him them and Every of
them att a Certaine Day and under a Certaine pain therein to be
Limitted personaly to be and Appeare before yoʳ Lordship in this
Honᵇˡᵉ Court then and there to Answer all and Singular yᵉ pʳmisses
upon his and their Respective Corporall Oath and Oath's and further
to stand to and abide such Order Decree and Direction therein as
to your Lordship shall seem Meet And Your Orator shall Ever
pray &c.

Sam: Mead.

[1708/9, 17 Feb.]

The Answer of Henry Brett Esqʳ Defendᵗ to the Bill of
Complaint of Sʳ Thomas Scipwith Barronett Complainant

This Defendᵗ saveing to himselfe all advantage and benefitt of Ex-
cepcon to the many Imperfections and Insufficiencies of the said
bill of Complaint for Answer thereto or to soe much thereof as he
is advised is materiall for him to Answer unto saith that he hath
heard and beleives that the Complainᵗ might be Intitled to him
and his heires to some Interest in Certein Letters Pattents Granted
by his late Majesty King Charles the Second under the Great Seal
of England in or about the fourteenth Year of his said Majesties
Raigne unto Sʳ William D'avenant and his heires for the sole priviledge and Authority of acting all sorts of Stage Plays Opera's Interludes and other such like Entertainements within the Citty of
Westminster and Liberties thereof And alsoe in certaine other Letters Patents bearing date the [   ] day of [   ] in the
[   ] yeare of his said Maᵗⁱᵉˢ Reigne, Granted by his said late
Maᵗⁱᵉ to [   ] Killegrew Esqʳ of the like nature, and that the
Complainant vnder the said Letters Patents might bee Intituled
to seu'all parts & shares of the profitts benefitts & advantages ariseing by & vnder the said severall Letters Patents in or out of the
Playhouse or Theatre in Drury Lane and otherwise. But whether
hee were Intituled to three fifth parts thereof as in the bill is suggested, or to what part or proporcon thereof hee was intituled to
this Defendᵗ knows not But whether such interest Cost him for the
pchase thereof the summe of Two Thousand ffive hundred pounds
or what other summe it might Cost him or what profitts or advantages hee hath made thereout or thereby this Defendᵗ knows
not but is a stranger thereto But this Defendᵗ hath Great reason

to beleive from the frequent declaracons and Complaints of the
Compl^t himselfe made to this Defend^t that for more then twelve
Yeares last past he hath made nothing thereof And not only soe
But that by the Artifice of the Managers He was not only perswaded to part with considerable sumes of money under pretence
of carrying the business of the said Play house on But was apprehensive that hee was drawn in and subjected to Great Debts and
demands on that account All which the Comp^{lt} had frequently
owned and declared to this Defend^t in theire Intimacy's And that
it was of noe vallue but a Plague to him and had involved him in
severall Expensive Law Suits or to that effect And the Comp^{lt}
haveing for long time been under such a Malancholy apprehension
& prospect of the said affairs and frequently Expressed his desire
to be got rid of the same had often importuned this Defend^t to
accept the same as a present or Gift from him And this Defend^t
had often refused it being apprehensive it might not be worth his
while to Engage himselfe in such a perplext and improffitable affair
However the Complain^t takeing occasion sometime in the Month
of October in the Year One thousand seaven hundred and Seaven
to make a visit to this Defend^t att his house at Sandiwell in the
County of Glouceter (whether he [came] unexpectedly and without
any Invitacon from this Defend^t) he there took occasion to Renew
his former Importunities and desire that this Defend^t would accept from him a Grant or Guift of his Estate and Interest in the
premisses as a Marke of his friendshipp for him which this De-
fend^t being att length prevailed on to accept thereupon att the
Desire and Solicitation of the Comp^{lt} himselfe Humphry Brent
Esquire being att that time att this Defend^{ts} house att Sandiwell
(there not being any Attorney or Agent in the neighbourehood
proper for that purpose did prepare an Instrument or Deed of
Assignm^t bearing date the 6th day of October in the yeare One
thousand seaven hundred & Seaven whereby the Compl^t in Consideracon of the Love and ffriendshipp between the Comp^{lt} & this
Defend^t and in consideracon of Tenn Shillings therein menconed
to be paid by this Defend^t to the Comp^{lt} Did Grant and Assigne
to this Defend^t & his heires All his Estate right title and Interest
in and to the said Letters Pattents and shares and proporcons of
all benefitt and advantage thereby ariseing by Stage Plays Opera's
Interludes and such like Entertainements in as full and ample
manner as the said Complainant Could or might Enioy the same,
In and by which Indenture the Complainant Covenanted that hee
had not done any Act or thing whereby the p^rmisses were in any
Sort Incumbred, and that hee would make and execute all further
and other acts Deeds matters and things whatsoever for the further

and more effectuall settling and assuring the premisses to and vpon
this Defendant and his heires, And that hee would deliver to this
Defendant on or before the ffive and twentieth day of November
then next ensueing the said Letters Patents, and all other Deeds
and Writings relateing to the premisses which hee then had in his
Custody or power or could come at by suit in law or otherwise, as
by the said Indenture of Grant or Assignment whereto for cer-
tainety this Defendant referrs himselfe may appeare And this Defendant says that the Complainant Executed the said Deed on or
about the time of the date thereof, and that the Consideracon for
the same was as is Exprest in the said Indenture and noe other,
and says that the Complainant not only gave direccons for the pre-
pareing and drawing the said Deed to the effect and Import as
drawne and Ingrossed but the same was read by the Complainant,
or read to him, and by him approved off, before the Ingrossment
thereof, And therefore this Defendant apprehends it to bee a
strange aswell as very weake Excuse that the Complainant being
a Gentleman of a knowne figure & Capacity should vse such an
Excuse for his Executeing the said Deed as that hee was drawne in
Unadvisedly soe to doe And this Defendant doth absolutely deny
that at the time of Executeing the said Deed or at any time before
the Execucon thereof Itt was agreed or declared by this Defend^t
that the said Grant or Deed was to be in Trust for the Comp^{lt} or
that the Comp^{lt} insisted to have such Trust declared or Incerted
in the said Deed or that it was pretended that if it were soe this
Defend^t could not soe effectually serve the Comp^{lt} in the management of the said affaire Or that this Defend^t promised he woud
after the Execucon of the said Deed make a declaracon of the said
Trust in writing for the Comp^{lt} & his heires or to any such effect
as in the Comp^{lts} bill is Unworthily and untruly Suggested But
this Defend^t beleives this Deft did not Execute any Counterpart
thereof to the Comp^{lt} nor had the Comp^{lt} att that time any Coppy
thereof nor did he then insist thereon And if he had at that time
desired such Counterpart or Coppy this Defend^t would have lett
him have had the same And this Defend^t denyes that he used such
Insinuacons or Expressions to the Comp^{lt} to perswade him to
Execute the said Deed as that the Comp^{lt} might Trust him with
the Management of his Interest in the Play house & that if hee soe
did he would restore it in a flourishing Condicon to him again as
in the bill is pretended Nor had this Defend^t any reason to take
upon himselfe so hazardous and Troublesome an Office as with his
own Care trouble and losse of time and Expence to Improve for
the Complain^t an Estate which hee had in Effect plainly abandoned
as haveing been of no advantage to him and worth nothing att all

for many Yeares together as the Compl^t himselfe had often own'd
and declared And notwithstanding the great pretences of the
Compl^{ts} ffriendshipp and kindnesse for this Defend^t as the Ground
or Motive of the said Grant or Guift to this Defend^t He this De-
fend^t hath Great reason to apprehend the true reason was to remove an Inconveniencie from himselfe and to bestow it on this
Defend^t the Compl^t being Jealous of Great charges debts and demands likely to pursue him Unlesse he parted therewith And for
as much as it appears by the said Deed and alsoe of the Compl^t
own Shewing that the pretended Trust was not declared nor is declared nor manifested by any writing Signed by this Defend^t or
any person Authorized by him This Defend^t is advised and doth
humbly insist upon it that by the Stat made in the Twenty Ninth
Yeare of his said late Maj^{ty} King Charles the Second for prevencon
of ffrauds and perjuryes The said pretended Trust for the Com-
plain^t & his heires if any such then were which yett this Defend^t
doth deny) ought not to be Established but is absolutely void And
this Defend^t humbly hopes he shall have the benefitt of the said
Statute and by this his Answer he relyes upon the same and this
Defend^t further says that the Compl^t haveing in kindnesse freely
and absolutely bestowed and Granted the premisses to this De-
fend^t He ever retained a Gratefull Intention and designe in case
the premisses should by his Dilligence or Interest be brought into
an Improved Condicon to bestow the same on the Compl^{ts} family
as a return and meer Act of Gratitude from this Defend^t but this
Defend^t absolutely denyes he was or is under any Trust Obligacon
or promise whatsoever to restore it to the Compl^t But this Defend^t
was left and is a ffree Agent in the said Matter when ever he shall
think itt proper or seasonable to bestow the same And this De-
fend^t say's he has seen 3 letters which the Compl^t suggests he had
left with his Clerk in Court for this Defend^{ts} inspection and admitts
the same are of this Defend^{ts} own hand writeing But this Defend^{ts} insists and is advised that the same do in no sort Imply or raise any
Trust for the Defend^t And this Defend^t say's that since the Execucon of the said deed or grant to him he hath Concerned himselfe in
the management of the affaires relateing to the said Play house
and premisses and hath bestowed much time and been att considerable charge and very Great expence in bringing the same into
a better Posture and unto a considerable Improvem^t and greater
advantage then the same have hitherto been unless this Defend^t
be obstructed in his good design by the Compl^t and this Unneces-
sary and (as this Defend^t apprehends) vexacous Suit and prosecu-
cons And this Defend^t admitts that since the Execucon of the said
Deed he hath reced small summes of money out of the said Play

house or on account thereof which falls very Short of reinbursing the charges hee has been at of which as well as of his disburstm^{ts} relating to the premisses this Defend^t submitts to come to an account with the Comp^{lt} and to be Examined on Interrogatories touching the same soe soon as the Complainant shall make it out to this hon^{ble} Court that he hath any title to such discov'y or Account Till which done this Defend^t is advised and doth humbly insist upon it that hee need not give any further Answer to the matter of the said account And this Defend^t denyes all Combinacon and confederacy laid to his charge without that that any other matter or thing matteriall or effectuall in the Law for this Deft to make Answere unto and not by him herein and hereby Sufficiently Answer'd unto confess'd or avoided traversed or denyed is true to any knowledge or beleife of him this Def^t All which matters and things he this Def^t shall be ready to averr maintaine and prove as this Honble Court shall award and therefore prays to be hence dismissed with his reasonable Costs and charges in this behalfe most wrongfully sustein'd./

A Newnam

C10 545/39

[1709, 29 July]

The further Answere of Henry Brett Esqr Def^t to the Bill of Comp^{lt} of Sr Thomas Skipwith Bar^t Comp^{lt}

This Def^t saveing to himself all benefitt and advantage of Exception to the many imperfections and Insufficiencies of the said Bill of Comp^{lt} for Answere to soe much thereof as is not allready by this Def^t answered unto sayth that the Letters mentioned in the Comp^{lts} said Bill to have been left with the Comp^{lts} Clerk in Court were sent by this Def^t to the said Comp^{lt} and doe relate to the Playhouse concerne wch was convey'd to the Def^t by the Comp^{lt} in and by the said Deed of Assignm^t mentioned in the Comp^{lts} Bill, but how or in what manner this Def^t referreth himself to the purport of the said Letters And this Def^t denyeth that he doth suffer the Comp^{lt} to be sued troubled or molested for the rent or any part of the Rent or other charges of the Playhouse in the Bill mentioned that did accrew due happen or arrise since the Execution of the said writing of Assignm^t for that this Def^t did (as far as he had power by virtue of the before mentioned deed of Assignm^t direct Mr Zachary Baggs the then Casheer of the Playhouse to pay all rents and charges upon the House or business as shou'd become due from the Date of the said Deed of Assignm^t and believes the said Casheer did pay the same accordingly, to whom this Def^t referreth himself, the said Casheer haveing given him noe Acc^t and

if he the Comp^{lt} is sued or troubled for any such rent or Charges
this Def^t knoweth nothing thereof But saith that he hath heard
and doth believe that the Comp^{lt} hath been threatned to be sued
or troubled for rent for the said Playhouse or for some money or
charge upon acc^t of the said Playhouse due before the Execution
of the said Assignm^t & that a considerable summe of money (but
how much knoweth not) is now demanded or claimed from the
p^{lt} upon acc^t of rent or arreares of rent or in some other manner
for the said Playhouse, but how and in what manner the same is
claimed or to how much the same amounts this Def^t doth not know
nor can he sett forth And saith that he doth not know nor hath he
heard nor doth he believe that any summe of money whatsoever is
or hath been demanded or claimed from the Comp^{lt} upon the
Acc^t of rent or arrears of rent or in any other manner for the said
Playhouse or any Accon or Accons have been commenced or
brought against the said Comp^{lt} for any the matters aforesaid
which did accrew due or happen since the Execution of the said
Assignment nor did this Def^t at any time refuse to pay or discharge
the same And saith that whatever rent or other charge was due
from the s^d Comp^{lt} before the date of the said Assignm^t this Def^t
insists with Submission to this Honble Court he is not liable to pay
the same nor ought he to be charg'd therewith and therefore did
and doth refuse to pay the same without that . . . [etc.]

                                        A Newnam.

THE WILL OF CHRISTOPHER BEESTON, ALIAS HUTCHINSON

Principal Probate Registry, Somerset House, P.C.C. Lee 172

T[estamentum]
   Xρoferi
Hutchinson

In the name of God Amen the fowerth day of October 1638, and in
the fowerteenth yeare of the raigne of our Soveraigne Lord Charles
by the grace of god King of England Scotland ffrance and Ireland
defender of the faith &c. I Christopher Hutchinson of the parishe
of Saint Gyles in the fieldes in the County of Middlesex gentleman,
being sick and weake in body but of sound and perfecte memory
praise be therefore given unto Allmighty god, doe make and declare this my last will and testament in manner and forme followinge that is to say ffirst and principally and aboue all earthly things
I comend my soule into the handes of Allmighty god my Creator
and to his sonne Jesus Christ my only Saviour and Redeemer by
the Merrittes of whose most bitter death and bloody passion I doe
assuredly trust to be saued and haue remission for all my synns
and my body to the earth from whence it came to be buried in
Christian buriall in the parishe Church of St. Gyles in the fieldes
aforesaid And as touchinge such temporall goodes wherewith the
lord hath endowed me I dispose thereof [as] followeth Imprimis I
forthwith give will and bequeath unto my loving sonne William
Hutchinson his heires and assignes for ever All and singuler my
freehold land and the messuages or tenementes thereupon erected
and builte or upon any parte or parcell thereof scituate lyinge and
beinge in the parish of St. Leonard in Shoreditch in the County of
Middlesex And all and singuler the deedes writinges and Evidences
concerninge the same, and all leases thereof made to any person or
persons whatsoever, more I give and bequeath unto him all my
parte or parcell of ground nowe inclosed with a brick wall lyinge
and beinge in Lyncolns Inn fieldes in the parishe of St. Gyles in the
fieldes aforesaid the deedes whereof were by me delivered vnto
Master Thomas Vaughan to keepe in trust for me Item I give and
bequeath vnto my eldest daughter Anne Bird wife of Theophilus
Bird gentleman and to her sonne my godsonne Christopher Bird,
the some of three hundred poundes of lawfull money of England
if my twoe houses lately erected and built in Covent garden in the
parishe of St. Martin in the feildes in the said county of Middlesex
shalbe assured to amounte unto the some of six hundred poundes
sterling, and by reason I doe owe many great debtes and am en-
gaged for greate somes of mony which noe one but my wife under-

standes where or howe to receaue pay or take in I therefore make
her my beloued wife Elizabeth Hutchinson my full and sole executrix of this my presente last will and testament And I doe hereby
give unto my said executrix after my debtes paid legacies performed and funerall charges defraied the residue of all and singuler
my goodes and Chattelles whatsoever And Ouerseers hereof I doe
make nominate and appointe my Noble freind Captaine Lewis
Kirk and my Worthy respected freind Thomas Sheppard esquier
entreatinge them in the loue of a true and dyinge freind that to
theire utmost as occasion shall serve they wilbe ayding and assisting to my executrix for the performance of this my last will and
testament according to my true intent and honest meaninge here
specified and I doe giue unto either of them a gold ring to weare in
remembrance of me. And whereas I stand possessed of fower of
the six shares in the Company for the King and Queenes service at
the Cockpitt in Drury lane, I declare that twoe of my said fower
shares be deliuered vpp for the advancement of the said Company
and the other twoe to Remaine vnto my said executrix as fully and
amply as if I lived amongst them. And I will that my said executrix shall for the said twoe shares provide and finde for the said
Company a sufficient and good stock of apparell fittinge for theire
vse shee allowinge and payinge to my said sonne William Hutchinson for his care and industry in the said Company twentie poundes
of lawfull mony of England per annum, And I doe hereby charge
him by the loue of a Child to his ffather that he for my sake doe all
good concerninge this or any other busines to my said wife and her
twoe daughters. And I doe hereby will and order that the legacies
by me hereby given willed and bequeathed be paid by my said
executrix within eighteene monethes nexte after my decease. In
witnes whereof I the said Christopher Hutchinson to this my present last will and testament haue sett my hand and seale dated the
daie and yeares first aboue written Christopher Chutchinson [*sic*].
Read signed sealed and as the last will and testament of the said
Christopher Hutchinson published and delivered in the presence
of Bartho: Bramfield scrivener, The marke of Marie Haines, The
marke of Marie Wilkes, Bar: Church.

7° die Octobris 1638/

Memorandum that whereas the within named Christopher
Hutchinson haue willed ordered and devised by my last will and
testament within written that my executrix within named should
pay unto my within named sonne William Hutchinson the yearely
some of Twentie poundes of lawfull mony of England for his Care
and industry to be taken in and about the Company within men-

*ti*oned, Nowe my will and mynde is and I doe hereby order and devise that my said Executrix in liewe of the said twentie poundes p*er* ann*um* shall allowe unto him my said sonne William Hutchinson one halfe share of the twoe shares in the said Company within men*ti*oned for his care in the busines shee findinge and providinge a stock of app*a*rell for the said company as is within declared Witnes my hand the day and yeare abovesaid Christopher Hutchinson Subscribed in the presence of Bar*tholomew* Church. The marke of Marie Haines, The marke of Mary Wilkes, Bartholomew Bramfield scri*vener*.

ORDER FOR A GRANT TO KILLIGREW TO ERECT A COMPANY

9 July, 1660

Mr Killegrew to Erect a Playhouse with Players for his Maty.

To our Trusty and Wellbeloued Our atturney or sollicitor grall Our Will and Pleasure is that you prepare a Bill for our R^ll. Signature to passe our Gt. Seale of Engl^d conteyning a Grant Vnto our Trusty and Wellbeloued Tho: Killegrew Esq. . . . to erect one Company of players wch shall be our owne Company . . . and likewise to settle and Establish such payemts to be paid by those that shall resort to see the said representacons performed as either haue been accustomerly giuen and taken in the like Kind or as now shall be thought reasonable by him in regard of the great expences of scenes musick and new decoracons as haue not been formerly used . . . and in case they [*i. e.* the Company of Players] shall faile the payemt of those Covenants Wee doe hereby giue him full power to silence them from Playing and to eiect all mutinous persons from the said Comp^y and in regard of the Extraordinary Licence that hath bin lately used in things of this nature our pleasure is that there sall be noe more places of representacons or Companyes of actors or representacons of Scenes in the Cities of London or Westm^r . . . then the 2 Companyes now to be erected . . . and Wee doe by these presents declare all other Company or Companyes to be sylenced and surprest during our pleasure. . . .

Given, &c. at Whitehall the 9th day of July 1660

[State Papers, Domestic, Entry Book v, 158.]

INDENTURE BETWEEN SIR WM. DAVENANT AND SIR WM. RUSSELL
OF STRENSHAM IN WORCESTER, BART., 7 MARCH, 1660/1

Whereas the said Sir Wm. Davenant by virtue of authority to him
derived from Charles I by His Majesty's letters patent under the
greate Seale of England . . . March 26, 14 Charles I, & also by
virtue of a late authority from . . . Charles II hath constituted
and made Thomas Betterton, Thomas Sheppey, Robert Noke,
James Noke, Thomas Lovell, John Mosely, Cave Underhill Robert
Turner and Thomas Littleston and their associates to be a company publiquely to act comedyes, tragedyes and playes in London
or Westminster or the suburbs thereof and Whereas the said
Thomas Betterton . . . and the rest of the said company by cer-
tayne articles of agreement indentured tripartite dated the fifth
day of November last past made between the said Sr. William
Davenant of the first part and the said Thomas Betterton [and the
rest of the company] of the second parte, and Henry Harris of London paynter of the third parte are at one weekes notice to be given
by the said Sr. William Davenant to joine with the said Henry
Harris and other men and women (provided or to be provided by
the said Sr. William Davenant) to performe tragedyes, comedyes
Playes and representations in a new theatre to be provided by the
said Sr. William Davenant with scaenes, and *Whereas* by the articles of agreement the generall receipts of the said Theatre (after
the deduction of the generall charges thereof) are to be divided into
fifteene shares or propor*t*ions and thereof the said Henry Harris
and the said Thomas Betterton [and the rest of the company] are
to have five shares or proportions amongst them and the said Sir
William Davenant . . . to have the remaineing tenne shares for
the maintenance of women providing of habits and scaenes and
paying the rent of the said theatre and in recompence of his great
paynes as by the said Articles may more fully appeare and whereas
the said Sr William Davenant hath taken a lease of the tennis court
commonly called Lisles Tennis Court scituate in Lincoln's Inne-
fields in the co. of Middlesex and of two houses or tenements thereunto next adjoining at the making of the lease aforesaid one of the
which said houses is since demolished for the better enlarging and
convenient preparinge of the said theatre there and in the Tennis
Court and *whereas* the said Sr William Davenant hath contracted
and agreed for the fitting and furnishing of the said Theatre there
accordingly and doth intend the said persons their successours and
certaine women and other men publiquely to act comedyes, tragedyes, playes and representations therein as aforesaid, *Now this
Indenture witnesseth* that the said Sr. William Davenant for and in

consideration of the sum of six hundred pounds of lawfull money of England to him the s*ai*d Sr William Davenant by the said Sr Wm Russell in hand payd at or before the ensealing or delivery of these presents the receipt whereof the s*ai*d Sr William Davenant doth hereby acknowledge and thereof and every part thereof doth acquitt and discharge the said Sr William Russell . . . by these presents hath given, granted, bargained and sett over . . . unto the said Sr. William Russell, . . . one equall share of the generall receipts of the said new Theatre in fifteene equall shares to be divided that is to say one of the said tenne shares which by virtue of the recited articles was reserved to the said Sr. William Davenant of which the said Sr William Russell [is] to have and receive the cleare and neat profit arising ratably and in proportion as the said Sr. William Davenant [is] to have and receive for the remaining shares of the said tenne shares, and the s*ai*d Sir William Russell, [is] to contribute towards the charges and disbursements in respect of the said one share ratably and in proportion as the said Sr William Davenant is by the said articles to contribute for the said tenne shares that is to say the s*ai*d Sr William Russell [is] to pay one just part of tenne thereof saving that the charges of habitts and scaenes for the two first representations and of fitting and preparing of the said theatre and the rent to be payd for the same for the first yeare is to be soly defrayed by the said Sr. William Davenant, and the s*ai*d Sr William Russell . . . to be quitt thereof. and the s*ai*d Sr William Davenant . . . doth covenant, promise, and grant to and with the s*ai*d Sr William Russell . . . by these presents that he the said Sr. William Davenant . . . shall and will constantly and daily or weekly on the severall Saturdays of every weeke, at the said theatre pay or cause to be payd and every of them shall permitt to be payd, at such Theatre or Theatres respectively to the s*ai*d Sr. William Russell . . . from tyme to tyme from and immediately after the publique acting of any comedy, tragedy, play or representation in the said Theatre the said one parte or share of the generall receipts for and during all and every such tyme or tymes wherein they shall be acted or showed therein by and with the permission, order, direction, approbation privity or procurement of the s*ai*d Sr William Davenant . . . or by virtue of the said authority or by any of them or any grant, pattent, Licence, or dispensation made or to be made to the said Sr William Davenant . . . or to any person in trust for him . . . to his, their, or any of their use or benefitt. And the said Sr William Davenant for himself . . . doth covenant . . . to and with the said Sr William Russell . . . that in case he . . . shall remove or cause to be removed the Theatre or Theatres therein to act Comedyes . . . he [William Davenant] shall constantly daily or weekly on the severall saturdays . . . pay . . . one equall share . . .

In case such removall shall be made either through necessity or better conveniency and advantage of place for acting . . . he the said Sr William Russell . . . shal contribute according to his proportion, to the charges of erecting, fitting, and preparing of such Theatre or theatres.

And lastly is hereby mutually covenanted . . . that the aforesaid deduction shall be allowed by them . . . and that all such materialls scaenes habitts and other requisites as shall be imployed, bestowed, or used in the erecting, fitting, and preparing of such Theatre or theatres to which such removall may or shall be made . . . and that gratis and without any demand for the said materialls, scaenes, etc.

[British Museum, Additional Charters, 9296.]

Deed of Sale between George Porter and William Richards, 6 December, 1669

. . . *Whereas* Sir William Davenant of London Knt by his Indenture bearing date the one and twentieth day of June in the thirteenth yeer of the Raigne of *our* Soveraigne Lord Charles the second . . . made betwene the said Sir William Davenant of the one pte and the said George Porter of th'other pte for the consideracõn therein mencõnd did give grant bgaine sell assigne and set over to the said George Porter his Executors and Assignes one halfe of one equall pte or share of the genall receipts of the theatre then calld Lisles Tennis Court scituate in Lincolnes Inne feildes in the County of Middx & since removed to the Theatre now in Little Lincolnes Inne feildes on the backside of Portugall Rowe and removeably according to Articles of agreemt had and made on the first institucõn therof for the more conveniency of the psons intested in the benefitt and advantages therof in fifeteene equall ptes or shares to be devided that is to say one halfe of tenn shares (wch by virtue of the said Articles were reserved to the said Sir William Davenant) of wch the said George Porter his Executors Administrators and Assignes was and is to have and receive the cleere full and neate pffitt ariseing rateably and in pporcõn as the said Sir William Davenant his Executors Administrators and Assignes are to have and receive for the remayning shares of the said tenn shares as in and by the said Indenture amongst divers other covents grants articles and agreemts therein conteyned more fully and at

large it doth and may appeare *Now* know yee that I the said George
Porter . . . Doe fully cleerly and absolutely bgaine sell assigne
and set over unto the said William Richards his Executors Administrators and Assignes as well the said halfe share and Indenture aforesaid as alsoe all th'estate right title Intest ppty clayme
and demand wch I the said George Porter have or may can might
shuld or ought to have in or to the same by force and vertue of the
said Indenture or anythinge therin conteyned or otherwise how-
soever *And* the said George Porter for himselfe and Executors and
Administrators doth covent pmise and grant to and wth the said
William Richardes his Executors administrators and assignes by
these presents in mann' and forme following that is to say that he
the said George Porter now hath lawfull authority to give grant
bgaine and sell the said halfe share in mann' and forme aforsaid
and that heretofore he hath not made any former bgaine sale gift
grant surrender or Assignmt charge or incumbrance wtsoeuer of
the said halfe share or any pte thereof nor that he the said George
Porter hath donne nor hereafter at any time shall doe comitt or
suffer to be donne any act deed or thing wtsoeuer wherby the said
William Richards his Executors administrators or assignes shall
or may be hindred or letted of or in the haveing receiving and en-
ioying of the said halfe share or any pte therof And that the said
William Richardes his Executors Administrators (or) assignes shall
and may from time to time and at all times here after for and dureing the continuance of such (intludes and representacons) lawfully
quietly & peaceably have hold use occupie possesse and enioy the
said halfe share and evy pte and pcell thereof in as full ample &
beneficiall mann' as he the said George Porter may might shall or
ought to enioy the same wthout the let trouble molestacon in-
trupcon or disturbance of him the said George Porter or any other
pson or psons by his meanes title . . . In witnesse whereof I have
herevnto set my hand and seale the sixth day of December in the
one & twentieth yeer of the Raigne of *our* Soveraigne Lord Charles
the second by the grace of God . . . annoque dn 1669

[*signed*] G. Porter.

[*Endorsed:*] Sealed and deliuered in the
presence of
[*signed*] Will. Clifton
Will. Noyes

[British Museum Additional Charters, 26,514.]

Sir Henry Herbert's

License to George Jolly, 1 January, 1663

To all Mayors Sherifs Iustices of ye peace Baylifs Constables head boroughs . . . greeting . . . wheres George Jolly hath desired an Authority from me to raise a Company of Stage players to act Comedies Tragedies Trage-Comedies pastoralls and enterludes throughout Eng: These are therefore (by uertue of a Grant made unto me under the G: Seale of England) to authorize and license ye sd G. Jolly to raise a company of Stage players or less to act Comedies &c throughout England with exception onely to ye Cities of London and Westm: and the suburbs of each respectiue city requiring you yr sd Sheriffs Iustices of ye peace, bayliffes, Constables, Headboroughs and all other his Maties officers in his Maties name to permitt and suffer ye sd company quietly to pass without any of your letts and molestacons and to bee aiding and assisting to them or any of them if any wrong or iniury bee offered them or any of them you affording them some conuenient place as aforesaid and to continue in any one place during ye space of 40 days, and what company soeuer either Stage players musicians, mountebanks, or such as go about with monsters and strange Sights shall repaire unto any of ye cities towns corporate hamlets or villages, not hauing their authority immediately from me or confirmed by mee and sealed with ye seale of ye office of ye reuells, that forthwith you take from ym any grant or Commission whatsoever they beare and send it to mee according to ye warrts of former Ld Chamberlains and ye present warrts of the Right honoble Edw: E of Manchester: Ld Chamberlaine of his Maties houshold prouided that they or any of ym do not act any thing offensiue against ye laws of god ye land and yt they act as aforesaid at lawfull times with ye exception of ye Lds day or any other day in ye time of publique diuine Services or on any day prohibited by proclamation: or other lawfull authority and this license to continue in force during the terme of my life. Given at his Maties office of ye reuells under my hand and the seale of ye sd office ye 1st day of Jan: in ye 14th year of ye raigne of our Soueraigne Ld K Ch 2 by ye Grace of god K &c in ye year of Our Ld 1662.

[State Papers, Domestic, Entry Book xlviii, 6a.]

The King's License to Jolly

29 January, 1663

G. Jolly to keep stage playes &c. Charles &c To all Mayors Sheriffs . . . Whereas Wee have appoynted & authorized George Jolly of London Gent & such . . . persons . . . as he shall choose . . . to exercise such playes Opperas Maskes Showes Scenes & ffarces & all other presentations of ye Stage w^hso-ever . . . Now know yee y^t Wee . . . doe . . . grant full . . . Licence & authority notwithstanding any former grant unto ye sd George Jolly . . . as aforesd in any convenient place . . . before any others to exercise & practise ye sd Playes . . . at all times & seasons Sondayes onely excepted & that w^thin any Towne Towne-hall Moted-halls Guildhalls Schooles or other convenient places within ye libertyes & freedomes of any Citty or University Towne or borough w^thin Our Kingdomes of England & Scotland & Do-minion of Wale Our Cities of London & West^er with ye suburbes adjacent onely excepted any former order set downe by any Citty Corporation or borough whatsoever & any Law Statute Acts of Parliament Proclamations Provisions restraint matter cause or thing whatsoever to the contrary thereof . . . notwithstanding . . .

[Here follow instructions to assist and protect George Jolly in his exercising of plays.]

West^er 29th Jan. 1662/3

[State Papers, Domestic, Entry Book ix, 247–250.]

Revocation of Jolly's License

2 April, 1667

Charles &c To all Mayors Bayliffs &c

Whereas Wee were graciously pleased by ye Writ under Our Roy^ll Signett and Signe Manuall bearing date 24 day of Dec in ye 12th yeare of our Reigne, to grant Power & Authority to Geo. Joliffe Gent to erect on Company to consist of so many persons as he shall thereto choose & appoint for ye representation of Tragedyes, Comedes, Playes, Operas Farces & all other Entertainments of that nature, wth other necessary Power and authority . . . and whereas wee have found fitt for ye better regulation of these En-tertainments & Representations that ye same be confined to the two companyes . . . authorized by Us by vertue of Letters Patente . . . und^er [Thomas Killigrew and William Davenant] W^th prohibiĉon to any other person . . . wh^tsoeu^er to erect any other company . . . in . . . London & Westm . . . We have thought fitt to revoke, determine, & annull *our* sd Grant of the 24 dec to ye sd Joly as aforsd, & every part, pow^er, & clause therein contained straightly charge & require ye sd G. Jolly & all other persons w^tso^ever that from henceforth they forbeare to act or doe anything by vertue of the aforesd Grant . . . whereof wee will that as well asd G. Joliffe as all others . . . all to . . . give due obedience to the same as they will answ^er the contrary at their perill . . .

[*Endorsed:*]

Jolly/

[State Papers, Domestic, Charles II, lxxvii, 39.

The draft of the warrant in full, issued 2 April, 1667 and signed 'Arlington' is found in State Papers, Domestic, Charles II, cxcviii, 39.]

INDEX

INDEX